T0180338

Lecture Notes of the Institute for Computer Sciences, Social Informatics and Telecommunications Engineering 429

More information about this series at https://link.springer.com/bookseries/8197

Zhihan Lv · Houbing Song (Eds.)

Intelligent Technologies for Interactive Entertainment

13th EAI International Conference, INTETAIN 2021
Virtual Event, December 3–4, 2021
Proceedings

Springer

Editors
Zhihan Lv (iD)
Uppsala University
Uppsala, Sweden

Houbing Song (iD)
Embry-Riddle Aeronautical University
Daytona Beach, WV, USA

ISSN 1867-8211   ISSN 1867-822X (electronic)
Lecture Notes of the Institute for Computer Sciences, Social Informatics
and Telecommunications Engineering
ISBN 978-3-030-99187-6   ISBN 978-3-030-99188-3 (eBook)
https://doi.org/10.1007/978-3-030-99188-3

This Springer imprint is published by the registered company Springer Nature Switzerland AG
The registered company address is: Gewerbestrasse 11, 6330 Cham, Switzerland

Preface

We are delighted to introduce the proceedings of the 2021 European Alliance for Innovation (EAI) International Conference on Intelligent Technologies for Interactive Entertainment (INTETAIN). This conference brought together researchers, developers, and practitioners around the world who are leveraging and developing interactive entertainment technology for a smarter and more resilient grid.

This year's edition of INTETAIN 2021 put emphasis on the future of 'Digital Twins for Interactive Entertainment'. The conference sought novel, innovative, and exciting work in areas including the art, science, design, and engineering of computer-based systems (models, software, algorithms, and tools) or devices (digital cameras, smartphones, etc.) that provide intelligent human interaction or entertainment experience.

The technical program of INTETAIN 2021 consisted of 25 full papers at the main conference tracks. Aside from the high-quality technical paper presentations, the technical program also featured eight keynote speeches. The keynote speeches were given by Feiyue Wang from the Institute of Automation, Chinese Academy of Sciences (CASIA), China; Mohsen Guizani from the Computer Science and Engineering Department of Qatar University, Qatar; Alberto Del Bimbo from the University of Firenze, Italy; Marc Baaden from the Centre national de la recherche scientifique (CNRS), France; Yongtian Wang from Beijing Institute of Technology, China; Zhigeng Pan from the Nanjing University of Information Science and Technology, China; Haibo Li from the KTH Royal Institute of Technology, Sweden; and Dongdong Weng from the Beijing Institute of Technology, China.

Coordination with the steering chair, Imrich Chlamtac was essential for the success of the conference. We sincerely appreciate his constant support and guidance. It was also a great pleasure to work with such an excellent organizing committee team for their hard work in organizing and supporting the conference. In particular, we are grateful to the Technical Program Committee who completed the peer-review process for technical papers and helped to put together a high-quality technical program. We are also grateful to Conference Manager Rupali Tiwari for her support and all the authors who submitted their papers to the INTERTAIN 2021 conference and workshops.

We strongly believe that INTERTAIN provides a good forum for all researchers, developers, and practitioners to discuss all science and technology aspects that are relevant to interactive entertainment. We also expect that the future INTERTAIN conferences will be as successful and stimulating this year's, as indicated by the contributions presented in this volume.

Zhihan Lv
Houbing Song

Organization

Steering Committee

Imrich Chlamtac   University of Trento, Italy

Organizing Committee

General Chair

Zhihan Lv   Uppsala University, Sweden

Technical Program Committee Chair

Houbing Song   Embry-Riddle Aeronautical University, USA

Sponsorship and Exhibit Chair

Enrico Natalizio   Université de Lorraine, France

Local Chair

Shanchen Pang   China University of Petroleum (East China),
                                   China

Workshops Chair

Minh-Son Dao   National Institute of Information and
                                   Communications Technology, Japan

Publicity and Social Media Chair

Gwanggil Jeon   Incheon National University, South Korea

Publications Chair

Fabio Poiesi   Fondazione Bruno Kessler, Italy

Web Chair

Haibin Lv   North China Sea Offshore Engineering Survey
                                   Institute, China

Posters and PhD Track Chair

Neil Vaughan   University of Exeter, UK

Panels Chair

Po Yang   University of Sheffield, UK

Demos Chair

Carlos Tavares Calafate   Technical University of Valencia, Spain

Tutorials Chair

Jun Shen   University of Wollongong, Australia

Technical Program Committee

Ali Kashif Bashir	Manchester Metropolitan University, UK
Anna Maria Vegni	Roma Tre University, Italy
Bouziane Brik	Burgundy University, France
Btissam Er-Rahmadi	Huawei Edinburgh Research Centre, UK
Carlos Tavares Calafate	Technical University of Valencia, Spain
Enrico Natalizio	Technology Innovation Institute, Abu Dhabi, UAE and LORIA, Université de Lorraine, France
Fabio Poiesi	Fondazione Bruno Kessler, Italy
Joel J. P. C. Rodrigues	Federal University of Piauí, Brazil
Jerry Chun-Wei Lin	Western Norway University of Applied Sciences, Norway
Jun Shen	University of Wollongong, Australia
Junli Zhao	Qingdao University, China
Konstantinos Psannis	University of Macedonia, Greece
Michel Kadoch	University of Quebec, Canada
Minh-Son Dao	National Institute of Information and Communications Technology, Japan
Moayad Aloqaily	Al Ain University, Abu Dhabi, UAE
Mohsin Raza	Edge Hill University, UK
Muhammad Naeem	COMSATS University Islamabad, Pakistan
Nasreddine Lagraa	University of Laghouat, Algeria
Neil Vaughan	University of Exeter, UK
Po Yang	University of Sheffield, UK
Qingqi Pei	Xidian University, China
Shehzad Ashraf	Istanbul Gelisim University, Turkey
Shui Yu	University of Technology Sydney, Australia
Waleed Ejaz	Lakehead University, Canada

Wei Xian	La Trobe University, Australia
Yang Xiao	University of Alabama, USA
Zehui Xiong	Singapore University of Technology and Design, Singapore
Zhi Liu	University of Electro-Communications, Japan
Zhiyuan Tan	Edinburgh Napier University, UK

Contents

Augmented Reality

Virtual Reality

Emerging Applications

Some Questions Regarding the Nature of Experience and Interaction in Media

Kenneth Feinstein(✉) ⓘ

Sunway University, Jalan Universiti, o. 5, 47500 Bandar Sunway, Selangor, Malaysia
kenf@sunway.edu.my

Abstract. Our relationship to and use of media is predicated on it helping us develop a sense of self within the context of our society. This is both a technological and ontological issue. If we turn to media theory, we can start to understand how the development of various media leads us to different types of engagement. Some are more intellectual; some merely diversion and others are deeply personal. What is not looked at is how does the form of the medium contribute to a more resonant and personal media experience.

In order to answer this question, we need to look at our relationship with media through the filters of media form and how it determines personal experience. With the understanding that a mediated experience has the potential to be as formative as a lived experience. Primarily through creating a relationship to the world through otherness. Different media will present such an experience to greater or lesser extent. Here I would like to look at various media from photography through to gaming and mixed-reality and analyze them through a framework defined by Roland Barthes stadium and punctum as well as Marshall McLuhan's idea of hi and low-definition media (hot and cold). By doing this we will be looking at the idea of interaction in a different manner, moving away from reaction as a definition of interaction to one where the work becomes a space of personal memory or emotion.

Keywords: Media theory · User experience · Interaction · Memory

1 Introduction

In *The Cult of Information*, Theodore Roszak tells us about the importance of the relationship of memory and physical space [1]. How we tend to remember things, facts, personal experiences, etc., by associating them with a physical space. So, that when we read a text, we remember a quote as being halfway through the text on the lower half of a right-hand page. His point was that when we receive all our information from a singular space, a television screen or computer monitor, we tend to not remember the information as well. He says that this explains why even as a public may be better informed through the content of television news, they seem to not retain the information presented. This idea of the specialization of memory relates both to Francis Yates' work on memory palaces and other memory systems [2], as well as Marshall McLuhan's contention that

Z. Lv and H. Song (Eds.): INTETAIN 2021, LNICST 429, pp. 3–12, 2022.
https://doi.org/10.1007/978-3-030-99188-3_1

the written word has to first be seen as existing in visual space [3]. In both cases memory is linked to the visual. Yet the critical language developed to address memory and technology has been one that valorises the word over the image and programmed meaning over experience.

According to Eric McLuhan his father Marshall's thinking was influenced by Practical Criticism, a methodology of literary analysis based on traditional rhetoric. Rhetoric itself is an exercise in how argumentation is created in the form of content [4]. It is about how to manage affect, how the rhetorical arts convince a public. It is based on a relationship with an audience that separates the speaker from the public. One of planned manipulation and at the end of the day based on the supremacy of the speaker's will over their opponent and the public. This methodology is not one of conversation, but of oration. Speech over talking.

We find a very similar focus with the semioticians. If we look at Roland Barthes' essay *The Rhetoric of the Image*, the idea of understanding or reading the visual image, in his case an advertisement, is clearly centred on an idea of oral argumentation [5]. The key is to convince people, to persuade them of the correctness of one's point of view. In this formula we find that the idea of mass communication, speech addressed to an amorphous mass that is identified as those who are affected. For Barthes, the role of the photographer is, like an orator, to make a convincing image. In *The Photographic Message*, Barthes focuses on journalistic photography in the same way he looks at advertising photography in *The Rhetoric of the Image*. In both cases we are expected to read, not see images with a goal of finding the programmed meaning [5]. The important function of the systems, news and advertising, is to limit the meaning of the image to a specific message. While it can utilize our emotions, it is made with a very specific message in mind. In Barthes analyses, visual media in a systematic way where meaning, the sign, is transmitted to only allow for specific readings. The idea of readings assumes not only specific programmed messaging, but also a structure where the receiver is distanced from the sender. Very much like cybernetics, these are information-based theories where the system is built as an information delivery system and the resulting analysis focuses on the efficiency of that delivery. How an individual responds to the information contained in the system is only important in relation to a predetermined and expected response. This is why advertising was used as a model of how visual media works. It is very confined in its intent and very controlled in its creation and delivery. So, arguments are made by reducing the variables and then the results are abstracted back out into a world where the variables exist.

By contrast, Roszak was looking at memory as a personal activity that affects each individual in a unique way. This was done in a work that was critical of the development of information technology and cybernetic theory. As much as his warnings are prescient, they have not been developed into a form of critical theory from which we can develop a new way to talk about media and how it affects personal memory.

As we develop our questions, we will use McLuhan and Barthes writings as a framework to try to develop a new way of talking about how we experience media and how media creates our experiences. This will be done by asking a series of questions and from there we will try to parse out a relationship of media and its forms to individual memory as well as what is the difference of interaction as reaction to that of the creation of experiences which generate memory. This essay is in the form of a series of questions as the ideas here are open ended and intended to provoke further investigation.

2 Question 1: What is the Difference Between Interaction and Experience?

Our first question regards of how we understand the nature of interaction in media. We need to define what it is and how it is different from other media. For example, do we define a playing Red Dead Redemption 2 as different from call and response in gospel and pop music? What are the defining rules of one as opposed to the other? How do we understand varying forms of participation and what is demanded of the user?

When we look at gaming, we should note the level of identification with characters found in the experience of playing the game. In major genres, like role playing games (RPG) or first-person shooters (FPS) we are involved in the action through the perspective of a specific character, our identification with that character is of a lower level than that found in a novel such as In Search of Lost Time or films like Star Wars. Here the chief form of engagement is through identifying with the main character. Yet we seem to be more alienated from the characters whose bodies we occupy. The idea of the character having a consciousness that we can connect to is missing. The mechanics of the game, the way that we move around and encounter that world, become a form and conscious part of how we experience the game. The mechanics and the idea of goals that we are tasked with achieving focus our own consciousness towards engaging in reflexive action. Our reflective thought is focused to the mechanics (process) much like |Joseph K in Kafka's The Trial (Der Prozess). We are caught in a world of process over meaning. We are thrust into a world of which we need to make sense of rules that define how we behave before having space to reflect [6]. If we are more engaged with mechanics than content it would seem that the function of the content would be to provide ever more unique ways to employ the mechanics. In such a situation we should ask what it the nature of the experience we find in such games? Where does it place us and is this action/reaction system something that we should call interactive or just reflexive?

To look at this we can look at works through the lens of McLuhan's idea of media participation. He defines our relationship to media using both the terms hot and cold or high and low definition. Hot and cold has been used to explain a medium in relation to a user's feeling of engagement. This engagement is not necessarily the same as interaction nor need it be experiential on a personal level. So, for McLuhan television is cool because of its liveness. The idea that all views are conscious of the fact that watching (a passive experience) is happening to thousands or millions of other people at the same time is enough for his definition. I would like to use high and low-def to refer to how we act with such works. How much agency does the work give us as users and does it or can it actually change our experiences in the world? We need to ask about how our systems are designed and if it is for impact or reaction.

There are many situations where that call on a person or an audience to participate. Call and response in a concert or religious service is a good example. Here we could say that it is cold in that it has high participation. Feelings of inclusiveness are very temporary, and the enduring quality of the experience tends to be low. What we have here is a highly conventionalized situation where the "maker" is creating a situation which the viewer completes a prescribed action. The viewer is meant to feel included while still alienated from the creative process. The audience/viewer knows coming in what is expected of them as this is a highly conventionalized action. Roles are clearly proscribed and what is demanded of the participant is very little. When an action becomes conventionalized, it removes any creativity from within the action. This heightens the maker's control giving us a high-definition work. In this way the user becomes a reactor instead of an actor. The logic of the work is one of cause and effect masked as choice. In games where the effects are known, and the narrative is built around levels or saving points the narrative is giving more of an illusion of choice than allowing for it. It is hoped that the illusion will keep the user engaged, but as Vilém Flusser pointed out all games either end when there are no more unique combinations or the action is repetitive and the user is bored [7]. This way of understanding how we relate to media identifies how alienation plays into the game. By contrast, works that allow for an intimate relationship between users either through or with the work would be low-def. Amateur photography and smartphone-based video would be examples of this. Here we are interacting with the recording device according to a set of rules that define our play. We can also engage with others through the act of recording in a similar low-definition way.

For Barthes the Maker and the Reader are in a struggle for supremacy over the image. He sees the ability to create meaning as being possessed by the image maker or the reader as interpreter. He tends to side with the reader as this is where he identifies. Meanwhile, those of us depicted in the image (the subject) are supposed to passively accept our fate of being transformed from a subject into an object [8]. But his way of understanding communication maintains a power relationship within a zero-sum game.

In Camera Lucida, Barthes defines how we interpret images as either learned, the studium, or that which is has meaning only to the individual, the punctum. These are forms of experiencing a photograph are only available to the reader of the image. It is closed to the maker and the subject [8]. In the book he seems to struggle with how to explain how the punctum exists because it only exists for the reader. He sees it as activated by seeing, but not understood until one is removed from the work. It exists best where the being with that which is in excess of the Self, the Other, is relegated to just a memory. He sees the punctum as a device that reaches out to Otherness, but only as a reflecting back on to the Self. That which is other than the reader may be objectified but is not allowed active agency in creating either meaning or experience. Understanding media this way expects interactive works as we know them to only exist in the realm of being reactive. We can only be given choices that are either right or wrong as determined by the Maker. While the impact from these choices is given to the reader in retrospect.

Combining Barthes definitions of the parties involved in the semiotic process with McLuhan's idea of interactivity within this process we expand the relationship of the Maker and the Reader to the include the possibility of a User. Where Barthes doesn't allow for the possibility of an active participant in his media world, by adding in the idea of the user/participant as separate from the reader we can develop a way of opening up the very emotional reaction to media works that he was trying to define through the punctum. By incorporating McLuhan's Participant with Barthes' Reader, we come to a way of being able to speak of how an individual work affects an individual, not just how a structure allows for communication. It reshapes the relationship away from a cause-and-effect model of communication exemplified by the advertising model and allows for the experiential to have impact. It is of significance that McLuhan's model of the most low-def form of media is the telephone. This is one where the awareness of the structure of the medium becomes the most invisible as the two users are in direct connection and the role of the medium as mediator is minimal.

In The Space of Literature, Maurice Blanchot speaks of the relationship of the work to the audience as a coming together. He places the author outside this formulation [9]. This is not to deny the influence of the maker or McLuhan's dictum about medium and content, rather it acknowledges that the relationship between the work and the user/reader is more intimate and personal. He speaks of meaning as created in a space, an interval, in between the work and the user. It is in this space that each party brings their knowledge and experiences together to negotiate a meaning. This meaning adds experience and richness to each party after the fact. This presumes that although intended meaning can be put into the work, the experience of it carries an excess beyond what can be programmed by the Maker. This moves an interaction between a work and a user away from base action/reaction. McLuhan talks about how a medium frames how information as it is presented, here we are talking about how meaning is created by the active event of interacting with a work within said medium. It central to and beyond the function of the medium. The idea of high and low definition can be seen as an expression of this and as such helps us in conceptualizing a language to talk about how works affect us. Further we could redefine the studium as what is brought to us by the work, be it information or a set of determined actions, and that the punctum is our finding meaning through an excess created in the act of encountering the work. This way of looking at the punctum moves it was from a detached reading found after the experience and makes it an active part of developing meaning through experience. Expanding from Barthes, the punctum becomes not just a point that we hang an experience onto as much as the acknowledgment of the experience itself as a defining act. One that changes how we see and interact with the world. This was what Victor Burgin was moving towards, but stopped short of in his essay The Remembered Film [10]. Burgin expanded the idea of the punctum by using it as a tool to understand cinematic experience. His work tries to understand the effects of memory on the psyche through a Freudian analysis. What is significant in his work is the idea that what we remember is detached from the narrative of the film, leaving the linkage of meaning to experience to scenes and fragments of the work. It acknowledges that the impact of a work is a fragmentary image and feeling invoked by the viewer, rather than the story as a whole. Here the punctum defines both the act of an experience creating a memory and as well as the object that is linked to that memory. It is through how we take on the image and its feeling that creates a meaning and knowledge that we incorporate into our lives.

3 Question 2: What is the Relationship of Experience to Knowledge?

In discussing how memory works Henri Bergson lays out two forms of memory, what we can call active memory and habitual or muscle memory. Both are learned, but one is based on reaction instead of reflection and thought. This is habitual memory; it is learned, but bypasses knowledge. While pure memory is where events from the past are activated into conscious thought [11]. This division of memory allows us to distinguish between reflex memory and memory as thought. Since the habitual specifically works through bypassing thought, it may be learned, but we cannot call what is learned knowledge. While we do learn habitual memory through repeated experience as seen in learning a sport, the distinction between these forms if memory is that the habitual operates without awareness of memory, while pure memory is conscious of the fact that memory is actively invoked in thought. It draws us into experience through time.

When look at the punctum as a phenomenon it is an act derived from pure memory. It is the activation of memory as the framework to understand the present through experience. What makes it different from the studium as pure memory is that it is not about the practicality of knowledge. But on a certain level both are pure memory. While Bergson used cinema as an analogy in his work, he wasn't concerned with relation of media to memory in a specific way.

As pure memory how does the studium and punctum relate back to the idea of hi-def and low-def media? This leads us to ask what McLuhan meant by hi-def and low-def. Should we only read it as a way of understanding a mechanical function or as a way of being able to talk about how it affects us as individuals. How can media have the capacity to create memory and help create our sense of self? For McLuhan low-def is an indication of openness in meaning, the ability of one to create meaning within or through a work. This is why he writes so much about art and how to understand it. Art is inherently low-def since it must carry meaning beyond what is inscribed on the surface. And whne he said, "Art is anything you can get away with" [12] he is indicating the importance of how an event can be communicate through a medium which can change us. This return to art is his way of trying to approach something akin to the punctum. His grounding in Practical Criticism tended to move him away from a psychological reading of how media works. Just as much as Barthes' work was moving in a Lacanian direction. In both cases they are trying to find a way of understanding how we can gain experience which can be transformed into knowledge that will change how we act in the world.

Key to either reading of media is that we learn from experience and incorporate it into our psyche as personal experience. Knowledge and creativity are then drawn from that. As an event this is both personal and ambiguous. Both writers seem to find it difficult to speak of experience in way that may appear to be systematic. Both come from a perspective of being readers, not creators and this does limit how they can conceive of how media can be understood. They see readers as separated from the work as an event. Readers may feel that they experience the events of a novel, but is always at a remove, essentially after the fact. Just as Josef K is moving through events, but remaining detached from them, so are Barthes and McLuhan's readers. For both, creation is done elsewhere, and we just react and analyse what is before us. Distance is required in order for meaning to occur and the effects of meaning are deferred to a future date. The idea that the user can be participatory in the creation of meaning in an active way is not really addressed. McLuhan does allow for a conversational aspect to media and it does help define hi and low-def, but not in a prescriptive way. So, the fact that like the telephone it can help define its function, but how that can affect the medium is not of interest to him. Barthes on the other hand can only see a participant's role in a struggle for control of meaning with the author/creator. In both cases the idea of cooperative systems or viewing the encounter with the work as facing Otherness is not possible. Yet, in both cases, by opening up to the excess found in art or the image in general, they as acknowledging the need for this type of view.

4   Question 3: Should We Be Treating Our Experiences with Media as a Being-With-Otherness?

Our question is how do we use media is to create situations of low definition where moments of significance can be made such as alleviating PTSD via gaming? As opposed to when each of us link media events to ourselves as a punctum. Should we see the punctum as a subset of low def, as a way of explaining how it works and can it be programmed? How can we understand the underlying functions that allows this to operate and in understanding this where can we go in developing new media?

To understand how media objects can have meaning beyond the work we need to see how we relate to media in a different way. We have to understand that we actually interact with it as we do other people. We face it in as real in a way as we face each other. It is the act of encountering the media work as a living experience that defines this. It is not that we confuse it with reality in the act, rather that we are open to the reality of the experience that it presents us. In this way we treat the media experience as a life experience, and this opens us up to this event as an encountering of the Other. How is this possible?

In order to see how media and memory do interact, let's look at Bergson's concept of thought and memory. For Bergson all stimulus that can be perceived are images. All of existence including our body are images. "All these images act and react upon one another in all their elementary parts" [11]. We take in images not to reduce them to a symbolic language, but to interact and make sense of the world. Memory is a function where we link the image or event before us to previous images in order to make sense of the present. So that we live in a world where past and present are always in active conversation with each other. It is through how we interact with and understand these images that memory is created. It opens up a new way of understanding ontology and from there our relationship to media.

According to Emmanuel Lévinas, we have to understand that our understanding of self has to be grounded in our relationship to Otherness. For him the idea of Being (Dasein) as separate individuals who manage their way through the world is a fallacy. Where Heidegger places Dasein in the world, it still sees the conflict between one's will and being-in-the-world as a struggle for authenticity. He sees anything that alters or modifies the will as inauthentic. In such a structure modern media as a system is a battle ground for authenticity. Media is to be is a ground for resistance. While Lévinas redefines ontology as the study of, "all knowledge of relations connecting or opposing beings to one another implies an understanding of the fact that these beings and relations exist" [13]. He squarely places the concept of being in relationship to the other as central of our understanding of the world. Because we live in a world of relatedness and relationships, we have a fundamental responsibility to the other that exceeds our individuality and also defines it. This goes beyond an intellectual concept of the world and acts out in our daily life. Being-in-the-world is living within this system of desires and responsibilities. This means that that to face the other we cannot reduce our relationships to it to our reading a series of images in a symbolic language. We have to face them in their reality, not as extensions of ourselves. It is the facing of the other as beyond systems of meaning that places us in-the-world. Subjectivity can only exist through our interrelationship with the world. We move from a world understood through the studium and the punctum as reflective acts of reading to one where we see the punctum as an act of being-in-the-world. This facing of the other calls for us to be responsible to the other through the media experience. We place ourselves in a position of where the significance of the interaction is to create a space of otherness, where it has the ability to be in dialogue with us. We find such a relationship in the act of amateur photography. When we hand a camera over to another person and ask them, "can you take a picture of me?" In this act we are handing over a responsibility towards to another through the media device [14]. In this way of experiencing the world through media, it is the act of photography rather than the image produced where the true interaction is produced. Where experience becomes more important than artifact. Where the artefact can be read, the experience is not found in the object. Although this may produce a highly conventionalized image, it is not the image but rather the act of creating the image that has significance. By turning a camera over to another to hand responsibility for a the creatin of a sense of self to another without reservation or dictates. S/he must be willing to take on this responsibility for the event to occur. This is an event, a moment of the self and the other in a direct face-to-face beyond meaning specifically created through the media technology. This connects with the idea of the punctum as experience and the image as record of that experience. We try to make sense of the connection between the remembered scene and the individual not as reading, but as memory. We have created a system that moves beyond understanding as an act that happened in the future to the act as presence having meaning. The experience moves beyond symbolic meaning into affective memory.

This is why we see games being used and developed as medical therapy. As an example, EndeavorRx is a new game that has been approved by the FDA in the US as a way of helping people manage ADHD. It recognises that focus and attention, not just repetition should be central to a gaming experience for it to be effective. There is the act of presence within the situation, the reality of the act. Such games move away from an alienated reactive world into one that demand our being present with in it.

This understanding brings images into the world as having impact beyond the symbolic and grounds our ethical relationship to the other as fundamental to being. Within this function we take on responsibility for the world before us as we incorporate the world into us to create our consciousness. This places our consciousness, thought and memory, into the world demanding that we have an ethical responsibility to it.

Along with these medical developments that recognise the importance of presence as a factor in creating punctum like media experiences, there have also been artists such as Shimon Attie who use the idea of presence as a way of creating this face-to-face between a media work and a viewer. His *Writing on the Wall* (1992), was a series of images of the pre-War Jewish community in Berlin, projected back into the neighbourhood that they were first taken. As often as possible they were projected onto the specific location of the original image. Attie is creating media images that demands a relationship of the viewer to the image that is one of a face-to-face. We cannot see these images among the ruined buildings without confronting the history giving them their context [14]. Because it demands such a direct emotional reaction form the viewer, we can say that it creates a punctum in the city space. We are put in a situation that places us into an ontological act of *being-in-the-world*. It places us in a here and now that demands us to be present. We can also see how this can be defined as a low-def work in the McLuhan sense. While such works can seem to be outliers compared to the vast majority of gaming and other environments, we are finding more and more development of media work.

5 Conclusion

If we are to look at how media and especially the new developing technologies can have a fundamental effect on our lives, we need to find a language to about what these effects are and how we incorporate them into media development. Structuralist and the McLuhan analysis leaves off at the level effect on a society and ignores the individual. It mechanizes us as parts in a system that appears to be more about power and control than communication. While it warns us to the dangers and possibilities of that system it still sees us as powerless cogs. Understanding the hopelessness of this view of the world they both look to art as the escape valve. They see it as carrying an unspecified excess that exceeds the structure of mechanism of meaning and control. What is missing in this interpretation of media is our individual relationship to an individual media work/object. An ontological view of our interaction as one of being-with the work/object as a facing of otherness that allows for a true interaction instead of a programmed communication. By facing the understanding of how media works, be it a film, podcast, game installations or multimedia performances, are experienced by us as if they were others in the world, we can find ways of developing interactions and works that where the focus is on meaning through a different set of standards or ideology.

In order to accomplish this, we need to find a way to talk about such issues in relation to media critique and development. This is where joining of Barthes' studium and punctum to McLuhan's hi-def and low-def can start to move us into that direction. Not to find a way to create cleverer and cleverer ways of engaging our time in reactive models of use, but rather to centre meaning and the individual in developing media works. To begin to conceptualize a language and perspective of critique is just a step in that direction.

References

1. Roszak, T.: The Cult of Information: The Folklore of Computers and the True Art of Thinking, 1st edn. Pantheon, New York (1986)
2. Yates, F.A.: The Art of Memory. Routledge, London (1999)
3. McLuhan, M., McLuhan, E.: Laws of Media: The New Science. University of Toronto Press, Toronto (1988)
4. McLuhan, E.: 'Marshall McLuhan's Theory of Communication: The Yegg'. Global Media J. Canadian Ed., 1(1) (2008)

5. Barthes, R., Heath, S.: Image, Music, Text. Hill and Wang, New York (1977)
6. Kafka, F., Mitchell, B.: The Trial, 1st edn. Schocken Books: Distributed by Pantheon Books, New York (1998)
7. Flusser, V.: Towards a Philosophy of Photography. Reaktion, London (2000)
8. Barthes, R.: Camera Lucida: Reflections on Photography. Hill and Wang, New York (1981)
9. Blanchot, M.: The Space of Literature. University of Nebraska Press, Lincoln (1982)
10. Burgin, V.: The Remembered Film. Reaktion, London (2004)
11. Bergson, H., Paul, N.M., Palmer, W.S.: Matter and Memory. G. Allen & Co., The Macmillan Co., London (1912)
12. McLuhan, M., Fiore, Q.: The Medium is the Massage: An Inventory of Effects. Gingko Press (2001)
13. Lévinas, E.: Entre Nous: On Thinking-of-the-Other. Columbia University Press, New York (1998)
14. Feinstein, K.: The Image That Doesn't Want to be Seen. Atropos Press, New York (2010)

Exploring the User Interaction with a Multimodal Web-Based Video Annotator

Rui Rodrigues[1,2(✉)], Rui Neves Madeira[1,2], and Nuno Correia[1]

[1] NOVA LINCS, NOVA School of Science and Technology,
NOVA University Lisbon, Lisbon, Portugal
nmc@fct.unl.pt
[2] Sustain.RD, Setúbal School of Technology, Polytechnic Institute of Setúbal, Setúbal, Portugal
{rui.rodrigues,rui.madeira}@estsetubal.ips.pt

Abstract. People interact with their surroundings using several multimodal methods. Human-computer interaction is performed using these capabilities in order to provide, as much as possible, the most natural and productive experiences through speech, touch, vision, and gesture. The Web-based application used in this paper is a multi-platform video annotation tool that supports multimodal interaction. MotionNotes has the primary goal of fostering the creativity of both professional and amateur users. It is possible to interact with this tool using keyboard, touch, and voice, making it possible to add different types of annotations: voice, drawings, text, and marks. Furthermore, a feature of human poses identification in real-time was integrated into the annotation tool, enabling the identification of possible annotations. This paper presents and discusses results from a user study conducted to explore the user interaction with the tool, evaluating the prototype and its different interaction methods. User feedback shows that this approach to video annotation is stimulating and can enhance the user's creativity and productivity.

Keywords: Multimodal interfaces · Video annotations · Performing arts · User study · HCI

1 Introduction

Human poses and human motion are essential components in video footage, particularly in activities related to performing arts. The tool explored in this paper proposes applying multimodal annotation input/output with AI algorithms for pose estimation to improve Human-Computer Interaction [1–3]. MotionNotes development was part of the EU-funded project called CultureMoves [4], which follows a user-oriented approach and has the primary goal of developing software tools to "access and augment educational and cultural content" such as the one contained in Europeana [5]. MotionNotes enables its users to record, replay, and add new information to the video footage by working with multiple annotations and machine learning algorithms to increase productivity and creativity.

© ICST Institute for Computer Sciences, Social Informatics and Telecommunications Engineering 2022
Published by Springer Nature Switzerland AG 2022. All Rights Reserved
Z. Lv and H. Song (Eds.): INTETAIN 2021, LNICST 429, pp. 13–22, 2022.
https://doi.org/10.1007/978-3-030-99188-3_2

New AI techniques such as 2D human pose estimation are becoming very reliable in recent years [6], and they can be applied with promising results in Human-Computer Interaction and Multimodal Systems.

Therefore, three main research questions have been posed while developing and testing this Web-based tool as an input interface to add and manipulate multimodal time-based annotations over video:

1. Is it preferable to carry out annotation work during or after recording?

    a. Moreover, for each mode, what are the differences in annotation type usage?

2. Regarding the user devices used for annotation work, is there a preference between laptop and mobile devices?

    a. Additionally, for each device type, what are the differences in annotation type usage?

3. Could the human pose estimation feature be an asset to users when carrying out annotation work?

This work will contribute with a preliminary evaluation of the prototype and its interactions by answering these research questions, which brings insights regarding users' preferences. We collected this feedback through questionnaires and informal interviews. As a result, we concluded that our users accepted the general idea of replacing previous annotation methods with this web-based solution during our lab days. Moreover, we can state that people who work with video annotation are receptive to exploring different tools and interactions.

This paper is structured as follows. We start by analysing the related work, followed by the MotionNotes description. Afterwards, we present the testing environment and the results that were obtained. Finally, in the last section, we conclude with a summary, highlighting the tool's potential, and plan the future work.

2 Related Work

Video annotation is a valuable resource in different application areas, including analysing and studying human body motion. Furthermore, they are essential tools for encouraging collaborative teamwork by enabling information sharing [7]. These reasons motivated the development of several tools over the last years.

ELAN [8] is one of the most well-known and used tools in manually annotating or transcribing non-verbal communication. The work of Goldman [9] explored video annotations with object tracking methods. However, this work does not support touch or pen-based annotations; the tracking feature could not perform in real-time. The Choreographer's Notebook [10] was designed specifically for Choreography workflow, allowing digital-ink and text annotations. The WML tool [11] is another Web-based tool specifically designed to annotate, archive, and search dance movements.

In contrast, a pen-based video annotation tool was developed by Cabral et al. [12] to track motion. Their solution used frame differences, and they later tried similar methods on video editing [13]. Silva et al. [14] presented a work that enables real-time object tracking using the same pen-based video annotations following the same path. After that, as part of the BlackBox project [15], a prototype was developed to experiment with annotations in a 3D environment using Microsoft Kinect. Commercial video annotation applications, such as Wipster [16], Camtasia [17], Frame.io [18], and Vimeo Pro Review [19], have simplified the process of annotating and sharing videos for users. However, none of them supports automatic human pose detection.

Human pose estimation is a valuable computer vision technique in several areas, such as gaming, virtual reality, and video surveillance. This technique seeks to detect the human body parts computationally from video frames, and the goal is to identify the head, elbows, shoulders, knees, hips and feet. To address this issue, a few approaches have been proposed over the years.

By the end of the 2000s, state of the art was based on algorithms using features selected by human specialists, like gradient histograms [20–22]. Later, deep learning techniques have motivated a great deal of attention over the AI community [23], and human pose estimation was no exception. Deep learning-based methods can extract more and better features from training data, being possible to find literature with superior results [24–28]. Our proposal will explore implementations based on this last technique.

3   MotionNotes

MotionNotes [29] is a web-based real-time multimodal video annotation tool based on keyboard, touch, and voice inputs. This tool can support professional and amateur users working on creative and exploratory processes. MotionNotes enables the capture of multimodal annotations while and after recording video. The annotation types available to be used can be text, ink strokes, audio, or user-configured marks.

3.1   MotionNotes Implementation Overview

The prototype was designed to run on any regular Web browser, exploring multiple input modes, such as keyboard and touch interaction. The interface is responsive in order to enable users with different screen sizes to enjoy adequate interaction. The MotionNotes user interface has a video display area in the centre of the screen where it is possible to add new annotations or update current ones. In order to improve user feedback, there is a graphical representation of all annotated moments right below the video area (Fig. 1). Moreover, we included a machine learning technique in MotionNotes to perform real-time human pose predictions. PoseNet [30], a pre-trained neural network, in conjunction with tensorFlow.js, is used to process the body part classification in the client's machine. Predicted points are drawn on an HTML canvas object located in the same position as the video but at a higher layer position. Finally, straight lines are calculated between the points, with the skeleton staying visible, giving the user another resource to identify possible annotations (Fig. 2).

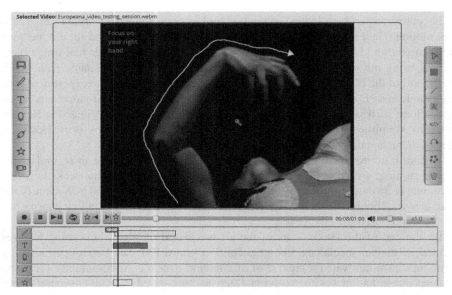

Fig. 1. Tool GUI and annotation types (Green: drawing; Red: text; Blue: mark) (Color figure online).

3.2 MotionNotes Interaction Example

After an initial interaction and reflecting on testing scenarios, a procedure was created for MotionNotes. In order to better understand the interaction, we follow Mary while she annotates her video with the MotionNotes.

First, Mary opens MotionNotes as she would like to load a video that she recorded in a recent dance competition. Mary goes to the File menu and clicks on the import video option; MotionNotes immediately opens a new window. Mary browses and selects her video. Once done, she needs to click on the play button, so the video instantly starts playing. She notices that the right-hand movement could be better and feels the need to highlight this. Mary pauses the video and then thinks about which annotation types are appropriate to express her thoughts. She decides to add one text annotation; to do that, she selects the text annotation type in the left menu and clicks above the video on the preferred location. MotionNotes immediately creates a new textbox and give focus to it. Next, Mary starts typing, "Right-hand position improvements were needed here", and clicks enter. MotionNotes saves several details about the annotation, for instance, the text, font, colour, position over the video, and the exact timestamp. To give more details about the objective, Mary decides that a draw annotation could help. She clicks on the draw annotation option, and MotionNotes activates the draw functionality; Then, she creates a line across the location where the arm and hand should be. Finally, Mary believes that this section is crucial for the performance and adds a mark annotation. For that, she selects the mark annotation, and MotionNotes opens a popup with the predefined images. She selects a key icon and concludes the procedure by clicking above the video on the desired location where the icon should be (Fig. 1).

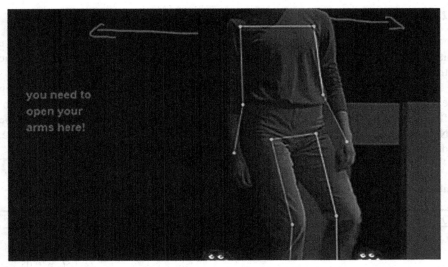

Fig. 2. MotionNotes with pose estimation. (Green: pose predictions; Red: manual annotation) (Color figure online).

4   User Study

The study was composed of three phases, each one to understand a different question. The study's first phase focused on collecting data regarding the annotation experience both while and after recording. The second phase was focused on understanding the user behaviour regarding different devices. Finally, the last one assessed if human pose estimation could add value to video annotation software.

4.1   Design and Participants

We performed a user study with 27 participants. The user test started with the users watching a 15-min tutorial. The next step was for participants to interact with the software, which was achieved by asking them to complete a set of proposed tasks.

Regarding the participants, the most representative age interval was between 25 and 34 years old. The gender representation was nearly even, with 51% female and 49% male. Regarding the testing group education levels, 37% had a master's degree, 29.6% had a bachelor's degree, 18.5% had studied until high school, and the remaining 14.8% held a PhD degree. Most of the participants reported they frequently annotate their work in some way (77.8%). The preferred method used to annotate is a regular paper notebook (63.6%), with the laptop devices being the second most popular way (36.4%), and mobile phones appearing right after (27.3%).

The questionnaire included 23 questions using the five-point Likert Scale. We used paired-samples t-tests and one-way ANOVA to analyse the feedback.

4.2   Results and Discussion

The three tables present in this section summarise the results, including descriptive statistics, t-test, and ANOVA regarding each one of the research questions posed in the introduction.

Table 1 focuses on results related to RQ1. Participants classified the tool regarding the annotation experience during and after a recording. The t-test returned a significant difference, showing preferences for using the tool in playback mode. Moreover, the ANOVA test has shown a substantial difference concerning this after recording mode, indicating that text was the most popular annotation type, followed by drawing.

Table 1. Descriptive statistics, t-test, and ANOVA for the different annotation type experience.

Question	A[1]	B	C	D	E	M	SD	t-test / ANOVA
1. Consider the annotation experience								
1.1. Annotating while recording	2	3	10	6	6	2.59	1.16	t=-3.56; p<0.05
1.2. Annotating in playback mode	12	4	5	2	4	3.67	1.47	
2. Consider the recording phase								
2.1. Classify the sketch usage	8	4	4	3	8	3.04	1.62	
2.2. Classify the text usage	6	4	4	5	8	2.81	1.54	f=0.32; p>0.05
2.3. Classify the audio usage	5	6	5	3	8	2.89	1.49	
2.4. Classify the marks usage	3	5	7	3	9	2.63	1.39	
3. Consider the after recording								
3.1. Classify the sketch usage	9	7	4	3	4	3.52	1.42	
3.2. Classify the text usage	14	7	3	2	1	4.15	1.11	f=2.89; p<0.05
3.3. Classify the audio usage	5	8	4	7	3	3.19	1.31	
3.4. Classify the marks usage	6	9	3	3	6	3.22	1.47	

[1] A: strongly useful, B: useful, C: ok, D: not useful, E: strongly not useful

Regarding RQ2, classifying the experience when using different devices, a mobile touch-based device (less than 576 px wide) was compared to a regular laptop. Again, the t-test returned a significant difference, showing preferences for using the tool in a regular laptop with larger resolutions. The ANOVA test did not show significant differences regarding the usage of different annotation types. However, it is possible to verify that text annotation is slightly more prevalent when using laptops, while mark annotation leads in mobile. Table 2 summarises the results.

Regarding RQ3, which addresses classifying the overall experience with the human pose estimation feature active, the feedback was positive, as shown in Table 3. However, when users were asked if they could consider using this feature during annotation work, the results were just ok. Users' comments about this feature were collected, which let us understand they were expecting more options to work with it, such as recording only the pose or reproducing the movements in isolation (e.g., without video and sound) and adding annotations in this mode.

Table 2. Descriptive statistics, t-test, and ANOVA for the device interaction experience.

Question	A[1]	B	C	D	E	M	SD	t-test / ANOVA
1. Consider the tool interaction								
1.1. Classify when using a laptop	11	11	3	2	1	4.11	0.99	$t=6.93; p<0.05$
1.2. Classify when using a mobile device	1	3	16	3	4	2.78	0.96	
2. User experience using a laptop								
2.1. Classify the sketch usage	9	5	7	3	3	3.52	1.34	
2.2. Classify the text usage	13	10	3	0	1	4.26	0.93	$f=2.06; p>0.05$
2.3. Classify the audio usage	14	6	4	2	1	4.11	1.13	
2.4. Classify the marks usage	12	5	8	1	1	3.96	1.10	
3. User experience using mobile								
3.1. Classify the sketch usage	3	3	15	2	4	2.96	1.10	
3.2. Classify the text usage	1	2	15	7	2	2.74	0.84	$f=1.77; p>0.05$
3.3. Classify the audio usage	2	5	16	2	2	3.11	0.92	
3.4. Classify the marks usage	4	5	15	2	1	3.33	0.94	

Table 3. Descriptive statistics, t-test for the pose estimation experience.

Question	A[1]	B	C	D	E	M	SD	t-test
1. Classify the overall experience	2	8	11	3	2	3.19	0.98	
2. Consider the annotation work								
2.1. Classify it using pose estimation	4	5	10	4	4	3.0	1.23	$t=-0.9; p<0.05$
2.2. Classify it without pose estimation	3	6	13	2	3	3.1	1.07	

The user statements during the test were mostly positive. One user (U3) said: "Easy to learn; the multiple annotation types complement each other very well." Another user (U15) stated: "The marks was a good idea, very fast to apply, even in small screen devices". Regarding human pose estimation, another user (U24) stated the following: "There were scenarios where having the pose helped in the creation of new annotations".

5 Future Work

The feedback obtained while testing MotionNotes was positive. However, we discussed and collected a couple of new ideas for additional developments.

Participants mentioned a few scenarios in which they considered human pose estimation and MotionNotes could benefit in a future version. The first scenario discussed by some participants was the background subtraction. That means, for instance, reproducing the body parts motion on a skeleton format in the same timeframe as the source video, but with a clean background. Additionally, the skeleton colour, background colour and audio should allow personalisation. The second scenario was based on having a particular type of annotation associated with the pose. This type of annotation should be optional and could be activated or deactivated depending on motion tracking status. This scenario brings several advantages like users could concentrate only on pose in a specific annotation iteration, leaving other elements for future work; another advantage is the movement correction, where users could edit several frames by drawing the correct pose.

Regarding the annotation types, the most discussed were the marks, where participants showed great interest given its novelty. Again, we stimulated the participants to give suggestions and ideas, and 3D was the subject of debate for this type of annotations. Right now, these marks are predefined 2D icons or images uploaded by users, and participants commented about how interesting it could be to upload 3D models and add them to a scene as annotations. We think most of these ideas could foster the users' creativity, which is one of our main goals, and we are already designing a new MotionNotes version containing some of these features.

6 Conclusion

The multimodal Web video annotation tool MotionNotes described in this paper enables users to add different annotation types and identify human poses in real-time. The tool was tested in order to address three main research questions concerning user preferences and interaction.

From our results, we can conclude that annotation software users prefer to work after the recording session and not during it. Additionally, they preferred to work in a traditional environment with a larger screen over the more modern and popular mobile devices. Finally, we observed a significant curiosity about both automatic human pose recognition and marks annotation type. Future work should focus on these features providing additional research.

Acknowledgements. This work is funded by Fundação para a Ciência e Tecnologia through a Ph.D. Studentship grant (2020.09417.BD). It is Supported by the project CultureMoves, Grant Agreement Number: INEA/CEF/ICT/A2017/1568369. It is also supported by NOVA LINCS RC, partially funded by project UID/CEC/04516/2020 granted by FCT.

References

1. Turk, M.: Multimodal interaction: a review. Pattern Recogn. Lett. **36**, 189–195 (2014)
2. Dumas, B., Lalanne, D., Oviatt, S.: Multimodal interfaces: a survey of principles, models and frameworks. In: Lalanne, D., Kohlas, J. (eds.) Human Machine Interaction. LNCS, vol. 5440, pp. 3–26. Springer, Heidelberg (2009). https://doi.org/10.1007/978-3-642-00437-7_1
3. Abuczki, Á., Esfandiari Baiat, G.: An overview of multimodal corpora, annotation tools and schemes. Argumentu **9**, 86–98 (2013)
4. CultureMoves: Culture Moves. https://culturemoves.eu/. Accessed 17 Jun 2021
5. Europeana: Europeana. www.europeana.eu. Accessed 16 May 2021
6. Cao, Z., Simon, T., Wei, S.E., Sheikh, Y.: Realtime multi-person 2D pose estimation using part affinity fields. In: Proceedings of the 30th IEEE Conference on Computer Vision and Pattern Recognition, CVPR 2017 (2017)

7. Cabral, D., Valente, J., Silva, J., Aragão, U., Fernandes, C., Correia, N.: A creation-tool for contemporary dance using multimodal video annotation. In: Proceedings of the 2011 ACM Multimedia Conference and Workshops, MM 2011 (2011)
8. Wittenburg, P., Brugman, H., Russel, A., Klassmann, A., Sloetjes, H.: ELAN: a professional framework for multimodality research. In: Proceedings of the 5th International Conference on Language Resources and Evaluation, LREC 2006 (2006)
9. Goldman, D.B., Gonterman, C., Curless, B., Salesin, D., Seitz, S.M.: Video object annotation, navigation, and composition. In: Proceedings of the 21st Annual ACM Symposium on User Interface Software and Technology, UIST 2008 (2008)
10. Singh, V., Latulipe, C., Carroll, E., Lottridge, D.: The choreographer's notebook-a video annotation system for dancers and choreographers. In: Proceedings of the 8th ACM Conference on Creativity and Cognition, C and C 2011 (2011)
11. El Raheb, K., Kasomoulis, A., Katifori, A., Rezkalla, M., Ioannidis, Y.: A web-based system for annotation of dance multimodal recordings by dance practitioners and experts. In: ACM International Conference Proceeding Series (2018)
12. Cabral, D., Valente, J.G., Aragão, U., Fernandes, C., Correia, N.: Evaluation of a multimodal video annotator for contemporary dance. In: Proceedings of the Workshop on Advanced Visual Interfaces AVI (2012)
13. Cabral, D., Correia, N.: Video editing with pen-based technology. Multimedia Tools Appl. **76**(5), 6889–6914 (2016)
14. Silva, J., Fernandes, C., Cabral, D., Correia, N.: Real-time annotation of video objects on tablet computers. In: Proceedings of the 11th International Conference on Mobile and Ubiquitous Multimedia, MUM 2012 (2012)
15. Ribeiro, C., Kuffner, R., Fernandes, C., Pereira, J.: 3D annotation in contemporary dance: Enhancing the creation-tool video annotator. In: ACM International Conference Proceeding Series (2016)
16. Wipster | Review Software. https://wipster.io/. Accessed 15 Jun 2021
17. Camtasia. https://www.techsmith.com/video-editor.html. Accessed 2 Jun 2021
18. Frame.io. https://www.frame.io/. Accessed 25 May 2021
19. Vimeo. https://vimeo.com/features/video-collaboration. Accessed 5 Jun 2021
20. Felzenszwalb, P., McAllester, D., Ramanan, D.: A discriminatively trained, multiscale, deformable part model. In: 26th IEEE Conference on Computer Vision and Pattern Recognition, CVPR (2008). https://doi.org/10.1109/CVPR.2008.4587597
21. Andriluka, M., Roth, S., Schiele, B.: Pictorial structures revisited: people detection and articulated pose estimation, pp. 1014–1021 (2010). https://doi.org/10.1109/CVPR.2009.520 6754
22. Yang, Y., Ramanan, D.: Articulated pose estimation with flexible mixtures-of-parts. In: Proceedings of the IEEE Computer Society Conference on Computer Vision and Pattern Recognition, pp. 1385–1392 (2011). https://doi.org/10.1109/CVPR.2011.5995741
23. Markoff, J.: Scientists See Promise in Deep-Learning Program. Nyt. (2012)
24. Toshev, A., Szegedy, C.: DeepPose: human pose estimation via deep neural networks (2014)
25. Insafutdinov, E., Pishchulin, L., Andres, B., Andriluka, M., Schiele, B.: DeeperCut: a deeper, stronger, and faster multi-person pose estimation model. In: Leibe, B., Matas, J., Sebe, N., Welling, M. (eds.) ECCV 2016. LNCS, vol. 9910, pp. 34–50. Springer, Cham (2016). https://doi.org/10.1007/978-3-319-46466-4_3
26. Sun, K., Xiao, B., Liu, D., Wang, J.: Deep high-resolution representation learning for human pose estimation. In: Proceedings of the IEEE Computer Society Conference on Computer Vision and Pattern Recognition, pp. 5686–5696 (2019)
27. Wei, S.E., Ramakrishna, V., Kanade, T., Sheikh, Y.: Convolutional pose machines. In: Proceedings of the IEEE Computer Society Conference on Computer Vision and Pattern Recognition, pp. 4724–4732 (2016)

28. Newell, A., Yang, K., Deng, J.: Stacked hourglass networks for human pose estimation. In: Leibe, B., Matas, J., Sebe, N., Welling, M. (eds.) ECCV 2016. LNCS, vol. 9912, pp. 483–499. Springer, Cham (2016). https://doi.org/10.1007/978-3-319-46484-8_29

29. Rodrigues, R., Madeira, R.N., Correia, N., Fernandes, C., Ribeiro, S.: Multimodal web based video annotator with real-time human pose estimation. In: Yin, H., Camacho, D., Tino, P., Tallón-Ballesteros, A.J., Menezes, R., Allmendinger, R. (eds.) IDEAL 2019. LNCS, vol. 11872, pp. 23–30. Springer, Cham (2019). https://doi.org/10.1007/978-3-030-33617-2_3

30. PoseNet. https://learn.ml5js.org/#/reference/posenet?id=posenet. Accessed 15 Nov 2021

A Fast Region Segmentation Algorithm for Water Meter Image Based on Adaptive Seed Point Selection

Hongchao Zhou[1], Yongjun Liu[2], and Zhenjiang Qian[2($\boxtimes$)]

[1] Huzhou University, Huzhou 313000, Zhejiang, People's Republic of China
[2] Changshu Institute of Technology, Changshu 215500, Jiangsu, People's Republic of China
qianzj@cslg.edu.cn

Abstract. This paper presents a fast region segmentation algorithm segmentation based on adaptive selection of seed points and without distance evaluation for water meter image. When the binary image of water meter is segmented, in order to better balance the precision and efficiency of segmentation, the algorithm adaptively selects some points in a specific line of the image as seed points. At the same time, the algorithm adopts a method similar to the connected component analysis algorithm, which takes the value of the point to be detected rather than the distance between the seed point and the point to be detected as the basis for region growth, which not only preserves the characteristics of high segmentation accuracy of the region segmentation algorithm, but also improves the segmentation efficiency. By analyzing the segmentation results of different algorithms for the same water meter image and their algorithm complexity, it is shown that the proposed algorithm has the highest segmentation efficiency, but the accuracy is not lower than other algorithms.

Keywords: Image processing · Region segmentation · Water meter · Connected component analysis

1 The Introduction

The traditional manual water meter reading is time-consuming and laborious, which is gradually replaced by the modern and automatic water meter digital reading. Some methods are installing smart water meters and reading the meter digital directly, but the original meter needs to be replaced [1–3]. Another method is to directly take images of the original water meter dial and send the images back to the server for image recognition. This method does not need to replace the water meter, has lower cost and simple operation, and becomes a better choice in some cases [4, 5].

There are many methods for water meter image recognition, some of which use deep learning to directly recognize water meter digital on the image, but this method requires a large amount of training for the algorithm and sufficient training samples [5–7]. Another approach is to segment the single digital of water meter and then recognize

Z. Lv and H. Song (Eds.): INTETAIN 2021, LNICST 429, pp. 23–35, 2022.
https://doi.org/10.1007/978-3-030-99188-3_3

them easily using existing image recognition algorithms. In the face of different styles of water meters, this method is obviously more robust.

Therefore, the process of using the second method is usually to first segment the dial digital and then recognize the digital. In the process of digital segmentation of water meters, the main methods used are manual segmentation algorithm, vertical projection algorithm and connected component analysis algorithm [8–10]. The accuracy of manual segmentation method is very low, requiring a high degree of consistency of each water meter image, and the segmentation results are prone to appear unrelated connected component. Vertical projection algorithm segmentation accuracy and efficiency are not high. Although the connected component analysis algorithm is accurate in image segmentation, it needs to analyze all pixel points, so the algorithm has low efficiency. In the face of water meter images of complex scenes, its shortcomings will be more obvious.

Region segmentation algorithms are usually used to process color images or grey images [11]. Therefore, aiming at the binary image of water meter, this paper tries to improve the region segmentation algorithm, so as to improve the segmentation efficiency while maintaining a high segmentation accuracy.

The content structure of this paper is arranged as follows: The Sect. 2 analyzes the principles and shortcomings of manual segmentation algorithm, vertical projection algorithm, connected component analysis algorithm and region segmentation algorithm. The Sect. 3 describes the algorithm principle of the improved region segmentation algorithm in detail, including adaptive seed point selection and the realization of these operations without distance evaluation; The Sect. 4 analyzes the segmentation effect and complexity of manual segmentation algorithm, vertical projection algorithm, connected component analysis algorithm and improved region segmentation algorithm through experiments. The Sect. 5 is the summary of the paper.

2   Disadvantages of Binary Image Segmentation Algorithms

Manual segmentation algorithm is based on prior knowledge, directly in a specific position to segment the image. Although this method is simple and efficient, it relies too much on prior knowledge and requires highly consistent features of the images to be segmented, so the robustness of the algorithm is poor.

Vertical projection algorithm is usually used to deal with binary images. As shown in Fig. 1, assume that the image size is m * n. There are four connected components in the image: L1, L2, L3 and R, among which L1, L2 and L3 are the target connected components. The sum of the pixel values of each column is counted:

$$z = \sum_{1}^{n} g \tag{1}$$

Where "z" is the sum of the pixel values for each column of pixels, and "g" is the pixel value for each point. Since the processed image is a binary image, the pixel values are only 0 and 1, so the value of "z" is actually the sum of the number of pixels with a pixel value of 1 per column.

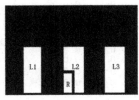 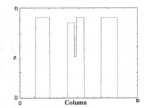 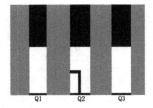

Fig. 1. Binary image   **Fig. 2.** The statistical results   **Fig. 3.** Segmentation results

Statistics on the z of each column, the statistical results of m columns were plotted (see Fig. 2). The statistical graph presents the feature of "peak - trough - peak". Since the sum of pixel points with the value of 1 between the target components are 0, they correspond to the trough position in the statistical graph. Therefore, the trough position is taken as the image segmenting line to complete image segmentation. Through segmentation, Q1, Q2 and Q3 are obtained. The connected component R is not the target region, but it is segmented as a part of Q2 (see Fig. 3). Therefore, the accuracy of vertical projection method is poor.

Connected component analysis is a common binary image segmentation algorithm. The function of the algorithm is to find the connected component in the image. Before segmenting, you need to create an tag array of the same size as n * n, with the element value initialized to 0.

First, line-by-line detection is carried out from the first row of pixels in the image. If the value of the pixel point is 0 or the value of the element in the corresponding position of the tag array is 1, the pixel point is directly skipped. When finding the pixel value is 1, and its position in tag array element has a value of 0, will immediately change the value of the corresponding position of the tag array is 1, and to detect the four-neighbors, after the detect, if found a pixel value of 1 point, regard it as the point in the same connected component, the next point of the surrounding, until connected component cannot expand a new point came in, This segmentation is over.

As shown in Fig. 4 below, when the pixel point at position (1,2) is detected, its value is found to be 1, and the corresponding element value on the tag array is 0, so the value at position of the tag array (1,2) is changed to 1. When detecting the elements of four-neighbors, it is found that the elements at the positions (2,1) and (1,3) can also be extended in. Similarly, four-neighbors detection is performed on the elements at position (2,1) and (1,3), and the elements at position (2,3) are extended. At this time, no new points can be expanded. The segmentation is over. Figure 5 shows the tag array after the segmentation.

Next, the pixel point at position (1,3) is detected. Although its value is 1, the corresponding element of the tag array is 1, so it is skipped directly. Next, (1,4), (1,5)…(n,n) are detected in sequence. According to the rule of line-by-line detection, when the pixels at position (n,n) are detected, the image segmentation is completed and the algorithm is finished. The segmentation result is shown in the Fig. 6.

```
0 1 1 0 0 0 0 0 0 0          0 1 1 0 0 0 0 0 0 0
0 1 1 0 0 0 0 0 0 0          0 1 1 0 0 0 0 0 0 0
0 0 0 0 0 0 0 0 0 0          0 0 0 0 0 0 0 0 0 0
0 0 0 0 0 0 0 0 0 0          0 0 0 0 0 0 0 0 0 0
0 1 0 0 0 0 0 0 0 0          0 0 0 0 0 0 0 0 0 0
0 1 1 0 0 0 0 0 0 0          0 0 0 0 0 0 0 0 0 0
0 1 1 0 0 0 0 0 0 0          0 0 0 0 0 0 0 0 0 0
0 0 0 0 0 0 0 0 0 0          0 0 0 0 0 0 0 0 0 0
0 0 0 0 0 0 0 0 0 0          0 0 0 0 0 0 0 0 0 0
0 0 0 0 0 0 0 0 0 0          0 0 0 0 0 0 0 0 0 0
```

Fig. 4. Binary image   **Fig. 5.** Tag array

```
0 0 0 0 0 0 0 0 0 0          0 0 0 0 0 0 0 0 0 0
0 0 0 0 0 0 0 0 0 0          0 0 0 0 0 0 0 0 0 0
0 0 0 0 0 0 0 0 0 0          0 0 0 0 0 0 0 0 0 0
0 0 0 0 0 0 0 0 0 0          0 0 0 0 0 0 0 0 0 0
0 1 0 0 0 0 0 0 0 0          0 1 0 0 0 0 0 0 0 0
0 1 1 0 0 0 0 0 0 0          0 1 1 0 0 0 0 0 0 0
0 1 1 0 0 0 0 0 0 0          0 1 1 0 0 0 0 0 0 0
0 0 0 0 0 0 0 0 0 0          0 0 0 0 0 0 0 0 0 0
0 0 0 0 0 0 0 0 0 0          0 0 0 0 0 0 0 0 0 0
0 0 0 0 0 0 0 0 0 0          0 0 0 0 0 0 0 0 0 0
```

Fig. 6. Segmentation results

As can be seen from the above, the algorithm needs to detect all pixels and find all connected components, which are not all connected components. Therefore, a large number of irrelevant connected components need to be screened, and the efficiency of the algorithm is reduced.

The region segmentation algorithm first needs to determine the seed points and thresholds. The determination of seed points can be divided into manual selection and automatic selection. The determination of threshold needs to select an appropriate value according to prior knowledge. As shown in Fig. 7, suppose the coordinates of the seed point S is (i,j), and the threshold is T. Sequentially detect $a(i-1,j-1)$, $b(i-1,j)$, $c(i-1,j+1)$, $d(i,j-1)$, $e(i,j+1)$, $f(i+1,j-1)$, $g(i+1,j)$, $h(i+1,j+1)$ these eight points. Perform the following calculation, where "x" is the pixel value of the current point:

$$T \leq |S - x| \tag{2}$$

If the above formula holds, then this point is merged and used as the seed point for the next round of detection, otherwise the next point is detected. When all these points are calculated, the current round of detection is completed, and the next seed point is replaced. Create an output array with the same size as the image, mark the points that have been detected, and then not detect again. Suppose that when the detection is completed, points e, f, g, and h are merged in. Next time, points b, c, S, g, and h will not be detected when using e point as the seed point next time, as shown in Fig. 8. Until the last seed point is replaced, and no new seed points are merged in, the algorithm ends. At this time, the output array is the result of this segmentation.

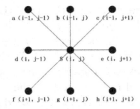

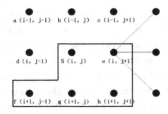

Fig. 7. Take S point as the seed point   **Fig. 8.** Take e point as the seed point

3 Improved Region Segmentation Algorithm

Since the image to be segmented is a binary image, according to its characteristics, an improved region segmentation algorithm is proposed. This algorithm can automatically select seed points and does not need distance evaluation. As shown in Fig. 9, it is assumed that the size of the image is m * n.

```
   ┌ middle row
0 │ 0  0  0  0  0  0  0  0  0  0  0  0  0  0
0 │ 0  0  0  0  0  1  1  0  0  0  0  0  0  0
1 │ 1  0  0  0  0  1  0  0  0  0  0  0  0  0
  ┌───────────────────────────────────────┐
  │ 0  0  0  0  0  1  0  0  0  0  0  0  0  0 │
  └───────────────────────────────────────┘
1   1  1  0  0  0  1  0  0  0  0  0  0  0  0
0   0  0  0  0  0  0  0  0  0  0  0  0  0  0
0   0  0  0  0  0  0  0  0  0  0  0  0  0  0
```

Fig. 9. Image to be segmented

The abscissa of the middle row:

$$L = \lceil m/2 \rceil \tag{3}$$

Where "L" is the middle row, "m" is the height of the image. Because the digital in the water meter image must pass through the L line, all the pixel points in the L line of the image are taken as the alternative points of seed points. When a region segmentation is completed, the next seed point is found from the candidate points through the L line in order to segment all the connected components.

Therefore, the alternative point coordinates are (L,1), (L,2)…(L,n).

In addition to the output array with the size of m * n, A one-dimensional tag array A is set up to mark whether the elements in line L have been detected. The length of the array is equal to the number of alternative seed points. The array element value is initialized to 0, indicating that the corresponding pixel is not detected.

Start the detection from the point (L,1), and set the value of the array A[1] to 1, indicating that the element has been detected, and the detected point will not be detected. At this time, the value of point (L,1) is found to be 1, so the eight neighbors are detected with this point as the seed point.

First, detect (L-1,1). Instead of evaluating the distance between (L,1) and (L−1,1), check the value of (L−1,1), which is 1, mark it in the output array, merge it in and serve as the seed point for the next round of detection. Then, the abscissa of (L−1,1) is judged. Since L−1 ≠ L, the operation is finished. Next, check (L−1,2), (L,2), (L+1,2), and (L+1,1) in the same way. When check (L,2), in addition to completing the operation described before, since its abscis-axis is equal to L and its ordinate is 2, the value of A[2] needs to be set to 1. After the detection is completed with (L,1) as the seed points, the points just merged will be used as the seed points for a new round of detection until all the merged points are detected as the seed points and no new points are merged. The region segmentation is completed this time, and the output array is the connected component found.

Next, look for the next seed point based on array A and the binary image. The value of second alternative point (L,2) is 1, but because value of the A[2] is 1, it has already been detected, so it is skipped. Look at the third alternative (L,3) and set the value of A[3] to 1. The value of (L,3) is 0, skip this point and look at (L,4), (L,5), (L,6)..., when looking at (L,7), since the value of (L,7) is 1 and A[7] = 0, this point is taken as the seed point for A region segmentation. The operation of the final alternative points (L,N) is completed in the above way, the algorithm ends.

4   Experiment and Analysis of Result

4.1   Experiment Preparation

In order to verify the accuracy and efficiency of the improved region segmentation algorithm in water meter digital image segmentation, in this paper, four segmentation algorithms are used for experimental comparison, which are manual segmentation algorithm, vertical projection algorithm, connected component analysis algorithm and improved region algorithm. The experimental platform is MATLAB software, its version is 2018A.

(a)   (b)   (c)   (d)

Fig. 10.   Images of ordinary household water meter

The experimental images are grayscale images of general household water meters and they are from some residential areas. Here are four images of water meters, a, b, c and d, with size of 640 px * 480 px (see Fig. 10).

4.2 Preprocessing of Water Meter Images

Because these water meter images contain not only the dial digits, but also the dial contour, number and other information, it is necessary to extract the images of the digital range before the images are segmented. The dial digits are concentrated in the center of the image, and the grey values of the digital pixel are small and the pixel points are continuous, which is obviously different from the background. The digital region of the water meter can be located in the following ways.

First, if the water meter image is not a grayscale image, it is first transformed into a grayscale image. Since the experiment uses grayscale images directly, this step can be skipped.

Next, the edge detection of the image is carried out. Robert operator is used in detection, because as a first-order differential operator, Robert is simple, the amount of calculation is small, and the reaction is sensitive to details [12]. In this step, a binary image containing the edges of each component in the water meter image is obtained.

(a)   (b)

(c)   (d)

Fig. 11. Digital image of water meter extracted by positioning

After the edge detection image is obtained, corrosion operation and closed operation are carried out [13]. There are still many small clusters in the image after the image closing operation, which affect the location of the digital range of the water meter, so they can be removed. It can be seen that the white area of the final image is the approximate area of the water meter digital. The digital range of water meter is extracted by projection segmentation algorithm [14] (see Fig. 11).

Next, the extracted image is processed by binarization. Binary image refers to dividing the values of all pixels on the image into 0 and 1. Thresholds need to be determined in the division, which can be obtained by using OSTU [15, 16]. Through binarization processing, all the values representing the digital gray scale of the water meter are 1 and the background pixel value is 0.The resulting binarization image also needs to trim the upper and lower edges (see Fig. 12).

![Binary image strips showing digits 004430, 038522, 0114196, 058923](#)

(a)   (b)

(c)   (d)

Fig. 12. Binary image

4.3 Segmentation of Water Meter Images

Use manual segmentation, vertical projection algorithm, connected component analysis algorithm, and improved region segmentation algorithm to segment the binary image.Moreover, the more disconnected components of the image to be segmented, the more obvious the number gap will be.

Therefore, in addition to the manual segmentation algorithm, other methods are divided into two steps: one is to segment the image, the other is to screen the segmentation results. Here are the components that were segmented by different algorithm (for easy seeing, the components image is placed on a grey background, same below) (see Fig. 13, Fig. 14, Fig. 15 and Fig. 16):

(a)   (b)

(c)   (d)

Fig. 13. Manual segmentation algorithm

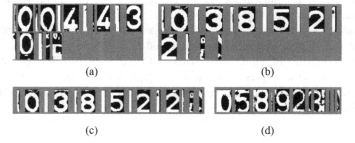

(a)   (b)

(c)   (d)

Fig. 14. Vertical projection algorithm

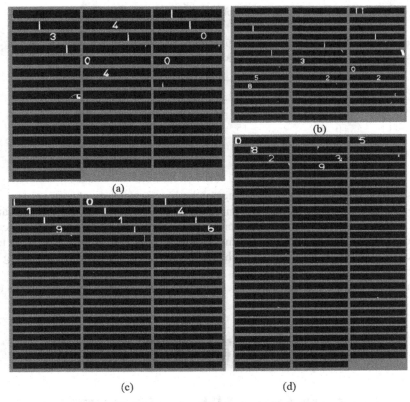

Fig. 15. Connected component analysis algorithm

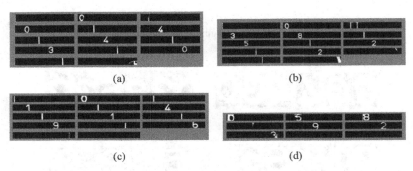

Fig. 16. Improved region segmentation algorithm

The following is the statistics of the total number of segmented components (Table 1):

Table 1. Components obtained by different algorithms

Segmentation algorithm	Manual segmentation	Vertical projection	Connected component analysis	Improved region segmentation
Image of a	6	16	43	14
Image of b	6	13	41	14
Image of c	6	15	57	14
Image of d	6	11	80	15

As can be seen from the above image and table, the total number of components segmented by the connected component analysis algorithm is far more than that of other algorithms. The total number of components segmented by the vertical projection algorithm and the improved region segmentation algorithm are similar. The more total number of obtained by segmentation, the more times of screening, thus reducing the segmentation efficiency.

The following are the results after screening the above connected components (see Fig. 17, Fig. 18, Fig. 19 and Fig. 20):

(a)   (b)

(c)   (d)

Fig. 17. Manual segmentation algorithm

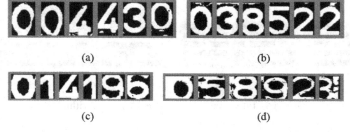

(a)   (b)

(c)   (d)

Fig. 18. Vertical projection algorithm

Fig. 19. Connected component analysis algorithm

Fig. 20. Improved region segmentation algorithm

From the screening results, it can be seen that the segmentation results of manual segmentation algorithm have a large number of unrelated connected components, and the segmentation accuracy is poor. The vertical projection algorithm also has a small number of disconnected components. Both the connected component analysis algorithm and the improved region segmentation algorithm have the best segmentation accuracy because they do not contain unrelated connected components.

The time complexity analysis of the four algorithms is as follows (Table 2):

Table 2. Time complexity of the four algorithms

Segmentation algorithm	Manual segmentation	Vertical projection	Connected component analysis	Improved region segmentation
Best situation	$O(1)$	$O(n^2)$	$O(n^2)$	$O(n)$
Worst situation	$O(1)$	$O(n^2)$	$O(n^2)$	$O(n^2)$

It can be observed from the above table that the time complexity of the improved region segmentation algorithm in this paper is only higher than that of manual segmentation in the best case. In the worst case, except the manual segmentation algorithm, the time complexity is $O(n^2)$. However, since the vertical projection algorithm needs to count the sum of pixel values in each column, and the connected component analysis algorithm needs to detect the whole graph, the constant term of their time complexity is greater than 1. However, the improved region segmentation algorithm in this paper usually only detects a limited number of pixels, and the time complexity constant term is usually less than 1. Therefore, the time complexity constant term of the improved region segmentation algorithm in this paper is less than the vertical projection method or the connected component analysis method. Summarizing the above experimental results and theoretical analysis, the following conclusions can be drawn:

(1) Since the improved region segmentation algorithm does not need to detect all the pixels of the image, while the connected component analysis algorithm needs to detect all the pixels of the whole image, the improved region segmentation algorithm significantly reduces the meaningless components segmented compared with the connected component analysis algorithm, thus improving the efficiency of screening the segmentation results.

(2) Since the improved region algorithm segmented specific connected components, while the manual segmentation algorithm and the vertical projection algorithm segmented connected components based on prior knowledge, the accuracy and robustness of the algorithm were higher than those of the manual segmentation algorithm and the vertical projection algorithm.

(3) In general, because the improved region segmentation algorithm can only detect a limited number of pixels, it can only detect all pixels of the image in extreme cases, so its constant term of time complexity is smaller than the connected domain analysis algorithm and vertical projection algorithm.

5 Conclusion

This paper presents a fast region segmentation algorithm for water meter images based on adaptive seed point selection. Firstly, the principles and disadvantages of manual segmentation algorithm, vertical projection algorithm and connected domain analysis algorithm are introduced. Then the principle of the improved region segmentation algorithm is described in detail, including the process of automatic seed point selection and the improvement of the algorithm. Finally, the above algorithms are used to test a household water meter image. The experiment includes image preprocessing, the extraction of digital range, and the analysis of the experimental results of various segmentation algorithms and the time complexity of the algorithm.

Through the analysis, it can be concluded that the algorithm proposed in this paper retains the advantages of accurate segmentation of the region segmentation algorithm, and the sum of components segmented by the algorithm is small, so it is convenient for screening. Since the proposed algorithm does not need to estimate the distance and detect the whole image point by point, the accuracy of the proposed algorithm is not lower than that of other algorithms and the efficiency is improved.

References

1. Suresh, M., Muthukumar, U., Chandapillai, J.: A novel smart water-meter based on IoT and smartphone app for city distribution management. In: 2017 IEEE Region 10 Symposium (TENSYMP), Cochin, India, 2017, pp. 1–5 (2017)

2. Saidi, A.H.K.S.A., Hussain, S.A., Hussain, S.M., Singh, A.V., Rana, A.: Smart water meter using power line communication (PLC) approach for measurements of accurate water consumption and billing process. In: 2020 8th International Conference on Reliability, pp. 1119–1122 (2020)
3. Hong, Y.-S., Lee, C.-H.: A design and implementation of low-power ultrasonic water meter. Smart Water **4**, 35–36 (2019)
4. Triantoro, T., Batubara, F.R., Fahmi, F.: Image based water gauge reading developed with ANN Kohonen. In: 2014 International Conference on Electrical Engineering and Computer Science (ICEECS), Kuta, Bali, Indonesia, pp. 74–78 (2014)
5. Azeem, A., Riaz, W., Siddique, A., et al.: A robust automatic meter reading system based on mask-RCNN. In: 2020 IEEE International Conference on Advances in Electrical Engineering and Computer Applications (AEECA), pp. 37–44. IEEE (2020)
6. Meng, L., Cheng, J.: Research on the visual recognition method of pointer water meter reading. In: 2021 IEEE 5th Advanced Information Technology, Electronic and Automation Control Conference (IAEAC), 15 November 2021, pp. 34–39. IEEE (2021)
7. Pan, S., Han, L., Tao, Y., Liu, Q.: Study on indicator recognition method of water meter based on convolution neural network. In: Tian, Y., Ma, T., Khan, M.K. (eds.) Big Data and Security: First International Conference, ICBDS 2019, Nanjing, China, December 20–22, 2019, Revised Selected Papers, pp. 594–602. Springer, Singapore (2020). https://doi.org/10.1007/978-981-15-7530-3_45
8. Mao, X., Zheng, L.: Locating micrometer in a digital image based on projection algorithm in space domain. In: 2010 5th International Conference on Internet Computing for Science and Engineering, Harbin, China, pp. 30–33 (2010)
9. Xia, H., Liao, D.: The study of license plate character segmentation algorithm based on vertical projection. In: 2011 International Conference on Consumer Electronics, Xianning, China, pp. 4583–4586 (2011)
10. Vishwanath, N., Somasundaram, S., Ravi, M.R.R., Nallaperumal, N.K.: Connected component analysis for Indian license plate infra-red and color image character segmentation. In: 2012 IEEE International Conference on Computational Intelligence, pp. 72–76 (2012)
11. Kumar, V., Lal, T., Dhuliya, P., Pant, D.: A study and comparison of different image segmentation algorithms. In: 2016 2nd International Conference on Advances in Computing, India, pp. 1–6 (2016)
12. Selvakumar, P., Hariganesh, S.: The performance analysis of edge detection algorithms for image processing. In: 2016 International Conference on Computing Technologies and Intelligent Data Engineering, Kovilpatti, India, pp. 1–5 (2016)
13. Cheng, X., Zhao, H., Liu, B.: Fast image dilation/erosion with cooperation of multiple neighbors. In: 2010 Chinese Conference on Pattern Recognition, Chongqing, China, pp. 1–4 (2010)
14. Ham, S., et al.: Myocardial territory segmentation on coronary computed tomography angiography images: comparison between projection and non-projection methods in a pig model. Inf. Med. Unlocked **19**, 100320 (2020)
15. Hou, J., Li, B.: An improved algorithm for horizon detection based on OSTU. In: 2015 7th International Conference on Intelligent Human-Machine Systems and Cybernetics, pp. 414–417 (2015)
16. Zhu, Q., Jing, L., Bi, R.: Exploration and improvement of Ostu threshold segmentation algorithm. In: 2010 8th World Congress on Intelligent Control and Automation, Jinan, China, pp. 6183–6188 (2010)

Enterprise Economic Forecasting Method Based on ARIMA-LSTM Model

Xiaofei Dong[1(✉)], Xuesen Zong[1], Peng Li[2], and Jinlong Wang[1]

[1] Qingdao University of Science and Technology, Qingdao, China
unsolvedcila@163.com
[2] Qingdao Yilian Information Technology Co. LTD, Qingdao, China

Abstract. Enterprise economic forecast is an important part of the development of enterprises, which can help the government to judge the development of enterprises quickly and effectively so as to make scientific decisions of China. With the development of Internet of Things (IOT) technology, enterprise's IOT data can bring strong data basis to enterprise's economic forecast. In order to obtain more accurate results of enterprise economic forecasting, a method of enterprise economic forecasting based on Auto regressive Integrated Moving Average and Long Short Term Memory networks (ARIMA-LSTM) model is proposed, which solves the problem that a single forecasting algorithm can only predict according to a single economic development data. The model uses ARIMA model to predict the linear data of time series such as IOT data, and LSTM to predict the nonlinear relationship. Combined with the historical economic data of enterprises, ARIMA-LSTM model is used to predict the future economic development of enterprises. Comparing the prediction results with ARIMA model and ARIMA-LSTM model without IOT data, it is found that the model has the smallest RMSE, MAE and MAPE. The results show that the model can effectively predict the economic situation of enterprises.

Keywords: Enterprise economic · IOT · ARIMA · LSTM · Forecast

1 Introduction

1.1 Research Significance

With the advent of the second Centenary Goal, many local governments have issued plans to support the acceleration of the development of leading enterprises and formulated development goals for leading enterprises. The State Council has also issued a number of opinions on promoting industrial development, guiding the development of emerging industries, expanding existing high-tech enterprises and fostering small and medium-sized technology-based enterprises. The government needs to monitor the development of enterprises and timely adjust the list of enterprises to be cultivated. To predict and estimate the specific economic status and future development trend of enterprises can help government personnel to have a clearer understanding of the economic development trend of enterprises, provide detailed information and data support

Z. Lv and H. Song (Eds.): INTETAIN 2021, LNICST 429, pp. 36–57, 2022.
https://doi.org/10.1007/978-3-030-99188-3_4

for decision-making, and ensure the accuracy of decision-making [1]. The operating income of an enterprise is one of the financial indicators that directly measure the scale of enterprise operation and indirectly reflect its operating results [2]. The management of enterprise operating income is an important aspect of enterprise financial management. However, it is difficult to judge the future development trend of an enterprise only by relying on the data reported by the enterprise, and a series of problems such as excess capacity and insufficient competitiveness of the enterprise may occur if the wrong large-scale investment is made. Therefore, it is of great significance for the government to monitor and manage enterprises and regions to study the future economic development trend of enterprises.

1.2   Research Background

Many scholars have conducted in-depth research on enterprise economic forecasting. Xiao et al. evaluated the performance of enterprise investment decision by Back Propagation (BP) neural network [3]. Wang et al. proposed an enterprise economic risk prediction model based on big data fusion to predict enterprise economic risk [4]. These methods are of great help to scientific decision making of China.

However, the above methods all use historical economic data for linear regression prediction. The factors affecting the economic development of enterprises are diversified, and the business operation and related data management can never be explained by a simple linear regression system. With the continuous development of learning technology, more and more scholars tend to use nonlinear regression model to model and analyze financial time series. Barker et al. constructed a unified modeling framework, adjusted the Machine Learning model hyperparameters and generated the prediction interval by using time series cross-validation, with good results [5]. Hryhorkiv et al. used artificial neural network to predict the nonlinear part of stock fluctuations and achieved good prediction results [6]. Feng et al. studied economic prediction based on wavelet neural network, which is used to predict nonlinear systems [7]. Huang et al. used support vector machine and other three different models to predict enterprise operating income data and evaluated the predictive ability of the models [8]. However, the nonlinear prediction are according to the nonlinear consolidation of economic data, without considering the other factors may be the effects on the economy, according to the analysis and forecasting of economic data, only can't analysis because the economic impact of other objective factors, lead to prediction has limitations, is not conducive to scientific decision-making of the government. In view of the method of using multiple factors to predict the economy, some scholars put forward the prediction model based on the traditional BP neural network and time series to predict the sales of the enterprise in the future unit time [9], but the training data are independent and cannot be combined with historical data for training. Wu used Long Short Term Memory networks (LSTM) model to forecast sales [10], avoiding the independent prediction problem of BP network and the long-term dependence problem of recurrent neural network. However, the model can only be used after obtaining all the data of influencing factors. If the data of current influencing factors has not been generated or missing, it cannot be predicted.

In view of the problems existing in the above existing methods, this paper will conduct in-depth studies on factors that can reflect the economic development status of enterprises. Internet of Things (IOT) data can truly reflect the characteristics of the operation process of enterprises [11–13], and excellent performance of Auto regressive Integrated Moving Average (ARIMA) in IOT data prediction [14–16]. A forecasting model of enterprise economic development based on ARIMA-LSTM is designed and implemented. The IOT data combined with the data of economic impact factors of Internet enterprises are used to train the economic development of enterprises. The ARIMA model is used to predict the changes of the data of influence factors in the future, and LSTM is used to integrate the data of historical economic data non-linear. The experiment shows that the model can accurately predict the future economic development trend of enterprises, and help government personnel to accurately control and timely adjust enterprises.

2   Correlative Knowledge

2.1   The Relationship Between IOT and Economic Development

The concept of the IOT was first put forward by the Massachusetts Institute of Technology in 1999. With the continuous development of information technology, the IOT is more and more widely used. The IOT can not only provide real and ordered data, but also bring great convenience to data calculation and analysis. Structured data of the IOT is also more convenient for researchers to sort out and study data, from which more valuable information can be found. And since IOT data is machine log data generated by networked devices, it is generally not allowed and does not need to be modified. For government departments, it avoids the situation that enterprises report false data, and the data is more real and reliable.

Many scholars have studied the connection between the IOT and economic development. Xu et al. analyzed the relationship between regional economic development and electricity consumption data and predicted the Gross Domestic Product growth rate of Jiangsu province with BP neural network algorithm, which achieved good results [11]. Wang et al. analyzed the connection between the IOT and the development of regional economy and proved that the IOT and regional economic development have a very strong correlation [12]. Chen et al. analyzed the significance and role of the IOT in economic development [13]. Research shows that the IOT data is closely related to economic development, and the economic development of enterprises can also be intuitively reflected through the IOT data.

2.2   Application of Time Series Model in IOT Data Prediction

IOT data is the data generated during the operation of equipment. The data must be time series data with time stamps, which is very important for the calculation and analysis of data and can be processed by using time series analysis algorithm. Moreover, the data flow of the IOT is stable and predictable, which makes the data of the IOT more suitable for stable prediction [17].

Many scholars applied the time series prediction model to the data prediction of the IOT. Tang et al. analyzed the practicability of three commonly used models in the prediction of three different types of parking lots, and the results proved that Autoregressive

Integrated Moving Average model (ARIMA) and Back Propagation (BP) neural network had good accuracy models in short-term prediction [14]. Lin used ARIMA model of geometric empirical mode decomposition to predict electricity sales and proved that ARIMA model has good prediction accuracy for electricity sales data [15]. Wang et al. used two forecasting methods combining BP neural network, ARIMA and Support Vector Regression (SVR) to predict the electricity consumption of 20 energy-intensive enterprises by taking into account macroeconomic indicators, upstream and downstream product output, and weather [16]. The experimental results show that ARIMA+SVR performs better in predicting power consumption. The above experiments show that the time series model can get good prediction effect in predicting the data of IOT, but only predicting the data of IOT is not enough to predict the economic development of enterprises, so it is necessary to redesign the method of predicting the economic development of enterprises.

3 Enterprise Economic Forecasting Method Based on ARIMA-LSTM Model

The overall process of the enterprise economic forecasting method based on ARIMA-LSTM model proposed in this paper is shown in Fig. 1. It is mainly composed of several ARIMA models and one LSTM model. The ARIMA model is mainly used to predict the original influencing factor data of each time series and get its predicted value respectively. Then, the training data, predicted value and other influencing factors are combined and normalized. The LSTM model is used to construct the functional relationship between the combined influencing factors and enterprise operating income, and the final enterprise operating income data is predicted.

3.1 Enterprise Development Environment

There are many factors related to economic development in the process of enterprise development. Faced with numerous data, data can be divided into Internet data and IOT data according to data sources. In the Internet data, the economic development of enterprises is closely related to the information of operating income of enterprises, the news and public opinion of enterprises, the number of highly educated talents. In the IOT data, the number of vehicles in the parking lot data, enterprise electricity consumption data, enterprise access control personnel information data, working hours data reflect the personnel situation of enterprises. Energy consumption and personnel activity can also reflect the economic development of enterprises.

When combining the IOT data to predict the enterprise economy, time series analysis and neural network model are used alone to predict accompanying by the following shortcomings. Time series analysis cannot predict the influence of other factors on the results. Neural network model can predict the results according to the existing influencing factor data, but can not predict the future results when there is no influencing factor data. In this paper, ARIMA which has good prediction results in time series analysis and LSTM which is suitable for long term series prediction in neural network are selected. Combined with the characteristics of the two, the time series influencing factor data and enterprise economic data are predicted, which can realize the enterprise economic forecast combined with the IOT data.

3.2 Model Principle

As mentioned above, the IOT data can accurately reflect the operating status of enterprise equipment, which can be predicted by the time series model, and the combined model can solve the limitation of single model prediction, so as to effectively predict enterprise economy.

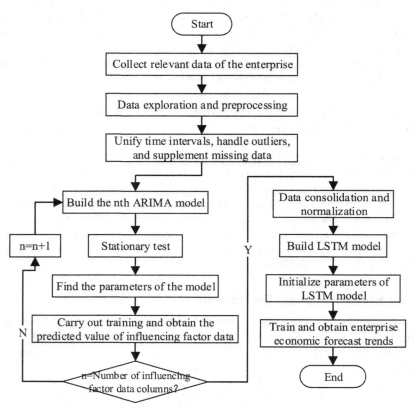

Fig. 1. The overall process of enterprise economic forecasting method based on ARIMA-LSTM model.

Table 1 shows the parameters of the main related variables of the model.

In most studies, the model is fixed and the validity is evaluated for different input characteristics, but there is a lack of research on hyperparameters [4]. After study, the model sets the data set of influencing factors as $F_t = \{O_{MR}, G_{MR}, H_t, P_t, E_t, N_t, W_t, m, P_{MR}, E_{MR}, N_{MR}\}$. Among them, O_{MR}, G_{MR}, P_{MR}, E_{MR}, N_{MR} is the lag data with the greatest correlation. In the process of forecasting the development of enterprise economy, the influence of data on enterprise economy also has certain characteristics. Generally, enterprise economy will not immediately show the change of enterprise economy with the change of data in the month, but there is a certain lag. Therefore, the most relevant IOT data are added into the influencing factors. Due to the absence of time series in Internet data, it is impossible to predict future data based on existing data. Therefore, the historical Internet data with the greatest correlation is added to the influential factor data set to predict enterprise operating income data. In addition, the data related to the current time is added to ensure the latest data. The current month data can be used to find the time characteristics of time series data.

Table 1. Variable parameter table.

Parameter	Parameter meaning
I^E	General term for Internet data
I^{OT}	General term for IOT data
M_t	The operating income data of the enterprise
O_t/O_{MR}	T time/maximum relevance of enterprise news public opinion information data
G_t/G_{MR}	T time/maximum relevance of enterprise positive information data
H_t/H	T time/all time data of highly educated talents
$P_t/P/P_{MR}$	T time/all time/maximum relevance of the number of vehicles in the parking lot
$E_t/E/E_{MR}$	T time/all time/maximum relevance of enterprise electricity consumption data
$N_t/N/N_{MR}$	T time/all time/maximum relevance of enterprise access control personnel information data
W_t/W	T time/all time working hours data
m	Month data
F_t/F	T time/all time general name of influencing factor data
F_{pre_n}	Influencing factor data for the nth month in the future

ARIMA model is responsible for predicting each time series data. Based on historical data, it predicts the vehicle access data of parking lot in the next year, electric power consumption data of enterprises, information data of access control personnel of enterprises, number of highly educated talents, working hours, etc.

Assume that the time series running data of an enterprise includes H, P, E, N and W.

The calculation formula of ARIMA model is as follows.

$$y_t = \sum_{m=1}^{p} \varphi_m y_{t-m} - \sum_{j=1}^{q} \theta_j a_{t-j} + a_t + c \tag{1}$$

Where $\varphi_m (m = 1, 2, ..., p)$ is the coefficient of the autoregressive model, $\theta_j (j = 1, 2, ..., p)$ is the average sliding coefficient, a_t is the white noise sequence, the mean value is 0, and c is a constant. The enterprise time series operation data H, P, E, N, W is used to obtain the prediction data results of time series through ARIMA model. Take parking lot data P as an example, if the white noise of parking lot time series is ε_t.

$$P_t = \sum_{m=1}^{p} \varphi_m P_{t-m} - \sum_{j=1}^{q} \theta_j \varepsilon_{t-j} + \varepsilon_t + c \tag{2}$$

The obtained prediction sequence is recorded as $P_{t+n}(n = 1, 2, ...)$.

The prediction results of each column of enterprise time series operation data in F in the next n months predicted by ARIMA model are recorded as $H_{t+n}, P_{t+n}, E_{t+n}, N_{t+n}$ and W_{t+n} respectively. Combining the monthly data and the maximum lag data, the predicted influencing factor data set F_{pre_n} is obtained.

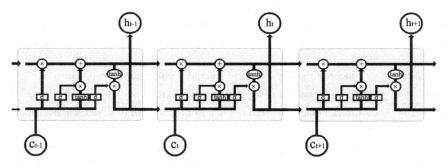

Fig. 2. LSTM model structure.

$$F_{pre\_n} = \{O_{MR+n}, G_{MR+n}, H_{t+n}, P_{t+n}, E_{t+n}, N_{t+n}, W_{t+n}, m_{t+n}, P_{MR+n}, E_{MR+n}, N_{MR+n}\} \tag{3}$$

The structure of LSTM model is shown in Fig. 2. Normalize the influencing factor data set F_t, prediction influencing factor data set F_{pre_n} and enterprise operating income data M_t as the input of LSTM model to make a nonlinear prediction of the enterprise's future economy. The prediction process is as follows:

Step 1: The forgetting gate reads the output of the last cell h_{t-1} and the input of the current cell c_t, and the sigmoid function σ outputs a value between 0 and 1. 1 means "keep completely" and 0 means "discard completely".

$$forget_t = \sigma(W_f \cdot [h_{t-1}, c_t] + b_f) \tag{4}$$

Step2: A sigmoid layer determines what information needs to be updated, and a tanh layer generates content $\tilde{C}_t$ for updating.

$$i_t = \sigma(W_i \cdot [h_{t-1}, c_t] + b_i) \tag{5}$$

$$\tilde{C}_t = \tanh(W_C \cdot [h_{t-1}, c_t] + b_C) \tag{6}$$

Then, update C_{t-1} to C_t. Multiply the old state by $forget_t$, discard the information to be discarded and add $i_t \cdot \tilde{C}_t$ as the new candidate.

Step3: Run a sigmoid layer to determine which part of the cell state will be output. The cell state is processed through tanh (to get a value between -1 and 1) and multiplied by the output of the sigmoid layer, and output the part that determines the output.

$$out_t = \sigma(W_o[h_{t-1}, c_t] + b_o) \tag{7}$$

$$h_t = out_t * \tanh(C_t) \tag{8}$$

It can be seen from the formula that the prediction results of LSTM model are closely related to historical data and stored by storage units. LSTM avoids the problem of gradient extinction and gradient explosion, and can still learn long-term dependence from corpus. Therefore, more accurate results can be obtained by using LSTM model to predict enterprise economic development sequence.

The prediction process of ARIMA-LSTM combined model is as follows:

$$forget_t = \sigma(W_f \cdot [h_{t-1}, \{F_t, F_{pre\_n}, M_t\}] + b_f) \tag{9}$$

$$i_t = \sigma(W_i \cdot [h_{t-1}, \{F_t, F_{pre\_n}, M_t\}] + b_i) \tag{10}$$

$$\tilde{C}_t = \tanh(W_C \cdot [h_{t-1}, \{F_t, F_{pre\_n}, M_t\}] + b_C) \tag{11}$$

$$out_t = \sigma(W_o[h_{t-1}, \{F_t, F_{pre\_n}, M_t\}] + b_o) \tag{12}$$

$$h_t = out_t * \tanh(C_t) \tag{13}$$

The optimization objective of ARIMA-LSTM combined model is to minimize the sum of the gap between the 16-month actual value E and the predicted value A in the predicted results:

$$Min \sum_{i=1}^{12} \left| \frac{A_i - E_i}{E_i} \right| \tag{14}$$

3.3 Model Process

The modeling process is mainly divided into two steps:

1) Data preparation

The model data preparation process is shown in Fig. 3.

Firstly, collect relevant data of the enterprise from relevant departments, sort out I^E, I^{OT} and M_t that may be associated, search for O_{MR}, G_{MR}, P_{MR}, E_{MR} and N_{MR}, preprocess the data, use 3sigma principle to find and delete outliers, and use multiple interpolation method to supplement missing data.

Considering the lag of enterprise economic data, we calculated the prediction effect of O_t, G_t, P_t, E_t and N_t data with one month lag, two months lag and three months lag respectively, and selected the forecast data with the best prediction effect as O_{MR}, G_{MR}, P_{MR}, E_{MR}, N_{MR}.

The results of correlation analysis by using Corel function of Excel are shown in Table 2.

As can be seen from the above table, the correlation of data with a lag of one month is the highest, so it can be concluded that $O_{MR} = O_{t-1}$, $G_{MR} = G_{t-1}$, $P_{MR} = P_{t-1}$, $E_{MR} = E_{t-1}$ and $N_{MR} = N_{t-1}$. Data set F_t of influencing factors can be expressed as $F_t = \{O_{t-1}, G_{t-1}, H_t, P_t, E_t, N_t, W_t, m, P_{t-1}, E_{t-1}, N_{t-1}\}$.

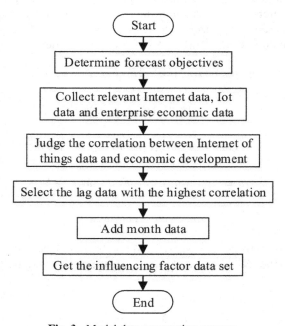

Fig. 3. Model data preparation process.

2) Construct ARIMA-LSTM combination model

The specific process of constructing the combined ARIMA-LSTM model is shown in Fig. 4.

Step1: Select a kind of time series data and test the stationarity of the time series. If the sequence is unstable, the difference operation is carried out to improve the stationarity until the time series meets the stationarity requirements. The number of differences is called d.

Table 2. Correlation between lag time and five kinds of data.

Correlation	O_t	G_t	P_t	E_t	N_t
Raw data	0.147	0.139	0.618	0.383	0.192
One month behind	0.183	0.169	0.911	0.712	0.192
Two month behind	0.122	0.131	0.424	0.033	0.168
Three month behind	0.101	0.128	0.151	−0.244	0.138

Step2: Find the parameter (p, d, q) that is most suitable for ARIMA model. Firstly, according to the number of differences, the number of differences of the model can be determined as d, thus transforming the problem into determining parameter C of the ARMA model. Then, we use the Akaike Information Criterion (AIC) minimum information criterion [18] to limit the range of p and q, and substitute the traversal mode of (p, q) into the AIC criterion to find a combination that minimizes AIC value. This is the optimal combination of parameters for the model.

Step3: The ARIMA model was constructed and trained according to the optimal combination parameter (p, d, q), and the prediction results in the next 16 months were obtained.

Step4: For time series data H_t, P_t, E_t, N_t, and W_t, construct ARIMA model respectively and obtain the predicted value H_{t+n}, P_{t+n}, E_{t+n}, N_{t+n} and W_{t+n} of each data. Combine monthly data and maximum lag data to get the data set of forecast influencing factors:

$$F_{pre\_n} = \{O_{t-1+n}, G_{t-1+n}, H_{t+n}, P_{t+n}, E_{t+n}, N_{t+n}, W_{t+n}, m_{t+n}, P_{t-1+n}, E_{t-1+n}, N_{t-1+n}\} \tag{15}$$

Step5: Merge influencing factor data F_t, forecast result data F_{pre_n} and enterprise business revenue data M_t, and represent them in the form of array: overall data set $X = [x_0, x_1, ..., x_{95}]^T$, training set $X_{train} = [x_0, x_1, ..., x_{83}]^T$, and test set $X_{test} = [x_{84}, x_{85}, ..., x_{95}]^T$. In order to unify the weight of data, G is normalized, which can retain data characteristics to the maximum extent and better fit the non-linear relationship between various data and enterprise operating income. In this paper, the maximum and minimum normalization method is adopted to normalize the data:

$$x_{norm} = \frac{x - x_{min}}{x_{max} - x_{min}} \tag{16}$$

Where, x represents sample data; x_{max} and x_{min} represent the maximum and minimum values in training data or test data respectively. Data of training set and test set after normalization are denoted as X_{train1} and X_{test1} respectively.

Step6: Initialize LSTM model parameters and build training network. The normalized training set X_{train1} is input into the network for training, and then the output result in the next month is obtained as the predicted value of enterprise economy.

Step7: Iterate the actual value of enterprise development on the model data and re-conduct the model process, and obtain the predicted value of the next 16 months successively as the final prediction result.

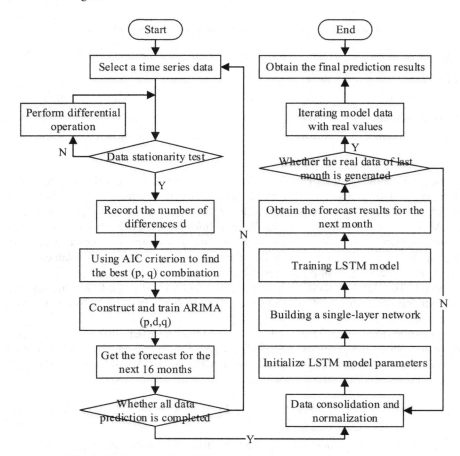

Fig. 4. The process for building a composite ARIMA-LSTM model.

ARIMA-LSTM combined model solves the limitation that ARIMA model can't make nonlinear prediction for a variety of influencing factors and LSTM model can't predict the situation without influencing factor data. Combined with the reflection of IOT data on enterprise economy, the model can predict the change of economic trend caused by emergencies. It has realized the more accurate forecast to the future enterprise economic trend.

Algorithm 1 gives the specific ARIMA-LSTM combination algorithm.

Algorithm 1 ARIMA-LSTM combination algorithm
Input: IOT data set, enterprise historical economic data, relevant Internet data, time data.
Output: Business economic forecasts for the next 16 months.

1: //Step 1: Data stationarity test.

2: data = ADF(train) // Data stationarity test

3: d = 0

4: if data >= 0.05

5:   d = d + 1;

6:   data = ADF(train).diff(d);

7: end if

8: //Step2: Traverses to find the best parameter.

9: for each

10:   for each

11:     temp = ARIMA(train, (p, d, q))

12:     AIC = AIC(temp)

13:   end for

14: end for

15: p, q = idxmin(AIC)

16: //Step3: Construct ARIMA model and predict each column time series value.

17: model = ARIMA(train, (p, d, q))

18: forecast1 = model. forecast(16)

19: //Step4: Repeat step1-Step 3 to predict other time series data.

20: forecast = [forecast1, forecast2, ..., forecast16]

21: //Step5: The predicted results are combined and normalized with the original training set.

22: trainData = train, forcast

23: norm = Normalization(trainData) // Normalize the data

24: //Step6: Create the LSTM model, initialize the parameters, and get the predicted values.

25: create LSTMmodel;

26: select the best parameters of LSTM;

27: predict = LSTM(trainData); // Get the predicted value for the next month.

28: //Step7: Iterate the data with true values and repeat Step22-Step27 for prediction.

4 Experiment and Analysis

4.1 Experimental Environment

The hardware environment of this experiment is a laptop computer equipped with I5-8250U CPU and 8 G memory. The software environment is Windows 10 operating system, the programming language is Python 3.7.1, and the LSTM neural network is constructed using Tensorflow deep learning framework.

4.2 Data Set Selection

The data set used in this experiment is from the data of an office building enterprise in Qingdao. Three IOT data, namely the number of parking lots, electricity consumption and working hours, and four Internet data including the total number of employees, the number of highly educated talents, the number of favorable enterprises and the number of online public opinions, are selected as well as the economic data of enterprises. A total of 96 groups of data were selected from January 2013 to December 2020.

Table 3. Some examples of training data of enterprise economic forecasting.

Time	O_{MR}	G_{MR}	H_t	P_t	E_t	N_t	W_t	m	M_t
2013/1/1	0	0	0	5575	5720	892	248	1	717.75
2013/2/1	0	0	0	3189	1524	892	224	2	628.24
2013/3/1	0	0	0	5393	4330	892	248	3	565.05
...	...	...	...	...	...	...	...	...	...
2016/11/1	0	0	9	5687	4239	1099	240	11	710.13
2016/12/1	0	0	9	5617	5426	1099	248	12	675.87
2017/1/1	0	0	11	5553	5623	1122	248	1	717.42
2017/2/1	0	0	11	3297	1557	1122	224	2	639.88
2017/3/1	0	0	11	5424	4337	1122	248	3	550.47
2017/4/1	0	0	10	6780	4287	1102	240	4	696.55
...	...	...	...	...	...	...	...	...	...
2019/10/1	0	0	27	7245	3981	1287	248	10	761.59
2019/11/1	0	0	27	5756	4136	1287	240	11	723.40
2019/12/1	0	0	27	6135	5558	1287	248	12	691.58

First of all, the data set is preprocessed to remove outliers in each column according to the most commonly used 3sigma principle [19] in anomaly detection, and the missing values are supplemented by multiple interpolation methods. After pre-processing, data from December 2019 and before were used as training sets, and data from the whole year of 2020 and the first half of 2021 were used as test sets. Since enterprise economic data is related to time series and other factors, and IOT data has a lag effect on the development of enterprise economy, enterprise economy will not immediately show a relationship with IOT data. Therefore, in order to obtain more accurate prediction results, we took the IOT data of the last month with the highest correlation as the input parameter of the model, and added them to the training of LSTM model after pretreatment, which can improve the prediction accuracy of LSTM. The processed data of the combined model are shown in Table 3.

The line chart of data of each influencing factor is shown in Fig. 5. It can be seen from the figure that parking data and electricity consumption data change with time with obvious regularity and have certain time series characteristics.

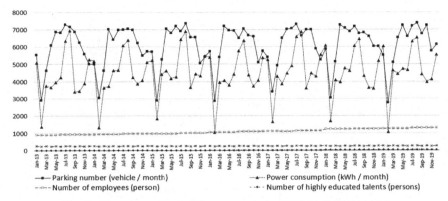

—•— Parking number (vehicle / month)   --▲-- Power consumption (kWh / month)
---◇--- Number of employees (person)   --+-- Number of highly educated talents (persons)

Fig. 5. The process for building a composite ARIMA-LSTM model.

4.3 Experimental Process

ARIMA-LSTM combined model predicts the influencing factor data of each column of time series to obtain the time series forecast data in the next 16 months. Taking parking data as an example, $P_{train} = \{P_1, P_2, ..., P_{84}\}$ is used as training data and $P_{test} = \{P_{85}, P_{86}, ..., P_{102}\}$ is used as test set. ARIMA model is used to train the training data. In order to eliminate the adverse effects of pseudo-regression of time series model, stationarity test of data is required. The most commonly used methods for stationarity testing are Autocorrelation Function (ACF) and Partial Autocorrelation Function (PACF) analysis. ACF and PACF diagrams of vehicle access data (a), enterprise electricity consumption data (b), and enterprise access control personnel information data (c) are shown in Fig. 6. Due to the limitation of space, we only take the total number of vehicles visited by enterprises in one month as an example to introduce the process and results of stationarity test in detail.

As can be seen from Fig. 6 (up (a)), the ACF graph fluctuates up and down instead of rapidly approaching 0, which is trailing. In addition, the Augmented Dickey-Fuller (ADF) test result P = 0.38 > 0.05 accepts H0, which also indicates that the sequence is non-stationary and difference is required to make the sequence stable. The data sequence diagram after first-order difference is shown in Fig. 7. It can be seen that the sequence fluctuates stably around 0. At this point, ADF test result P = 0.004 < 0.05 rejects H0, indicating that the sequence is stable and can be used for prediction of ARIMA model.

After ARIMA's prediction, the prediction result of parking data in the nth months in the future is denoted as P_{t+n}. Similarly, other sequences were input into ARIMA model to obtain the prediction results of all influencing factor data in the nth months in the future, which were denoted as H_{t+n}, P_{t+n}, E_{t+n}, N_{t+n} and W_{t+n} respectively. Data set F_{pre_n} of influencing factors was obtained by combining monthly data and maximum lag data.

After the data is merged and normalized, the LSTM model is created and parameters are set. Initialize the LSTM argument using Python's Keras library. The activation function of LSTM module was tanh, the fully connected artificial neural network receiving LSTM output was set as Linear, and the rejection rate of each network node was set

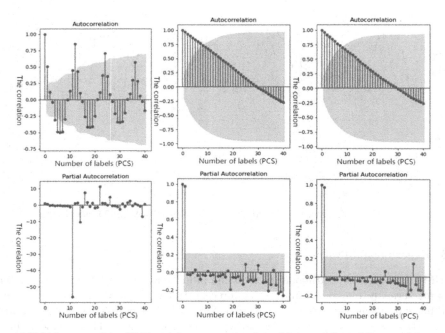

(a) Vehicle access data   (b) Electricity consumption data   (c) Access Control Personnel data

Fig. 6. ACF and PACF graphs of IOT data.

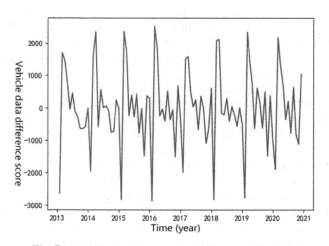

Fig. 7. Vehicle data diagram after first order difference.

as 0.2. RMSprop algorithm suitable for RNN is used for iterative updating of mean square error and weight parameters. The epoch interval for model training was set to 100 and the Batch size was set to 500. Train and get a forecast for the next month. As the test data of one and a half years is set, the results of the next month are continued to be predicted after the iteration results of the true value of the current month, until the enterprise economic data of the next year and a half is predicted as the final model prediction result.

4.4   Results and Analysis

In order to reflect the advantages of the combination model combined with IOT data in enterprise economic forecasting, we choose a single ARIMA model, a single LSTM model and a combination model without IOT data to compare the enterprise forecasting results.

In this paper, Root Mean Square Error (RMSE), Mean Absolute Error (MAE) and Mean Absolute Percentage Error (MAPE) are selected as the calculation of prediction accuracy.

1) RMSE

$$RMSE = \sqrt{\frac{1}{n} \sum_{i=1}^{n} (\hat{y}_t - y_t)^2} \qquad (17)$$

Where $\hat{y}_t$ represents the predicted value of time t, y_t represents the actual value of time T, and n represents the total predicted time. The RMSE range is $[0, +\infty)$, and the smaller the value is, the higher the prediction accuracy is. When the predicted value is in perfect agreement with the real value, the value is 0. The greater the error, the greater the value.

2) MAE

$$MAE = \frac{1}{n} \sum_{i=1}^{n} |\hat{y}_t - y_t| \qquad (18)$$

MAE range is $[0, +\infty)$, the smaller the MAE value is, the higher the prediction accuracy is. When the predicted value is in perfect agreement with the real value, the value is 0. The greater the error, the greater the value.

3) MAPE

$$MAPE = \frac{100\%}{n} \sum_{i=1}^{n} \left| \frac{\hat{y}_i - y_i}{y_i} \right| \qquad (19)$$

MAPE range is $[0, +\infty)$, similarly, the smaller the value, the higher the prediction accuracy.

The ARIMA-LSTM model proposed in this paper is combined with the IOT data to predict the enterprise economy, and is compared with the original data, the single ARIMA model and the combined model without the IOT data. Figure 8 shows the line chart of the comparison between the predicted value and actual value of enterprise economic forecast by the ARIMA-LSTM combination model combined with IOT data in this paper. As can be seen from Fig. 8, since 2020, due to the impact of COVID-19, the operating revenue of an enterprise has been low for nearly half a year, and gradually approaches the level of previous years in the later period. By June 2021, the operating revenue trend is similar to that of previous years. The difference between the overall predicted value and the real value of ARIMA-LSTM model is small and the error tends to be stable, indicating that ARIMA-LSTM model combined with Internet of Things data can well predict the economic development of enterprises. It shows that ARIMA-LSTM model combined with IOT data can well predict the economic development of enterprises.

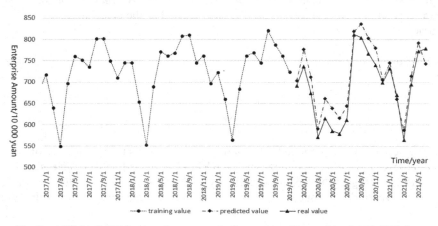

Fig. 8. ARIMA-LSTM enterprise economic forecast results combined with IOT data.

The error and trend prediction between the predicted value and the real value are shown in Table 4. The error is the difference between the predicted value and the true value. When the predicted value is less than the true value, the error is negative. When the predicted value is greater than the true value, the error is positive. The error interval is $[-9.58, 33.39]$, the error percentage interval is $[-1.2\%, 4.5\%]$, and the overall prediction accuracy is higher than 95%. In terms of trend prediction, the combination ARIMA-LSTM model with IOT data can well predict the future trend of enterprise economy and help the government and departments to better control the enterprise economy.

In order to verify the universality of the model, we selected relevant training data input models of several different types of enterprises for training and verification. In order to verify the universality of the model, we select several relevant training data input models of different types of enterprises for training and verification. The prediction results of enterprise A and enterprise B are shown in Fig. 9 and 10 respectively.

The comparison of prediction results between original data, single ARIMA model, combined model without IOT data and the method proposed in this paper is shown in Fig. 11. For easy observation, several types of predictions are shown in the same graph. The solid line is the actual value. The combination model can combine a variety of factors to forecast the economy, which takes more factors into account than the single

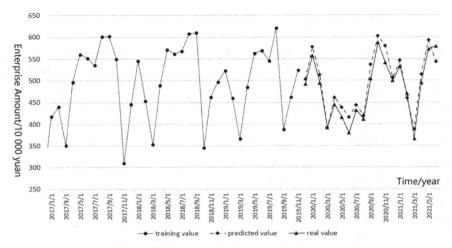

Fig. 9. ARIMA-LSTM economic forecast results of Enterprise A.

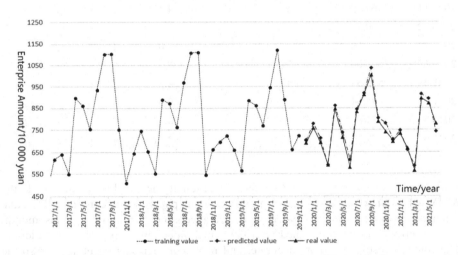

Fig. 10. ARIMA-LSTM economic forecast results of Enterprise B.

model, so the forecast effect is more accurate. In addition, the combined model with IOT data can predict the impact on the enterprise economy in the case of sudden decrease of IOT data caused by shutdown in emergencies (epidemics), because it takes into account the IOT data that can directly reflect the operation status of enterprises. As can be seen from the figure, the original data began to decline from April 2020 and continued until July, when the data did not exceed 650. The prediction curve of the combined model with IOT data is closest to the original data curve. ARIMA and the combined model without IOT data have similar prediction curves, which are closer to the time series data rules of previous years, and cannot predict the economic impact caused by the abnormal operation of enterprises in the early stage of the epidemic. Since 2021, the

Table 4. The prediction results of ARIMA-LSTM combined model.

Time	True value	Predictive value	Error	Trend	
				True	Pridict
2020.1	691.58	703.60	12.02	–	–
2020.2	737.15	770.54	33.39	↑	↑
2020.3	674.53	695.14	20.61	↓	↓
2020.4	571.87	580.27	8.4	↓	↓
2020.5	615.09	637.13	22.04	↑	↑
2020.6	586.00	618.78	32.78	↓	↓
2020.7	579.34	599.48	20.14	↓	↓
2020.8	612.01	635.42	23.41	↑	↑
2020.9	811.59	802.01	−9.58	↑	↑
2020.10	803.82	804.48	0.66	↓	↓
2020.11	767.10	762.93	−4.17	↓	↓
2020.12	740.40	744.18	3.78	↓	↓
2021.1	732.58	745.67	13.09	↓	↓
2021.2	669.64	659.87	−9.77	↓	↓
2021.3	565.34	587.66	22.33	↓	↓
2021.4	694.34	713.99	19.66	↑	↑
2021.5	771.88	792.22	20.34	↑	↑
2021.6	778.79	745.88	−32.91	↑	↓

prediction accuracy of traditional models has gradually declined over time, while the ARIMA-LSTM combination model proposed in this paper, which combines IOT data, can make short-term forecasts based on the actual economic situation of the last month. Smooth errors can be maintained with the actual values in all periods of prediction. The forecast results are more accurate, and more conducive to accurately grasp the direction of future economic development. It can be seen that the predictive value of ARIMA-LSTM model combined with IOT data is the closest to the actual value, and the predictive performance is better than the other three models. It can solve the problems that a single model can't solve, and more accurately predict the direction and value of enterprise economic development. Three evaluation criteria are used to evaluate the two models. The indicators of enterprise economy predicted by different models in the next 16 months are shown in Table 5.

The evaluation results show that the single LSTM model cannot predict the nonlinear relationship with the factors related to economic development, so no comparison is made. The three indexes predicted by single ARIMA model are all larger than those of combination model. Because the single ARIMA model can only predict the time series of future data based on the business revenue data of enterprises, the influencing

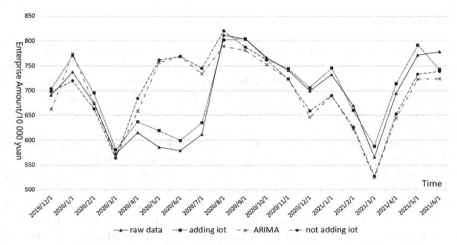

Fig. 11. Comparison of prediction results of different models.

Table 5. Three evaluation indexes of enterprise economy predicted by different models.

Model	RMSE	MAE	MAPE
ARIMA	8683.35	5609.75	9.06%
BP	5663.28	4901.85	8.15%
WNN	5738.10	5012.67	7.63%
The combined model without IOT data	8444.38	5491.72	9.02%
The combined model with IOT data	1913.05	1591.33	2.47%

factor data is single and cannot deal with emergencies. The training data of BP neural network are independent, not affected by other data, and the prediction results are not accurate enough. The number of nodes in the hidden layer of wavelet neural network and the initialization parameters of weights and scale factors between layers are difficult to determine, and the prediction results can not reach the optimal. The three indicators of the combined model without adding IOT data are all medium. It can predict slightly better than a single linear model. However, due to the inability to deal with the impact of emergencies, the prediction results are not accurate enough. The three index values of the combined ARIMA-LSTM model, which combines IOT data, are the smallest compared to other prediction models. It can not only predict the non-linear relationship between a variety of influencing factors on the economic development of enterprises, but also combine the characteristics of the IOT data can reflect the operation of enterprises. It can be timely improved according to the actual situation, making the prediction result more accurate.

5 Conclusion

This paper presents an enterprise economic forecasting method based on ARIMA-LSTM model. ARIMA model is used to predict the influencing factors of the IOT to get the linear predicted value of each column of data. Then LSTM model is used to establish the relationship between the predicted value of IOT data, the influence value of time factor, and the IOT data value of last month, which is important to the forecast result, and predict the final result of enterprise economic data. By comparing the prediction results of other neural network models, it can be seen that ARIMA-LSTM model combined with IOT data solves the problem that a single model cannot predict the impact of multiple influencing factors. At the same time, the addition of IOT data enables the model to predict the impact of emergencies on enterprise economy according to the changes of IOT data. The prediction results are more accurate than other models and combined models without IOT data. Therefore, ARIMA-LSTM model combined with IOT data can more accurately reflect the future economic trend and economic situation of enterprises, which can help government departments better monitor the development prospects of various enterprises and contribute to better decision-making.

References

1. Zhang, C.: Intelligent Internet of things service based on artificial intelligence technology. In: 2021 IEEE 2nd International Conference on Big Data, Artificial Intelligence and Internet of Things Engineering (ICBAIE), Nanchang, China, pp. 731–734 (2021)
2. Wang, X.: The difference analysis of enterprise operating income and VAT taxable sales. Journal **2019**(09), 25–27 (2019)
3. Xiao, D., Chen, R., Wang, Z.: Performance integration evaluation of investment decision-making of firm based on fuzzy set and BP neural network. Journal **2005**(03), 163–166 (2005)
4. Wang, T.: Research on enterprise economic risk forecast model based on Big Data fusion. In: 2020 International Conference on Big Data and Informatization Education (ICBDIE), Zhangjiajie, China, pp. 5–9 (2020)
5. Barker, J., Gajewar, A., Golyaev, K.: Secure and automated enterprise revenue forecasting. Journal **32**(1), 7657–7664 (2018)
6. Hryhorkiv, V., Buiak, L., Verstiak, A.: Forecasting financial time series using combined ARIMA-ANN algorithm. In: 2020 10th International Conference on Advanced Computer Information Technologies (ACIT), Deggendorf, Germany, pp. 455–458 (2020)
7. Feng, J., Li, H.: Research on macroeconomic forecasting technology based on optimized wavelet neural network. Journal **42**(07), 181–183, 186(2019)
8. Lei, H., Cailan, H.: Comparison of multiple machine learning models based on enterprise revenue forecasting. In: 2021 Asia-Pacific Conference on Communications Technology and Computer Science (ACCTCS), Shenyang, China, pp. 354–359 (2021)
9. Sheng, W., Zhao, H., Sun, Y.: Sales forecasting model based on BP neural network optimized by improved genetic algorithms. Journal **28**(12), 200–204 (2019)
10. Wu, J., Ren, S., Zhang, W.: A daily sales forecasting method based on LSTM model. Journal **30**(2), 133–137 (2020)
11. Xu, M., Ji, C., Zhong, C.: GDP growth forecast method based on electricity consumption. In: Proceedings of 2017 Power Industry Informatization Annual Conference, pp. 224–227. Posts and Telecommunications Press, China (2017)

12. Wang, R., Long, Z.: Research on the relationship between Internet of things and regional economic development. Journal **2020**(12), 147–148 (2020)
13. Chen, Q.: Significance and function of Internet of things in economic development. Journal **2020**(02), 24–25 (2020)
14. Tang, K., Hao, Z., Yixie, B.: Evaluation of prediction methods for parking occupancy rate. Journal **45**(04), 533–543 (2017)
15. Lin, N.: ARIMA model based on ensemble empirical mode decomposition for industry electricity sales prediction. Journal **34**(02), 128–133 (2019)
16. Wang, Z., Zhao, G., Wang, L.: Power consumption forecast of energy-intensive enterprises based on power marketing business data. In: 2020 IEEE 5th International Conference on Cloud Computing and Big Data Analytics (ICCCBDA), Chengdu, China, pp. 241–245 (2020)
17. Boštjančič, R., Timčenko, V., Kabović, M.: Industrial Internet: architecture, characteristics and implementation challenges. In: 2021 20th International Symposium INFOTEH-JAHORINA (INFOTEH). East Sarajevo, Bosnia and Herzegovina, pp. 1–4 (2021)
18. Akaike, H.: A new look at the statistical model identification. Journal **19**(6), 716–723 (1974)
19. Liu, Y., Li, Q.: Fundamentals of Statistics. Northeast University of Finance and Economics Press, Shenyang, China (2019)

eXtended Reality (XR) Experiences in Museums for Cultural Heritage: A Systematic Review

Manuel Silva$^{(\boxtimes)}$ and Luís Teixeira

CITAR-School of Arts, Universidade Católica Portuguesa, Porto, Portugal
{mosilva,lteixeira}@ucp.pt

Abstract. The incorporation of different types of media promotes a multimodal approach to the dissemination, communication and exploitation of Cultural Heritage in Museums. By utilizing digital technologies allows new forms of interactions with cultural content. Cultural spaces such as museums have been integrating new digital tools, presenting their audiences immersive, interactive, and multisensory experience that is not possible in traditional exhibitions. Withing these approaches a new term of Extended Reality (XR) is emerging and increasing its role in these cultural spaces. XR is the umbrella that englobes all forms of immersion and interaction such as Augmented Reality (AR), Mixed Reality (MR) and Virtual Reality (VR). This article aims to provide a comprehensive state of the art of XR experiences for Cultural Heritage in Museums. To support this goal, a systematic review of the peer-reviewed articles was gathered from the Scopus and Web of Science databases. Results are analyzed and the case studies are presented in this paper.

Keywords: Cultural heritage · Extended reality · Museums · Experience

1 Introduction

According to Fast-Berglund et al. (2018), XR defines a spectrum of new media technologies such as Augmented Reality (AR), Virtual Reality (VR), and Mixed Reality (MR). These technologies provide us with the possibility to create more immersive and meaningful experiences and to reach a bigger range of audiences with different demands and expectations. Such technologies and approaches have a short history in cultural heritage, virtual museums, and tourism.

Cultural Heritage (CH) can be referred to as the selection of physical artefacts and intangible attributes selected by the society that creates a legacy of tangible culture (physical objects) and intangible culture (traditions, languages, knowledge, and folklore) from past generations (Aikawa 2004). Museums, according to the International Council of Museums (ICOM), a division of UNESCO, have the mission to acquire, conserve, research, communicates and exhibits the tangible and intangible heritage of humanity and its environment for education, study, and enjoyment (ICOM 2007).

In the last years, cultural environments, such as museums have been merging new and more engaging immersive, interactive, and multi-sensorial approaches, to allow their

© ICST Institute for Computer Sciences, Social Informatics and Telecommunications Engineering 2022
Published by Springer Nature Switzerland AG 2022. All Rights Reserved
Z. Lv and H. Song (Eds.): INTETAIN 2021, LNICST 429, pp. 58–79, 2022.
https://doi.org/10.1007/978-3-030-99188-3_5

publics a direct way to exposition space and contents, proving information, prevailing over the traditional methods. To achieve their mission, museums have been incorporating new technologies to reach, engage and educate their audiences, by preserving the CH and democratize access to culture, and opening a space for dialogue and promotion of the exchange of ideas and knowledge. These approaches will benefit not only elderly or disabled people but all types of publics. It is foreseen that this trend will grow in a post COVID19 scenario (Agostino et al. 2020).

The goal of this paper is to present the state of the art of XR experiences in museums, synthesizing trends in the development of research in the field of XR within the subject area CH, more specifically Museums.

In order to do so, the authors followed guidelines for conducting systematic reviews of research (Okoli and Schabram 2010) and analyze XR case studies that contain experiences in terms of objectives, results, locations, software, hardware and evaluation, with the aim to answer the following research questions:

RQ1: What is the total distribution and volume by geographic source, location and time of issued studies on XR Technologies in Museums Experiences?

RQ2: What authors, journals, and research articles have had the highest impact on studies focusing on XR Technologies in Museums Experiences?

RQ3: What type of experiences are being developed with XR technologies in Museums Experiences?

2 Reality-Virtuality Continuum

With Augmented Reality (AR), the reality is enhanced by adding extra digital content over the real world. AR is a disruptive technology as it provides a positive result by engaging with the users (Amin and Govilkar 2015; Khan et al. 2015). Burkard et al. (2017) divides AR experiences into four types of AR applications:

1. Area Information: this displays specific information about the user's environment in the camera image like tourist attractions, parks, lagoons, public spaces, etc.
2. Object information: delivers information on a particular object in the immediate environment like sculptures, monuments, buildings, etc.
3. Navigation: provides georeferenced waypoints in the camera image along a navigation route.
4. Games: Lets the user play with game elements on top of the camera image. This permits the real world to become the players playing field like Pokemon Go (Ling 2017).

While AR overlaps the real world with digital content, VR creates a whole virtual world around the user (Milgram et al. 1994). The user enters these virtual worlds by using headsets to fully immerse in a computer-simulated reality. These headsets generate realistic images and sounds, engaging two senses to create an interactive virtual world.

With Mixed Reality (MR), the real-world and the virtual world blend together, combining interactivity and immersion offering immersive-interactive experience to view the real-virtual world, thus uniting different properties of the continuum into a single immersive reality experience (Milgram et al. 1994, Rahaman et al. 2019).

From a technology point of view, a new term has been introduced, designated by eXtended Reality (XR) (Fraunhofer HHI 2019). According to Fast-Berglund et al. (2018), XR defines a spectrum of new media technologies such as AR, VR, and MR, as well as all future realities such technologies, might bring. XR covers the full spectrum of real and virtual environments. This new concept can be proposed as a vehicle for promoting enhanced cultural experiences that allow people to virtual travel to other areas and fascinatingly experience local history and lore. Margetis et al. (2021).

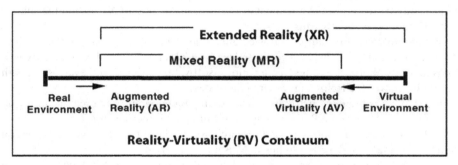

Fig. 1. Extended Reality Continuum (Authors)

In Fig. 1, the Reality-Virtuality Continuum, present by Milgram et al. (1994), is extended by the new umbrella term. As seen in Fig. 1, a less-known term is presented, called Augmented Virtuality. This expression concerns an approach, where the reality, e.g. the user's body, shows in the virtual world that is typically referred to as mixed reality.

XR development requires high-end computer hardware and specialized software. For software, experiences typical use game engines such as Unity3D and UnrealEngine4, integrating SDK's (software development kit) like Vuforia. A game engine is a fully integrated development platform that provides features to create interactive experiences with 3D content, and export experiences to multi-platforms (PC, Web, iOS, Android) (Kim et al. 2017). Regarding hardware, equipment depends on the experience they are intended for. To use AR applications, terminal devices such as smartphones, tablets, or systems like Google Glasses and Hololens are necessary (Amin and Govilkar 2015). For VR experiences, the development of optimized hardware as HMD (Head Mount Display) systems is becoming the mainstream consumer device, and CAVE displays the most common choice (Bekele et al. 2018). Examples of HMD devices are HTC Vive, Oculus Rift, Google VR and Samsung Gear VR (Gugenheimer et al. 2017).

By combining these technologies, it is possible to create virtual experiences and even Virtual Museums (VM). VM is a collection of digital objects integrate with a variety of media, providing more ways of interaction and deepening the connection between visitors and objects (Schweibenz 1998).

3 Research Methodology

This article followed Okoli and Schabram's (2010) systematic review methodology, beginning with the setting of a review protocol: systematic search process, practical screening, literature search, and data synthesis.

3.1 Data Sources and Search Strategies

We performed a systematic literature search for articles published from January 2000 and August 2021 based on Scopus and Web of Science digital libraries. We include articles written in English, related to Extended Reality and Museums and Cultural Heritage, with a transparent methodology and from trusted resources and journals. We exclude those who were not submitted to peer-reviewed process or whose study's full text is not available.

The search strategy was designed to retrieve publications that were evaluated for eligibility and inclusion. The quality of the search strategy is vital as it affects what items may have been missed. The chosen keywords and the relationships between these keywords were the same for searches in each database.

By utilizing the search string: [(TITLE-ABS-KEY (extended AND reality) AND TITLE-ABS-KEY (museum) AND TITLE-ABS-KEY (cultural AND heritage))] we retrieved 14 results from Scopus and 24 from Web of Science.

After applying our selection criteria presented in Table 1 and checking for crossed results we ended up with 27 results.

Table 1. Systematic review process

Institute for scientific information–SCOPUS	
Criteria	Filters
Restriction	Topic (Title, Abstract, Keywords)
Documents type	Articles and conference proceedings
Language	English

By not applying any restrictions to the subject area, the first results included papers from other research fields. So, we performed a manual check of the content of the full articles, the abstracts, and the title, then, defined which studies should be included or excluded for our case studies.

By applying these criteria, Esmaeili et al. (2014) and Petriaggi (2016) were excluded since the authors never relate to or approach XR or XR technologies such as AR/MR/VR in their articles being left with 25 results.

For the analysis of our case studies, we added the keyword "Experience" to our search string which left us with 17 results in total from both databases.

Data Extraction Results
From the total of 25 publications, 13 publications were in journals and 12 in conference proceedings (Fig. 2).

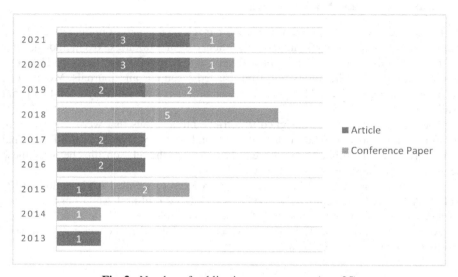

Fig. 2. Number of publication type per year (n = 25)

Analyzing articles publications, six articles in the first six years (2013–2018) and since 2019, eight articles (this number can increase as the period ends in 1st August 2021).

As for conferences publication, 2018 was an exceptional year, with 5 conferences publications. This is the same number in the period before 2018. After 2018, 4 conferences publications already.

Table 2. Distribution of results by country of contribution (n = 25)

Country	Contribution
Greece, Italy	20%
England, Romania	12%
Portugal	8%
Bosnia and Herzegovina, China, Denmark, Malaysia, South Korea, United States of America, Uzbekistan	4%

Table 2 presents the contribution of each country to the XR in the museums for the CH area. Of the total of 12 countries, Greece and Italy are on the top of the list with 20% each followed by England and Romania with 12% which make them the top contributors with 64% of the total publications. Then Portugal contributes with 8% and the rest of the countries all contributed with 4% each. This allows observing which countries are investing the most in the implementation of XR technologies in museums for CH.

Table 3. Top 5 authors of the field

Authors	Publication	Cites	Cites/Year
(Madsen and Madsen 2015)	Journal on computing and cultural heritage	16	2.29
(Banfi et al. 2019)	Virtual archaeology review	15	2.14
(Katyal 2017)	California law review	8	1.14
(Spiridon and Sandu 2016)	International journal of conservation science	7	1
(Anastasovitis et al. 2018)	3DTV-Conference	3	0.43

It is also possible to extract the top 5 authors on the field by citation numbers which are demonstrated in Table 3. The citations to the articles begin in the year 2015, not existing previous citations, which permits to observe the average citation number per year from 2015 to 2021, with a maximum average of 2.29 citations per year from the Madsen and Madsen, authors. For the Publication areas present in the table, show that the authors are publishing their work in different areas such as applied conservation sciences, arts, technologies and engineering.

We also explore the distribution of articles per journal, where the MDPI journal has the highest impact of publication with 31% of the publications from the 13 articles Fig. 3. This is a journal that has a mission to foster open scientific exchange in all forms across all disciplines.

4 XR Experiences in Museums Case Studies

Earlier XR experiences have emerged in recent years in several fields of applications. For example, touristic operators working with cultural destinations are constantly investing in new technologies, following the current trend of mobile use. These investments allow companies to stay competitive in the global market since many tourist attractions face a lack of funds to maintain these sites (Fritz et al. 2005).

In this section, we will answer Research Question Q3 regarding what type of experiences are being developed with XR technologies in Museums Experiences. As mentioned in Sect. 3.1 we have obtained 17 results.

Minucciani and Garnero (2013), discuss virtual tourism, presenting two different scenarios: a virtual trip in a virtual world and a real trip augmented with digital content.

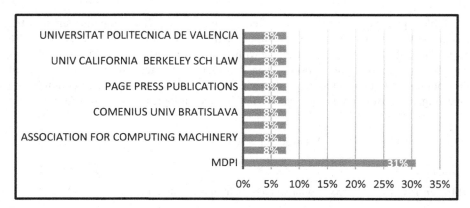

Fig. 3. Articles distribution per journal (n = 13)

This discussion is supported by research and implementation of techniques available to transpose their content to the virtual world in a prototypal station installed in the Politecnico di Torino (Fig. 4). The station allows visitors to explore a tour simulation with three basic features. One feature offers the visitor a real and immersive vision of what he would see across the places he's visiting, without turning to city models or synthetic worlds. A second feature brings together the virtual displacement on sites with a physical motion made by the visitor and the final feature is the use of shared databases about historic architecture and cultural heritage.

Fig. 4. Prototypal station. Retrieved from (Minucciani and Garnero 2013)

The prototype station can be replicable in different contexts and situations of use, allowing the visitor to explore remote sites without using the traditional station in front of a monitor.

In 2015, Madsen and Madsen present an AR system with the objective to facilitate the presentation of information to visitors. This system is divided into two parts. The first installation uses a tablet connected to a large screen TV that allows a single visitor to operate the installation while the other visitors can experience the visualization as over-the-shoulder spectators (Fig. 5.a). The second installation is a handheld experience that allows multiple visitors to operate their viewfinder, enabling them to use it as a window to the past and create their own tour throughout the chapel (Fig. 5.b).

(a)   (b)

Fig. 5. Left to right–(**a**) Static installation, (**b**) Handheld version. Retrieved from (Madsen and Madsen 2015)

Partarakis et al. (2015), demonstrate an experience in the Museum Coffee Table that aims to augment the user experience within museum leisure spaces such as cafeterias, targeting family visitors. This system provides an AR physical surface extra information about artists and their creations for the parents while creating an entertainment environment for the children with the integration of popular games. As a result, the entire family can be sitting at the table drinking a coffee and having an extended (completed) visit to the museum.

In 2015 Ahn and Wohn, present what they have learned from four experiences that used a reconstruction of a virtual 3D "Grotto" they have created. The first experience is a VR movie displayed in the VR theater of Gyeongju Expo, the second a special exhibition at the National Museum of Korea, the third one a Stereoscopic film for digital heritage museum, and the last one is and Head Mounted Display (HMD) VR experience. The authors discuss several issues such as performance, physical immersion, interactivity and realism and conclude that exists difficulties to maintain high detail 3D models reality-based in steady frames for virtual interactive applications for CH.

Galdieri and Carrozzino (2017) develop the Muse-tools whit the objective to create a system that allows museum curators to be independent while creating reliable virtual spaces reducing the gap between curators and technology. The system is based on an extension of the Unity 3D game engine software to support new features and tools to allow the curator to plan real and virtual exhibitions without relying on expert programmers or artists. A full explorable Virtual Museum (Fig. 6) with four rooms, plus an external open space to demonstrate the possibility of abstracted VR in combination with human heritage exhibition was created using only the features of the author's system showing its capabilities to create virtual and concluding that it is unlikely for this demo to be recreated by a single museum curator.

Fig. 6. One of the four rooms from the Virtual Museum: The Egyptian Room. Retrieved from (Galdieri and Carrozzino 2017)

In 2018, Duguleana et al. demonstrate the process of building an AR application that can be used as a digital guide for outdoor museums, monuments or any other type of heritage site. They present three different scenarios of experiences, the visit to the remains of the Etruscan tomb where the application overlaps the real world with a 3D digital reconstruction of the Etruscan tomb (Fig. 7).

Fig. 7. Left to right–(a) Original actual site of the Etruscan tomb (Archaeological Museum of Cecina), (b) Site with the digitally reconstructed tomb overlapping the real world. Retrieved from (Duguleana et al. 2018)

The second experience allows the visitor to observe the famous poet Ovid wandering around the central square in front of the Rome Colosseum reciting one of his poems. The last experience is the 3D reconstruction of a destroyed Romanian Reformed Church monument, allowing the visitor to inspect an intangible monument that does not exist anymore.

Anastasovitis et al. (2018) presents three case studies of serious games created in the context of a European Union-funded project DigiArt (The Internet Of Historical Things And Building New 3D Cultural Worlds. These experiences allow the visitor to observe a simulation of the real world through the application of 3D models that can permit interaction, imagination and triggers immersion of the visitor. Figure 8, displays three examples of the case studies. The first experience is the Open site virtual experience of the Palace of Aigai in Greece where the visitor stands in the past oin 350 BC as an architect assistant (Fig. 8 (a)). The second experience is the virtual cave experience of Scladina Cave in Belgium where the visitor can explore the digital reconstruction of the site base on the scanned model of Scladina cave (Fig. 8 (b). The last shows the Anthropology virtual museum experience of the Liverpool John Moores University skeleton collection, where the visitor can explore the virtual space and observe 3D models of the skeleton collection (Fig. 8 (c)).

Fig. 8. Left to right–(**a**) Open site virtual experience (Palace of Aigai), (**b**) Virtual cave experience (Scladina Cave), and (**c**) Anthropology virtual museum experience (LJMU skeleton collection). Retrieved from (Anastasovitis et al. 2018).

The authors Adao et al. 2019 introduced the MixAR, a full-stack system with the capability to provide the visualization of virtual reconstructions seamlessly overlapping the real world with digital content (e.g. upon ruins). The system allows the visitor to freely explore the digital content and the archaeological site. To evaluate MixAR, a set of immersive and non-immersive experiences of the digitally reconstructed buildings that took place in the Vila Velha's Museum were implemented. In these experiences, the user could visualize the Chapel 3D digital reconstruction overlaying the real world, allowing to explore the interior of the 3D model. The overall user satisfaction, on a 1–100 scale, was 77.53 for the immersive experience and 71.34 for the non-immersive experience.

In 2019, Banfi et al. present a holistic approach to the Basilica of Sant'Ambrogio in Milan that starts from data collection such as 3D survey and historical records, followed by the creation of 3D models and ending with an XR experience (Fig. 9). These experiences offer an increased level of information and create an increased awareness of the intangible value and historic richness that would be possible by the traditional ways. With their research, they discuss the potential and challenges to the utilization of these technologies in the CH field. One of the potential uses is the already consider increased availability of information to the visitors, providing multiply outcomes with different levels of information. But at the same time, these outcomes create challenges themselves, like the problems faced for the parametrization of historical building shapes, difficulty to represent historical hypotheses and the communication of intangible values. For this, the authors propose that the creation process must be carried with communication between the creator's experts, restorers and art historians.

Fig. 9. Extended Reality and informative models for multiple devices. Retrieved from (Banfi et al. 2019).

In 2019 Cisternino et al. present the possibility to extended their previous work, an AR indoor experience, into MR outdoor experience, creating a set of virtual portals, accessible through a smartphone or a mobile device, generating in the visitor the sensation of time travel, between the real world (the present) and the virtual world (the past).

Duguleană et al. in (2020), present a thorough investigation that reveals significant progress from the technologies used to digitize CH and report the creation of a Virtual Assistant with artificial intelligence for CH in museums of Romania (Fig. 10). 3D VR avatars were considered innovative by young audiences. The introduction of virtual elements increased the levels of interaction of the visitors with the museum content and lead to an increase in visitor's numbers. The enhancement of the engagement and the attractiveness of cultural institutions are two crucial objectives, such as social and psychological points of view and economically.

Fig. 10. Virtual Assistant physical stand. Retrieved from: (Duguleană et al. 2020)

In 2020, Silva and Teixeira present a PhD project for the creation of an XR platform for immersive and interactive experiences for CH, designed for Serralves Museum and Coa Archeological Park, based on the study of the state of the art of XR applications/experiences from CH in museums and archaeological parks. The main objectives of the project are, the understanding of the potential of XR within CH and the development of an XR platform that could create multiple experiences for CH, contributing with new approaches to process and deliver immersive and interactive content for CH environments. The platform will provide and enhance the augmented experience for visitors to these sites. The system is based on new multilayered and narrative modalities.

Tennent et al. in (2020), show Thresholds, a VR experience that recreates the world's first photographic exhibition and toured multiple museums. The experience allows having multiple visitors at the same time in the real and virtual space, being replaced by ghostly avatars into the virtual world. The visitors can walk and explore the virtual world and experience the digital content such as high-quality scans from the original photographs (Fig. 11). Visitors were observed how they experienced the work to extract information for the design of VR user experiences for museums.

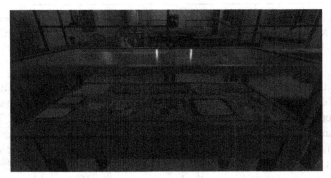

Fig. 11. Virtual wood and glass vitrine that hold several photographs. Retrieved from Tennent et al. in (2020)

In 2021, Rizvić et al. display four XR applications to bring visitors back in time, into the history of Bosnia and Herzegovina, by recreating digital objects, events and characters from the past. In the first experience, "Nine Dissidents", the authors record VR videos and create a VR movie to represent the conflicting opinions that existed on the character of the socialist regime in Yugoslavia. The second one, "Old Crafts Virtual Museum", uses VR technology to exhibit and preserve the crafts presented in Old Town Sarajevo Baščaršija since the 15th century. Actors dress as craftsmen who appear in a virtual world, telling stories about their crafts. The third one "Battle on Neretva VR" places the visitor in the middle of one of the most important battles in Yugoslavia during WWII. The visitor is giving the mission to destroy a bridge and save his wounded comrades. "Sarajevo 5D", the last experience, combines AR technology with the recreation of cultural monuments and objects that have disappeared from their original locations. Thus, allowing the visitor to learn about their historical significance and original appearance. All the applications are display in Fig. 12.

Fig. 12. From left to right (**a**) First application "Nine Dissidents", (**b**) Second application "Old Crafts Virtual Museum", (**c**) Third application "Battle of Neretva VR", (**d**) Forth application "Sarajevo 5D". Retrieved from Rizvić et al. (2021).

Harun and Mahadzir (2021), developed a 360° Virtual tour of the traditional Malay house, after having performed a literature review on VR photography and analyzing examples of other 360° systems that already exist mainly in the Asia area. They aim to preserve the architectural heritage for the future generation by providing local and digital visitors heritage information with effectiveness, simplicity, and a low-cost system. The system works with a simple but effective interface as shown in Fig. 13 and delivers detailed information of the building displayed around the 360° world as anchor points. Results show that the development of their Virtual Tour can indirectly attract the people's interest in the uniqueness of traditional Malay houses.

Banfi and Previtali (2021) propose a method to improve human-computer interaction between Heritage Building Information Modelling (HBIM) and advanced XR projects. This digital process allows the transmission and shares the tangible and intangible values of built heritage between different software, devices and formats to create a more sustainable way from a technological point of view. At the same time, it is possible to keep the high levels of parametricity, interoperability, orientation and virtual interactivity of digital models. Supported by these results, the authors developed an XR experience for the Church of San Valentino in Italy that allows the visitor to explore the virtual space of the 3D modelling from the Church implemented in a virtual world using VR and see the 3D model imposed into the real world by the use of AR.

Margetis et al. (2021) propose a synthesis of AR, VR and MR technologies to provide unified X-Reality experiences for "real" and virtual visits to the museum. Three XR definitions are proposed: a superset, an extrapolation, and a subset of MR. XR aims to fuse layered objects into the real world through immersive digital worlds. Two new

Fig. 13. 360° Virtual Tour Main Interface. Retrieved from Harun and Mahadzir (2021)

concepts to XR are introduced: Diminished Reality, to denote the fading of real parts of
the environment that are substituted by digital counterparts, and True Mediated Reality,
to define the need for delivering realistic virtual characters. The first results show that
XR allows museum visitors to interact with the physical environment while immersed
in an XR application.

5   XR Case Studies Tables Analysis

In this chapter, to answer RQ1 and RQ2, we organize the information into two tables: the
first table (Table 4) displays the case studies in terms of locations, objectives, evaluations,
and results, and the second table (Table 5) contains data regarding technology, software
and hardware used in the experiences. For this analysis, the case studies (Silva and
Teixeira 2020) and (Margetis et al. 2021) are not included because of being conceptual
articles and not having an implementation of an experience, thus being not present most
of the information required to the table.

In Table 4, Location is referred to the place where the experience was tested: Museum,
University Lab or Other (standing for city spaces, conferences, etc.). The Objective
is the main goal of the experience, and Evaluation reports if any type of assessment
was performed and if it occurs, how it was evaluated. For Results, we consider three
possibilities: R1 – for Prototype; R2 – for Pilot and R3 for Product.

From Table 4 we can observe that near 47% of the experiences was tested/presented
in a University Lab were 86% from the 47% were only on University Lab. And the
remaining 14% were tested/presented in University Lab and Other. Then 40% were
tested/presented in Museums in which half of the 40% were tested/presented only in
Museums and the other half was tested in Museums and Other locations. As for Other
locations only was 13% since some of the experiences were tested in both Museums and
Other or University Lab. and Other in a total of 33%.

In terms of evaluation, 53% of the experiences were evaluated, using mostly qualitative methods, typically questionnaires, with the number of participants ranged from
12 to over 250 answers. 47% did not report any kind of evaluation of the experience.

Table 4. Locations, objectives, evaluations and results of the XR case studies.

Authors	Location	Objective	Evaluation	Result
(Minucciani and Garnero 2013)	University lab	Prototypal Station: allows the visitor to visit remote sites without turning to the traditional station in front of a monitor	n/a	R1
(Partarakis et al. 2015)	University lab	Museum Coffee Table: allows the visitors to extend (complete) their visits within leisure spaces of the museum such as cafeterias	Questionnaire, twelve participants, recording the use of the system to be analyzed offline	R2
(Madsen and Madsen 2015)	Museum	Two installations for the visualization of a 3D reconstruction of a castle chapel, running autonomously, at interactive framerates on modern tablets, during open hours	Anonymously logged data from the visitors, number of times the application was used	R2
(Ahn and Wohn 2015)	Museum/ Other	Virtual 3D reconstruction of the Seokguram Grotto (four projects)	n/a	R2
(Galdieri and Carrozzino 2017)	University lab	Create a toolbox system to support the development of digital experience by curators, diminishing the gap between curators and technology	Questionnaires to evaluate the technology acceptance sent to over 350 museum curators, 63 answers received	R3
(Anastasovitis et al. 2018)	University lab	Design and development of three desktop serious games for promoting European CH	n/a	R1

(*continued*)

Table 4. (*continued*)

Authors	Location	Objective	Evaluation	Result
(Duguleană et al. in 2020)	Museum/ Other	Demonstrate the use of AR applications with three different experiences	Questionnaire, 92 participants distributed by the 3 experiences, 8 in the first, 63 in the second and 12 in the third	R2
(Adao 2019)	Other	Implement the MixAR system to allow visitors access of *in situ* experiences of reconstructed buildings that no longer exist	Questionnaire, 18 participants where 56% were students of technological areas	R1
(Banfi et al. 2019)	University lab	3D survey and gather data of historical records of the church, to create an XR experience that reaches a new level of interactivity for different types of devices (desktop, mobile, VR headset) and users (experts, non-experts)	n/a	R1
(Cisternino et al. 2019)	University lab/Other	Evaluate the feasibility to extend an existing AR indoor experience, to a MR experience with the creation of outdoor points of interest (Virtual Portals)	n/a	R1
(Duguleană in et al. 2020)	Museum	To develop an intelligent conversational agent (Virtual Assistant) to improve the accessibility to information inside a history museum	User Acceptance Evaluation questionnaire, 2 min duration, over 250 students	R3

(*continued*)

Table 4. (*continued*)

Authors	Location	Objective	Evaluation	Result
(Tennent et al. in 2020)	Museum	To recreate into a VR experience the world's first photographic exhibition	Evaluate the top 15 items of the experience using the time spent by each visitor for each item	R3
(Banfi Previtali 2021)	University lab	Improve human-computer interaction between HBIM and advance XR projects, by design a new digital process and implementing it on XR experience	n/a	R1
(Harun and Mahadzir 2021)	Other	Development of a 360° virtual tour of the traditional Malay house to preserve Malay architectural heritage for future generations	n/a	R3
(Rizvić et al. 2021)	Museum/ Other	To present four projects that bring back visitors to the history of Bosnia and Herzegovina and recreated objects, events, and characters from its past	Two different UX evaluation methods: (1) qualitative studies for exploring new modalities of expression and pilot solutions (2) quantitative studies to obtain a reliable measure of the success of VR/AR applications	R2

Regarding results, 40% are prototypes, 33% pilots and 27% already products. Although almost all prototypes were present in a University Lab, only one in seven experiences were evaluated, while on the other hand, 80% of the pilots, located mostly in Museums, were evaluated.

Table 5 presents information regarding the technology used to implement the experiences: XR modality (AR/VR/MR/360°/XR), software platforms and hardware devices.

Table 5. Software and Hardware used on XR case studies.

Authors	XR modality	Software	Hardware
(Minucciani and Garnero 2013)	VR	GraphDB, Google Maps	n/a
(Partarakis et al. 2015)	AR	Microsoft Byte Tag/Microsoft Surface SDK/Protégé/SPARQL	Mobile device
(Madsen and Madsen 2015)	AR	Arduino/Unity 3D/123D Catch/ Maya	Arduino/iPad/TV Screen/iPhone
(Ahn and Wohn 2015)	VR	Unreal engine 4	Desktop/Head mount display
(Galdieri and Carrozzino 2017)	VR	Unity 3D	Desktop
(Anastasovitis et al. 2018)	VR	Unity 3D	Desktop/Head mount display
(Duguleana et al. 2018)	AR	n/a	Mobile device
(Banfi et al. 2019)	XR	Autodesk A360/Unreal engine 4	Desktop/Oculus Rift/Mobile device
(Adao 2019)	AR/MR	Unity 3D/Metaio SDK /Blender	Mobile device
(Cisternino et al. 2019)	MR	Unity 3D/ARcore/ARKit	Mobile device
(Duguleană et al. in 2020)	VR	Google cloud speech to text/ proprietary using NLU programming language and RASA platform	Desktop/Large TV Screen
(Tennent et al. in 2020)	VR	Orion SDK/Unity 3D/Autodesk 3D Studio max	Laptop/HTC Vive/Leap motion sensor
(Banfi and Previtali 2021)	AR/VR	Unreal engine/Twinmotion	Desktop/Head mount display/Mobile device
(Harun and Mahadzir 2021)	VR/360°	n/a	n/a
(Rizvić et al. 2021)	XR	Unity 3D	Desktop/Head mount display/Mobile device

According to Table 5, 53.3% of the experiences use only VR, 33.3% use only AR, 13.3% use MR or XR. If we consider the use of each of the XR modalities, AR, MR or VR, then 66% uses VR, 46% uses AR and 26% use MR.

Analyzing the software and hardware components, two publications (Duguleana et al. 2018) do not mention which software was used and two publications (Minucciani and Garnero 2013 and Harun and Mahadzir 2021) do not mentions which hardware was used.

Regarding the 13 publications that have refer software or hardware, 54% use Unity 3D and 23% use Unreal Engine as software platforms, and 31% use mobile devices only (such as cellphones, tablets), while the remaining 69% use desktop mixing with other types of hardware such as Head Mounted Display, Large TV Screens, Leap Motion Sensors and Mobile Devices. With this we can observe that 77% of the authors are using Game Engines to develop their experiences and utilizing more common approaches in terms of hardware with Mobile Devices and Desktops, indicating a path to standardization in Software and Hardware for the creation of XR experiences.

6 Discussion and Future Directions

In this paper, we explore and analyze a literature review of research made in the Scopus and Web of Science digital libraries from the string Extended Reality in Museums for Cultural Heritage and Extended Reality in Museums for Cultural Heritage Experiences for the analysis of case studies. The relatively small number of publications indicates that the use of XR technology is still in its early phases in the CH area in Museums. With these results, we answered our three research questions for the XR in the Museums Experiences. The first question, "What is the total distribution and volume by geographic source, location and time of issued studies on XR Technologies in Museums Experiences?" showed us that after the year 2018 we start to see a growing number of publications and the countries Greece and Italy are the ones contributing the most for these publications; The second question, "What authors, journals, and research articles have had the highest impact on studies focusing on XR Technologies in Museums Experiences?" present us that the authors Anastasovitis et al. (2018); F. Banfi et al. (2019); Katyal (2017); Madsen and Madsen (2015); Spiridon and Sandu (2016) are the top 5 authors with more impact in the studies of XR technologies in Museums and as for the journals demonstrated us that MDPI has more impact with 31% publications from 13. The last question, "What type of experiences are being developed with XR technologies in Museums Experiences?" presented us that the majority of the authors are developing VR experiences, resorting to game engine software to develop their experiences. From our results, it is present that the XR will be adopted by even more institutions XR since it has clear benefits for attracting visitors and encouraging revisits, where the visitors can experience more engaging, immersive, and meaningful CH content (Banfi et al. 2019; Margetis et al. 2021). Also was present that these technologies can help to preserve and reviving CH lost content (Harun and Mahadzir 2021; Madsen and Madsen 2015; Rizvić et al. 2021). Nevertheless, the XR technologies have a positive influence on the CH giving several different tools to this area to develop better and enhanced experiences for its visitors, but there is still present a gap between museum curators and these new technologies which can't be filled without the help of new categories of professionals that can understand museums and new technologies at the same time (Galdieri and Carrozzino 2017).

For future works, there is the option to do a literature review of XR with AR/VR/MR terms to see how much influences the number of results. Also, the geographic distribution can be further explored to find if exists a difference between the selection of

XR technologies when developing experiences in different countries. The design of the experiences and evaluation process can be thoroughly explored and compared between articles to understand the existing difficulties when creating XR experiences for CH in Museums.

Acknowledgements. This article is a result of the project (CHIC-Cooperative Holistic View on Internet and Content (POCI-01-0247-FEDER-024498) and CCD-Centro de Criatividade Digital (NORTE-01-0145-FEDER-022133), supported by Norte Portugal Regional Operational Programme (NORTE 2020), under the PORTUGAL 2020 Partnership Agreement, through the European Regional Development Fund (ERDF).

References

Adao, T., et al.: MixAR: a multi-tracking mixed reality system to visualize virtual ancient buildings aligned upon ruins. J. Inf. Technol. Res. **12**(4), 1–33 (2019). https://doi.org/10.4018/JITR.201 9100101

Agostino, D., Arnaboldi, M., Lampis, A.: Italian state museums during the COVID-19 crisis: from onsite closure to online openness. Museum Manage. Curatorship, 1–11 (2020). https://doi.org/ 10.1080/09647775.2020.1790029

Ahn, J., Wohn, K.: Lessons Learned from Reconstruction of a Virtual Grotto - From Point Cloud to Immersive Virtual Environment. In: Guidi, G., et al. (eds.) 2015 Digital Heritage International Congress, Analysis and Interpretation Theory, Methodologies, Preservation and Standards Digital Heritage Projects and Applications, pp. 651–654. IEEE (2015)

Aikawa, N.: An historical overview of the preparation of the UNESCO international convention for the safeguarding of the intangible cultural heritage. Museum Int. **56**(1–2), 137–149 (2004). https://doi.org/10.1111/j.1350-0775.2004.00468.x

Amin, D., Govilkar, S.: Comparative study of augmented reality Sdk's. Int. J. Comput. Sci. Appl. **5**(1), 11–26 (2015). https://doi.org/10.5121/ijcsa.2015.5102

Anastasovitis, E., Ververidis, D., Nikolopoulos, S., Kompatsiaris, I.: Digiart: building new 3D cultural heritage worlds. 3DTV-Conference, 2017, 1–4 (2018). https://doi.org/10.1109/3DTV. 2017.8280406

Banfi, F., Brumana, R., Stanga, C.: Extended reality and informative models for the architectural heritage: from scan-to-bim process to virtual and augmented reality. Virtual Archaeol. Rev. **10**(21), 14–30 (2019). https://doi.org/10.4995/var.2019.11923

Banfi, F., Previtali, M.: Human-computer interaction based on scan-to-bim models, digital photogrammetry, visual programming language and extended reality (XR). Appl. Sci. Basel, **11**(13) (2021). https://doi.org/10.3390/app11136109

Bekele, M.K., Town, C., Pierdicca, R., Frontoni, E., Malinverni, E.V.A.S.: A survey of augmented, virtual, and mixed reality. ACM J. Comput. Cult. Heritage **11**(2), 36 (2018). https://doi.org/10. 1145/3145534

Burkard, S., Fuchs-Kittowski, F., Himberger, S., Fischer, F., Pfennigschmidt, S.: Mobile Location-Based Augmented Reality Framework. In: Hřebíček, J., Denzer, R., Schimak, G., Pitner, T. (eds.) ISESS 2017. IAICT, vol. 507, pp. 470–483. Springer, Cham (2017). https://doi.org/10. 1007/978-3-319-89935-0_39

Cisternino, D., et al.: Virtual Portals for a Smart Fruition of Historical and Archaeological Contexts. In: De Paolis, L.T., Bourdot, P. (eds.) AVR 2019. LNCS, vol. 11614, pp. 264–273. Springer, Cham (2019). https://doi.org/10.1007/978-3-030-25999-0_23

Duguleană, M., Briciu, V.-A., Duduman, I.-A., Machidon, O.M.: A virtual assistant for natural interactions in museums. Sustainability (Switzerland), **12**(17) (2020). https://doi.org/10.3390/SU12176958

Duguleana, M., Voinea, G.D.: Enhancing the Experience of Visiting Outdoor Heritage Sites Using Handheld AR. In: Stephanidis, C. (ed.) HCI 2018. CCIS, vol. 852, pp. 184–191. Springer, Cham (2018). https://doi.org/10.1007/978-3-319-92285-0_26

Esmaeili, H., Woods, P.C., Thwaites, H.: Realisation of virtualised architectural heritage. In: Proceedings of the 2014 International Conference on Virtual Systems and Multimedia, VSMM 2014, pp. 94–101 (2014). https://doi.org/10.1109/VSMM.2014.7136676

Fast-Berglund, Å., Gong, L., Li, D.: Testing and validating Extended Reality (xR) technologies in manufacturing. Proced. Manuf. **25**, 31–38 (2018). https://doi.org/10.1016/j.promfg.2018.06.054

Fraunhofer, H.H.I.: XR4ALL Moving The European XR Tech Industry Forward. **95** (2019)

Fritz, F., Susperregui, A., Linaza, M.T.: Enhancing cultural tourism experiences with augmented reality technologies. In: The 6th International Symposium on Virtual Reality, Archaeology and Cultural Heritage VAST (2005). http://citeseerx.ist.psu.edu/viewdoc/download?doi=10.1.1.622.4265&rep=rep1&type=pdf

Galdieri, R., Carrozzino, M.: Towards dedicated software tools to assist the creation of virtual exhibits. Scires It Sci. Res. Inf. Technol. **7**(1), 17–28 (2017). https://doi.org/10.2423/i22394 303v7n1p17

Gugenheimer, J., Stemasov, E., Frommel, J., Rukzio, E.: ShareVR: Enabling co-located experiences for virtual reality between HMD and Non-HMD users. In: Conference on Human Factors in Computing Systems - Proceedings, 2017, 4021–4033 (2017). https://doi.org/10.1145/302 5453.3025683

Harun, N.Z., Mahadzir, S.Y.: 360° virtual tour of the traditional malay house as an effort for cultural heritage preservation. IOP Conf. Series Earth Environ. Sci. **764**(1) (2021). https://doi.org/10.1088/1755-1315/764/1/012010

Haynes, R.: Eye of the Veholder: AR Extending and Blending of Museum Objects and Virtual Collections. In: Jung, T., tom Dieck, M.C. (eds.) Augmented Reality and Virtual Reality. PI, pp. 79–91. Springer, Cham (2018). https://doi.org/10.1007/978-3-319-64027-3_6

Hsiao, P.-W.: The LOHAS digital and interactive vitalization community for heritage and sustainability of the ruins of St. Paul. In: Meen, T.H. (Ed.), Proceedings of 2019 IEEE EURASIA Conference on Biomedical Engineering, Healthcare And Sustainability (IEEE ECBIOS 2019), pp. 79–82. IEEE (2019)

ICOM. (2007). Museum Definition. https://icom.museum/en/resources/standards-guidelines/museum-definition/

Kakarountas, A., Dragoumanos, S., Kakarountas, K.: Extending visitor's reality at museums. In: 5th International Conference on Information, Intelligence, Systems And Applications, IISA 2014, 196 (2014)

Katyal, S.K.: Technoheritage. California Law Rev. **105**(4), 1111–1172 (2017). https://doi.org/10.15779/Z38PN8XF0T

Khan, A., Khusro, S., Rauf, A., Mahfooz, S.: Rebirth of augmented reality – enhancing reality via smartphones. Bahria Univ. J. Inf. Commun. Technol. **8**(1), 110–121 (2015)

Kim, S.K., Kang, S.J., Choi, Y.J., Choi, M.H., Hong, M.: Augmented-reality survey: from concept to application. KSII Trans. Internet Inf. Syst. **11**(2), 982–1004 (2017). https://doi.org/10.3837/tiis.2017.02.019

Koterwas, T., Suess, J., Billings, S., Haith, A., Lamb, A.: Augmenting Reality in Museums with Interactive Virtual Models. In: Jung, T., tom Dieck, M.C. (eds.) Augmented Reality and Virtual Reality. PI, pp. 365–370. Springer, Cham (2018). https://doi.org/10.1007/978-3-319-64027-3_25

Ling, H.: Augmented reality in reality. IEEE Multimed. **24**(3), 10–15 (2017). https://doi.org/10.1109/MMUL.2017.3051517

Madsen, J.B., Madsen, C.B.: Handheld visual representation of a castle chapel ruin. J. Comput. Cult. Heritage, **9**(1) (2015). https://doi.org/10.1145/2822899

Margetis, G., Apostolakis, K.C., Ntoa, S., Papagiannakis, G., Stephanidis, C.: X-reality museums: unifying the virtual and realworld towards realistic virtual museums. Appl. Sci. (Switzerland) **11**(1), 1–16 (2021). https://doi.org/10.3390/app11010338

Milgram, P., Takemura, H., Utsumi, A., Kishino, F.: Augmented reality: a class of displays on the reality-virtuality continuum. Telemanipulator and Telepresence Technologies, **2351**, 282–292 (1994). https://doi.org/10.1117/12.197321

Minucciani, V., Garnero, G.: Geomatics and virtual tourism. J. Agricult. Eng., 44(2s) (2013). https://doi.org/10.4081/jae.2013.s2.e100

Okoli, C., Schabram, K.: Working papers on information systems a guide to conducting a systematic literature review of information systems research. Inf. Syst. **10** (2010). https://doi.org/10.2139/ssrn.1954824

Partarakis, N., et al.: Digital Heritage Technology at the Archaeological Museum of Heraklion. In: Stephanidis, C. (ed.) HCI 2018. CCIS, vol. 852, pp. 196–203. Springer, Cham (2018). https://doi.org/10.1007/978-3-319-92285-0_28

Partarakis, N., Zidianakis, E., Antona, M., Stephanidis, C.: Art and Coffee in the Museum. In: Streitz, N., Markopoulos, P. (eds.) DAPI 2015. LNCS, vol. 9189, pp. 370–381. Springer, Cham (2015). https://doi.org/10.1007/978-3-319-20804-6_34

Petriaggi, R.: Management strategies for conservation restoration and fruition of underwater archaeological parks. Archaeologia Maritima Mediterranea Int. J. Underwater Archaeol. **13**, 55–72 (2016)

Rahaman, H., Champion, E., Bekele, M.: From photo to 3D to mixed reality: a complete workflow for cultural heritage visualisation and experience. Digital Appl. Archaeol. Cult. Heritage, **13** (2019). https://doi.org/10.1016/j.daach.2019.e00102

Rizvić, S., Bošković, D., Okanović, V., Kihić, I. I., Prazina, I., Mijatović, B.: Time travel to the past of bosnia and herzegovina through virtual and augmented reality. Appl. Sci. (Switzerland), **11**(8) (2021). https://doi.org/10.3390/app11083711

Schweibenz, W.: The '"Virtual Museum"': new perspectives for museums to present objects and information using the internet as a knowledge base and communication system. In: Internationalen Symposiums Für Informationswissenschaft, pp. 185–200 (1998). http://www.informationswissenschaft.org/wp-content/uploads/isi/isi1998/14_isi-98-dv-schweibenz-saarbruecken.pdf

Silva, M., Teixeira, L.: Developing an eXtended Reality platform for immersive and interactive experiences for cultural heritage: serralves museum and coa archeologic park. In: Adjunct Proceedings of the 2020 IEEE International Symposium on Mixed and Augmented Reality, ISMAR-Adjunct 2020, pp. 300–302 (2020). https://doi.org/10.1109/ISMAR-Adjunct51615.2020.00084

Spiridon, P., Sandu, I.: MUSEUMS IN THE LIFE OF THE PUBLIC. INTERNATIONAL JOURNAL OF CONSERVATION SCIENCE 7(1), 87–92 (2016)

Tennent, P., et al.: Thresholds: embedding Virtual Reality in the Museum. ACM J. Comput. Cult. Heritage, **13**(2) (2020). https://doi.org/10.1145/3369394

Zyla, K., Montusiewicz, J., Skulimowski, S., Kayumov, R.: VR technologies as an extension to the museum exhibition: a case study of the Silk Road museums in Samarkand. Muzeologia A Kulturne Dedicstvo-Museology And Cultural Heritage, **8**(4), 73–93 (2020). https://doi.org/10.46284/mkd.2020.8.4.6

Mesh2Measure: A Novel Body Dimensions Measurement Based on 3D Human Model

Tao Song$^{(\boxtimes)}$ ⓘ, Rui Zhang, Yukun Dong, Xixi Tao, Hongcui Lu, and Baohua Liu

China University of Petroleum (East China), Qingdao 266580, China
{tsong,dongyk}@upc.edu.cn

Abstract. In this work, we propose an anthropometric dimensions measurement method based on 3D human model, namely Mesh2Measure. In our method, Human body features in the front and side images are firstly extracted and fused. And then, the feature vectors are attached to the template mesh model SMPL by using Graph-CNN, and 3D coordinates of the model vertices are regressed. Anthropometric dimensions of height, length, width and depth are calculated by scale conversion based on the model vertex coordinates. A novel general dense elliptic model is developed for the curve dimension or closed circumference dimension, which obtains human body dimensions by accumulating the length of elliptic segments with different coefficients. Data experiments are conducted by measuring 100 subjects. Experimental results show that our Mesh2Measure model can measure 38 main dimensions of human body in 15 s, and more importantly, the accuracy rate is 97.4% compared with the ground truth dimensions by manual measurements.

Keywords: Anthropometric dimensions · 3D Human reconstruction · Dense elliptic model

1 Introduction

Anthropometry is a branch of anthropology, focusing on anthropometrics and observation methods, and exploring the characteristics, types, variation and development of the human body through measurements of human body. Under the framework of industry 5.0, remote acquisition of anthropometric dimensions is of great significance to theoretical research of anthropology. It also has vital applications in medical care, forensic anthropology, sports, monitoring, garment customization and other fields. In health care, for example, it can help detect potential health problems in people. For instance, abdominal obesity was associated with gastroesophageal reflux disease (GERD) and Barrett's esophagus (BE), and by abdominal diameter index, we can predict the existence of BE better than body mass index (BMI) and waist-to-hip ratio (WHR) [1]. Koning et al. [2] showed a stronger correlation between waist-to-hip ratio and cardiovascular disease, and suggested that these measurements should be included in cardiovascular risk assessment. In addition, dimensions such as cervical spine height, high hip depth, and high hip circumference can be used to detect postural disorders [3]. According to the waist depth

Z. Lv and H. Song (Eds.): INTETAIN 2021, LNICST 429, pp. 80–99, 2022.
https://doi.org/10.1007/978-3-030-99188-3_6

data, we can analyze the metabolic triad of atherosclerosis [4], and waist circumference can be used to analyze obesity and lung function [5]. In health care, the risk of heart disease and premature death can be estimated by thigh circumference [6]. Using chest circumference data can detect the risk of coronary heart disease [7]. Hip circumference can be used to measure pelvic tilt an d analyze the incidence rate and mortality of cardio-vascular diseases [8]. It is obtained in [9] that people with too small calf circumference are prone to carotid plaque and atherosclerosis, leading to myocardial infarction and stroke, and the probability of insulin resistance increases, leading to diabetes [10].

Traditional anthropometric dimensions measurement methods mainly adopt contact measurement. These methods are intuitive and easy to use, but their applicability is limited and affected by many other factors. Surveyors with different skills and experience levels will make different human errors, and multiple operations of one surveyor will be different. Non-contact body measurement methods based on 2D images can be found in [11, 12, 16, 18, 31]. These methods require all subjects to take the front, side images in a required posture to calculate the length, width and other dimensions of all part of the human body.

In recent years, it has become one of research directions of anthropometric measurement to obtain dimensions based on 3D human model [13–15]. There are still many problems in current methods of accurately obtaining anthropometric dimensions based on 3D human body model. Firstly, the 3D model based on single image reconstruction has inherent fuzziness in shape estimation, which cannot meet the requirements of accurate measurement. Secondly, taking linear length accumulation between points as measurement dimensions may lead measurement error. Thirdly, there is no robust method to adapt to various body types.

We propose here a novel anthropometric dimensions measurement method based on 3D human body model, namely Mesh2Measure. In our method, the typical depth convolution neural networks Resnet-50 are used to extract and fuse human features in 2D images, and then the feature vector is attached to a standard mesh model SMPL from [17]. Vertex coordinates of the reconstructed model are obtained by using GraphCNN to deform vertices of model point by point. Dimensions of model are calculated by using these vertexes coordinates and the measurement datum points. In order to improve accuracy of model to meet the requirements of our dimension measurement, we used two view images of human body in MeshNet stage to reconstruct 3D human body model. Data experiments are conducted by measuring 100 subjects. Experimental results show that our Mesh2Measure model can measure 38 main dimensions of human body in 15 s, and the accuracy rate is 97.4% compared with the ground truth dimensions.

Our contributions can be summarized as follows.

1) Mesh2Measure uses two views to reconstruct the 3D human body model. This avoids the inherent ambiguity of single-view reconstruction of the human model.
2) A dense elliptic model is proposed. The length of the elliptic segment with different coefficients is accumulated as the calculation method of the curve dimension and the closed circumference dimension to reduce the error.

2 Our Mesh2Measure Model

We design Mesh2Measure in a cascaded architecture, which consists of MeshNet and Measure. Figure 1 describes the overall architecture of the system.

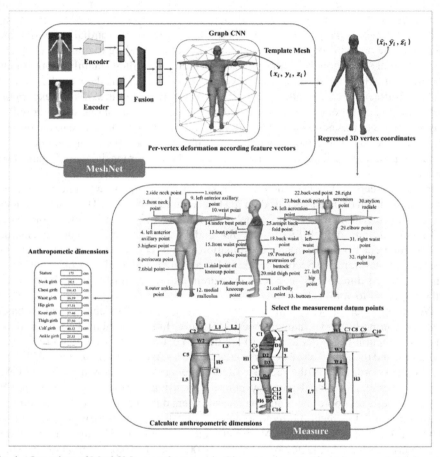

Fig. 1. Overview of Mesh2Measure framework. Given two images (front image and side image), MeshNet architecture performs 3D human body reconstruction based on the given images, and then the Measure architecture obtains human body dimensions based on the reconstructed human body model.

MeshNet is responsible for reconstructing the human body mesh model based on images from different perspectives, Measure is responsible for the selection of measurement points and the calculation of dimensions. Our Mesh2Measure can measure all the dimensions mentioned in GB/T 16160–2017 [29], and compare the main 38 dimensions of human body measured with the truth dimensions to determine that the error is within the allowable range of the tolerance standard of all dimensions of clothing, and our method is more robust to the special body type of people.

2.1 MeshNet

MeshNet architecture is mainly responsible for 3D human model reconstruction using two 2D images with architectures from [24, 27]. Human body features of two view images are extracted and fused based on Resnet-50 network to get a 2048-D feature vector. And then these features are attached to vertices of a template mesh model SMPL, using Graph-CNN deforms vertices of the mesh model point by point. Finally, MeshNet outputs vertexes coordinates of the deformed mesh model.

Feature Extraction and Fusion Network Based on Resnet-50

The first part of MeshNet architecture consists of a feature extractor, which extracts the human feature information from the image for model reconstruction. In order to reduce the error of body shape estimation by complex posture and make the network extract body shape features better, we consider separating posture feature extraction from body shape feature extraction. The accuracy of feature extraction affects the accuracy of model reconstruction. It is difficult to extract the comprehensive three-dimensional information of human body with traditional single view feature extraction. We propose here a multi view feature extraction and fusion network, which uses two view images as input. The two implementation methods of multi view feature fusion strategy is shown in Fig. 2. The fusion strategy of the former is to decouple the image features from different angles, so we use the former method to extract human features for images with different viewing angles by using separate subnets. Multiple subnets work in parallel. Finally, the feature vectors obtained from different subnets are weighted and averaged as the final feature representation. Experiments show that the two view images reconstruction model can meet our accuracy requirements.

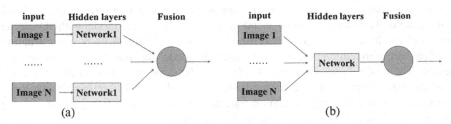

Fig. 2. Multi-view fusion strategy. (a) One view corresponds to one network strategy. (b) Multiple views correspond to one network strategy.

Our feature extraction and fusion network is composed of two ResNet-50 [27] networks trained on ImageNet. Of course, there are many other feature extraction networks, such as AlexNet [32],VGG16 [33] and GoogLeNet [34]. Based on their performance on image classification tasks, we decided to still use ResNet-50 to complete our feature extraction task. According to our requirements, the final fully connected layer of Resnet-50 network is removed, the 2048-D feature vectors output by the average pooling layer are retained, and the feature vectors extracted from different subnets are input into the feature fusion layer for weighted average fusion operation. The architecture of feature extraction and fusion network is shown in Fig. 3.

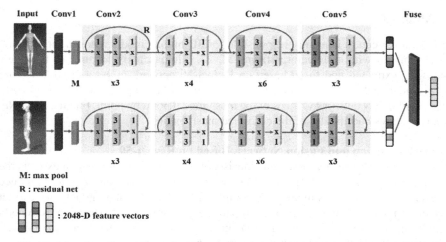

Fig. 3. The network architecture of feature extraction and fusion based on ResNet-50.

3D Human Model Reconstruction Network Based on Graph-CNN

SMPL (Skinned Multi-Person Linear Model) is a vertex-based and most widely used parameterized human body mesh model, which contains 6980 vertices, 13776 triangular patches, and a skeleton with 24 joint points. Among them, from the left to the right of the model is the positive direction of the X axis, from the bottom to the top, that is, the standing direction of the human is the positive direction of the Y axis, and the direction of the line of sight of the human eye perpendicular to the X axis and Y axis is the Z axis, as shown in Fig. 4. The SMPL parametric model includes 10 β parameters representing human body shape and 75 θ parameters representing human motion posture and joint relative angle. By modifying the pose and shape parameters, a 3D model with 3D human joints and mesh vertex coordinates can be generated. 3D human body reconstruction based on deep convolution neural network includes model-based method and model-free method. The model-based method [19–22] trains the network and estimates the SMPL parameters from the input image; the model-free [23–26] method directly estimates mesh vertex coordinates. In this paper, the model-free method is used to regress the vertex coordinates of the mesh instead of the model parameters.

The second part of MeshNet architecture is to deform the extracted human features to get the 3D coordinates of the mesh model vertices. Since our goal is to regress the vertex coordinates to meet the measurement requirements, rather than output the model parameters, we learn the method given by kolotouros et al. [24], and use Graph CNN to simplify the regression. Human features extracted from feature extraction and fusion network are added to the vertices of SMPL template mesh, and Graph-CNN is responsible for processing them on the mesh structure. The vertex coordinates after point by point deformation are output to restore the complete 3D geometry of the mesh.

Graph CNN is performed by a series of graph convolutions [28]. The formula is defined as,

$$Y = \tilde{A}XW \tag{1}$$

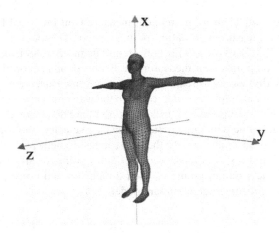

Fig. 4. SMPL model.

where A is the row normalized adjacency matrix, X is the input eigenvector, and W is the weight matrix. In this experiment, the weight data of Kolotouros training is used for regression. The full loss is defined as,

$$L = L_{\text{joint}} + L_{\text{mesh}} \tag{2}$$

$$L_{\text{joint}} = \sum_{k=1}^{M} \left\| \widehat{J_k} - J_k \right\|_1 \tag{3}$$

$$L_{\text{mesh}} = \sum_{i=1}^{N} \left\| \widehat{V_i} - V_i \right\|_1 \tag{4}$$

J_k is the ground truth 2D joints locations, $\widehat{J_k}$ is obtained by projecting 3D joint points of the predicted 3D mesh shape onto the image plane , L_{joint} is the L_1 loss of the predicted joints locations and the ground truth joints. L_{mesh} is a per-vertex L_1 loss about the predicted 3D mesh shape and the ground truth 3D mesh shape. $\widehat{V_i}$ represents our predicted 3D mesh vertices and V_i represents the ground truth of 3D mesh vertices.

2.2 Measure

As the second part of Mesh2Measure architecture, Measure mainly selects measurement datum points on the 3D human body mesh model, and calculates dimensions according to the spatial relationship between the points. We first introduce the selection basis and strategy of measurement points based on mesh model. Then, the method of dimension calculation based on the measurement datum points is introduced.

Measurement Point Selection Based on 3D Human Body Mesh Model

Whether it is contact measurement or non-contact measurement, most of them rely on measurement datum points highly related to the body parts. The measurement based on 3D human body model can make better use of 3D information of the human body, and the effect is almost equivalent to the manual measurement on a real human body. We mark corresponding measurement datum points on the 3D model in accordance with the provisions of GB/T 38131–2019 [30] on a template mesh model, and determine corresponding dimension points near measurement datum points according to dimensions measurement definition, so as to realize the automatic measurement of all 3D human model dimensions. For example, in order to obtain the waist measurement points, first the front waist point, side waist point and back waist point are determined, then the vertices on the same horizontal line with these datum points are selected, the waist measurement points are recorded in turn, and finally the waist measurement points are obtained, as shown in Fig. 5. Figure 6 shows measurement datum points of all marks, and Table 1 shows the measurement datum points of each dimension and corresponding vertexes serial numbers on the reconstructed human model.

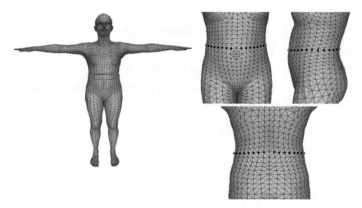

Fig. 5. Schematic diagram of waist measurement point selection.

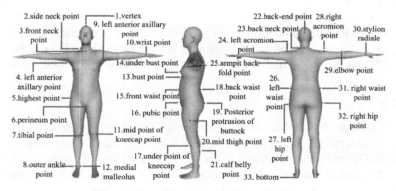

Fig. 6. The datum points of anthropometry.

Table 1. Anthropometric dimensions and characteristic points.

Classification	Body dimension	Dimension mark	Auxiliary measurement points	Corresponding vertex number on the model
Height	Stature	H1	1,33	411,3426
	Torso height	H2	6,23	1208,3164
	Waist height	H3	18,33	3502,3426
	Hip height	H4	19,33	1246,3426
	Straight body rise	H5	6,15	1208,3504
	Knee height	H6	11,33	4533,3426
Length	Upper-arm length	L1	28,29	5342,5112
	Lower-arm length	L2	29,30	5112,5568
	Under-arm length	L3	9,10	1545,2112
	Back neck point to waist	L4	18,23	3502,3164
	Outside-leg length	L5	5,31,33	4332,4310,3426
	Thigh length	L6	6,7	1208,4635
	Inside-leg length	L7	6,8	1208,6727
Width	Shoulder width	W1	24,28	3011,5342
	Chest width	W2	4,9	5013,1545
	Waist width	W3	26,31	676,4310
	Hip width	W4	27,32	1447,4920
Depth	Chest depth	D1	13	3042
	Waist depth	D2	15,18	3504,3502
	Hip depth	D3	16,19	1807,1246
	Thigh depth	D4	20	904
	Calf depth	D5	21	1183
Circumference	Neck circumference	C1	2,23	3721,3164
	Neck-base circumference	C2	2,3,23	3721,3168,3164

(continued)

Table 1. (*continued*)

Classification	Body dimension	Dimension mark	Auxiliary measurement points	Corresponding vertex number on the model
	Chest circumference	C3	4,9,13	5013, 1545, 3042
	Under-chest circumference	C4	14	1329
	Waist circumference	C5	15,18,26,31	3504, 3502, 676, 4310
	Hip circumference	C6	19,27,32	1246, 1447, 4920
	Armscye circumference	C7	24,25	3011,1879
	Upper-arm circumference	C8	28,29	5342, 5112
	Elbow circumference	C9	29	5112
	Wrist circumference	C10	20,30	904, 5568
	Thigh circumference	C11	6	1208
	Mid-thigh circumference	C12	20	904
	Knee circumference	C13	11	4533
	Under-knee circumference	C14	17	1073
	Calf circumference	C15	21	1183
	Ankle circumference	C16	8,12	6727,6833

Calculation of Anthropometric Dimensions Based on Dense Elliptic Model

Based on the measurement point list of the model, we calculated 38 main dimensions of human body, including 6 height dimensions, 7 length dimensions, 4 width dimensions, 5 thickness dimensions and 16 circumference dimensions, as shown in Fig. 7. Once the real height of the subject is known, the ratio of the real height to the model height is used as the conversion scale of dimensions of other parts.

It needs to calculate the coordinate difference or vector length of several measurement feature points in a certain direction according to the human body measurement points. For special arc lengths such as L4 and H1, they are composed of several small arc

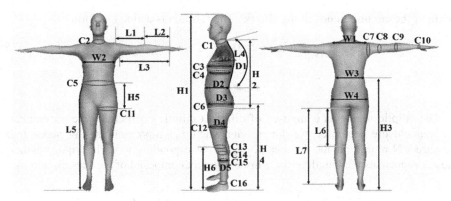

Fig. 7. Anthropometric dimensions obtained from 3D human model.

lengths. The length of each arc is approximated by its inscribed chord, and the length of the whole arc can be regarded as the sum of the lengths of several inscribed chords. We take the enclosed circumference as the result of the stitching of elliptic curve segments with different ellipse coefficients, and propose a dense elliptic model. In other words, the measurement points corresponding to the enclosed circumference dimension are projected towards a certain direction to obtain the corresponding two-dimensional curve. The two-dimensional curve can be regarded as composed of elliptic segments with different elliptic coefficients, and the calculated circumference dimension is obtained by accumulating the lengths of multiple elliptic curve segments, as shown in Fig. 8 (a).

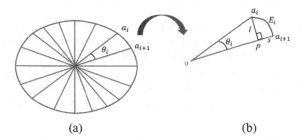

(a)   (b)

Fig. 8. Closed curve size fitting diagram.

As shown in Fig. 8 (b), given the centre point O and coordinates of the point sequence constituting the closed curve, a_i and a_{i+1} are the boundary points of the elliptic segment, Oa_i and Oa_{i+1} are the length of the edge, and the included angle θ_i can be calculated by the line segments Oa_i and Oa_{i+1}. The point P can be obtained by taking the endpoint of the relatively short side of Oa_i and Oa_{i+1} as a vertical line to the longer side, and the lengths of OP, Pa_i and Pa_{i+1} can be obtained respectively. Taking P as the coordinate origin, the relatively long side of Pa_i and Pa_{i+1} as the long half axis l and the short side as the short half axis s, the elliptic equation L is established, and the arc length E_i is one fourth of the circumference of the elliptic. The formula is defined as follows,

$$C_{L_i} = 2\pi s_i + 4(l_i - s_i) \tag{5}$$

$$E_i = \frac{1}{4} C_{L_i} \tag{6}$$

The elliptic segments composed of different elliptic coefficients are accumulated to obtain closure circumference dimensions, where E_{all} represents the dimension to be measured, N represents the number of angles corresponding to each elliptic segment, and E_N represents the length of the elliptic segment composed of vertices a_N and a_1.

$$E_{all} = \sum_{i=1}^{N-1} \frac{1}{4}[2\pi s_i + 4(l_i - s_i)] + E_N \tag{7}$$

3   Results and Discussion

3.1   Datasets

Human3.6M: This is an indoor shot 3D pose dataset that contains 11 professional actors (6 male, 5 female) in 17 scenarios like smoking, taking photo, taking on the phone, eating. Based on our needs, we selected pictures from two perspectives of a subject in different scenarios. In order to improve the robustness of the model, the selected angles are not strict front and side photos. The data sets selected from S5, S7, S8 and S9 are used for training, and the data sets selected from S10 and S11 are used for testing.

Human-Measure: We collected a data set including the front and side images, and anthropometric dimensions to test our proposed algorithm. These data are from 100 volunteers, as shown in Table 2, including 52 females and 48 males, aged between 20 and 55 years old, and include a wealth of body types. People in the images are all dressed in tight clothes and stand in an upright position so that the outline of the body can be clearly seen. Figure 9 shows the scatter plots of age and BMI distribution of subjects in the data set.

Table 2. Dataset parameters.

Number of volunteers	Sex	Age	Weight(kg)	Body mass index
52	Female	19–76	42–92	18.3–33.3
48	Male	18–72	53–103	17.4–32.6

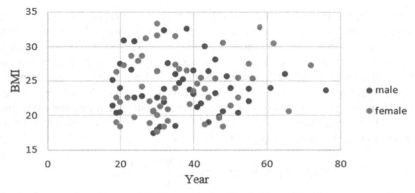

Fig. 9. Scatter plot of age and body mass index distribution of the data sets we collected.

3.2 Experimental Results

We used reconstruction error and MPJPE [38] to evaluate the pose reconstruction result of our model on Human3.6M. Table 3 showed the comparison of our method with other excellent 3D reconstruction methods, and the data of different methods are the best results they report. Our method is better than the optimized baseline, which shows that our improved method has a clear improvement on the effect of reconstruction.

According to dimensions definition and method requirements of clothing specific anthropometry, three experienced surveyors measured the actual dimension of 100 volunteers for two consecutive days and calculated the average dimension G_k as the truth value of the dimension. During the measurement, the subjects should wear tight clothes to avoid the clothing affecting the human body shape or hindering the accuracy of the dimension. The height of the human body is measured with a human altimeter, and all horizontal and other dimensions are measured with a tape. The tape should be properly tightened and the human body should not be oppressed by the tape.

$$G_k = \frac{1}{a} \left(\sum_{i=0}^{a} \left(\frac{1}{c} \sum_{j=1}^{c} m_{ij} \right) \right) \tag{8}$$

Table 3. Comparison with other methods on Human3.6M (Protocol 2[19]).

Method	MPJPE (mm)	Reconstruction error (mm)
Lassner et al. [36]	-	93.9
SMPLify [35]	-	82.3
Pavlakos et al. [20]	-	75.9
NBF [37]	-	59.9
HMR [19]	87.97	56.8
CMR [24]	102.1	50.1
Ours	100.87	48.9

Here, G_k represents true value of the kth dimension, a represents the number of surveyors, c is the number of measurements, and m_{ij} represents the jth measurement value of the ith surveyor. There are inevitably two kinds of errors in face-to-face manual measurement, one is the inter-observer error when different surveyors measure the same dimension, the other is the intra-observer error caused by multiple measurements of a certain dimension by the same surveyor. In order to evaluate the influence of these two manual measurement errors on our experimental results, the measurement technical error (TEM) and reliability coefficient (R) of 100 volunteers were calculated for each dimension, and the formula was defined as follows,

$$TEM = \frac{\sum_1^n \left[\left(\sum_1^a m_a^2 \right) - \left(\left(\sum_1^a m_a^2 \right) / a \right) \right]}{n(a-1)} \tag{9}$$

$$R = 1 - \left(\frac{TEM^2}{S^2} \right) \tag{10}$$

In the above formula, n is the number of volunteers to be measured, a is the number of measurement personnel to perform the measurement, when calculating the first type of intra-observer error, the number of measurements is a, when calculating the second type of inter-observer error, the number of measurements is 2a. Therefore, in this experiment, each surveyor needs to make two measurements. s^2 is the sample variance. The results of the calculated intra-observer and inter-observer reliability coefficients are shown in Table 4.

Table 4. Reliability of manually measured dimensions.

Dimension	Inter-observer reliability	Intra-observer reliability		
	R	Surveyor1	Surveyor2	Surveyor3
H1	0.87	0.91	0.96	0.94
H2	0.84	0.88	0.89	0.86
H3	0.86	0.85	0.93	0.89
H4	0.82	0.83	0.89	0.91
H5	0.81	0.86	0.94	0.96
H6	0.84	0.94	0.98	0.98
L1	0.90	0.87	0.91	0.84
L2	0.92	0.85	0.96	0.92
L3	0.78	0.84	0.84	0.81
L4	0.83	0.89	0.91	0.93
L5	0.87	0.91	0.96	0.83
L6	0.83	0.89	0.9	0.92

(*continued*)

Table 4. (*continued*)

Dimension	Inter-observer reliability	Intra-observer reliability		
	R	Surveyor1	Surveyor2	Surveyor3
L7	0.89	0.90	0.93	0.89
W1	0.82	0.93	0.86	0.93
W2	0.79	0.88	0.97	0.87
W3	0.88	0.87	0.90	0.98
W4	0.94	0.82	0.96	0.92
D1	0.94	0.96	0.93	0.96
D2	0.85	0.92	0.87	0.89
D3	0.96	0.90	0.93	0.87
D4	0.92	0.95	0.86	0.93
D5	0.79	0.86	0.90	0.75
C1	0.93	0.88	0.88	0.85
C2	0.87	0.89	0.90	0.93
C3	0.85	0.85	0.89	0.86
C4	0.83	0.98	0.92	0.95
C5	0.91	0.86	0.97	0.87
C6	0.90	0.96	0.94	0.93
C7	0.89	0.94	0.85	0.94
C8	0.88	0.96	0.89	0.95
C9	0.94	0.85	0.92	0.91
C10	0.81	0.82	0.85	0.83
C11	0.76	0.83	0.96	0.89
C12	0.85	0.88	0.89	0.95
C13	0.86	0.94	0.93	0.91
C14	0.84	0.92	0.95	0.94
C15	0.95	0.85	0.84	0.79
C16	0.82	0.86	0.91	0.98

As shown in Table 4, after calculation, the average value of inter-observer reliability is 0.864 (range: 0.75–0.96), which shows good reliability. In addition, the mean intra-observer reliability of the three measurers are 0.889 (range: 0.83–0.98), 0.912 (range: 0.84–0.98) and 0.901 (range: 0.78–0.98). From the calculation results, it can be seen that the human body dimensions measured manually is reliable and within the allowable measurement error range.

Next, we evaluate our Mesh2Measure measurement method. The measurement values obtained by our method are affected by two factors: (1) the degree of relaxation of the subject's clothes and the complexity of the background lead to the inaccurate display of the body shape, which affects the estimation of the body shape, resulting in the generation of size measurement errors. (2) the distance between the camera and the subject. These factors should be adjusted in the test process to obtain more favorable measurement results. The measurement error of a dimension is absolute difference between dimension obtained by our method and measured manually dimension. The mean absolute difference (MAD) between dimension obtained automatically and dimension measured manually is taken as the accuracy evaluation standard of our method. MAD of the kth dimension is defined as,

$$MAD_k = \frac{1}{n} \sum_{i=1}^{n} |M_i - G_i| \tag{11}$$

Among them, M_i is the dimension of the ith subject measured by our method, G_i is the average size of volunteers measured by all surveyors, and N is the number of volunteers.

In this paper, 38 main dimensions of 100 volunteers were evaluated. Firstly, three-dimensional human models were reconstructed based on single image, dual image and three images respectively, and the dimensions were measured on the models. The curve dimension and circumference dimension were calculated by point-to-point linear distance accumulation method, and the MAD values were MAD-1-pp and MAD-2-pp, MAD-3-pp. In addition, we use the dense ellipse model to calculate the curve dimension and circumference dimension based on the 3D model reconstructed from double image to evaluate the accuracy of our dense ellipse model, and the MAD value was expressed by MAD-2-e, as shown in Table 5.

Table 5. Comparison table of human body size measurement accuracy.

Classification	Dimension mark	MAD-1-pp(mm)	MAD-2-pp(mm)	MAD-3-pp(mm)	MAD-2-e(mm)	MAE
Height	H1	3.4	3.4	3.4	3.4	6
	H2	4.5	4.4	4.4	4.4	×
	H3	5	4.8	4.8	4.8	7
	H4	5.8	5.5	5.5	5.5	×
	H5	6.8	6.5	6.5	6.5	×
	H6	2.1	2	2	2	3
Length	L1	2.6	2.6	2.7	2.6	6
	L2	4.3	4.3	4.3	4.3	6
	L3	4.4	4.3	4.3	4.3	6
	L4	6.2	5.9	5.9	4.7	×
	L5	5.3	5.3	5.3	5	×
	L6	6.5	6.1	6.1	6.1	×
	L7	4.8	4.8	4.7	4.8	×

(*continued*)

Table 5. (*continued*)

Classification	Dimension mark	MAD-1-pp(mm)	MAD-2-pp(mm)	MAD-3-pp(mm)	MAD-2-e(mm)	MAE
Width	W1	5.2	5.1	5.2	5.1	8
	W2	3.5	3.5	3.5	3.5	8
	W3	3.6	3.5	3.5	3.5	7
	W4	4.2	4.1	4.1	4.1	7
Depth	D1	2.6	2	2	2	4
	D2	2.8	2.1	2.1	2.1	4
	D3	4.6	4	4	4	8
	D4	3.1	2.5	2.5	2.5	9
	D5	2.6	2.3	2.3	2.3	9
Circumference	C1	6	5.5	5.4	4.3	6
	C2	7.2	6	5.9	5.1	6
	C3	9.8	7.4	7.2	5.9	15
	C4	8.3	7.5	7.4	6.2	15
	C5	9.4	7.9	7.2	6.6	11
	C6	9.7	7.4	7.2	6.4	12
	C7	8.5	7.5	7.5	7	9
	C8	7.8	7.2	7.1	6.1	9
	C9	6.2	5.3	5.2	4.9	×
	C10	6.8	5.7	5.4	4.6	×
	C11	9.4	8.6	8.4	7.2	9
	C12	8.6	7.7	7.5	6.6	9
	C13	8.4	7.1	7	6.2	×
	C14	9.1	8.6	8.3	7.2	×
	C15	9.2	8.8	8.5	6.4	9
	C16	7.9	7.3	7.2	5.8	×

It can be seen from Table 5 that the MAD value of MAD-1-pp is similar to that of MAD-2-pp and MAD-3-pp in height, length and width dimensions. It is worth noting that MAD-2-pp and MAD-3-pp are smaller than MAD-1-pp in depth, circumference dimensions. The results show that multi view images reconstruction method is more effective than the single view image reconstruction method. In addition, by comparing the values of MAD-2-pp and MAD-3-pp, it is found that the mean absolute difference of two methods is similar in most dimensions, and only in a few dimensions, values of MAD-3-pp method are smaller than that of MAD-2-pp method. Therefore, experiments show that dual image can contain enough body shape information. Considering users experience and measurement accuracy, the number of images used in the final multi view strategy is n = 2. On the other hand, comparing the MAD value of MAD-2-pp with mad value of MAD-2-e, the application of dense elliptic model algorithm in curve dimension (L4, L5) and circumference dimension reduces the measurement error. The results show that our dense ellipse model algorithm can get smaller error than the point-to-point linear distance accumulation method.

In the process of measurement, the absolute difference of a dimension larger than MAE is inevitable, which is regarded as an abnormal value. In this paper, PA value is used as an index to evaluate the stability of measurement method. The PA value calculation formula of the kth dimension is defined as follows,

$$PA_k = \left(\frac{s}{n}\right) \times 100 \tag{12}$$

Where n is the number of volunteers and s is the number of outliers. We calculated PA values of some dimensions of 100 volunteers obtained by our method and other methods, and drew a bar chart, as shown in Fig. 10. Through analysis, we found that the average PA value of all dimensions of our proposed method was 95%, Murtaza's [16] method is 93%, and Liu's [12] method is 94.2%. Therefore, compared with other methods, our measurement method is more stable and accurate.

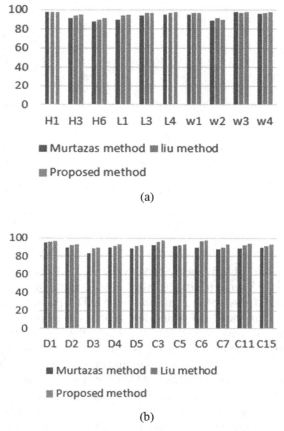

(a)

(b)

Fig. 10. The PA comparison of dimensions obtained by proposed method with other methods.

4 Conclusions

In this work, we present Mesh2Measure, an anthropometric dimensions measurement method based on 3D human body model. Compared with methods based on 2D human body contour, our method can extract more datum points and is more robust. The effect is almost the same as the manual measurement on a real human body. To make the reconstruction model more accurate, we fully extract and fuse human features of two view images. In addition, we propose a dense elliptic model method to calculate curve dimensions and closed circumference dimensions, which has higher fitting degree. The experimental results show that the proposed method is suitable for various body types, and the error of 38 main dimensions are smaller than that of existing methods. Therefore, anthropometric dimensions measured in our experiment can be used to assist medical health detection, sports, human body data analysis, garment customization and other fields. Future work can explore the anthropometric of a variety of postures and complex backgrounds, making the measurement more convenient and suitable for more situations.

Acknowledgments. This work was supported by National Natural Science Foundation of China (Grant Nos. 61873280, 61873281, 61972416), Taishan Scholarship (tsqn201812029), Major projects of the National Natural Science Foundation of China (Grant No. 41890851), Natural Science Foundation of Shandong Province (No. ZR2019MF012).

References

1. Baik, D., Sheng, J., Schlaffer, K., Friedenberg, F.K., Smith, M.S., Ehrlich, A.C.: Abdominal diameter index is a stronger predictor of prevalent Barrett's esophagus than BMI or waist-to-hip ratio. Diseases Esophagus **30**(9), 1–6 (2017)
2. De Koning, L., Merchant, A.T., Pogue, J., Anand, S. S.: Waist circumference and waist-to-hip ratio as predictors of cardiovascular events: meta-regression analysis of prospective studies. European Heart J. **28**(7), 850–856 (2007)
3. Dunk, N.M., Lalonde, J., Callaghan, J.P.: Implications for the use of postural analysis as a clinical diagnostic tool: reliability of quantifying upright standing spinal postures from photographic. J. Manipulative Physiol. Therapeutics **28**(6), 386–392 (2005)
4. Lemieux, I., Pascot, A., Couillard, C.: Hypertriglyceridemic waist: a marker of the atherogenic metabolic triad (hyperinsulinemia, hyperapo B, small, dense LDL)? Conf. 72nd Sci. Sessions Am. Heart Association (AHA) **102**(2), 179–184 (2000)
5. Chen, Y., Rennie, D., Cormier, Y.F., Dosman, J.: Waist circumference is associated with pulmonary function in normal-weight, overweight, and obese subjects. Am. J. Clinical Nutrit. **85**(1), 35–39 (2007)
6. Scott, I.A.: Thigh circumference and risk of heart disease and premature death. BMJ **339**(7723), 704–705 (2009)
7. Smith, D.A., et al.: Abdominal diameter index: a more powerful anthropometric measure for prevalent coronary heart disease risk in adult males. Diabetes Obesity Metabol. **7**(4), 370–380 (2005)
8. Heitmann, B.L., Frederiksen, P., Lissner, L.: Hip circumference and cardiovascular morbidity and mortality in men and women. Obesity Res. **12**(3), 482–487 (2004)
9. Debette, S., Leone, N., Courbon, D., et al.: Calf circumference is inversely associated with carotid plaques. Stroke **39**(11), 2958–2965 (2008)

10. Park, J.S., Cho, M.H., Ahn, C.W., et al.: The association of insulin resistance and carotid atherosclerosis with thigh and calf circumference in patients with type 2 diabetes. Cardiovasc. Diabetol. **11**(1), 62 (2012)
11. Lu, J.M., Twu, L.J., Wang, M.J.J.: Constructing 3D human model from front and side images. Expert Syst. Appl. **39**(5), 5012–5018 (2012)
12. Wang, X., Liu, B., Dong, Y., et al.: Anthropometric landmarks extraction and dimensions measurement based on ResNet. Symmetry **12**(12), 1997 (2020)
13. Xiao, Q.I., Zhongping, J.I.: Size measurement and fitting based on 3D human body model. College Comput. Sci. Eng. **643**(7), 76–83 (2019)
14. Wang, J., Jin, X.: three dimensional body measurement based on cnns and body silhouette. Master Thesis Zhejiang Univ. (2018)
15. Xu, L., Wu, X.: Research on the automatic measurement of 3D model of human body. Master Thesis Harbin Inst.Technol. (2019)
16. Aslam, M., Rajbdad, F., Khattak, S., Azmat, S.: Automatic measurement of anthropometric dimensions using frontal and lateral silhouettes. IET Comput. Vision **11**(6), 434–447 (2017)
17. Loper, M., Mahmood, N., Romero, J., et al.: SMPL: a skinned multi-person linear model. ACM Trans. Graphics **34**(6), 248 (2015)
18. Xiao, Y., Zhang, D.: Design and development of a garment and human body measurement system based on photography. Master Thesis Zhejiang Univ. (2019)
19. Kanazawa, A., Black, M.J., Jacobs, D. W., Malik, J.: End-to-end recovery of human shape and pose. IEEE Conf. Comput. Vision Pattern Recogn (CVPR) (2018)
20. Pavlakos, G., Zhu, L., Zhou, X., Daniilidis, K..: Learning to Estimate 3D Human Pose and Shape from a Single Color Image. In: The European Conference on Computer Vision and Pattern Recognition (CVPR), (2018)
21. Kolotouros, N., Pavlakos, G., Black, M.J., Daniilidis, K.: Learning to reconstruct 3D human pose and shape via model-fitting in the loop. In: International Conference on Computer Vision (ICCV), pp. 2252-2261 (2019)
22. Gabeur, V., Franco, J.S., Martin, X., Schmid, C., Rogez, G.: Moulding humans: non-parametric 3D human shape estimation from single images. In: IEEE/CVF International Conference on Computer Vision (ICCV), pp. 2232-2241 (2019)
23. Choi, H., Moon, G., Lee, K.M.: Pose2Mesh: Graph Convolutional Network for 3D Human Pose and Mesh Recovery from a 2D Human Pose. In: Vedaldi, A., Bischof, H., Brox, T., Frahm, J.-M. (eds.) ECCV 2020. LNCS, vol. 12352, pp. 769–787. Springer, Cham (2020). https://doi.org/10.1007/978-3-030-58571-6_45
24. Kolotouros, N., Pavlakos, G., Black, M.J., Daniilidis, K.: Convolutional mesh regression for single-image human shape reconstruction. In: The IEEE Conference on Computer Vision and Pattern Recognition (CVPR), pp. 4501–4510 (2019)
25. Moon, G., Lee, K.M.: I2L-MeshNet: Image-to-Lixel Prediction Network for Accurate 3D Human Pose and Mesh Estimation from a Single RGB Image. In: Vedaldi, A., Bischof, H., Brox, T., Frahm, J.-M. (eds.) ECCV 2020. LNCS, vol. 12352, pp. 752–768. Springer, Cham (2020). https://doi.org/10.1007/978-3-030-58571-6_44
26. Moon, G., Lee, K.M.: Pose2Pose: 3D positional pose-guided 3D rotational pose prediction for expressive 3D human pose and mesh estimation. In: The IEEE Conference on Computer Vision and Pattern Recognition (CVPR) (2020)
27. He, K., Zhang, X., Ren, S., Sun, J.: Deep residual learning for image recognition. In: IEEE Conference on Computer Vision and Pattern Recognition (CVPR), pp. 27–30 (2016)
28. Kipf, T.N., Welling, M.: Semi-supervised classification with graph convolutional networks. In: The International Conference on Learning Representations (ICLR) (2017)
29. GB/T 16160–2017: Anthropometric Definitions and Methods for Garment; Standards Press of China: Beijing (2017)

30. GB/T 38131–2019: Acquisition Method of Datum Points for Clothing Anthropometry; Standards Press of China: Beijing, China (2019)
31. Dibra, E., Jain, H., Oztireli, C., Ziegler, R., Gross, M.: HS-nets: estimating human body shape from silhouettes with convolutional neural networks. In: Fourth International Conference on 3D Vision (3DV), pp. 108–117 (2016)
32. Technicolor, T., Related, S., Technicolor, T.: ImageNet Classification with Deep Convolutional Neural Networks. Curran Associates Inc, NIPS (2012)
33. Simonyan, K., Zisserman, A.: Very deep convolutional networks for large-scale image recognition. Comput. Sci. (2014)
34. Szegedy, C., Liu, W., Jia, Y.: Going deeper with convolutions. In: Proceedings of the IEEE Conference on Computer Vision and Pattern Recognition, (pp. 1-9) (2014)
35. Bogo, F., Kanazawa, A., Lassner, C., Gehler, P., Romero, J., Black, M.J.: Keep It SMPL: Automatic Estimation of 3D Human Pose and Shape from a Single Image. In: Leibe, B., Matas, J., Sebe, N., Welling, M. (eds.) ECCV 2016. LNCS, vol. 9909, pp. 561–578. Springer, Cham (2016). https://doi.org/10.1007/978-3-319-46454-1_34
36. Lassner, C., Romero, J., Kiefel, M., Bogo, F., Black, M.J., Gehler, P.V.: Unite the people: closing the loop between 3D and 2D human representations. In: CVPR (2017)
37. Omran, M., Lassner, C., Pons-Moll, G., Gehler, P., Schiele, B.: Neural body fitting: unifying deep learning and model based human pose and shape estimation. In: 3DV (2018)
38. Zhou, X., Zhu, M., Pavlakos, G., Leonardos, S., Derpanis, K.G., Daniilidis, K.: Monocap: monocular human motion capture using a CNN coupled with a geometric prior. PAMI 41(4), 901–914 (2019)

Charting Science Fiction in Computer Science Literature

Philipp Jordan[1]([✉]) and Paula Alexandra Silva[2]

[1] Communication and Information Sciences, University of Hawaii at Manoa,
Honolulu, USA
philippj@hawaii.edu

[2] Department of Informatics Engineering, University of Coimbra, Coimbra, Portugal
paulasilva@dei.uc.pt

Abstract. Studies concerning the usage of 'science fiction' in computer science research are scarce and rely mostly on anecdotal evidence and scattered oral accounts. For this reason, we present a content analysis of a random sample of 500 publications, retrieved from the IEEE *Xplore* Digital Library via a faceted, full-text search for 'science fiction'. We analyze the type of research paper and the contextual usage of the science fiction referral and show that science fiction, in the grand scheme of things, is a niche topic in computer science research. Furthermore, results demonstrate that science fiction referrals appear primarily in opinion-type contributions, largely with the purpose of drawing inspiration and innovation into the research paper. The implications of this study can guide computer scientists to consciously utilize science fiction in their research and scholarship and therefore, contribute to innovative HCI and computer science research and application.

Keywords: Science fiction · Human-computer interaction · Computer science · Science studies · Content analysis

1 Introduction

Both literary and audio-visual SF [22] propose important ethical questions and dilemmas to the general public—from the role and agency of technology in our lives, to the moral utilization of autonomous robots; or as well highlight the conflict zone of technology, privacy and security in the 21st century. Science Fiction (SF) and real-world technological development intersect in a variety of ways, and a bi-directional relationship between both domains seems not too far-fetched. Especially SF films and shows inevitable focus—to a lesser or larger extent—on yet-to-come Human-computer Interaction (HCI), speculative user interfaces, interactions and future human-machine integration. SF movies and shows can further provide visual use cases and compelling scenarios, allowing conjecture on technological foresight of, for instance, beneficial and detrimental technology outcomes of the society of the future.

© ICST Institute for Computer Sciences, Social Informatics and Telecommunications Engineering 2022
Published by Springer Nature Switzerland AG 2022. All Rights Reserved
Z. Lv and H. Song (Eds.): INTETAIN 2021, LNICST 429, pp. 100–126, 2022.
https://doi.org/10.1007/978-3-030-99188-3_7

Commonly, depictions of advanced devices, innovative interactions and future technologies in SF are a regular topic in popular news and tech magazines. However, their usage in computer science research has not been comprehensively charted. Such investigations are critical to better understand the potential utility and latent shortcomings of SF for computing research and HCI innovation and, as such, through a content analysis of science communication, this study endeavors to shed light on the relationship between both domains.

2   Background

While still a nascent topic, distinct aspects of the mutual relationship and crossings of SF and HCI have been partially studied [31,40–42,55], including studies examining research indexed in the Association of Computing Machinery (ACM) Digital Library (DL), which:

- Investigated the patterns of use of SF in the CHI proceedings over three decades of computing research [24];
- Described the evolutionary usage of the popular SF franchise STAR TREK [25];
- Assessed the utilization of 18 SF robots and AIs [45].

Related work concerning SF/HCI found a convergence of the depiction and real-world progress of computer technology [33]. More recently, researchers did delineate SF-based shape-changing interfaces [65] and hand gestures [16] from SF movies. In addition, catalogues of SF movies and shows, relevant to HCI research, have been made available recently [48,49,60]. In the larger arena of computer science research, the SF/real-world R&D link has been noted by many [11,14,15,21,62,63,69], including Kay and Dourish's [12] special issue on SF and ubiquitous computing.

SF can also stimulate creativity of students in computer science and a diversity of other STEM fields [67], such as computer-ethics [9,10] or -security [30], through an alternative viewpoint extending traditional technical foci in computing education. In fact, as early as in the 1970s, the value of SF literature for educational purposes has been discussed in, for example, Michalsky's essay [43] on the integration of SF into formal education, which presents an early notion of speculative fiction as a means to benefit student creativity. While the topic lately gained traction [3,4,20,37,54], SF in educational settings seems to be a double-edged sword, as has been viewed critically as well [46]; an indicator for a mindful integration of these materials in classroom and educational contexts in the time to come.

Furthermore, Aaron Marcus [40] has presented an overview detailing an HCI travelogue of Hollywood SF movies and shows, and has coordinated two Computer-Human Interaction (CHI) conference plenaries [41,42] on the topic. Similarly, Schmitz, Endres and Butz [58] surveyed various instances of a convergence of SF movies and HCI, outlining a collaboration scheme between researchers and filmmakers through a continuous, inspirational dialogue wherein films (or filmmakers) are inspired by technology (or by scientists). David Kirby [26–29] speaks extensively about the impact of SF on both, the public perception and the Research and Development (R&D) of technology in his comprehensive, qualitative studies investigating the collaboration schemes of scientists and movie-makers. From a theoretical standpoint, hardly any models describe the relationship of SF and computer science research fully and comprehensively (e.g. [25, 29, 44, 58]).

HCI researchers have as well followed up on the concept of design fiction, which has, since the 2010s, been popularized by a small number of design researchers and labs in HCI and computer science research [6–8, 13, 38, 39, 50, 64]. Design fictions are closely related to film theory fundamentals, such as Kirby's [28] 'diegetic prototypes' or Frank's [17] notions of 'perceived and referential realities'. For example, Tanenbaum [64] refers to Kirby's [28] concept of diegetic prototypes and extends design fiction it into an emerging research and design method in HCI for innovative interface design research, which is currently used as i) a method to envision new futures and technologies, ii) a tool for communicating innovations to other researchers and the public and, iii) an inspirational and motivational vehicle to explore design affordances and constraints within fictional scenarios. Extending traditional academic research, the mutual relationship of SF/HCI is furthermore well recognized in applied settings, including Experience Professionals Association (UXPA) [66], Nature Careers [61] and the Los Angeles based Science and Entertainment Exchange [47].

Research Rationale. Notwithstanding the earlier introduced commonalities and existing body of research, Marcus [40] states that the history, relationship and synergy effects of of SF and HCI/computer science research, are poorly documented and insufficiently described. Thus far, no studies which explore the usage of SF in scientific publications, with a focus on computer science, are available up to this date with the existing work on the subject matter being:

- limited on specific aspects and applications of SF and computer science research, such as specific interaction types [16, 65];
- having a selection bias (e.g. toward a specific subset of selected SF films) and lack accountable and longitudinal data to describe the relationship of SF and computer science research over time and across fields of computer science research [33, 58];
- or using a limited sample size and restricted query (e.g. investigations for 20 SF films) without a focus on SF and computing research [34, 35].

As a result, SF appears like a related, but yet uncharted topical domain in computer science research. Be that as it may, such investigations are important, as they highlight missed opportunities and future potentials of SF for computing research.

3 Method

Utilizing a methodological framework provided by [23–25,45,52], we present in the following procedure for a detailed, qualitative analysis and discussion of a large sample of computer science records, which refer to SF.

Research Questions. Our study is organized around the following research questions (RQ):

- RQ1: What are the metadata characteristics of computer science publications which reference SF?
- RQ2: What SF particulars co-occur in the context of computer science publications which reference general SF?
- RQ3: What is the purpose of references to SF, and SF particulars which co-occur in the context of SF references, in computer science publications?

Potential Repositories. Both, the ACM DL and Institute of Electrical and Electronics Engineers (IEEE) *Xplore* DL were identified as potential repositories. As an considerable body of research by [23,24,45] already analyzed records retrieved from the ACM DL, the decision was made to search in the IEEE *Xplore* DL for relevant publications which reference SF.

Metadata versus Full-text Retrieval. The question if a metadata, full-text or a hybrid search (e.g. full-text span retrievals) is the most effective method to generate relevant datasets in search and retrieval tasks is of substantial importance for the current study. Contrasting metadata and full-text searches, Beall [5] lists 25 disadvantages of full-text searches, including the failure to recognize abbreviations and acronyms (e.g. "science fiction" and "SF", "sci-fi", or "scifi") and synonyms.

On the other side, Salton and Harman [57] find common problems of metadata-based search and retrieval queries in digital collections, among those, the indexing qualification and individual expertise of those which generate the metadata of the records in the first place. It seems clear that both approaches stand in diametrical opposition to each other and research [19,36,68] shows that an integrated combination of both, metadata and full-text searches, can generate the best results with regards to the relevance of the retrieved documents in specific circumstances.

Comparative Queries. On Dec 30, 2017, a total of eight queries were conducted in the IEEE *Xplore* Digital Library. These initial searches—through the usage of synonyms and the instantiation of different search fields, Boolean operators, synonyms of SF and related concepts—increased in complexity. As a result, two potential candidate sets were identified, introduced next.

C_7 retrieved 353 records in the IEEE *Xplore* Digital Library for a metadata-based search for a variety of SF synonyms:

— *Displaying results 1-25 of 353 for ("science fiction" OR "science-fiction" OR "sciencefiction" OR "sci-fi" OR "scifi" OR "sci fi" OR "sf film" OR "sf movie" OR "sf show" OR "sf story" OR "sf author" OR "sf novel" OR "space fiction" OR "space fictions" OR "space opera")*

C_4, a full-text search, over all fields of the records, returned at that date 2784 records for a search for the single search term "science fiction":

—*Displaying results 1-25 of 2,784 for ("science fiction")*

As RQ2 and RQ3 focus on the *contextual usage* of SF in computer science research publications, it can be reasoned that a full-text retrieval (which includes obvious SF referrals in the metadata) is the more fruitful and inclusive approach, especially if one aims to understand the usage of the concept *in situ* of the publication under scrutiny. Therefore, the authors agreed to move forward with C_4 for further analysis.

Facets and Sampling — C_4. Before the application of repository-specific facets (see Table 1), C_4 retrieved of a total of 2784 records (1262 Journals & Magazines, 1086 Conference Proceedings, 429 Books, 7 Early Access Articles) in the IEEE *Xplore* DL. After the application of the facets *My Subscribed Content, Content Type: Journals & Magazines, Conference Publications,* and *Early Access Articles,* C_4 is reduced to 1647 records—$C_{4(1647)}$.

Due to its notable size of 1647 research papers mentioning SF, $C_{4(1647)}$ was deemed unfeasible for a full qualitative review. Therefore, a random sample was drawn to create a subset called $C_{4(500)}$ representing about 30% of the records in $C_{4(1647)}$. Lastly, a random sample of 125 records was drawn from $C_{4(500)}$ and utilized for a subsequent Inter-rater Reliability (IRR) analysis of two interpretative variables. Table 1 shows the sampling process and step-wise reduction of records per set from the initial full-text retrieval as described in C_4.

Variable Overview. With regards to the variables and attributes reviewed for each record in $C_{4(500)}$, Table 2 presents the nine final variables, along with an abbreviation, the scale type they are measured on, the attribute per variable, data type, coding approach and the prevalence or absence of mutual exclusivity. From these nine variables, seven are reviewed solely by the leading author while the remaining two, the type of research contribution (Pub_{Type}) and the contextual usage of the SF referral (SF_{Cont}) were subjected to an independent, two-person IRR analysis.

Inter-rater Reliability — Pub_{Type} and SF_{Cont}. The lead author and Rater 1 (R1) randomly drew $C_{4(125)}$, as part of the random sample from $C_{4(500)}$, using a random number generator and proceeded to qualitatively review the publications for the variables in Table 2. After an independent coding by R1 of $C_{4(125)}$ for the two interpretative variables in this study—i) the type of research contribution (according to Wobbrock and Kientz [70]) and ii) the contextual usage of the SF referral—the initial coding scheme was established and $C_{4(125)}$ was made available to the second rater (R2).

Table 1. Reduction of C_4 via facets and sampling.

Set	Records	Sampling and reduction
$C_{4(2784)}$	2784	Initial full-text retrieval
$C_{4(1647)}$	1647	After application of facets
$C_{4(500)}$	500	Random sample of $C_{4(1647)}$
$C_{4(125)}$	125	Random sample of $C_{4(500)}$

Table 2. Variable overview.

#	Variable	Scale	Type	M.E.	Coding
1	Pub_{Year}	Interval	Quan	Yes	R1/in vivo
2	Pub_{Type}	Nominal	Qual	Yes	IRR
3	SF_{Freq}	Ratio	Quan	Yes	R1/in vivo
4	SF_{Loc}	Nominal	Qual	No	R1/in vivo
5	SF_{Cont}	Nominal	Qual	Yes	IRR
6	SF_{Auth}	Nominal	Qual	No	R1/in vivo
7	SF_{Books}	Nominal	Qual	No	R1/in vivo
8	SF_{Movies}	Nominal	Qual	No	R1/in vivo
9	SF_{Char}	Nominal	Qual	No	R1/in vivo

Following a general introduction to the coding scheme by R1 with a focus on the two interpretative variables—Pub_{Type} and SF_{Cont}—R2 coded independently $C_{4(125)}$ using the coding rubric for the two interpretative variables and attributes provided by R1. After R2 provided the assessment of $C_{4(125)}$, an IRR evaluation by means of cohen's κ (and Krippendorff's α as alternative) coefficient(s) was calculated. Two check-ins (one after R2 did code 50% of $C_{(4125)}$, one after R2 finished coding $C_{4(125)}$ by R1 served to resolve disagreements and finalize the final coding scheme. Specifically, R2 did indicate in 33 of the 125 records in $C_{4(125)}$ (36 of 250 possible codes) alternative codes for either, the type of research contribution, or the contextual usage of the SF referral. These 36 alternative codes were reviewed and consolidated between the raters, hence allowing R1 to proceed to code the remaining 375 records in $C_{4(500)}$.

Rater Background. Rater 1 is the lead researcher on this project and has been conducting research on SF and HCI/computer science research for the last 5 years. Rater 2 is a HCI and design innovation researcher and practitioner with 15+ years experience. Rater 2 volunteered her time and expertise to rate $C_{4(125)}$ for no compensation or reimbursement.

3.1   Coding the Type of Research Paper—Pub$_{\text{Type}}$

In order to judge which type of research contribution is under scrutiny, the main contribution of the paper was coded along 7 mutually exclusive categories following Wobbrock and Kientz [40–43, 70]. This variable is of categorical nature, mutually exclusive and has the following eight attributes:

1. **Empirical contributions**—e.g. experiments, user tests, field observations, interviews, surveys, focus groups, diaries, ethnographies, sensors, log files, quantitative lab experiments, crowdsourced study
2. **Artifact contributions**—e.g. input device, system, hardware toolkit, envisionment
3. **Methodological contributions**—e.g. method adaption, method application, method innovation, new measures, new instrument
4. **Theoretical contributions**—e.g. frameworks, conceptual models, design criteria, quantitative models
5. **Dataset contributions**—e.g. test corpi, benchmark results, repositories, datasets
6. **Survey contributions**—e.g. surveys on techniques, emerging topics, tools, domains and technologies, meta-analyses
7. **Opinion contributions**—e.g. arguments on specific research topics or a domain, for example, new prospects in evaluation, application or vision of the future
8. **Other contributions**[1]—e.g. Newsletters, Editor's Notes, Interviews, Readers Letters, Obituaries, Tutorials, Presentation Slides, Keynote Speaker Introductions, or Book Reviews, which do not fit in any of the other categories.

3.2   Coding the Contextual SF Referral—SF$_{\text{Cont}}$

In order to classify the contextual usage[2] of the SF referral(s) in the publication(s) under review, a mutually exclusive variable called 'Contextual usage of the SF referral' with eight attributes was coded. These attributes did emerge from the prior introduced analysis of $C_{4(125)}$ and can be conceptually classified into three broader domains:

---

[1] This category has been added and is not listed as part of the original 7 categories from Wobbrock and Kientz [40–43, 70]. In contrast to *opinion contributions*, these publications are coded as *other, non-research-focused contributions*, as they do not cite extensive, related research or work, commonly found in *opinion contributions*.

[2] In cases where multiple SF referrals occur in a publication, a judgment by the respective Rater across all referrals in the paper under review is made, therefore yielding one code for the overall usage of the SF referrals in the respective paper.

1. **SF Referrals, with a focus on drawing innovation from SF in the research paper:**
   (a) **Coming from SF**— This attribute sums up the usage of a SF referral to draw from a general SF concept, technology, device or idea, originating, as seen in or known from SF, and potentially inspiring research. Conceptually, this attribute describes references to SF, which in contrast to 1.(b) or 1.(c), refer to a known SF concept, but do neither stress the realization or impossibility of the concept.
   (b) **Making SF a Science Reality**— This attribute encapsulates a SF reference, which stresses the realization of a SF concept, technology, device, or idea (or approximation of), by crossing over into or being reality. Conceptually, this attribute describes SF references the authors use to stress that an innovation moved from SF into science. Conceptually, this attribute is a sub-attribute of 1.(a)
   (c) **Unreal SF**— This attribute describes a SF reference, which emphasizes a SF concept, technology, device or idea, as seen in, or known from SF, but, at the time of the publication, not possible in the real world. Conceptually, this attribute is a sub-attribute of 1.(a).
2. **SF referrals, with a focus on individuals, the scientific community and/or the general public:**
   (a) **SF and the Individual**—This attributes codes the contextual usage of a SF referral win regards to the relationship of the author, or another person (e.g. other researcher, SF author, or research participant), who is also involved with SF. Conceptually, this attribute encapsulates the usage of a SF referral with a focus on the external implications and consequences for people and communities. Conceptually, this attribute encapsulates the usage of a SF referral with a focus on specific individuals.
   (b) **SF and the Community or Public**—This attributes codes contextual usages of SF in reference to an the relationship of SF with the understanding, expectations, or imaginations of science in the public or research communities. Conceptually, this attribute encapsulates the usage of a SF referral with a focus on the external implications and consequences for general people and the larger community and society.
3. **SF referrals, integrated as part of the research paper.**
   (a) **SF and the Paper Research Method**—This attributes summarizes contextual usages of SF referrals in regards to the research background, method, objective, application, or outcome of the paper. Conceptually, this attribute encapsulates the usage of a SF reference with the purpose of the utilization within the research contribution itself.
   (b) **SF in the References**—In reference to SF reference, listed in the references section of a publication. Conceptually, this attribute reflects the usage of a SF referral in the references section of a research contribution.

3.3   Contextual SF Particulars—SF$_{\text{Cont}}$

This variable represents explicit SF particulars, which co-occur in the publication which references SF in $C_{4(500)}$. This variable is of nominal nature and structured in the following sub-variables:

1. **SF Authors:** (e.g. ARTHUR C. CLARKE or H.G. WELLS)
2. **SF Books, Novels, Short Stories, Magazines**[3]: (e.g. NEUROMANCER or I, ROBOT)
3. **SF Movies or Shows:** (e.g. 2001: A SPACE ODYSSEY or BLACK MIRROR)
4. **SF Characters:** (e.g. MR. DATA from STAR TREK or HAL from 2001: A SPACE ODYSSEY)

Research Tools. With regard to the research tools, the author used Atlas.ti v8 to qualitatively code $C_{4(500)}$. In addition, Microsoft Excel was used to calculate descriptive measures of $C_{4(125)/(500)}$ and further utilized to create the graphs and figures for the data presentation in this paper. For the IRR analyis, IBM SPSS Statistics was used to calculate the IRR coefficients for cohen's κ, respectively, Krippendorff's α.

4   Results

In the remainder of this paper, only results pertaining to $C_{4(125)}$ and $C_{4(500)}$ will be presented. The IRR results were calculated using $C_{4(125)}$, the Publication Years results and Referral Frequency and Location results contrast both $C_{4(125)}$ and $C_{4(500)}$. All other results used $C_{4(500)}$.

Inter-rater Reliability (IRR). As all other variables are of non-interpretative nature and coded in vivo (see Table 2), only the variables Pub$_{Type}$ and SF$_{Cont}$ are subjected to an IRR assessment. The IRR coefficients of cohen's κ, respectively Krippendorff's α as an alternative measure, were calculated through IBM SPSS Statistics. The IRR analysis of the agreement of R1 and R2 with regards to the type of research paper (Pub$_{Type}$) of $C_{4(125)}$ showed a substantial agreement (κ between 0.61–0.80) between R1 and R2, with a κ of 0.71, respectively, resulted in an α coefficient of 0.71 ($\alpha \geq 0.667$ [32]) allowing for tentative conclusions to be drawn. The IRR analysis of the agreement of R1 and R2 with regards to the type of the contextual SF referral (SF$_{Loc}$ in $C_{4(125)}$ showed a substantial agreement (κ between 0.61–0.80), with a κ of 0.65, respectively, resulted in an α coefficient of 0.68 ($\alpha \geq 0.667$ allowing for tentative conclusions to be drawn.

---

[3] There might be instances where it is not possible to identify if a specific SF referral is toward a movie or a book. Most SF media is rooted SF literature, however, in cases where it is not clear if an author refers to a specific SF book, or rather the equivalent SF film, a judgment by the Rater is conducted and either the *SF Books* or *SF Movies* categories is chosen.

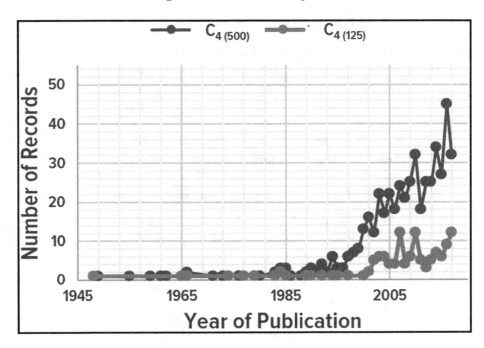

Fig. 1. Distribution of publication years: $C_{4(500)}$ and $C_{4(125)}$

Publication Years. Figure 1 shows the distribution of records per year of $C_{4(500)}$. The earliest record in $C_{4(500)}$ dates from 1948 while the most recent papers in $C_{4(500)}$ were published in 2017. Figure 1 also shows that 72 out of the 500 records (14%) in $C_{4(500)}$ were published before 2000, while the bulk of retrieved papers (n = 428, 86%) was published in the year 2000 or later. $C_{4(500)}$ is overall representative of the distribution patterns of publications years of records in comparison to the IRR Set $C_{4(125)}$.

SF Referral Frequency and Location. Table 3 shows the distribution of SF referrals in $C_{4(125)}$ and in $C_{4(500)}$.

In total, 899 referrals to 'science fiction' are identified with the vast majority of referrals (n = 761, 84.6%) being found in the body of the reviewed publications, n = 64 in the references, n = 49 in the abstracts, n = 21 in the titles and n = 4 in the footnotes. With a total of 899 SF referrals in 500 records, on average, every publication in $C_{4(500)}$ did refer 'science fiction' 1.55 times/record, with a maximum of 31 referrals in one single record. Table 4 shows that the majority of the records (380 out of 500 records, 76%) in $C_{4(500)}$ refer 'science fiction' one time. This frequency and location distribution re-ensembles closely the frequency and location distribution in $C_{4(125)}$.

Table 3. SF Referral frequency and location: $C_{4(125)}$ and $C_{4(500)}$.

SF_{Loc}	Records	% of $C_{4(500)}$	Records	% of $C_{4(125)}$
Title	21	2.3%	2	1%
Abstract	49	5.5%	12	6%
Body	761	84.6%	152	81%
Footnote	4	0.4%	2	1%
References	64	7.1%	19	10%
Total	**899**	**100%**	**187**	**100%**

Table 4. SF Referral frequency: $C_{4(500)}$ and $C_{4(125)}$.

SF_{Freq}	Records	% of $C_{4(500)}$	Records	% of $C_{4(125)}$
1	380	76.0%	98	78.4%
2	60	12.0%	15	12.0%
3	21	4.2%	3	2.4%
4	12	2.4%	4	3.2%
5	9	1.8%	2	1.6%
6	3	0.6%	1	0.8%
7	2	0.4%	1	0.8%
8	1	0.2%	—	—
10	2	0.4%	—	—
11	2	0.4%	1	0.8%
12	2	0.4%	—	—
15	1	0.2%	—	—
20	1	0.2%	—	—
22	1	0.2%	—	—
24	1	0.2%	—	—
25	1	0.2%	—	—
31	1	0.2%	—	—
Total	500	100%	125	100%

4.1   Type of Research Paper

Figure 2 shows the frequency distribution of the type of research paper across $C_{4(500)}$. With almost one out of three papers (n = 153, 31%), opinion research contributions represent the clear majority with regards to the publication type in $C_{4(500)}$. On the lower end of the spectrum, methodological contributions (n = 38, 8%) are found to be the least common type of research paper. Note that dataset contributions[4] (n = 0), as visualized in Fig. 2, were not found in $C_{4(500)}$.

---

[4] As dataset contributions are quasi non-existent in $C_{4(500)}$, this attribute of Pub_{Type} will be disregarded in the following analysis.

4.2 Contextual SF Referral

Figure 3 shows the frequency distribution of the context of the SF referral across $C_{4(500)}$.

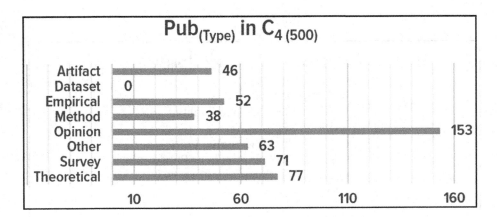

Fig. 2. Type of research paper: $C_{4(500)}$.

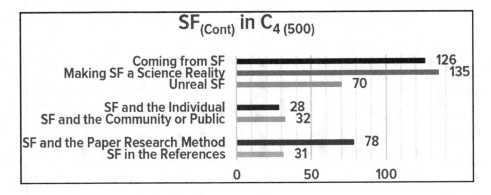

Fig. 3. Contextual SF referral: $C_{4(500)}$.

In $C_{4(500)}$, SF referrals are primarily used for two main reasons: First, in the context of introducing ideas, concepts, technologies, devices, or interactions originating in, seen in, or known from SF (n = 126, %25). Second, in the context of converting these ideas, concepts, technologies, devices, or interactions into reality (n = 135, %27), or an approximation thereof. Contrasting the three domains of the contextual usage of the SF referrals, it is clear that scientists primarily refer to SF with the purpose to draw innovation and inspiration from SF into the research contribution (331[5] out of 500 records, 66%).

---

[5] 331 = Coming from SF (n = 126) + Making SF a Science Reality(n = 135) + Unreal SF (n = 70).

4.3   Type of Research Paper/Contextual SF Referral

Figure 4 shows the frequency distribution of the type of research paper in relationship to the contextual usage of the SF referral (combination of Fig. 2 and Fig. 3).

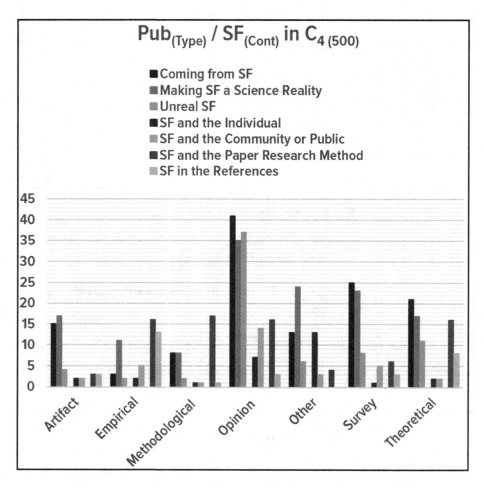

Fig. 4. Type of research paper/context of SF referral: $C_{4(500)}$.

An investigation of the most frequent contextual uses of SF references across all seven identified research paper types reveals that in three categories of contributions (Opinion, Survey, Theoretical), SF referrals are most often used to introduce concepts, originating in SF. In addition, SF referrals in the context of converting a SF concept into a reality are found most often in two categories of paper types (Artifact, Other).

The two remaining research contribution types (Empirical, Methodological) use SF referrals most frequently as an integrated part of the research paper introduction, background, application, method or discussion. These types of referrals (SF and the Paper Research Method) are also the third-most common type of referral in the Theoretical paper category. Furthermore, across the majority of all seven research contribution types in Fig. 4 (with Opinionated and Other paper types being the exception), SF referrals, with a focus on individuals, the scientific community and/or the general public are, - relative to all referrals within the individual category under review, the least common type of referrals.

4.4   SF Authors

A total of 72 unique SF authors, spread across 528 full-text referrals, in 201 records were identified in vivo in $C_{4(500)}$. Table 5 shows the partial results of this analysis by means of a cut-off for the 14 most frequent SF authors for binary counts[6].

Table 5. Most frequent SF Authors: $C_{4(500)}$.

	Author	bin. ref.	% of $C_{4(500)}$
1	Isaac Asimov	28	13.9%
2	Arthur C. Clarke	19	9.5%
3	William Gibson	15	7.5%
4	Robert Heinlein	9	4.5%
5	Jules Verne	7	3.5%
6	Karel Čapek	7	3.5%
7	Neal Stephenson	7	3.5%
8	Philip K. Dick	7	3.5%
9	John Brunner	5	2.5%
10	Vernor Vinge	5	2.5%
11	George Orwell	4	2.0%
12	Ray Bradbury	4	2.0%
13	Frank Herbert	3	1.5%
14	H. G. Wells	3	1.5%
	Subtotal	**123**	**61.2%**
...	...	...	...
72	William F. Nolan	1	0.2%
	Total records	**201**	**100%**

---

[6] The analysis of the binary counts in $C_{4(500)}$ disregards the coding frequency and counts the presence of a referral to a specific SF author as 'yes' if present, regardless how often, or 'no', if not present. This allows a differentiated analysis. For example, NORBERT WIENER is the second most often mentioned SF author absolutely (n = 80), however only appears in n = 3 papers in the binary counting.

Herein, ISSAC ASIMOV (28 records, 13.9%) appears the most frequent in the research papers, followed by ARTHUR C. CLARKE (19 records, 9.5%) and WILLIAM GIBSON (15 records, 7.5%). The fourteen SF authors who appear the most often in research papers in Table 5 account for the majority (123 records, 61.2%) of the 201 records in $C_{4(500)}$, which mention at least one of the 72 SF authors identified.

4.5   SF Writings

A total of 162 unique SF books, novels, short stories and magazines, spread across 328 full-text referrals, in 224 records were identified in vivo in the random sample of 500 records in $C_{4(500)}$. Table 6 shows the partial results of this analysis by means of a cut-off for the 14 most frequent books and short stories, by binary count.

The binary frequency analysis in Table 6 shows that NEUROMANCER (10 records, 4.5%) appears the most frequent in the research papers in $C_{4(500)}$, followed by references to ASTOUNDING SCIENCE FICTION (7 records, 3.1%) and RUNAROUND (7 records, 3.1%). The 14 SF novels which appear the most often in research papers (binary counting) in Table 6 account for a little less than a third (65 records, 29%) of the 224 records in $C_{4(500)}$, which mention at least one of the 162 unique SF books, novels, short stories or magazines.

4.6   SF Movies and Shows

A total of 103 unique SF shows and movies, spread across 429 full-text referrals, in 205 records were identified in vivo in the random sample of 500 records in $C_{4(500)}$. Table 7 shows the partial results of this analysis by means of a cut-off for the 14 most frequent SF movies and shows, by binary count.

The analysis shows that STAR TREK (28 records, 13.7%) appears the most frequent in the research papers in $C_{4(500)}$, followed by 2001: A SPACE ODYSSEY (23 records, 11.2%) and the movie THE TERMINATOR (13, 6.3%). The 14 SF movies and shows which appear the most often in research papers (binary counting) in Table 7 account for more than $\frac{2}{3}$ (141 records, 68.8%) of the 205 records in $C_{4(500)}$, which mention at least one of the 103 unique SF movies or shows.

4.7   SF Characters

A total of 38 unique SF characters (humans, robots, androids, computers), spread across 100 full-text referrals, in 55 records were identified in vivo in the random sample of 500 records in $C_{4(500)}$. Table 8 shows the partial results of this analysis by means of a cut-off for the 14 most frequent books and short stories, as a binary count.

The analysis shows that HAL 9000 (11 records, 20%) appears the most frequent in the research papers in $C_{4(500)}$, followed by R2-D2 (3 records, 5.5%) and DICK TRACEY (3 records, 5.5%). Accordingly, the 14 SF characters which appear the most often in research papers (binary counting) in Table 8 account for more than half (31 records, 56.4%) of the 55 records in $C_{4(500)}$, which mention at least one of the 38 unique SF characters.

5 Discussion

SF Referral Frequency and Location. The study outcome demonstrates that SF referrals occur in the majority of cases one single time in the full-text of a publication (i.p 78% in $C_{4(125)}$, respectively 77% in $C_{4(500)}$). In addition, the results indicate that SF referrals occur the most often in the body of the reviewed records (i.p. 81% in $C_{4(125)}$, respectively 84.6% in $C_{4(500)}$). This suggests that the majority of scientific authors who refer to SF do not focus ultimately on SF in their research contributions per se, but instead most often introduce, draw, refer, discuss or exemplify, a general or specific aspect of a SF idea, concept, device or technology in the context of the individual research contribution. From a frequency and referral location analysis point-of-view, it can be reasoned that

Table 6. Most frequent SF writings: $C_{4(500)}$.

	Books, Novels, Short stories	bin. ref.	% of $C_{4(500)}$
1	Neuromancer	10	4.5%
2	Astounding Science Fiction	7	3.1%
3	Runaround	7	3.1%
4	Snow Crash	6	2.7%
5	HH Guide to the Galaxy	4	1.8%
6	The Shockwave Rider	4	1.8%
7	R.U.R.	4	1.8%
8	Do Andr. Dream of E. Sheep?	4	1.8%
9	I, Robot	4	1.8%
10	True Names	3	1.3%
11	From the Earth to the Moon	3	1.3%
12	Nineteen Eighty-Four	3	1.3%
13	The Diamond Age	3	1.3%
14	2001: A Space Odyssey	3	1.3%
	Subtotal	**65**	**29%**
...	...	...	...
162	Young Lady's Ill. Primer	1	0.4%
	Total records	**224**	**100%**

Table 7. Most frequent SF movies and shows: $C_{4(500)}$.

	Movies, Shows	bin. ref.	% of $C_{4(500)}$
1	Star trek	28	13.7%
2	2001: A Space Odyssey	23	11.2%
3	The Terminator	13	6.3%
4	Minority Report	12	5.9%
5	Star Wars	11	5.4%
6	The Matrix	9	4.4%
7	I, Robot	9	4.4%
8	Fantastic Voyage	8	3.9%
9	Star Trek: TNG	7	3.4%
10	Blade Runner	7	3.4%
11	Gattaca	4	2.0%
12	Metropolis	4	2.0%
13	Forbidden Planet	3	1.5%
14	Battlestar Galactica	3	1.5%
	Subtotal	**137**	**68.8%**
...	...	...	...
103	Westworld	1	0.5%
	Total records	**205**	**100%**

Table 8. Most frequent SF Characters: $C_{4(500)}$.

	Movies, Shows	bin. ref.	% of $C_{4(500)}$
1	HAL 9000	11	20.0%
2	R2-D2	3	5.5%
3	Dick Tracy	3	5.5%
4	Captain Kirk	2	3.6%
5	Borg	2	3.6%
6	C-3PO	2	3.6%
7	Wintermute	1	1.8%
8	Princess Leia	1	1.8%
9	Waldo	1	1.8%
10	David	1	1.8%
11	Dr. Frankenstein	1	1.8%
12	Mr. Data	1	1.8%
13	Terminator (robot)	1	1.8%
14	Agent Smith	1	1.8%
	Subtotal	**31**	**56.4%**
...	...	...	...
38	Victor Frankenstein	1	1,.8%
	Total records	**55**	**100%**

SF rather often acts as a 'supportive vehicle' in computer science research. This interpretation is supported by the analysis of the usage of SF in the paper types, in context. Furthermore, this finding supports results found by [24], where the majority of the reviewed records in the ACM DL (30%) did as well refer one single time, one (of six possible) SF search term(s).

Type of Research Paper. In cases where researchers refer to SF, the analysis shows clearly that opinion research papers are *the* preferred outlet of research contributions for (computer) scientists who publish in the IEEE *Xplore* DL. This finding confirms work by [45], which identified philosophical and opinion papers as the most frequent category of research contribution type when searching for SF robots.

Unsurprisingly, this dominance of opinion research contributions stems from the fact that SF—etymologically and historically—is a powerful mediator, effectively bridging the arts and technical fields. In this study, SF was often utilized via its main intended function, a commentary and envisionment on future, sociotechnical possibilities.

It is therefore likely that SF appears the most frequently in research papers which are placed in that niche of opinion research papers, essays and philosophical arguments. A remarkable result, however, is that SF references occor in opinion research contributions (n = 153 records) twice as much as they do in the second most frequent category, theoretical papers (n = 77 records).

In addition, methodological papers – after dataset papers with n = 0 referrals – are the least frequent type of research paper in which references to SF appear. This may be due to the fact that the contextual SF referral in methodological papers typically involves a practical integration of SF into the research method or application, for example as a method to recommend entertainment content among SF movies. In other words, SF in methodological-type papers is not often used to introduce innovation, creativity, or reflection into the research paper or study, despite that being the ample opportunity SF offers in the first place.

Putting aside both extremes, opinion (n = 153 records) and dataset contributions (n = 0), another interesting observation is the more-or-less even distribution of the remaining five paper research contribution types, ranging between = =38–77 records per category. Perhaps this indicates that SF referrals can serve as a 'jack-of-all-trades', as scientists utilize them in a broad range of research settings, from empirical studies to theoretical/conceptual research papers, from artifact and interface contexts, to surveys/overviews on emerging research topics.

This broad and almost universal applicability of SF, as a source of inspiration, as part of a research method, or as a vehicle to assess future developments in the realm of technology and society allows a selective utilization of preferred aspects of SF across different types of research. For example, theoretical and survey articles on the topic of smart, autonomous drones (e.g.[1,2]) outline the proliferation and beneficial technology outcomes of as the coming-of-age of SF dreams. Barfield [2],[810], based on Asimov, introduces three laws of robotics for drones, which he calls 'flyborgs', including navigational heuristics for a strategic airspace. The laws call for a protection of first, 'friendlies' and second, 'protection of its own existence', in order to avoid in-air collisions with other drones or manned aircraft. However, what laws or heuristics are relevant for autonomous drones, which share an airspace with 'hostiles' are not presented, nor any sort of explanation what would happen in such case. As a reminder, Issac Asimov's original laws did mention in fact 'humans' instead of 'friendlies' and 'hostiles'. On the other hand, these important ethical questions and concerns seem to be addressed in opinion-and other-type research papers (e.g. [18,59]), who do in fact warn, that scientists are on the verge of crossing the Rubicon to create 'Killer Robots', but seem less relevant in methodological-, theoretical- or survey-based research contributions.

While the above-mentioned efforts are noteworthy and important, one main function of SF is to actually show the public the broad range of potential outcomes of technologies as part of our lives, positive and negative. The *unintended consequences* of this rapid transition and transformation toward the information society are in fact barely understood, and even more difficult to predict. SF can provide either, an admonition or commendation of these forthcoming changes – scientists should consider both equally and critically.

Contextual SF Referral. The analysis of the contextual usage of the SF referrals in this dataset shows that four specific attributes, from two conceptual domains, are utilized the most often:

The group of SF referrals, with a focus on drawing innovation from SF in the research paper emerges as the preferred utilization of SF across paper types . SF is most often referenced in the context of a fictional idea, concept or technology crossing over from fantasy to reality (Making SF a Science Reality, $n = 135$). Also, SF references which emphasize the origin, inspiration, acknowledgment or linkage to a SF writing or movie represent the second most-frequent category with 126 referrals. The fourth most often contextual SF referrals are associations with far-fetched, unrealistic or impossible SF concepts ($n = 70$).

From the domain of SF referrals, integrated as part of the research paper and representing the third most-often utilized category overall, 78 referrals are utilized as part of the research method application, implementation or evaluation. This attribute reflects a SF reference as a integrated component of a method, an empirical evaluation or study, rather than e.g., a vehicle for inspiration or blueprint of a future technology. For instance, SF referrals in the context of user preferences in the evaluation of a movie recommendation system or as part of a content analysis of an online community are found in this category. It should be noted that a subset of records in this category reflects papers, which utilize SF in i) traditional engineering and computer science education, ii) in the context of design research via SF prototyping and, iii) SF as a means to forecast future technological developments.

These results show that SF in scientific articles is abundantly utilized by scientists as an inspiration, a blueprint, an envisionment and pacemaker of past, present and future technological developments, across usage contexts. SF references herein range from innovative medical devices to the SF depiction of AI and robotics, from new interaction modalities through gesture and speech to utopian visions of teleportation, light speed travel and space elevators. The three categories of this domain – providing inspiration and innovation through SF for the research paper – account for a total of 331 out of 500 SF referrals in our dataset. This is both a remarkable result and a powerful display of the inherent strength and advantage SF can provide to scientists. This diversity of SF imaginations can be traced back to the search strategy in this study, an inclusive retrieval of a full-text search for 'science fiction', instead of a focus on a specific SF author, book or movie or concept.

SF Authors and Writings. The analysis of the SF particulars, i.e. the presence and frequency of referrals to SF authors and writings, reveals interesting, although anticipated trends.

With regards to the SF authors, ISSAC ASIMOV is referenced in 28 records in $C_{4(500)}$ and succeeded by ARTHUR C. CLARKE (n $=$ 19 binary referrals) and WILLIAM GIBSON (n $=$ 15 binary referrals). Suitably, the works of the most frequent SF authors are reflected in the distribution of the most popular SF novels per record accordingly, with WILLIAM GIBSON'S NEUROMANCER being the most often (n $=$ 10 binary referrals) cited SF writing in $C_{4(500)}$. ISSAC ASIMOV'S short story I, ROBOT (n $=$ 4 binary referrals) originally appeared in ASTOUNDING SCIENCE FICTION, n $=$ 7 binary referrals) is the second most often referred SF writing. As such, the analysis of the referred SF authors and books complements itself – the most frequent works of the most often mentioned SF authors are both found in $C_{4(500)}$. It is well known that ISSAC ASIMOV, ARTHUR C. CLARKE, and ROBERT HEINLEIN held a 'SF triumvirate' in the first golden age of SF [51],[81] which:

> "[...] largely dominated American (and, though to a lesser extent, Anglo-American) science fiction during the 1940s, the 1950s and well into the 1960s [...].

In this study, the analysis of the SF authors in $C_{4(500)}$ places the these three SF authors – informally referred to as the 'Big Three' – in the Top 4 most often named SF authors per record. Interestingly, Roberts [31,53] finds that:

> "[...] the so-called 'Golden Age' of science fiction, from the late 1930s through to the early 1960s [...] referred to a particular body of texts that were, specifically, founded in science and the extrapolation of science into the future."

As this study explores the utilization of SF in computer science, it can be reasoned that these influential SF authors, including their works from the first golden age of SF, are the preferred choices of scientists, expressed by their explicit referrals in the publications in $C_{4(500)}$. Although negligible in the larger context of all records in the full collection of the IEEE *Xplore* Digital Library, the specific analysis of $C_{4(500)}$ shows a clear manifestation of this first golden age of SF in scientific research, a remarkable reflection of influential pop-culture in science communication. This is an overall plausible conjecture supported by anecdotal evidence, for instance, by Carl Sagan, who stated in a New York Times essay in 1973 [56] that SF had been a seminal factor and forerunner to pursue his scientific career as astronomer, science communicator and SF author.

5.1 SF Movies, Shows and Characters

With regards to the referrals of specific SF movies and characters, the study results show that the STAR TREK (n=28 binary referrals) and STAR WARS (n=11 binary referrals) franchises, as well as the SF films 2001: A SPACE ODYSSEY (n=23 binary referrals), THE TERMINATOR (n=13 binary referrals) and MINORITY REPORT represent the top SF franchises and films in $C_{4(500)}$. The density of STAR TREK referrals, including spin-offs of the franchise (e.g. STAR TREK: TNG and others, see Table 7), was anticipated due to work by conducted by [23], who investigated exclusively STAR TREK references in the ACM Digital Library.

Yet another interesting discovery is that the 38 SF characters, referenced in $C_{4(500)}$, are more often 'robots/AIs' than 'human characters', with the most frequent SF character, HAL 9000 from 2001: A SPACE ODYSSEY, accounting for 20% of all binary referrals. This indicates that scientists preferably resort to SF robots and depictions of an AI, instead of the human counterparts found in SF stories and movies and more importantly, introduces a speculation space for such rationale.

An obvious explanation could be that fictional robots and AIs, through the utilization of a bandwidth of technologies, from speech interfaces to sentient systems, can serve as both ways—as utopian imaginations of future human-robot cooperation or dystopian horrors of technological disobedience and men-versus-machine scenarios, either-ways, providing full-fledged examples, highly relevant to computer science research. for instance, work by [45] did not only identify 18 SF robots in a different repository, the ACM Digital Library, but also confirmed that the contextual referrals of these robots was mostly to communicate (SF) concepts to the readers.

6   Limitations

First of all, we acknowledge that the IRR coefficients for both interpretative variables, Pub_{Type} and SF_{Cont}, were acceptable but did not reach the desired levels of agreement. With regards to the type of research contribution, Wobbrock and Kientz [70] state that very often, multiple primary contribution types might co-occur in a single publication, complicating a one-dimensional, mutually exclusive coding. With regards to the contextual usage of the SF referral, the above-average IRR results can be explained due to the fact, that the mutually exclusive seven attributes chosen for this variable were not perfectly defined and hence did partially overlap. This is an expected result, especially in consideration that an emerging coding approach was utilized, which generated the coding scheme from $C_{4(125)}$, and not $C_{4(500)}$.

As a second limitation we acknowledge is the deliberate choice to use a singular search/query term—"science fiction"—for a full-text search in the IEEE *Xplore* DL. This choice might have affected the results as it can not be reasonably assumed that every record, which discusses SF, will use *this* search query term, instead of, for instance, an appropriate synonym, such as "SF" or "sci-fi". Nevertheless, the query for "science fiction" in C_4 does represent an inclusive, full-text retrieval returning the largest cache of records while minimizing Type 1 Errors and false-positive retrievals, effectively establishing high precision and recall.

As mentioned earlier, the records in $C_{4(500)}$ are retrieved for a full-text search for 'science fiction' in the IEEE *Xplore* Digital Library. One drawback for such an inclusive search in a large technical repository is that of institutional subscription limitations. As a consequence, the initial set of records $C_{4(2784)}$ was not fully accessible for a retrieval. Therefore, facets were applied, among those, the filter 'subscribed content only'. This reduced the potential set of records for analysis to $C_{4(1647)}$, effectively decreasing the initial retrieval cache by 40%. As the initial body of retrieved records, $C_{4(1647)}$, was deemed unfeasible for a full qualitative review by the author, due to its massive size, a random sampling was conducted to review about 30% of records in $C_{4(500)}$. While this was a necessary reduction of the retrieval cache at hand for simple study feasibility, this sampling might, in contrast, not necessarily be representative of $C_{4(1647)}$. However, a comparative publication year analysis of all C_4 sets did show a distribution of records of $C_{4(500)}$, which did principally re-ensemble the distributions of records per year in both, $C_{4(1647)}$ and $C_{4(2784)}$.

7   Conclusions

This work provides a broad and in-depth investigation analysis of records, which discuss SF in the IEEE *Xplore* DL. Although, SF is clearly a niche topic in the overall IEEE *Xplore*, which lists about 4.5 million records, its influence is explored and established in specific types or research contributions and contextual usages, i.p. by means of researchers resorting to SF concepts, ideas, technologies, devices or interfaces in mostly opinionated research contributions. Therefore, future researchers, professionals and educators in computer science and HCI research might be able to use this work to recognize the potentials and opportunities, as well as the challenges and limitations, SF can provide them with, including their peers, their students, their research and ultimately, their future work. The SF particulars (authors, books, movies and characters) identified in this study show that researchers predominately resort to Western SF, with a clear minority of SF references stemming from Non-Western materials. This leads to believe that personal cultural upbringings and influences play a significant role in the context of researcher creativity, motivation, objectivity and ultimately, bias.

7.1   Future Work

Supplementing the data and results in the presented content analysis with empirical data (i.p. interviews with researchers) seems like a logical, next step to better comprehend the link of SF and computer science/HCI research. Such studies could shed light on the reasons scientists write, or do not write, about SF in their publications. This then could lead to the exploration of the influence of popular culture on the works of researchers. For instance, the analysis of $C_{4(500)}$ revealed multiple instances where scientists stated to be inspired to begin a research career, based on past exposure to a SF novel or movie. Additional potential directions to extend the presented work would be to investigate if the most frequent SF particulars, found in this study, are representative of the distribution when searching directly for them. Such a study could then be cross-referenced with the presented results and, as a consequence, provide further support or further extend the results of this research.

References

1. Allen, R., Pavone, M., Schwager, M.: Flying smartphones: when portable computing sprouts wings. IEEE Pervasive Comput. **15**(3), 83–88 (7 2016). https://doi.org/10.1109/MPRV.2016.43
2. Barfield, F.: Autonomous collision avoidance: the technical requirements. In: Proceedings of the IEEE 2000 National Aerospace and Electronics Conference. NAECON 2000. Engineering Tomorrow (Cat. No.00CH37093), pp. 808–813 (2000). https://doi.org/10.1109/NAECON.2000.894998
3. Barnett, M., Wagner, H., Gatling, A., Anderson, J., Houle, M., Kafka, A.: The impact of science fiction film on student understanding of science. J. Sci. Educ. Technol. **15**(2), 179–191 (2006). https://doi.org/10.1007/s10956-006-9001-y
4. Bates, R., Goldsmith, J., Berne, R., Summet, V., Veilleux, N.: Science fiction in computer science education. In: Proceedings of the 43rd ACM Technical Symposium on Computer Science Education. SIGCSE '12, Association for Computing Machinery, New York, NY, USA, pp. 161–162 (2012). https://doi.org/10.1145/2157136.2157184
5. Beall, J.: The Weaknesses of Full-Text Searching. J. Academic Librarian. **34**(5), 438–444 (2008). https://doi.org/10.1016/j.acalib.2008.06.007
6. Bleecker, J.: Design Fiction: A Short Essay on Design, Science, Fact and Fiction (2009), blog.nearfuturelaboratory.com/2009/03/17/design-fiction-a-short-essay-on-design-science-fact-and-fiction/
7. Blythe, M., Encinas, E.: Research fiction and thought experiments in design. Found. Trends® Human Comput. Interact. **12**(1), 1–105 (2018). https://doi.org/10.1561/1100000070
8. Blythe, M., Encinas, E., Kaye, J., Avery, M.L., McCabe, R., Andersen, K.: Imaginary workbooks: constructive criticism and practical provocation. In: Proceedings of the 2018 CHI Conference on Human Factors in Computing Systems. Association for Computing Machinery, New York, NY, USA, pp. 1–12 (2018). https://doi.org/10.1145/3173574.3173807
9. Burton, E., Goldsmith, J., Koenig, S., Kuipers, B., Mattei, N., Walsh, T.: Ethical considerations in artificial intelligence courses. AI Magazine **38**(2), 22–34 (2017). https://doi.org/10.1609/aimag.v38i2.2731

10. Burton, E., Goldsmith, J., Mattei, N.: How to teach computer ethics through science fiction. Commun. ACM **61**(8), 54–64 (2018). https://doi.org/10.1145/3154485
11. Clarke, A.C., Stork, D.G.: HAL's Legacy: 2001's Computer as Dream and Reality. MIT Press, Cambridge, Mass., USA (1998). mitpress.mit.edu/books/hals-legacy
12. Dourish, P., Bell, G.: "Resistance is futile": reading science fiction alongside ubiquitous computing. Personal Ubiquit. Comput. **18**(4), 769–778 (2013). https://doi.org/10.1007/s00779-013-0678-7
13. Dunne, A., Raby, F.: Speculative Everything: Design, Fiction, and Social Dreaming. MIT Press, Cambridge, Mass., USA (2013). mitpress.mit.edu/books/speculative-everything
14. Ferro, D., Swedin, E.: Computer fiction: "A Logic Named Joe". In: Impagliazzo, J., Järvi, T., Paju, P. (eds.) History of Nordic Computing 2, pp. 84–94. Springer, Heidelberg (2009). https://doi.org/10.1007/978-3-642-03757-3_9
15. Ferro, D.L., Swedin, E.G.: Science fiction and computing: essays on interlinked domains. Co, M., Jefferson, N.C. (2011). airandspace.si.edu/research/publications/science/fiction/and/computing/essays/interlinked/domains
16. Figueiredo, L.S., Gonçalves Maciel Pinheiro, M.G., Vilar Neto, E.X., Teichrieb, V.: An open catalog of hand gestures from sci-fi movies. In: Proceedings of the 33rd Annual ACM Conference Extended Abstracts on Human Factors in Computing Systems. CHI EA '15, Association for Computing Machinery, New York, NY, USA, pp. 1319–1324 (2015). https://doi.org/10.1145/2702613.2732888
17. Frank, S.: REEL REALITY: science consultants in hollywood. Sci. Cult. **12**(4), 427–469 (2003). https://doi.org/10.1080/0950543032000150319
18. Guizzo, E., Ackerman, E.: When robots decide to kill. IEEE Spectr. **53**(6), 38–43 (2016). https://doi.org/10.1109/MSPEC.2016.7473151
19. Hemminger, B.M., Saelim, B., Sullivan, P.F., Vision, T.J.: Comparison of full-text searching to metadata searching for genes in two biomedical literature cohorts. J. Am. Soc. Inf. Sci. Technol. **58**(14), 2341–2352 (2007). https://doi.org/10.1002/asi.20708
20. Jeon, M.: Analyzing novel interactions in science fiction movies in human factors and HCI courses. Proceed. Human Factors Ergon. Soc. Ann. Meeting **62**(1), 336–340 (2018). https://doi.org/10.1177/1541931218621078
21. Johnson, B.D.: Science Fiction Prototyping: Designing the Future with Science Fiction. Morgan and Claypool Publishers LLC (2011). https://doi.org/10.2200/s00336ed1v01y201102csl003
22. Jordan, P.: Science Fiction in HCI – A nuanced view. In: Cockton, G. (ed.) IX Blogs. Association for Computing Machinery (2018). interactions.acm.org/blog/view/science-fiction-in-hci-a-nuanced-view
23. Jordan, P., Auernheimer, B.: The fiction in computer science: a qualitative data analysis of the ACM digital library for traces of star trek. In: Ahram, T., Falcão, C. (eds.) Advances in Usability and User Experience, pp. 508–520. Springer International Publishing, Cham (2018). https://doi.org/10.1007/978-3-319-60492-3_48
24. Jordan, P., Mubin, O., Obaid, M., Silva, P.A.: Exploring the referral and usage of science fiction in HCI literature. In: Marcus, A., Wang, W. (eds.) Design, User Experience, and Usability: Designing Interactions. pp. 19–38. Springer International Publishing, Cham (2018). https://doi.org/10.1007/978-3-319-91803-7_2
25. Jordan, P., Mubin, O., Silva, P.A.: A conceptual research agenda and quantification framework for the relationship between science-fiction media and human-computer interaction. In: Stephanidis, C. (ed.) HCI International 2016 - Posters' Extended Abstracts, pp. 52–57. Springer International Publishing, Cham (2016). https://doi.org/10.1007/978-3-319-40548-3_9

26. Kirby, D.A.: Science consultants, fictional films, and scientific practice. Soc. Stud. Sci. **33**(2), 231–268 (2003). https://doi.org/10.1177/03063127030332015
27. Kirby, D.A.: Scientists on the set: science consultants and the communication of science in visual fiction. Public Understandin. Sci. **12**(3), 261–278 (2003). https://doi.org/10.1177/0963662503123005
28. Kirby, D.A.: The future is now: diegetic prototypes and the role of popular films in generating real-world technological development. Soc. Stud. Sci. **40**(1), 41–70 (2010). https://doi.org/10.1177/0306312709338325
29. Kirby, D.A.: Lab Coats in Hollywood: Science, Scientists, and Cinema. MIT Press, Cambridge, Mass., USA (2011). mitpress.mit.edu/books/lab-coats-hollywood
30. Kohno, T., Johnson, B.D.: Science fiction prototyping and security education: cultivating contextual and societal thinking in computer security education and beyond. In: Proceedings of the 4nd ACM Technical Symposium on Computer Science Education. SIGCSE '11, Association for Computing Machinery, New York, NY, USA, pp. 9–14 (2011). https://doi.org/10.1145/1953163.1953173
31. Kurosu, M.: User interfaces that appeared in SciFi movies and their reality. In: Marcus, A. (ed.) Design, User Experience, and Usability. Theories, Methods, and Tools for Designing the User Experience, pp. 580–588. Springer International Publishing, Cham (2014). https://doi.org/10.1007/978-3-319-07668-3_56
32. Landis, J.R., Koch, G.G.: The measurement of observer agreement for categorical data. Biometrics **33**(1), 159–174 (1977). www.jstor.org/stable/2529310
33. Larson, J.: Limited imagination: depictions of computers in science fiction film. Futures **40**(3), 293–299 (2008). https://doi.org/10.1016/j.futures.2007.08.015
34. Levin, L.G.: Which movies and what for? analysis of "Patterns of use" of the science fiction films in scientific journals. In: Donghong, C. (ed.) Public Communication of Science and Technology Archive (2014). pcst.co/archive/paper/2293
35. Levin, L.G., De Filippo, D.: Films and science: quantification and analysis of the use of science fiction films in scientific papers. J. Sci. Commun. **13**(3) (2014). https://doi.org/10.22323/2.13030207
36. Lin, J.: Is searching full text more effective than searching abstracts? BMC Bioinf. **10**(1) (2009). https://doi.org/10.1186/1471-2105-10-46
37. Lin, K.Y., Tsai, F.H., Chien, H.M., Chang, L.T.: Effects of a science fiction film on the technological creativity of middle school students. Eurasia J. Math. Sci. Technol. Educ. **9**(2), 191–200 (2013). https://doi.org/10.12973/eurasia.2013.929a
38. Lindley, J.: A pragmatics framework for design fiction. In: Proceedings of the 11th European Academy of Design Conference. (2015). eprints.lancs.ac.uk/id/eprint/73456/
39. Lindley, J., Coulton, P.: Back to the future: 10 years of design fiction. In: Proceedings of the 2015 British HCI Conference. British HCI '15, Association for Computing Machinery, New York, NY, USA, pp. 210–211 (2015). https://doi.org/10.1145/2783446.2783592
40. Marcus, A.: The past 100 years of the future: HCI and user-experience design in science-fiction movies and television. In: SIGGRAPH Asia 2015 Courses. SA '15, Association for Computing Machinery, New York, NY, USA (2015). https://doi.org/10.1145/2818143.2818151
41. Marcus, A., Norman, D.A., Rucker, R., Sterling, B., Vinge, V.: Sci-Fi at CHI: cyberpunk novelists predict future user interfaces. In: Proceedings of the SIGCHI Conference on Human Factors in Computing Systems. CHI '92, Association for Computing Machinery, New York, NY, USA, pp. 435–437 (1992). https://doi.org/10.1145/142750.142892

42. Marcus, A., Soloway, E., Sterling, B., Swanwick, M., Vinge, V.: Opening pleanary: Sci-Fi @ CHI-99: science-fiction authors predict future user interfaces. In: CHI '99 Extended Abstracts on Human Factors in Computing Systems. CHI EA '99, Association for Computing Machinery, New York, NY, USA, pp. 95–96 (1999). https://doi.org/10.1145/632716.632775

43. Michalsky, W.: Manipulating our futures: the role of science fiction in education. Clearing House J. Educ. Strat. Issues Ideas **52**(6), 246–249 (1979). https://doi.org/10.1080/00098655.1979.10113595

44. Mubin, O., et al.: Towards an agenda for Sci-Fi inspired HCI research. In: Proceedings of the 13th International Conference on Advances in Computer Entertainment Technology. ACE '16, Association for Computing Machinery, New York, NY, USA (2016). https://doi.org/10.1145/3001773.3001786

45. Mubin, O., Wadibhasme, K., Jordan, P., Obaid, M.: Reflecting on the presence of science fiction robots in computing literature. J. Hum. Robot Interact. **8**(1) (2019). https://doi.org/10.1145/3303706

46. Myers, J.Y., Abd-El-Khalick, F.: "A Ton of Faith in Science!" nature and role of assumptions in, and ideas about, science and epistemology generated upon watching Sci-Fi film. J. Res. Sci. Teaching **53**(8), 1143–1171 (2016). https://doi.org/10.1002/tea.21324

47. National academy of sciences: the science and entertainment exch ange (2021). scienceandentertainmentexchange.org/

48. Noessel, C.: Sci-Fi Interfaces (2021). scifiinterfaces.com/

49. Noessel, C.: O'Reilly Webcast: how sci-fi and real world interfaces influence each other (2013). www.youtube.com/watch?v=E5EIJla51Bw

50. Pargman, D., Eriksson, E., Comber, R., Kirman, B., Bates, O.: The futures of computing and wisdom. In: Proceedings of the 10th Nordic Conference on Human-Computer Interaction. NordiCHI '18, Association for Computing Machinery, New York, NY, USA, pp. 960–963 (2018). https://doi.org/10.1145/3240167.3240265

51. Parrinder, P.: Learning from Other Worlds: Estrangement, Cognition, and the Politics of Science Fiction and Utopia (Post-Contemporary Interventions). Duke University Press Books (2001). www.dukeupress.edu/learning-from-other-worlds/

52. Pohl, H., Muresan, A., Hornbæk, K.: Charting subtle interaction in the HCI literature. In: Proceedings of the 2019 CHI Conference on Human Factors in Computing Systems. Association for Computing Machinery, New York, NY, USA, pp. 1–15 (2019). https://doi.org/10.1145/3290605.3300648

53. Roberts, A.: Science fiction. Routledge, London and New York (2005). https://www.routledge.com/Science-Fiction/Roberts/p/book/9780415366687

54. Rogers, M.L.: Teaching HCI design principles using culturally current media. Proceed. Human Factors Ergon. Soc. Ann. Meeting **54**(8), 677–680 (2010). https://doi.org/10.1177/154193121005400806

55. Russell, D.M., Yarosh, S.: Can we look to science fiction for innovation in HCI? interactions **25**(2), 36–40 (2018). https://doi.org/10.1145/3178552

56. Sagan, C.: Growing up with science fiction. The New York Times (1978). www.nytimes.com/1978/05/28/archives/growing-up-with.html

57. Qian, M., et al.: Auto-learning convolution-based graph convolutional network for medical relation extraction. In: Lin, H., Zhang, M., Pang, L. (eds.) Information Retrieval. CCIR 2021. LNCS, vol. 13026. Springer, Cham (2021). https://doi.org/10.1007/978-3-030-88189-4_15

58. Schmitz, M., Endres, C., Butz, A.: A survey of human-computer interaction design in science fiction movies. In: Proceedings of the 2nd International Conference on INtelligent TEchnologies for Interactive EnterTAINment. INTETAIN '08, ICST (Institute for Computer Sciences, Social-Informatics and Telecommunications Engineering), Brussels, BEL (2008). dl.acm.org/doi/10.5555/1363200.1363210

59. Sharkey, N.: Automated killers and the computing profession. Computer **40**(11), 124–123 (11 2007). https://doi.org/10.1109/MC.2007.372

60. Shedroff, N., Noessel, C.: Make it so: interaction design lessons from science fiction. Rosenfeld media, Brooklyn N.Y. USA (2012). rosenfeldmedia.com/books/make-it-so/

61. Smaglik, P.: Media consulting: entertaining science. Nature **511**(7507), 113–115 (2014). https://doi.org/10.1038/nj7507-113a

62. Stork, D.G.: From HAL to office appliances: human-machine interfaces in science fiction and reality. In: Proceedings of the 3rd International Conference on Intelligent User Interfaces. IUI '98, Association for Computing Machinery, New York, NY, USA, p. 181 (1998). https://doi.org/10.1145/268389.295093

63. Stork, D.G.: Keynote address: the HAL 9000 computer and the vision of 2001: a space odyssey. In: Proceedings of the 33nd Conference on Winter Simulation. WSC '01, IEEE Computer Society, USA, p. 3 (2001). dl.acm.org/doi/10.5555/564124.564126

64. Tanenbaum, T.J.: Design fictional interactions: why HCI should care about stories. In: Interactions. Association for Computing Machinery, New York, NY, USA, vol. 21, pp. 22–23 (2014). https://doi.org/10.1145/2648414

65. Troiano, G.M., Tiab, J., Lim, Y.K.: SCI-FI: shape-changing interfaces, future interactions. In: Proceedings of the 9th Nordic Conference on Human-Computer Interaction. NordiCHI '16, Association for Computing Machinery, New York, NY, USA (2016). https://doi.org/10.1145/2971485.2971489

66. UXPA: Science Fiction. User Experience Magazine **13**(2) (2013). uxpa.org/user-experience-magazine-issue-13-2/

67. Vrasidas, C., Avraamidou, L., Theodoridou, K., Themistokleous, S., Panaou, P.: Science fiction in education: case studies from classroom implementations. Educ. Media Int. **52**(3), 201–215 (2015). https://doi.org/10.1080/09523987.2015.1075102

68. Waugh, L., Tarver, H., Phillips, M.E., Alemneh, D.G.: Comparison of full-text versus metadata searching in an institutional repository: case study of the UNT Scholarly Works. CoRR abs/1512.07193 (2015). arxiv.org/abs/1512.07193

69. Westfahl, G., Yuen, W.K., Chan, A.K.s.: Science fiction and the prediction of the future: Essays on foresight and fallacy, Critical explorations in science fiction and fantasy. McFarland, Jefferson, N.C., USA, vol. 27 (2011) mcfarlandbooks.com/product/science-fiction-and-the-prediction-of-the-future/

70. Wobbrock, J.O., Kientz, J.A.: Research contributions in human-computer interaction. Interactions **23**(3), 38–44 (2016). https://doi.org/10.1145/2907069

Deep Learning Based Video Compression

Kang Da Ji and Helmut Hlavacs$^{(\boxtimes)}$ (iD)

University of Vienna, Research Group Entertainment Computing Vienna,
Vienna, Austria
helmut.hlavacs@univie.ac.at

Abstract. Our goal is to test the capability of deep learning for compressing the size of video files, e.g., for sending them over digital networks. This is done by extracting keypoint and affine transformation tensors, using a pre-trained face model and then reducing the data by quantization and compression. This minimal information is sent through a network together with full source images used as starting frames for our approach.

The receiver device then reconstructs the video with a generator and a keypoint detector, by transforming and animating the keypoints of the source image according to the video keypoints. We minimized the required data by using LZMA2 compression and a quantization factor of 10 000 for keypoints and 1 000 for transformations.

Lastly, we determined limitations of this approach and found that in regard to file size reduction, our approach was noticeably better, while the quality of the resulting video in comparison to the original one was only half as good.

Keywords: Deep learning · Video compression · Video reconstruction

1 Motivation

Due to the 2020 pandemic, the quantity of video data sent over the Internet has dramatically increased, be it for interactive video conferences, game streaming, video clip and movie streaming, or a multitude of many other applications [1].

Currently, codecs for encoding and decoding videos are commonly used for transmitting videos by compressing the video files for faster transmission to the user. However, by using machine learning, it might be possible to reduce the size of video data even further than with video codecs, while only suffering little quality losses.

The main goal of this work is to implement a tool that takes a few frames and is able to reconstruct the original video with little additional information. The neuronal network should be trained on a certain video or a category of videos and be able to reproduce them so that the result is similar to the original video.

We thus implemented a system that is based on Aliaksandr Siarohin's implementation of his "First Order Motion Model for Image Animation" approach [17,18], which extracts the keypoint information from the source image and

© ICST Institute for Computer Sciences, Social Informatics and Telecommunications Engineering 2022
Published by Springer Nature Switzerland AG 2022. All Rights Reserved
Z. Lv and H. Song (Eds.): INTETAIN 2021, LNICST 429, pp. 127–141, 2022.
https://doi.org/10.1007/978-3-030-99188-3_8

sends these pieces of information and the source image itself to the receiver. We modified Aliaksandr Siarohin's project by including quantization and zip compression methods to reduce the scope of the required keypoint information. By doing this, we were able to generate a video that is similar to the original video, while sending less data than codecs like AV1 and H.264 [2,3,10].

These results were further evaluated by us and compared to the AV1 and H.264 video codecs. Additionally, we analyzed the limitations of the system and formulated what type of videos this project works well on and what should be avoided.

2   Related Work

There is a similar idea to this project coming from Wang et al., a software product called "One-Shot Free-View Neural Talking-Head Synthesis for Video Conferencing" [20]. Wang et al. also extracted the keypoints of a video for use in fast and high quality video conferencing. They took the first frame and discarded the rest of the video. With only using the head position and facial expression, they upsampled the frames and created a video that is similar in quality to the original one. Even though our project sounds similar to this software product, there are several differences.

First, Wang et al. [20] focused on real time video conferencing, while our project aims to send as little data as possible over the network. We are condensing the keypoint and transformation data with the LZMA2 compression algorithm and quantize it, so they take even less bandwidth to transfer.

Secondly, we do not have to limit ourselves to generating face videos. According to the First Order Motion Model [17,18], we can train a model to use taichi movements instead of human faces. Generally, any structured motion with clear movements can be used, as long as it is trained properly. This is an advantage over something that will mainly be utilized as a video conferencing tool or a generator for face videos.

Another technology that is similar, are deep learning video compression algorithms like the one from Djelouah et al. [7]. They try to encode and decode an arbitrary video by decoding the information into latent space, which represents motion and blending coefficients. To mitigate prediction errors, they still require residuals between the original frame and the interpolated one. This rivals the efficiency and quality of state-of-the-art codecs, namely H.264 and H.265, with comparable bits per pixel.

But while they have better quality than codecs, this paper focuses more on quality retention than on data reduction by encoding and decoding it more efficiently. Our main aim is to reduce the file size while retaining as much quality as possible.

Moreover, Kazantsev et al. [12] suggested the much more straight forward idea of using machine learning to tune the encoder configurations for a given codec, treating it as an optimization problem. According to their paper, this would save 9–20% of the bitrate compared to the original H.264 encoded video.

It can also be used for other codecs, but since there is no training data available, one has to collect their own. This approach can be used to complement existing and future codecs.

Using codecs is not the only way of reducing data. By using a procedure called "Video Inbetweening" it is also possible to reduce the transmitted data. This type of technique focuses on interpolating images between two adjacent frames, raising the frames per second. A sender could split a video into its frames and send every second image. The receiver can then synthesize the missing frames and reproduce the original video. Such an inbetweening systems was proposed by Wu et al. [21]. Systems only implementing the inbetweening algorithm were for example proposed by Bao et al. [6] or Li et al.[14].

3   Implementation

First of all, the service "Google Colab" was used as the environment of our project to utilize their GPU/TPU and CPU resources. Since extensive computation was expected, we decided to outsource it to Google Colab, to speed up the development process and prevent issues that are linked to hardware requirements. This enabled us to focus less on the setup of the project and more on how to achieve our goals. Furthermore, many machine learning projects already included a demo for Google Colab in their GitHub repository, which reduced the research time to find a suitable basis for the development process.

Secondly, we used a GitHub repository from Siarohin et al. called "First Order Motion Model for Image Animation" [17,18]. We decided to use their work, because, like several other machine learning projects, they already had a demonstration on Colab where we were able to test its capabilities. This also included a few pre-trained neuronal network models that would otherwise require extensive time, experience and resources to train. It turned out his project was working with keypoints, which gave us the idea of trying to send this data over the network, similar to Wang et al. [20].

Another service we utilized is letsenhance.io [13]. It is a neuronal network-based web service that charges a fee or is only usable as a demo, that is able to enhance images without changing the resolution of the picture. Although the exact network architecture is not specified, the website claims that they use a neuronal network which is able to upscale images and remove compression artifacts of pictures. Any other service we found was focused on upscaling the picture or did not work as well as we wanted, for example, they did not sharpen the image like letsenhance.io did without changing the resolution. The utilization of said service improved the output image quality. This was necessary since the 256256 image was often blurry, which resulted in even blurrier results in our project. By enhancing the source image, we were able to counteract this partially.

One of the tools we utilized was the "MSU Video Quality Measurement Tool 13.1" [8], which helped evaluate data. This tool is able to compare two videos and ascertain their differences in quality. The VQMT tool is very helpful in detecting artifacts and inaccuracies that are not visible to the naked eye, which is achieved by using a value called "Peak signal-to-noise ratio" in each frame.

7zip was our preferred zipping software. Unlike the standard zipping method, we were able to use different and more up-to-date compression algorithms. By testing various algorithms, we figured out that LZMA2, which is an improved version of the LZMA compression algorithm, outperformed the other algorithms and produced significantly smaller files than the standard zipping method [4,5].

Lastly, we used the video editing software FFmpeg, more specifically the version 2021-07-04-git-301d275301-full_build. This tool allowed us to manually extract frames from the video, convert videos to another codec, change the resolution, cut videos, and remove audio tracks. It is a powerful and versatile tool for editing videos without using a complicated interface, and is able to perform operations normal video editing tools are not capable of.

4 Design and Approach

The "First Order Motion Model for Image Animation" project by Siarohin et al. was used as the basis for our project [17,18]. This project uses a motion module which can determine which pixels correspond to which object and a generation module that is able to use the information of the motion module and generate an image based on it. The challenge was to find a way to extract the information that contains fewer data than the actual video itself.

Our reason for choosing this project is that contrary to images, binary files are far easier to compress, because images are often already heavily reduced. Since standard zipping is not efficient enough, we often used LZMA2 compression, which performed better than other zip formats [4,5]. The compressed data size was only a fraction of the original video, which was encoded with an AV1 codec [3].

Figure 1 shows the process of our project. We took one frame from a driving video and a source frame. Driving frames are the original video frames processed into readable data. Afterwards, we detected the keypoints and local affine transformations of both images. The local affine transformations were used for object motion in the neighborhood of each predicted keypoint and acted as a guide to describe the motion of each keypoint.

Important to note is that even though the keypoint of a color in the visualization has a consistent placement on the face, it does not mean that it will necessarily have the same color placement on a different face. The keypoints only need to be understandable by the neuronal network, and does not necessarily have to make sense to the user.

The next step was to use relative motion transfer, so we were able to extract the image movements from the driving frame to the source frame. Relative motion was done by comparing the motion of the first frame of the driving video and the currently processed frame and transferring this difference to the source image. By doing this, each frame could then be processed independently of the other video frames.

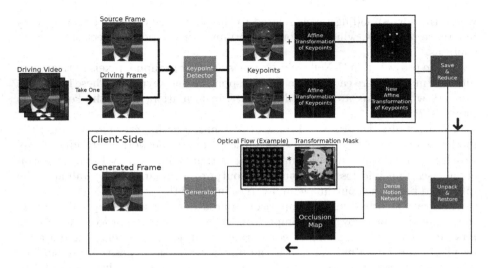

Fig. 1. Overview of the frame generation process

After generating the output from the relative motion transfer, we saved and quantized it, turned them into binary files, and compressed the output using LZMA2 compression. These files were then sent to the receiver to be decompressed, loaded and reversed to approximately its original float values.

The dense motion network continued to generate an optical flow and a transformation mask, which together told us which areas had to move where and how far. While the optical flow described the motion of a frame, the transformation mask indicated which areas were affected. The occlusion map dictated which areas needed to be inpainted by the generator and which areas just needed to be warped. This information was then used to generate the final output, a frame that was close to being identical to the frame it tried to duplicate, while only sending a fraction of the size to the receiver.

This process only shows how one frame will be generated. This needs to be done for each frame of the driving video, which requires more time and resources the longer the video gets. If it reads too many frames at once, it will overstrain the RAM, which is applicable to long videos. This is why we divide the video into multiple smaller segments and discard the frames that are already generated to clear out RAM space.

5   Theoretical Background

The "First Order Motion Model for Image Animation" that we use utilizes a U-Net for keypoint detection and dense motion prediction, which are a part of the motion module [17]. U-Nets are a subtype of convolution neural network that is used for image segmentation. More specifically, semantic segmentation, which means that the neural network not only knows what is inside the picture, but where the corresponding pixels related to the object are on [15]. This is a stark difference to CNNs, which can only determine what type of object the picture contains.

In the project, this U-Net architecture is used for grouping pixels in the image into heatmaps, where each heatmap correspond to one keypoint. These heatmaps indicate which areas are affected by the transformation, when the keypoint is moved [17].

Additionally, the project also uses the Johnson architecture for training the model, which is a deep residual convolutional neural network. A residual CNN is helpful to recognize more complex images that require many layers. Johnson et al. uses multiple loss functions that outputs a scalar, which evaluates the difference between input image and target image [11].

Contrary to other image comparison approaches, it uses perceptual comparison instead of pixel by pixel comparison. A perceptual comparison determines how similar two pictures are by comparing the style and content, while a pixel by pixel comparison only checks if the pixels in the same position are similar. This would mean that even though an image that would only have an offset of one pixel, pixel by pixel would detect it as a completely different image, while a perceptual comparison will detect it as the same [11].

For image generation, a specialized generation module is used, which is able to warp the features of an object in an image. Similar warping techniques can be found in [9,16,19]. This architecture allows us, if properly trained, to generate an image that warps the object of the foreground according to an optical flow map, a transformation mask and an occlusion map.

6   Result Evaluation and Discussion

6.1   File Size Comparison

The aim of our project was to compress the video file in such a way that we only needed to send little data to a receiver. We compared our LZMA2 files that contain kp_norm.pickle files to the standard H.264 encoding and AV1 encoding to determine how much data is needed to be transmitted [3,10].

Figure 3 shows the difference in file size. The nicknames of the used videos are written on the x-axis, while the file size is on the y-axis. All videos here are only a few seconds long and contain less than 2000 frames. The computation time of each of them lasted a few minutes and generated a single kp_norm.pickle file, which is a binary representation of the keypoints and their affine transformations. The kp_norm.pickle file was then zipped by the LZMA2 algorithm to reduce the file size further [4].

As shown in the bar chart, our approach approximately stayed around 20 and 40 KB for each video, while the AV1 encodings were noticeably bigger. This showed, that short videos were much more effectively than other by state-of-the-art encodings compressed. In these experiments we used a factor of 10 000 for keypoints and a factor of 1 000 for the affine transformations for quantization,

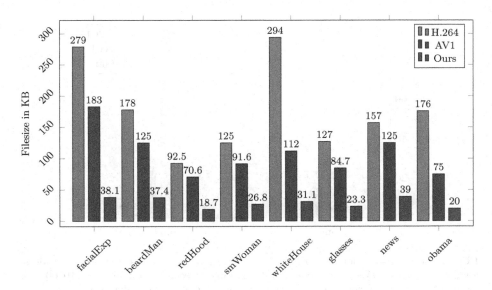

Fig. 2. Comparison between different transferred data sizes. Quantization Ours: 10 000 keypoints, 1 000 transformations. The source image file is not considered here.

but the source images that we used for generation were not considered in the bar charts, since the file size depends on the image type.

We further tested the file size reduction of our approach to see if the video size reduction also works for longer videos. By looping the same video, we extended the video length, since it was difficult to find longer videos that fit our requirements. For example, a person moving out of the picture or the camera changing positions would drastically reduce the quality of the generated videos. As we can see in Fig. 3 our approach performs even better, when the videos are longer. Here we managed to reduce the video size to 1/10 compared to the AV1 encoding on the longNews and even more on the longObama video.

These experiments helped answer the question, if we are able to find an artificial intelligence that can generate files that are much smaller than the original video. In this area, our approach was very efficient and not only beat the older H.264 encoding, but even beat the cutting edge AV1 encoding. The downside is that the process of creating and sending these files is not fully automated, which can lead to errors and consume more time.

The user should also consider that the source image can also take a few kilobytes depending on the image format, so the image format should be picked carefully, according to the user's aim. While .png are compressed losslessly and give better quality, these formats are a few times bigger than .jpg files, which are considerably smaller but use a lossy compression.

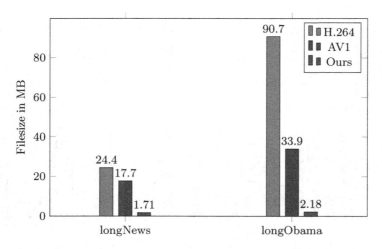

Fig. 3. Comparison between different transferred data sizes for longer videos. longNews: 46 min 05 sec, longObama: 1h 17 min 44 sec. Quantization is 10 000 for keypoints and transformations. The source image file is not considered here.

6.2   Quality Measurement

Besides comparing the file size, we also need to consider the image quality of the generated video. Here we used the MSU Video Quality Measurement tool, VQMT for short, to compare the difference between the original video in H.264 and our generated video [8].

Figure 4, an error bar chart, shows us how much AV1 reduces the quality of a H.264 video and how much our approach does.

As previously mentioned, we used a tool called letsenhance.io to improve our image quality by sharpening edges of the source image and making it less blurry without changing the 256×256 resolution. Although image enhancement is not required to get a result, the data that is collected in this work used enhanced images from said website. While it enhances the output, the difference in quality might be marginal. If there is a method to sharpen an image drastically without upscaling or changing the resolution of 256×256, the quality of the output should be equal to the ones that were used in this project.

VQMT is able to determine the "Peak signal-to-noise ratio" (PSNR) which is used to quantify reconstruction quality of a video in each frame. The higher the PSNR value is, the more similar the frames are to each other. The highest PSNR value is 100 which indicates that they are identical.

On the y-axis we can see the mean of each video comparison, and on the x-axis we see the nicknames of the videos. The lines above each bar represent the standard deviation of the mean PSNR value. The error bar chart shows us that our approach is on average only approximately half as good as the AV1 encoding.

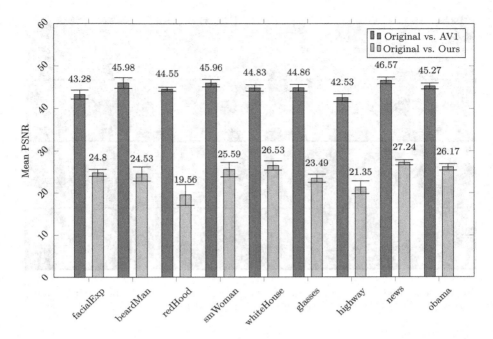

Fig. 4. Quality comparison with the MSU tool. Difference between AV1 encoding quality and Our encoding quality. Max PSNR is 100. Quantization Ours: 10 000 keypoints, 1 000 transformations.

Unfortunately, when we compare the videos side by side, they perceptually look very similar, but sometimes there are major artifacts like weird face and background warping and inaccurate facial movements as seen in Fig. 7. This happens more often on longer videos, since we are using segmentation, which does not always start in the same position as the original frame. This causes the project to misinterpret the movement and translate the motion incorrectly. This can be mitigated by choosing a video with little movement and similar positions throughout the video.

The best generations that were perceptually similar were the news anchor, obama and the facialExpression videos. The news anchor had almost no artifacts, besides the fact that the blinking was not working properly. The obama video had lighting issues, since the generator was not able to learn that the lighting would change when the head moves and the background also was warped by the movement of the head. And lastly, the facialExpression video had issues in filling in hair information that was outside the image and could not reproduce all facial expressions accurately, but it was still very well generated.

Other videos were also performing well, since they perceptually looked similar to the original video, but often had big issues such as weird distortions and inaccuracies that were visible even without knowing the driving video. However,

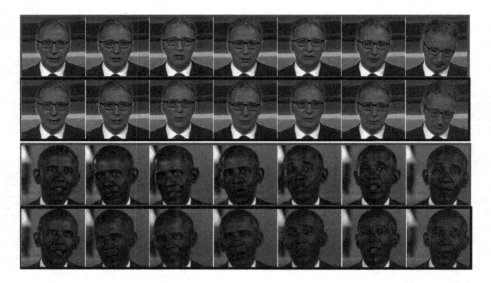

Fig. 5. Generated and original video frames. Green (top row) are the original frames, blue (bottom row) are the generated. (Color figure online)

most of the problems can be resolved by carefully choosing the driving video and understanding what the underlying limitations are.

Most of the time, the generated video resembles the original, as seen in Fig. 5, but it still has drawbacks in quality compared to AV1 or other codecs. Even though our goal to have minimal quality loss is not met entirely, the generated video is still perceptually close to the source.

6.3   Quantization

Since we used the method of quantization, by dividing the keypoint values and cut off the last few numbers, we reduced the accuracy of the keypoints and affine transformations. This has an impact on the quality of the generated video.

We tried different quantization factors depending on the maximal signed integer value that the int format is able to hold. For example, the int16 format can only assume values from −32,768 to 32,767.

We concluded that any power of ten under 1 000, no matter if keypoint or affine transformation tensors, resulted in much more visible artifacts. These artifacts were often noticeable on edges of the person, like the shoulders or the face. In each frame, the edges of the person seemed to shift rapidly and then shift back to their correct position, which looks like the person "glitched". This was not very noticeable if one stopped in a single frame, but it was visible when looking at it as a video. The smaller the power of ten it was, the more artifacts appeared. This is why we had to find a factor that made the file as small as possible, while not creating more artifacts.

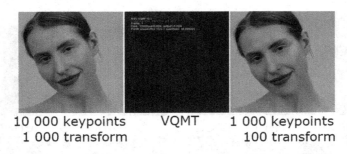

10 000 keypoints   VQMT   1 000 keypoints
1 000 transform   100 transform

Fig. 6. The difference in quantization shown with the MSU Video Quality Management Tool.

At the end, we chose to use a factor of 10 000 for keypoints and a factor of 1 000 for the transformations, since it seemed to retain most of the quality, while reducing the file size drastically. Using 1 000 for keypoints was also possible, although there was very little difference in file size and quality, so we decided to choose a bit more quality over file size.

Figure 6 shows us how much of an effect quantization has on images. By comparing our normal 10 000 keypoint and 1 000 transformation approach to a generated video with one power less, we can make the inaccuracies visible. Even though the changes are not visible to the naked eye, the VQMT tool was able to show us the difference in quality.

6.4   Limitations

It is very important to understand what this project is capable of before using it. Besides using a square video format, optimally 256×256 and not expecting high-resolution outputs, we also have to consider perceptual information and filter out videos that do not fit these requirements.

First of all, this software is not very good at filling in data that is not visible in the source image. For example, if the person moves their head, areas that were not in the original source image might appear. This information needs to be filled in by coloring or warping the missing information in the area, which is done, but sometimes it does not work well. Figure 7 in the upper left corner, shows how such a result could look like. Even though this can produce some valid information, it does not do its job perfectly, thus the image quality suffers from this issue.

The fact that the generator can not generate new information is a big issue. Use cases like moving backgrounds, occluded areas, turning heads or, objects, and excessive movement in general often lead to unsatisfying output videos. This needs to be considered when picking an appropriate driving video.

One has to be careful that the background does not move. If it does, it warps not only the moving parts, but it also might warp the face, which will result in minor distortions. These distortions can make the face more shaky and distracting. Even if the background is still, the generator might not have a clear

Fig. 7. Image examples of badly generated frames.

line indicating where the head ends and the background begins. This results in the background sometimes being warped by head movements.

Another important point is that the person in the image needs to have clear facial expressions. Things like barely moving lips or subtle eyebrow movement will not be picked up by the keypoint detector and generator. This will result in almost no visible motion in the output frames. Sometimes, it also does not translate blinking correctly. Often you can see a shift in the pixels that should represent the closing eyelid, but by closer inspection one can see that it does not look like a full blink. This can be seen in the lower left comparison in Fig. 7.

Additionally, turning the head too far to the side, for example by almost 90 °C, will result in a very faulty face position. Here it is not able to generate more information about the side view of the face and since the network only understands the front facing views, it will display a distorted front faced frame. This can be seen in the upper right comparison in Fig. 7.

Furthermore, the whole head of the person must be covering most of the frame area, optimally being centered and looking into the camera. It appears that if the head is not in focus, face features, like eyes, cannot be correctly detected. Figure 7 in the lower right corner is a good example. Here it almost works, but still does not seem close enough to detect all face features correctly.

The camera itself also should not move too much. The generator does not handle things like zooming very well. Since the background moves unproportionally to the face, the face will get distorted.

Important to note is that, even though the video does look very similar to the original, the video could have minor facial differences depending on the source image. For example, in Fig. 7 in the upper left corner, we can see that even though the comparison looks similar, there are still facial differences because the expression changed noticeably since the first frame. Since the project is not able to generate new information, it assumes that the face will stay the same throughout the video, thus creating frames that are not completely accurate.

A related issue is that if the source image is not in the same position as the first frame, we get very different facial expressions or movements that are faulty. This occurs when the video is too long and sthe project uses segmentation, where the head position in the first frame of the video differs immensely from the position in the source image. Because the starting position is wrong, the head will still use the same motion as in the driving video, which will cause inaccurate frame generation. This happened in our longNews video once and multiple times on the longObama video, because the news anchor did not move a lot, while Obama switched from side to side in his interview.

To sum it up, the best results can be produced when the video is short, contains a person, looking forward, with clear facial expressions, a still background, few head rotations and the person is covering most of the frame with a non-moving camera. These properties can be found, for example in news reporter videos.

6.5   Discussion and Future Work

Considering all problems and limitations of the project, the requirements are very restrictive. Many videos can not be used and even if the video fits, the user still needs to crop the video correctly and perform multiple operations by hand to achieve the goal, for example LZMA2 zipping. This could affect how quickly and well outputs can be generated.

In relation to this, there is a possibility to train a model or reuse the already trained face model to detect faces in videos and crop them accordingly with the help of video editing tools like FFmpeg.

Despite the shortcomings of this project, the results highly resembled the driving videos. Even with impressive breakthroughs in the area of artificial intelligence, it was surprising to see that the generated videos managed to replicate the original video so well.

What we did not expect was how little data was needed to create videos, and even more unexpected was the difference of data size compared to H.264 and AV1 codecs. It showed us that utilizing artificial intelligence as video codecs instead of years of development of a better algorithm is possible. This can lead to new codecs that utilize neural networks to encode videos and are better than normal codecs. There are still potential improvements on the shortcomings we did not succeed to fix in this project. Additionally, to the suggestion of reusing the face model for cropping, it is also possible to implement a neuronal network that improves the image quality of faces.

Another issue of the project is that it poorly handles longer videos with a lot of motion. Because the first frame of the segmentation likely starts from a different position than the source image, the motions will either move the face differently than in the original video or it can not handle the difference and generate frames that do not look pleasant.

One approach could be to send more source images to the receiver. For each segment, we would require to send a new source image, which would be the first frame of each segment, but at the cost of increasing the file transmission size. The source image also needs to be carefully selected, as seen in Fig. 7 what can go wrong. Even without careful selection of the source image, using multiple source images will probably increase the quality of longer generated videos, since major distortions are worse than blurry images.

At first, finding a neuronal network to outperform state-of-the-art codecs was hard, but even though many things are not fully satisfactory, the project gave us new views on what artificial intelligence is capable of and how much potential it still has. This project should encourage further research into that area and find even better ways to encode videos with neuronal networks.

7 Conclusion

We have posed the question if it is possible to generate videos with artificial intelligence that only requires little information extracted from a video and a source image, which can be sent over the network. By adapting the project from Siarohin et al. [17], we managed to extract the keypoint and local affine transformation from a neuronal network face model and compressed it to send the data to a receiver, which was able to reconstruct the original video approximately.

Although the results were not perfect, the partial success of this project showed us the potential of artificial intelligence for video codecs and should encourage further research into this area.

References

1. In-home media consumption due to the coronavirus outbreak among internet users worldwide as of March 2020, by country. www.statista.com/statistics/1106498/home-media-consumption-coronavirus-worldwide-by-country/. Accessed 14 Nov 2021
2. H.264 : Advanced video coding for generic audiovisual services. www.itu.int/rec/T-REC-H.264. Accessed 14 Nov 2021
3. AV1 Video Codec Homepage. aomedia.org/av1/. Accessed 14 Nov 2021
4. LZMA and LZMA2 7zip. www.7-zip.org/7z.html. Accessed 12 Nov 2021
5. LZMA2 7zip Documentation Page. sevenzip.osdn.jp/chm/cmdline/switches/method.htm#LZMA2. Accessed 12 Nov 2021
6. Bao, W., Lai, W., Ma, C., Zhang, X., Gao, Z., Yang, M.: Depth-aware video frame interpolation. CoRR abs/1904.00830 (2019)
7. Djelouah, A., Campos, J., Schaub-Meyer, S., Schroers, C.: Neural inter-frame compression for video coding. In: 2019 IEEE/CVF International Conference on Computer Vision (ICCV), pp. 6420–6428 (2019)
8. Dmitriy, V., et al.: MSU video quality measurement tool (MSU VQMT). www.compression.ru/video/quality/measure/videomeasurement/tool.html (2009)
9. Grigorev, A., Sevastopolsky, A., Vakhitov, A., Lempitsky, V.: Coordinate-based texture inpainting for pose-guided image generation (2019)

10. Han, J., et al.: A technical overview of av1 (2021)
11. Johnson, J., Alahi, A., Li, F.: Perceptual losses for real-time style transfer and super-resolution. CoRR abs/1603.08155 (2016)
12. Kazantsev, R., Zvezdakov, S., Vatolin, D.: Machine-learning-based method for finding optimal video-codec configurations using physical input-video features, pp. 374–374
13. Let's Enhance, Inc., Let's enhance.io. letsenhance.io/
14. Li, Y., Roblek, D., Tagliasacchi, M.: From here to there: video inbetweening using direct 3d convolutions (2019)
15. Ronneberger, O., Fischer, P., Brox, T. U-net: Convolutional networks for biomedical image segmentation. CoRR abs/1505.04597 (2015)
16. Siarohin, A., Lathuilière, S., Tulyakov, S., Ricci, E., Sebe, N.: Animating arbitrary objects via deep motion transfer (2019)
17. Siarohin, A., Lathuilière, S., Tulyakov, S., Ricci, E., Sebe, N.: First order motion model for image animation. In: Conference on Neural Information Processing Systems (NeurIPS) (2019)
18. Siarohin, A., Lathuilière, S., Tulyakov, S., Ricci, E., Sebe, N.: First order motion model for image animation repository (2019)
19. Siarohin, A., Sangineto, E., Lathuiliere, S., Sebe, N.: Deformable gans for pose-based human image generation (2018)
20. Wang, T.-C., Mallya, A., Liu, M.-Y.: One-shot free-view neural talking-head synthesis for video conferencing. In: Proceedings of the IEEE Conference on Computer Vision and Pattern Recognition (2021)
21. Wu, C.-Y., Singhal, N., Krähenbühl, P.: Video compression through image interpolation (2018)

Validating the Proposed Framework for Visualising Music Mood Using Visual Texture

Adzira Husain[1]([⊠]) [iD], Mohd Fairuz Shiratuddin[2] [iD], and Kok Wai Wong[2] [iD]

[1] School of Creative Industry Management and Performing Arts, Universiti Utara Malaysia, Changlun, Malaysia
`adzira@uum.edu.my`
[2] Discipline of Information Technology, Media and Communications, College of Arts, Business, Law and Social Sciences, Murdoch University, Perth, Australia

Abstract. There are several ways to search for songs in an online music library. A few types of visual variables to represent music information such as colour, position, shape, size, and visual texture have been explored in Music Information Retrieval (MIR). However, from a comprehensive literature review, there is no research focusing explicitly on the use of visual texture for browsing music. In this research, we define visual texture as an image of texture designed using the drawing application. In this paper, a framework for visualising music mood using visual texture is proposed. This proposed framework can be used by designers or software developers to select suitable visual elements when designing a clear and understandable visual texture to represent specific music moods in the music application. This research offers a new way of browsing digital music collection and assisting the music listener community to discover new song especially in mood category. To validate the framework, usability testing was conducted. This paper presents the process of developing and validating the proposed framework.

Keywords: Human-Computer Interaction · Information visualization · Music browsing · Music mood · Music information retrieval · Usability testing · Visual texture

1 Introduction

In the conventional way of displaying a music collection in most music library, the song titles were represented in a text list (see Fig. 1). An end-user or music listener will browse or scroll through this text list and select which song to play. However, this method of browsing is insufficient to maintain an overview of the music collection. Moreover, the traditional browsing method is not effective in response to the escalating growth of music collections [1]. As a result, music listeners will search for the same artist they are familiar with and will not be able to discover new and interesting songs available in their music collection. Therefore, Information Visualisation or InfoVis is a promising option for representing musical metadata [2, 3].

Z. Lv and H. Song (Eds.): INTETAIN 2021, LNICST 429, pp. 142–160, 2022.
https://doi.org/10.1007/978-3-030-99188-3_9

Fig. 1. The conventional way of displaying a music collection

InfoVis is a multidisciplinary research field that encompasses a wide range of areas, including computer graphics, cognitive psychology, and Human-Computer Interaction (HCI). Data images and structures are created toward assisting the exploration, performance of the specific task, analysis, and decision making [4]. Also, InfoVis is often evaluated as a tool that can support the performance of a certain task [5].

Previously, music users listened to music by browsing through the song title or artist's name list. Nevertheless, nowadays, the music segment that has become popular among music enthusiast is mood. Hence, mood has been identified as essential criteria in organising their music collection [6, 7].

In the MIR research field, various types of visual forms such as album cover, avatar, and mood picture have been introduced to represent mood.

Table 1. Related research and the type of visual variable used.

Related works	Visual variable
Moodo dataset [9]	Colour
Moodplay [7]	Colour, position
myMoodplay [1]	Colour, value, shape
Songrium [10]	Shape, size, position
Mood Pictures [11]	Pictures

Table 1 shows several related works that have explored visual variables in their research. Previous research has used other visual variables to associate music metadata, but they have not focused explicitly on textures [3, 8]. The look and feel of a surface are called texture. It can be classified into two types that are, tactile and visual textures. A tactile texture, also known as an actual texture, is the feature of a surface that can be touched and felt. A visual texture is the texture designed using a drawing application, scanned from actual textures, or photographed.

In consumer studies, ceramic art, textile design, and user interface research have discovered that texture has an emotional relationship to human moods [12, 13]. Still, until this research is carried out, visual texture has not been used to represent the music mood category in an online music library. Therefore, a framework for visualising music mood using visual texture is proposed.

In this paper, we proposed a framework for visualising music mood using visual texture. This framework can be used by designers or software developers to select suitable visual elements when designing a clear and understandable visual texture to represent specific music moods in the music application. A usability test was conducted to validate the framework. The process of developing and validating the proposed framework was presented in the next section.

2 Research Methodology

In HCI methodology, this research employed a User-Centered Design (UCD) science research method. The UCD has been identified as a multidisciplinary design method. This is based on the active participation of users towards improving the knowledge on user and task specification and the iteration of design and evaluation. [14]. Design science research has become popular methodology in multiple fields such as information system [15–17], Human-Computer Interaction (HCI) [18, 19], instructional design and technology [20], and educational research [21].

In design science research, purposeful artefacts are built and evaluated to understand the problem domain and its solution [22]. The artefacts can be constructs such as vocabulary and symbols. They can also be in the form of models such as abstractions and representations, methods such as algorithms and practices, or instantiations such as implemented and prototyped systems [22]. However, outcomes such as working prototypes, algorithms, user interfaces, processes, techniques, methodologies, and frameworks can also be considered valid artifacts under the design science research method [23].

In music recommendation research, several inventive artefacts such as prototypes and graphical representations for music retrieval and visualisation have been developed and evaluated [1, 6, 11, 24]. In particular, the outcomes of this research overlap with the list of artefacts mentioned in the previous paragraph. Therefore, the design science research method applies to this research.

In proposing and validating the framework, five phases are executed (see Fig. 2). A description of each phase is included in the following sub-sections below.

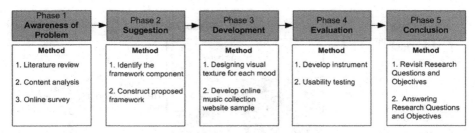

Fig. 2. Research phases

2.1 Phase 1: Awareness of the Problem

In Phase 1, an online survey was set up to determine which type of design element best represents the specific mood. The survey was divided into four mood sections which are angry, sad, happy, and calm. There are four different subsections in each section, namely colour, colour values, lines, and shapes (see Fig. 3). All possible types for the elements are listed in the answer options.

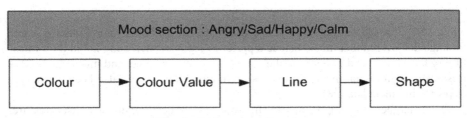

Fig. 3. Online survey flowchart

The respondents will then select an option from the list which they think best represents the mood before moving on to the next subsection and submitting the survey as soon as they have finished. Next, the respondents will select the type of element they think matches the mood from the list of design elements. Once the specific types of design element for each mood have been confirmed, they will be incorporated to construct the proposed framework in Phase 2.

2.2 Phase 2: Suggestion

After confirming the specific types of design element for each mood in Phase 1, a framework for visualising music mood using visual texture was proposed. Derived from the Visualisation Reference Model [25], the proposed framework was developed (see Fig. 4). The highlight of this framework is the visual mapping process. In the process, a specific visual texture was mapped to four different types of music mood category.

One of the components in the proposed framework is the music moods which include Angry, Calm, Happy and Sad. Previous research has shown that 30% of music listeners browse music based on the event's theme, such as birthday parties or weddings,

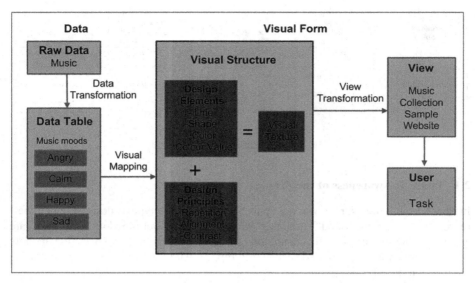

Fig. 4. The components of the proposed framework

while 15% is based on mood, such as sad or happy [26]. Furthermore, other research findings discovered that music listeners prefer to organise their song list in their music library based on mood rather than the song's title, artist's name, and music genre [27]. Besides that, in digital music library research, mood labels have also been considered as promising metadata [28].

Next, another key component in the framework is the design elements. Visual textures also consist of design elements such as colour, colour value, line, and shape, just like any other images. These design elements can represent mood. Different type of moods can be represented by a different type of design element [29]. For example, horizontal lines indicate a calm mood, while zigzag lines can express a feeling of excitement. A round and curved shape appears more friendly, while a sharp-angled shape conveys a negative mood. Certain colours also can convey a wide range of moods.

In this research, selected visual elements are combined using suitable design principles to develop a clear and understandable visual texture that can represent a specific music mood.

2.3 Phase 3: Development

This section discusses the processes in the development phase (see Fig. 5), and there are two activities in this phase. Firstly, the visual texture for each mood is designed. Next, the selected visual elements that were acquired from Phase 1 are combined using appropriate design principles. Then, the visual textures are applied in a music collection demo website to represent the respective music mood category.

Designing Visual Texture. Visual texture for each mood was designed based on the stage of Visual Mapping in the General Visualisation Reference Model [25]. This model

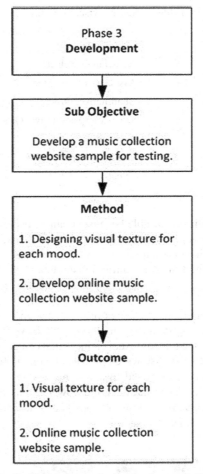

Fig. 5. The processes in the development phase

starts by converting raw data into a visual structure that the user can perceive. By going through the visual mapping process, the data table was then mapped onto visual structures. Visual structures are made of visual variables. Finally, a specific set of symbols can be applied to data to interpret information [30].

Table 2 shows seven essential visual variables that can create visual differences for a user to perceive and interpret the meaning of certain data. These visual variables can create an image or a symbol that has meaning to the audience [30]. The choice of a variable that would be the most suitable to represent each aspect of information depends on its characteristics. The characteristics comprise of selective, associative, quantitative, and order. Selective refers to visual variables that can be perceived as different; associative is defined by visual variables that can be perceived as similar; quantitative is perceived as variables that can be interpreted numerically, and order is identified as variables that support ordered reading. For example, colour is considered an

Table 2. Bertin's visual variable.

Visual variable	Characteristic
Colour	Associative, Selective
Orientation	Associative
Position	Quantitative, Order
Sizes	Selective, Quantitative, Order
Shapes	Associative
Texture	Selective, Order
Value	Selective, Order

associative and selective visual variable because it can be useful when choosing certain items from a group. However, colour should not be used to visualise quantity.

In the field of music visualisation, visual variables such as colour, position, size, and shape have been investigated in representing music data [6, 9, 11]. Texture is also one of the visual variables. It has been established that visual texture can represent a certain mood [29].

To design an understandable visual texture, the design elements are separated to explore their specific meaning in portraying the mood. To verify this, an online survey was set up towards finding the type of visual element that can be associated with a certain mood [31]. From the results, we discovered the visual element for each mood. Next, the selected design elements are composed by applying a suitable Gestalt principle. The Gestalt principle is a set of laws that describe how humans typically see objects by similar grouping elements such as colour or shape [32, 33]. Finally, the design of visual texture for each mood was finalised (see Fig. 6).

Angry   Calm   Happy   Sad

Fig. 6. Visual texture for Angry, Calm, Happy and Sad mood

Music Collection Demo Website. Visual textures that have been designed were applied to the music collection demo website. In this website, we represent four types of mood using four different images of visual texture. First, the website was designed using a free, website creation platform called WordPress. Then, it is published on the Internet using a web host service.

On the main page, mood categories such as Angry, Sad, Happy, and Calm were represented using four different visual images (see Fig. 7). Once the participants click on any of the visual texture, they will get a list of song suggestions according to the type of mood (see Fig. 8). Participants can browse through the suggested song list and press the play button to listen to the song and the pause button to stop.

Fig. 7. The main page of the music collection website sample

Fig. 8. List of suggested songs for Angry mood

2.4 Phase 4: Evaluation

This section discusses the processes in the evaluation phase (see Fig. 9). This phase aims to validate the proposed framework by conducting usability testing on the music collection demo website. Two outcomes were gathered from this usability testing. The first is the feedback on the suitability of the selected visual textures that represent each of the music moods. Secondly, it is the usability of browsing music by mood category using visual texture by measuring the Effectiveness, Efficiency, and Satisfaction.

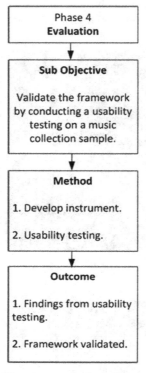

Fig. 9. The processes in the evaluation phase

Research Instrument: Task. In this research, one of the instruments developed to conduct usability testing is the task. The task contains a list of steps required to be completed by the participants during the usability testing procedure. The given task is used to ensure that participants can use and browse through the music collection website sample to look for songs in a particular mood category.

Table 3 shows an example of a task sheet for the Angry mood category. These task sheets are handed out randomly to each participant. Then, participants are given sets of questionnaires after each task to further clarify how much they agree with the suitability of the visual texture used to recommend a music mood.

Research Instrument: Questionnaire. The usability testing measures the suitability of the visual textures, the Ease of Use and the User Satisfaction while interacting with the visual textures to browse for music in the mood category. Hence, a scale type measurement was used to quantify these values. Accordingly, each item in the instrument is measured on a 7-point Likert scale ranging from strongly disagree (denoted by 1) to

Table 3. The task for the Angry mood category

No	Task
1.	Read the scenario below: "You just had a heated argument with your friend and need to listen to an angry song"
2.	You want to look for a song with the title "Mandatory Suicide" from the Angry mood category
3.	Click on any visual texture that you think represents an angry mood
4.	Look for the song from the list provided. If you cannot find it, click on the 'Home' button, and try clicking on another visual texture
5.	Once you have found the song, click on the Play button to listen to it
6.	Listen to the song for at least 30 s. You may also listen to the whole song if you like
7.	When you are ready, rate the suitability of the design elements in the visual texture in Section B of the questionnaire

strongly agree (denoted by 7). In addition, the instrument is partially used as a measure of outcome; hence, scale sensitivity becomes an important concern [34].

Usability Testing. In HCI research, the standard advice is to have 30 or more participants for the questionnaire testing method [35, 36]. However, it is advised to follow a similar number of employed participants from another related research. Assumed on that justification, 40 participants are recruited [11, 37, 38]. The participant recruitment was advertised through email, social media and posted on campus noticeboards. In the advertisement, we invited participants who enjoy listening to music and above 18 years old.

The usability testing is organised into two separate sessions. In Session 1, participants browse the music application demo website and answered a few sets of questionnaires. Next, two days after they have completed Session 1, participants receive a reminder note through email that contained a few simple tasks for them to accomplish. This session is conducted online. At the end of Session 2, they answer questionnaires on the Ease of Use and Satisfaction. As soon as Sessions 1 and 2 of the usability testing are completed, all data is prepared and organised for the data analysis process.

Demographic Data. In this usability study, there are 40 participants from different educational backgrounds involved. 43% of participants are male, and 57% are female. Most of the participants are university postgraduates and undergraduate students from universities around Perth, namely Curtin University, Murdoch University, and the University of Western Australia (UWA). All participants enjoy listening to music and able to use the computer. 75% of them listen to at least 1 to 3 h of music daily. 70% of the participants search for music by artist and band name, 55% by song title, 28% by genre, 45% by mood, and 28% by occasion. When asked if they searched for music according to their mood at a specific moment, 75% of participant selected 'Yes'. 80% of them also agreed that music undoubtedly has an impact on their mood.

Suitability of the Visual Texture for Each Mood. In measuring the suitability of the visual texture, participants were asked to answer a questionnaire right after they have completed each task. It is measured on a 7-point Likert scale ranging from 'strongly disagree' (denoted by 1) to 'strongly agree' (denoted by 7). The questionnaire's objective is to let the participants further clarify the suitability of the visual texture that represents each of the music moods. As Likert scales produces ordinal data, the median and Inter-Quartile Range (IQR) of each item is calculated. The median shows the participants' average response, while the IQR shows whether the responses are clustered together or scattered across the range of possible responses. The median and IQR for each type of mood are presented in the next section.

Angry Mood. Right after looking for a song with the title "Mandatory Suicide" from the Angry mood category, participants rated the suitability of the visual elements in the visual texture by answering the questionnaire. The following results are the median and IQR for each item.

Table 4. Median and IQR for each item in Task 1

No	Item	Median	IQR
1.	It is easy to look for the song in Task 1	7	1
2.	The visual texture matched the song that I found in Task 1	7	1
3.	The type of line used in the visual texture matched the song that I found in Task 1	7	1
4.	The type of shape used in the visual texture matched the songthat I found in Task 1	7	1
5.	The type of colour used in the visual texture matched the songthat I found in Task 1	7	1
6.	The colour value (tone) in the visual texture matched the songI found in Task 1	7	1

Table 4 shows that most participants agreed that looking for a song in the given task is easy (median = 7, IQR = 1). In addition, most participants considered that the visual texture used to represent the angry mood matched the song given (median = 7, IQR = 1). Also, most participants agreed that the type of line, shape, colour, and colour value integrated into the visual texture matched the given song in Task 1 (median = 7, IQR = 1).

Calm Mood. Next, in Task 2, after looking for a song with the title "Kiss of Life" from the Calm mood category, participants rated the suitability of the visual elements in the visual texture by answering the questionnaire. The following are the median and IQR for each item.

Table 5 shows that most participants seem to agree with the idea that looking for a song in the given task is easy (median = 6, IQR = 1.75). Furthermore, most participants

Table 5. Median and IQR for each item in Task 2

No	Item	Median	IQR
1.	It is easy to look for the song in Task 2	6	1.75
2.	The visual texture matched the song that I found in Task 2	5	3.75
3.	The type of line used in the visual texture matched the song that I found in Task 2	5	3.00
4.	The type of shape used in the visual texture matched the songthat I found in Task 2	5	2.00
5.	The type of colour used in the visual texture matched the songthat I found in Task 2	6	2.00
6.	The colour value (tone) in the visual texture matched the songI found in Task 2	6	3.75

somewhat agree that the visual texture suggested in the music collection demo website matched the song given in Task 2 (median = 5, IQR = 3.75). For the design elements, most participants show an agreement that the type of line (median = 5, IQR = 3.00), shape (median = 5, IQR = 2.00), colour (median = 6, IQR = 2.00), and colour value (median = 6, IQR = 3.75) in the visual texture matched the song given in Task 2. However, as shown in the above table, the IQR for items 3 and 6 are quite big. This means that opinion seems to be divided regarding the agreement on the type of line and colour value used in the visual texture that matched the calm mood.

Many respondents (N = 9, 23%) expressed either a strong disagreement or disagreement, but a roughly equal number (N = 14, 35%) indicate that they agreed or strongly agreed that the type of line used in the image matched the calm mood.

Happy Mood. After looking for a song with the title "Two of us" from the Happy mood category, participants rated the suitability of the visual elements in the visual texture by answering a questionnaire. The following are the median and IQR for each item.

Table 6 shows that most participants strongly agreed that looking for a song in the given task is easy (median = 7, IQR = 0.25). They also agreed that the visual texture suggested in the music collection demo website matched the song given in Task 3 (median = 6, IQR = 1). On the visual elements, participants also considered that the type of line (median = 6, IQR = 1), shape (median = 6, IQR = 1), colour (median = 7, IQR = 1.75), and colour value (median = 6, IQR = 2) in the visual texture matched the song given in Task 3.

Sad Mood. Soon after looking for a song with the title "Ain't No Way" from the Sad mood category, participants are asked to rate the suitability of the visual elements in the visual texture by answering the questionnaire. The following are the median and IQR for each item.

Table 6. Median and IQR for each item in Task 3

No	Item	Median	IQR
1.	It is easy to look for the song in Task 3	7	0.25
2.	The visual texture matched the song that I found in Task 3	6	1.00
3.	The type of line used in the visual texture matched the song that I found in Task 3	6	1.00
4.	The type of shape used in the visual texture matched the songthat I found in Task 3	6	1.00
5.	The type of colour used in the visual texture matched the songthat I found in Task 3	7	1.75
6.	The colour value (tone) in the visual texture matched the songI found in Task 3	6	2.00

Table 7. Median and IQR for each item in Task 4

No	Item	Median	IQR
1.	It is easy to look for the song in Task 4	7	1.00
2.	The visual texture matched the song that I found in Task 4	6	2.00
3.	The type of line used in the visual texture matched the song that I found in Task 4	6	1.00
4.	The type of shape used in the visual texture matched the songthat I found in Task 4	5	1.00
5.	The type of colour used in the visual texture matched the songthat I found in Task 4	7	1.00
6.	The colour value (tone) in the visual texture matched the songI found in Task 4	6	1.75

Table 7 shows that most participants agreed that the visual texture suggested in the music collection demo website sample matched the song given in Task 4 (median = 6, IQR = 2). Most participants also agreed with the idea that the type of line (median = 6, IQR = 1), shape (median = 5, IQR = 1), colour (median = 7, IQR = 1), and colour value (median = 6, IQR = 1.75) in the visual texture matched the song given in Task 4.

Usability. The ISO 9241–11 standard was employed to define the concepts of three usability elements. In the ISO 9241-11 model, usability consists of three elements: Effectiveness, Efficiency, and Satisfaction. Definition of each element is defined and measured according to the following:

- Efficiency – resources used in completing a task
- Effectiveness – level of completeness at which users achieve specified goals, and
- Satisfaction – positive attitudes toward using the system (ISO, 1998)

Each usability element was measured by adopting Jeng's usability assessment model [39] as follows:

- Efficiency – time spent to complete the tasks
- Effectiveness – the proportion of completed tasks
- Satisfaction – seven-point Likert scale from "not satisfied at all" to "very satisfied."

Efficiency. Efficiency is a measure of how quickly and easily a task can be accomplished. In this test, task time is used as a primary indicator to evaluate the Efficiency of using visual texture to browse for a song in the music mood category. Task time refers to the length of time it takes the participant to complete a task.

Table 8. Average time to complete all task

	Task 1	Task 2	Task 3	Task 4
Average time to complete (secs)	44.45	81.38	52.73	57.30

Overall, Table 8 presents the average time taken to complete all task. Participants completed Task 1 (Angry mood) significantly faster than others. The average time taken to complete Task 2 (Calm mood) is 81.38 s, Task 3 (Happy mood) is 52.73 s and 57.30 s for Task 4 (Sad mood). From these results, it can be concluded that the participants took a longer time to complete Task 2 than the other tasks. This is probably because some of the participants are confused by the design elements incorporated into the visual texture to represent the Calm mood.

Effectiveness: Completion Rate. Effectiveness can be calculated by measuring the completion rate. It is the percentage of tasks that users complete correctly. Referred to as the fundamental usability metric, the completion rate is calculated by assigning a binary value of '1' if the participant manages to complete a task and '0' if they do not complete it. The average completion rate is 78%.

In total, there are 40 attempts observed for each task. Of those attempts in Task 1, 35 participants are successful, and 5 are unsuccessful, and the completion rate for Task 1 (Angry mood) is 88.5%. In Task 2, an equal number of participants are successful and unsuccessful, making the completion rate for Task 2 (Calm mood) 50%. In Task 3, 39 participants are successful, and only 1 is unsuccessful. Thus the completion rate for Task 3 (Happy mood) is 97.5%. Finally, in Task 4, 37 participants are successful, and only 3 are unsuccessful, and the completion rate for Task 4 (Sad mood) is 92.5% (see Fig. 10). Overall, the completion rates for the tasks: Angry, Happy and Sad are above the average rate.

Effectiveness: Success Rate. The success rate is the percentage of participants who can complete the task given in their first attempt. In this usability testing, the success rate implies whether the participant can choose the right visual texture to find the song

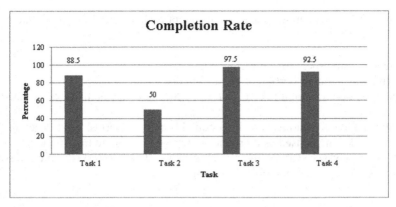

Fig. 10. The task completion rate for each task

in the mood category. A task will be considered a "success" and given one point if it is completed on the first attempt. Then, a task will be considered "partially success" and given half a point if it is completed on the second attempt. Finally, the task is considered a failure if the participant completed the task on the third attempt [27, 40].

Table 9. Success for each task

	Task 1	Task 2	Task 3	Task 4
Success rate (%)	91.25	67.5	96.25	93.75

Table 9 represents the summary of the success rate for all tasks. In Task 1, 35 attempts are considered successful, 3 attempts are partially successful, while 2 attempts are failed. Hence, the success rate for Task 1 (Angry mood) is 91.25%. In Task 2, 20 attempts are considered successful, 14 attempts are partially successful, while 6 attempts are failed. Hence, the success rate for Task 2 (Calm mood) is 67.5%. In Task 3, 37 attempts were successful, and 3 attempts are partially successful. As a result, the success rate for Task 3 (Happy mood) is 96.25%. In Task 4, 36 attempts are considered successful, 3 attempts are partially successful, and 1 attempt is failed. Hence, the success rate for Task 3 (Sad mood) is 93.75%. Overall, the success rate for all tasks is acceptable, and the percentage for Task 3 (Happy mood) is the highest among other tasks.

Ease of Use. After measuring the Efficiency and Effectiveness of browsing music in the mood category using visual texture have been analysed; Ease of Use is measured next. In the usability testing, participants are asked to rate the Ease of Use towards browsing music mood using the visual texture on two separate occasions. The first is after they have completed Session 1, and the next is after they have completed Session 2. The results for both sessions are compared to see if there are any changes in the Ease-of-Use rating between the first-time use and longer-term use.

Generally, most participants believe that browsing music by mood category using visual texture is clear and understandable. Moreover, they also think that it is easy to be skillful at browsing music by mood category using visual texture. From these findings, we can conclude that the participants find it easy to browse for music based on mood category using visual texture.

After using the music collection demo website for 2 weeks, the participants are asked to rate the Ease of Use once again, and both results are subsequently compared. A Wilcoxon signed-rank test shows that browsing music for 2 weeks does not elicit a statistically significant change in Ease of Use for first-time versus long-term use.

Satisfaction. Like Ease of Use, the participants are also asked to rate their Satisfaction (on two separate occasions) towards browsing music based on mood category using visual texture. The results for both sessions are compared to see if there are any changes in Ease-of-Use rating from the first-time use to the longer-term use.

Most participants were satisfied using visual texture in browsing music based on mood. They would recommend it to their friends, and they find that browsing music according to mood category using visual texture is fun. They also believe that the music collection demo website worked the way they wanted it to and browsing music based on mood category using visual texture is wonderful and pleasant.

After using the music collection demo website for another 2 weeks, the participants are asked to rate their Satisfaction once again. The results from both sessions are then compared. A Wilcoxon signed-rank test shows that browsing music for 2 weeks does not elicit a statistically significant change in Satisfaction for first-time use and long-term use.

3   Conclusion and Future Work

This paper presents the processes of validating a proposed framework for visualising music mood by using visual texture. Four visual textures are designed to represent Angry, Calm, Happy and Sad mood. The visual textures are used to represent music mood category in a music collection demo website. Usability testing was carried out to validate the proposed framework. In total, there were 40 participants browses through the website and respond to a few sets of questionnaires. During the usability testing session, activity on the computer screen is recorded.

From the findings, it can be concluded that the design elements that were suggested for each visual texture is acceptable and suits the assigned mood. Therefore, browsing music mood using visual texture is also perceived to be effective and efficient. Furthermore, most participants find that browsing music using visual texture is easy for them. They are also pleased with the new way of browsing music that has been introduced to them. Besides, they would like to suggest it to their friends. Generally, the majority of participants believe that browsing music by mood using visual texture is fun, wonderful, and pleasant to use. Therefore, it is firmly established that visual texture can be used as an alternative way of browsing music by mood.

In conclusion, all phases of validating the proposed framework are completed. Therefore, this framework will be a useful guideline to help the designers and software developers to select suitable visual elements when designing a clear and understandable visual texture to represent specific music moods in the music application.

To the music listener community in general, this research will offer a new way of browsing digital music collection, assisting listeners in discovering songs and artists they might not have been noticed otherwise using the traditional ways.

In the future, it would be more exciting if actual physical objects such as rocks, rugs or glass are used to portray music mood or music genre.

References

1. Allik, A., Fazekas, G., Barthet, M., Swire, M.: myMoodplay: an interactive mood-based music discovery app (2016)
2. Khulusi, R., Kusnick, J., Meinecke, C., Gillmann, C., Focht, J., Jänicke, S.: A survey on visualizations for musical data. Comput. Graph. Forum **39**(6), 82–110 (2020)
3. Marandi, Y.M.H., Sajedi, H., Pirasteh, S.: A novel method to musicalize shape and visualize music and a novel technique in music cryptography. Multimedia Tools Appl. **80**(5), 7451–7477 (2020). https://doi.org/10.1007/s11042-020-09962-8
4. Forsell, C.: Evaluation in information visualization: heuristic evaluation. In: 2012 16th International Conference on Paper Presented at the Information Visualisation (IV) (2012)
5. Baumer, E.P., Snyder, J., Gay, G.K.: Interpretive impacts of text visualization: mitigating political framing effects. ACM Trans. Comput. Hum. Interact. (TOCHI) **25**(4), 20 (2018)
6. Pradeep, A.A., Vispute, K.B., Bhavsar, V.S., Wadile, S.P., Pawar, V.N.: Emotion based music player. Int. J. Comput. Sci. Mobile Comput. **10**(2), 50–53 (2021)
7. Moscato, V., Picariello, A., Sperli, G.: An emotional recommender system for music. IEEE Intelligent Systems (2020)
8. Husain, A., Shiratuddin, M.F., Wong, K.W.: A proposed framework for visualising music mood using texture image. In 2013 International Conference on Research and Innovation in Information Systems (ICRIIS), pp. 263–268. IEEE
9. Pesek, M., Strle, G., Kavčič, A., Marolt, M.: The Moodo dataset: integrating user context with emotional and color perception of music for affective music information retrieval. J. New Music Res. **46**, 1–15 (2017)
10. Hamasaki, M., Goto, M., Nakano, T.: Songrium: a music browsing assistance service with interactive visualization visualisation and exploration of protect a web of music. In: Paper Presented at the Proceedings of the 23rd International Conference on World Wide Web (2014)
11. Lehtiniemi, A., Holm, J.: Using animated mood pictures in music recommendation. In: 2012 16th International Conference on Paper Presented at the Information Visualisation (IV) (2012)
12. Zhao, Z.: Emotional study of ceramic art texture in ceramic. Front. Art Res. **3**(1), 44–47 (2021)
13. Phillips, T.S.: Patterns of identity. Electronic theses and dissertations, 2184 (2020)
14. Mao, J.-Y., Vredenburg, K., Smith, P.W., Carey, T.: The state of user-centered design practice. Commun. ACM **48**(3), 105–109 (2005)
15. March, S.T., Smith, G.F.: Design and natural science research on information technology. Decis. Support Syst. **15**(4), 251–266 (1995)
16. Purao, S.: Design research in the technology of information systems: truth or dare. GSU Department of CIS Working Paper, vol. 34 (2002)

17. Kuechler, W., Vaishnavi, V., Kuechler Sr, W.L.: Design [science] research in IS: a work in progress. In: Proceedings of the Second International Conference on Design Science Research in Information Systems and Technology (DESRIST 2007), pp. 1–17, May 2007
18. Carroll, J.M.: Making Use: Scenario-Based Design of Human-Computer Interactions. MIT Press, Cambridge (2000)
19. Druin, A.: The role of children in the design of new technology. Behav. Inf. Technol. **21**(1), 1–25 (2002)
20. Reigeluth, C.M.: Instructional theory and technology for the new paradigm of education. RED. Revista de Educación a distancia **32**, 1–18 (2012)
21. Barab, S., Squire, K.: Design-based research: Putting a stake in the ground. J. Learn. Sci. **13**(1), 1–14 (2004)
22. Hevner, A., Chatterjee, S.: Design Research in Information Systems, pp. 9–22. Springer, Boston (2010). https://doi.org/10.1007/978-1-4419-5653-8
23. Norshuhada, S., Shahizan, H.: Design Research in Software Development: Constructing and Linking Research Questions, Objectives, Methods and Outcomes (2010)
24. Andjelkovic, I., Parra, D., O'Donovan, J.: Moodplay: interactive music recommendation based on Artists' mood similarity. Int. J. Hum. Comput. Stud. **121**, 142–159 (2019)
25. Card, M.: Readings in Information Visualization: Using Vision to Think. Morgan Kaufmann, San Francisco (1999)
26. Thompson, W.F., Russo, F.A.: The attribution of emotion and meaning to song lyrics (2004)
27. Wetzlinger, W., Auinger, A., Dörflinger, M.: Comparing effectiveness, efficiency, ease of use, usability and user experience when using tablets and laptops. In: Marcus, A. (ed.) DUXU 2014. LNCS, vol. 8517, pp. 402–412. Springer, Cham (2014). https://doi.org/10.1007/978-3-319-07668-3_39
28. Patra, B.G., Das, D., Bandyopadhyay, S.: Mood classification of Hindi songs based on lyrics. Paper Presented at the Proceedings of the 12th International Conference on Natural Language Processing (2015)
29. Husain, A., Shiratuddin, M.F., Wong, K.W.: Combining visual elements as a new method to browse and discover music mood. Paper Presented at the Proceedings of the 2nd International Virtual Conference on Advanced Scientific Results (2014)
30. Carpendale, M.: Considering visual variables as a basis for information visualisation (2003)
31. Husain, A., Shiratuddin, M.F., Wong, K.W.: Establishing a framework for visualising music mood using visual texture (2015)
32. Lester, P.M.: Visual Communication: Images with Messages. Cengage Learning, Wadsworth (2013)
33. Rodgers, P., Stapleton, G., Chapman, P.: Visualizing sets with linear diagrams. ACM Trans. Comput. Hum. Interact. (TOCHI) **22**(6), 27 (2015)
34. Cummins, R.A., Gullone, E.: Why we should not use 5-point Likert scales: the case for subjective quality of life measurement. In: Proceedings, Second International Conference on Quality of Life in Cities, vol. 74, p. 93, March 2000
35. Lazar, J., Feng, J.H., Hochheiser, H.: Research Methods in Human-Computer Interaction. Wiley, New York (2010)
36. MacKenzie, I.S., Castellucci, S.J.: Empirical research methods for human-computer interaction. Paper Presented at the CHI Extended Abstracts (2014)
37. Lehtiniemi, A., Holm, J.: Evaluating a potentiometer-based graphical user interface for interacting with a music recommendation service. Paper Presented at the 2011 15th International Conference on Information Visualisation (2011)
38. Lehtiniemi, A., Holm, J.: Designing for music discovery: evaluation and comparison of five music player prototypes. J. New Music Res. **42**(3), 283–302 (2013)

39. Jeng, J.: Usability of the digital library: an evaluation model. Coll. Res. Libr. News **67**(2), 78 (2006)
40. Nielsen, J.: Success rate: the simplest usability metric. Jakob Nielsen's Alertbox **18**, 3–5 (2001)

Interactive Art Therapy for Mental Health Using Microsoft Kinect

Ruzinoor Che Mat[(✉)] and Shumalee Cham Long

School of Creative Industry Management and Performing Arts, Universiti Utara Malaysia,
Changlun, Malaysia
ruzidatahp@gmail.com

Abstract. Nowadays, mental illness also called mental health disorders was becoming the most common illness among people. Many people who suffer from mental illness having difficulties in expressing their feeling and commit suicide because they normally do not or cannot open up in verbal communication such as traditional therapy. Interactive art therapy has the potential to decrease mental health among people. The main objective of this paper is to introduce an interactive art called Interactive Art Therapy (IAT) for people who are suffering from mental health that is needed non-verbal communication. The completed IPT application has been successfully developed by using Microsoft Kinect and Touchdesigner software which utilizing visual and audio elements for their interactivity. Based on the results from the usability testing, most of the respondents are agreed that this application is effective and usable for everyone especially those who are suffering from mental illness.

Keywords: Interactive art · Mental illness · Visual · Audio

1 Introduction

Mental illness has been one of the most common illnesses among people regardless of age today. Mental illness is also known as mental disorders which refers to different kinds of mental conditions and can affect the behavior and mood of people. Some mental illnesses are depression, anxiety disorders, schizophrenia, eating disorders, and addictive behaviors. Mental health is the potential to becomes a mental illness when signs and symptoms occur frequently due to stress. This will affect the brain's ability to function. A mental illness can make them feel miserable and can cause problems in their daily life which affects their daily productivity and when this happens constantly it would worsen the emotion of a particular person. People who are having a mental illness could treat their condition by taking medications and also through psychotherapy. Psychotherapists actually can help the person who has mental illness by listening to them in a non-judgmental and compassionate way. With their ability to listen in this way, the solutions to the problem could be solved and discuss. But some of the mental disorders could not be solved by psychotherapy. This is because some mental disorders

Z. Lv and H. Song (Eds.): INTETAIN 2021, LNICST 429, pp. 161–170, 2022.
https://doi.org/10.1007/978-3-030-99188-3_10

patients choose to suppress their emotions, and also choose to not open up their problem and discussed it with somebody. For a long time ago, the field of art therapy is effective in helping individuals explore and express feelings and improve overall wellbeing. Furthermore, interactive art has the potential as a therapy to decrease mental health among people. Through creating art and discovering its meaning, the process of making art itself becomes therapy. This unconventional approach assists the patients, especially those who don't or can't normally open up in traditional therapy and counseling sessions. Therefore, these group of people could undergo their therapy through non-verbal communication such as this interactive art which consists of both - visual and audio.

In this study, the concentrations on the problem of a group of people who suffer from mental health are given priority. Mental health is the level of psychological wellbeing or an absence of mental illness. It is the state of someone who is functioning at a satisfactory level of emotional and behavioral. Many people nowadays have been suffering especially from depression and anxiety. A mental health concern becomes a mental illness when ongoing signs and symptoms cause frequent stress and affect their ability to function. Depression plays a role in more than one-half of all suicide attempts, whereas the lifetime risk of suicide among patients with untreated depressive disorder is nearly 20%. Although depression and anxiety can be treated by medication which psychiatrists usually recommend that patients continue to take medication for six or more months after symptoms have improved. Longer-term maintenance treatment may be suggested to decrease the risk of future episodes for certain people at high risk which with all medicines, this change can cause side effects. Besides, the researcher has found that people commit suicide because they normally do not or cannot open up in verbal communication such as traditional therapy or counseling sessions. Increase the number of people who suffer from mental illness. People having difficulties in expressing their feeling or just keep them to themselves. People tend to take drugs or other dangerous medication to calm themselves. The objective of this paper is to introduce an interactive art therapy called IAT by using Microsoft Kinect for people who are suffering from mental health that is needed non-verbal communication.

2   Literature Review

Microsoft had launched the Kinect sensor at the end of 2010 [1]. This sensor is for the videogame system Xbox 360. However, this sensor has gained popularity not only in gaming [2, 3], but also in other areas such as robotics [4, 5], gestures [3, 6], medical [7], and rehabilitation [8–10] applications. Microsoft Kinect is a motion sensing input device that using state of the art motion sensing camera to allow full-body 3D motion capture, facial recognition, and voice recognition capabilities. This technology allows the users such as patients to interact with computer program which known as natural user interface. This kind of technology could be applied in many different types of medical setting such as for helping in mental health illness using art therapy. Mental health such as anxiety disorders and depression are very serious illness which could be affecting anybody. These kinds of mental health were the two most common mental disorders which brought great challenge to personal wellbeing. Based on latest trend, the need for private and home-based settings to act as therapy for mental illness is needed. The methods of interactive art as therapy for mental health not yet been fully established [11]. As mentioned before Kinect has potential to be used as art therapy. The Kinect used to allow the patient or the user to interact with the system in a 3D environment, where they perform multiple movement combinations without the need of an attached device or a controller. It is tackling issues related to act as therapy. Focusing on the rounded-particle and the relaxing audio added which would bring the user to feel the movement and feels along. This visual will be more effective with the dark surrounding with no outer sound disturbance. Some of the works related to Kinect conducted by Zao et al. [11]. He has conducted an experiment on 179 participants where there are required to walked on the footpath naturally while shot by the Kinect cameras. The result shows that by using different machine learning algorithms to train the regression models, the anxiety and depression levels were recognized. Other than that, Webster and Celik [12] present a review of research about Kinect-based elderly care and stroke rehabilitation systems. The results provide an overview of the state of the art, limitations, and issues of concern as well as suggestions for future work in this direction. Physiopedia [10] has discussed how Microsoft Kinect could be utilized for different kind of purposes which related to rehabilitation physiotherapy rehabilitation for stroke patients. Microsoft Kinect allows virtual rehabilitation to be conducted which has ability to provide more innovative and exciting ways to rehabilitate. Dove and Astell [13] in their Kinect project have demonstrated that learning and improvement over time of 23 participants for final analysis shown significant decreases in number of prompts per turn and turn duration and significant increases in turns completed independently.

3   Development of Interactive Art Therapy

The development of IAT consists of three phases which enable Kinect node and calibration at phase 1, design particle and motion at phase 2, and creating effects on particle visual at phase 3. It is very important to make sure each of the phases should be completed successfully before other phases could proceed. The development stage can be used as a guideline and identified as a strategic plan for developing the project.

At phase 1, the interactive sensor which is Kinect was used and set. The software used in this project called Touch designer [14]. Before this software could be used with the Kinect, it has to be enabled and test. Kinect sensors need to be tested to make sure that their sensor functioning well (refer Fig. 1). During the testing, the calibration needs to be performed. The calibration of the Kinect sensor needs to be tested with the human body part such as the hand, neck, shoulder, and leg. To merge the sensor with the visual, the setup needs to be performed. The setup involves by activating the Kinect calibration with the value of x, y, and z. When the calibration value appears and is verified successfully, the next phases could be started.

After the Kinect node is enabled, set and calibrate, phase 2 can be started. At this phase, the design of particle and motion are involved because the project is related to therapy visuals. The process of designing the particle and motion is very crucial and needs to make sure it is working properly. The process starts with creating the particle nodes to display visual and platform to merge with the Kinect. The size of this particle can be set in different sizes accordingly and could move randomly in motion. This process

Fig. 1. Testing the Kinect sensor

could be performed by settings up the property of this particle accordingly. When the particle is setup properly, this particle node needs to be merged with the Kinect node (refer Fig. 2). This merging could be performed by using node geometry as a bridge to connect both nodes. After that, the particle visual and motion will be appeared based on what being set before. When these phases are completed, phase 3 could be started.

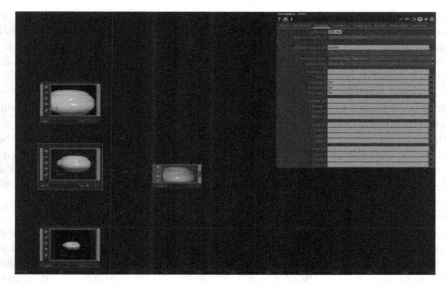

Fig. 2. Process of merging the visual node

After phase 1 and phase 2 are completed, phase 3 could be started. At this phase, the effects such as colours, shape, edge, and delay could be added into the particle that being created before at phase 2. First, the effects of colour could be set to the visual. Effects such as optical flow, feedbackEdge and RGBblur also can be set to the visual. After that, the delay effects can be added to the visual. Finally, audio can be added to the node to enable turn on audio in the project. When all these effects are set, the visual is ready. Then the process of calibration for hand to control and interact with visual could be performed. In order to perform this, have to turn back to phase 1 to make sure all effects were applied and calibrate well with the visual and also motion. At this stage, the particle attractor was added and merged. To produce calming visuals, some of the effects need to be reduced and maintain only certain effects. The particle must be set randomly. The purpose of adding effects is to give more therapy looks on visual. As mentioned before, to produce and boost more relaxing and calming feelings, the related and calm audio is added. The audio could help the user feel more relaxing and calming while interacting with the visual and motion. After all the phases are finished, the final look of the visual is ready and could be controlled with the hand gesture through the Kinect sensor. The demo of the IAT is released. The final visual is projected on the television screen. The setup is included Kinect Xbox 360 V.2, Kinect adapter, and television screen. The environment setup for IAT should be in the dark background to make sure that the visual representation of IAT could be seen clearly and affects more to the user. A few peoples are tested to interact with the visual. After testing with the demo project, there are some feedbacks given by the user. Therefore, some improvement needs to be done. Some of the changes or improvement is changing the size of the particle, shapes and add more particles to the project. After that, the final changes are made, and the final project is released. Figure 3 shows the final visual representation of the project which can be interacted by the users.

Fig. 3. Final IAT tested by the users

4   Results and Discussion

After finished the development of the IAT, the evaluation on the effectiveness of the IAT was conducted. The instruments have been developed for the purpose of the evaluation. These instruments consist of 5 questions. Below are the questions: -

Question 1: "Does the color of the visual, make you feel calm or relaxing?"
Question 2: "Do you agree that audio in this visual used could make you feel calm?"
Question 3: "After you interact with the visual, how do you feel?"
Question 4: "Do you think that this project could help others to improve their mental illness?"
Question 5: "So, based on your opinion, will you suggest this to those who have or facing with mental health problem?"

The questionnaire has been distributed to the 30 respondents randomly and all the respondents give their feedback by answering the questionnaire. Due to the pandemic covid-19, only 5 respondents could be tested IAT directly before they give the feedback. But the rest of the respondents are giving their feedback by watching the video of IAT. The results from these feedbacks are discussed in this section.

Question 1: "Does the color of the visual, make you feel calm or relaxing?".

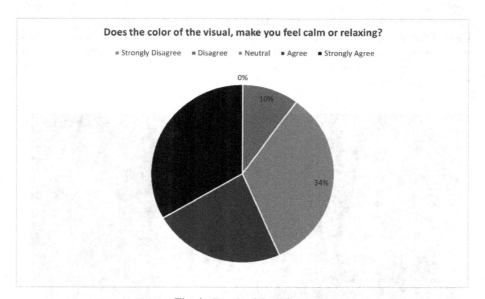

Fig. 4. Result of Question 1

The results for Question 1 shows in Fig. 4. From a total of 30 respondents, there are 33% respondents are strongly agreed that the color of the visual could make them feel calm and relaxing. While there are 23% of respondents are agreed that color of the visual helps them to feel calm and relaxing. Another 34% of respondents are feeling neutral with the color of the visual. And the rest of the respondents (10%) were disagreeing that the visual could make them feel calm and relaxing. This may be because they expected more variety of color on the visual to make them calm and relax.

Question 2: "Do you agree that audio in this visual used could make you feel calm?".

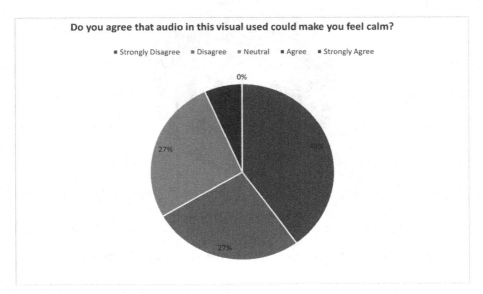

Fig. 5. Result of Question 2

The results for Question 2 shows in Fig. 5. From the total of 30 respondents, there are 40% respondents strongly agree that audio used in the visual could make them feel calm and relaxing. While 27% of respondents are agreed that the audio together with the visual could make them feel calm. The other 27% of respondents answered as feeling neutral and the rest 6% respondents have disagreed.

Question 3: 'After you interact with the visual, how do you feel?'

The results for Question 3 shows in Fig. 6. From a total of 30 respondents, there are 83% respondents feel very calm after interacting with the visual. While there are 14% of respondents feel no feeling on the visual. And there are 3% of respondents feel stressed with the visual after he or she interacts with the visual.

Question 4: 'Do you think that this project could help others to improve their mental illness?

The results for Question 4 shows in Fig. 7. From the total of 30 respondents, there were 64% respondents are strongly agreed that this project can help people who are suffering from mental illness. While 23% of respondents are agreed. Follow with 10% respondents answered neutral and only 3% respondent has disagreed. And there is no one who answered strongly disagree. This result has support by work done by Haeyen et al. [15]. Whereby in their work on quatitative research on finding the effects of art therapy with mental illness and health outcomes has concluded that art therapy has potential to promotes mental health and reduces the mental illness.

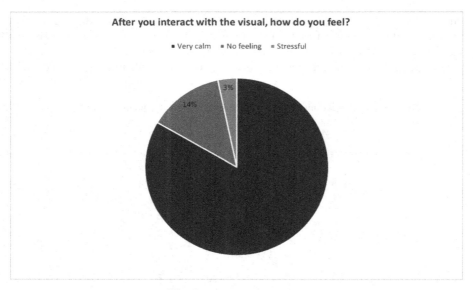

Fig. 6. Result of Question 3

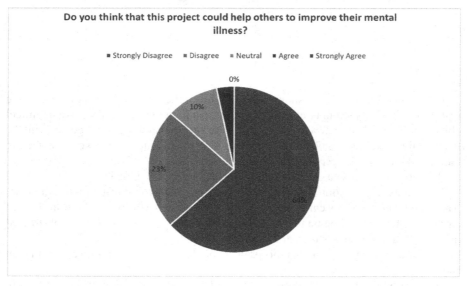

Fig. 7. Result of Question 4

Question 5: "So, based on your opinion, will you suggest this to those who have or facing with mental health problem?"

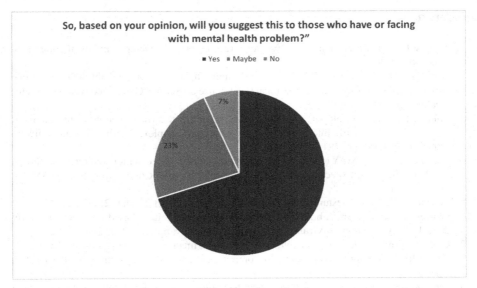

Fig. 8. Result of Question 5

The results for Question 5 show in Fig. 8. From a total of 30 respondents, there were 70% respondents answered 'Yes' to will suggest this project to those who have a mental health problem. While there are 23% of respondents voted for 'Maybe' and the last 7% of respondents voted for 'No'.

5   Conclusion

In conclusion, the project namely IAT has met in successful which achieve the objectives to improve mental health especially for the people who are needed non-verbal communication. The project has been successfully developed by using the latest technology which utilizing Microsoft Kinect and Touchdesigner software. Due to the pandemic of Covid-19, some of the respondents could not interact directly with the project. The results show that most of the respondents are agreed that IAT is effective and usable for people who are suffering from mental illness. The majority of the respondents select strongly agree with all aspects being asked in the questionnaires. They agreed that the IAT makes them feel calm and relax. The audio used with the visual art also makes them feel calm. When they interact with IAT, the majority feel very calm and would suggest this IAT for others to improve their mental health. In the end, this IAT has the potential to help and improve the health of people who are suffering from mental illness which needed non-verbal communication. For future work, the IAT could be improved and enhanced especially on the particle representation by adding more effects on the particle to improve the quality of the visual representation.

References

1. Microsoft Corporation: Kinect for windows (2021). https://developer.microsoft.com/en-us/windows/kinect/
2. Borghese, N.A., et al.: An intelligent game engine for the at-home rehabilitation of stroke patients. In: 2013 IEEE 2nd International Conference on Serious Games and Applications for Health (SeGAH), pp. 1–8 (2013)
3. Soltani, F., et al.: Developing a gesture-based game for deaf/mute people using microsoft Kinect. In: 2012 Sixth International Conference on Complex, Intelligent, and Software Intensive Systems, pp. 491–495 (2012)
4. Boyraz, P., et al.: UMAY1: a modular humanoid platform for education and rehabilitation of children with autism spectrum disorders. In: 2013 9th Asian Control Conference (ASCC), pp. 1–6 (2013)
5. Jayasurya, B., et al.: Gesture controlled AI-robot using Kinect. Studies **2**, 1 (2021)
6. Chaves, T., et al.: Human body motion and gestures recognition based on checkpoints. In: 2012 14th Symposium on Virtual and Augmented Reality, pp. 271–278 (2012)
7. Gallo, L., et al.: Controller-free exploration of medical image data: experiencing the Kinect. In: 2011 24th International Symposium on Computer-Based Medical Systems (CBMS), pp. 1–6 (2011)
8. Loayza, B.G., et al.: Application of Kinect technology and artificial neural networks in the control of rehabilitation therapies in people with knee injuries. Int. J. Adv. Comput. Sci. Appl. **11**(8), 509–515 (2020)
9. Milosevic, B., et al.: Kinect and wearable inertial sensors for motor rehabilitation programs at home: state of the art and an experimental comparison. Biomed. Eng. Online **19**, 1–26 (2020)
10. Physiopedia: The emerging role of Microsoft Kinect in physiotherapy rehabilitation for stroke patients (2020). https://www.physio-pedia.com/index.php?title=The_emerging_role_of_Microsoft_Kinect_in_physiotherapy_rehabilitation_for_stroke_patients&oldid=237924
11. Zhao, N., et al.: See your mental state from your walk: Recognizing anxiety and depression through Kinect-recorded gait data. PLoS ONE **14**, e0216591 (2019)
12. Webster, D., Celik, O.: Systematic review of Kinect applications in elderly care and stroke rehabilitation. J. Neuroeng. Rehabil. **11**, 108 (2013)
13. Dove, E., Astell, A.J.: Kinect project: people with dementia or mild cognitive impairment learning to play group motion-based games. Alzheimer's Dement. Transl. Res. Clin. Interventions **5**, 475–482 (2019)
14. Derivative: Touchdesigner by derivative (2021). https://derivative.ca/
15. Haeyen, S., van Hooren, S., van der Veld, W.M., Hutschemaekers, G.: Promoting mental health versus reducing mental illness in art therapy with patients with personality disorders: a quantitative study. Arts Psychother. **58**, 11–16 (2018)

Impact of Games on People: A Comprehensive Review

Hoshang Kolivand[1,2,3], Shiva Asadianfam[4(✉)], and Daniel Wrotkowski[1]

[1] Faculty of Engineering and Technology, School of Computer Science and Mathematics, Liverpool John Moores University (LJMU), Liverpool L3 3AF, UK
h.kolivand@ljmu.ac.uk
[2] School of Computing and Digital Technologies, Staffordshire University, Stoke-on-Trent, UK
[3] Bharath Institute of Higher Education and Research, Chennai, India
[4] Department of Computer Engineering, Qom Branch, Islamic Azad University, Qom, Iran
sh_asadianfam_stu@qom-iau.ac.ir

Abstract. It is clear from the beginning that video games are no cure for anything, like books and movies, they are often used in an antisocial way. Games clearly are a way of seeing reality differently through a person's eyes, and mostly nowadays, the games commonly come with violence and sometimes with abusive themes. Critics say that the things people learn from playing video games are not often the things that they expect. However, even the crudest critics agree with the ways we learn something from video games. Above the multibillion-dollar industry, higher than a fascinating toy for both children and adults or more than a passage to computer proficiency, the video game is highly profitable in ways that let people engage in a new world. It allows the player to think, speak, and act in a new way. Unquestionably, players come to possess roles that are unapproachable to them. This paper presents a comprehensive review of games and the impact of video games on them. Also, we will point out the qualities of Virtual Reality and its history. We will also point out the importance of development, which gives birth to new technology.

Keywords: Digital games · Games & Simulation · Integrated learning systems · Video games

1 Introduction

In the past, the form of digital games has initially been brimmed with a variety of different experiments and changes based on each new electronic creation. For example, a valve, silicon circuits, and televisions. This change has helped the researchers in many ways by seeking ways of improving the value of entertainment we could get from the new technology. Nowadays, the mass of older games can still be playable through purchasing the games on online auctions or through retro gaming companies or from using modern technology, which allows people to use the internet to play games on emulation software [1]. The way of defining the first computer games is somewhat

Z. Lv and H. Song (Eds.): INTETAIN 2021, LNICST 429, pp. 171–188, 2022.
https://doi.org/10.1007/978-3-030-99188-3_11

debatable, with claims pointing at the explanations and the chronological way of looking at it. In 1952, Alexander Douglas created a version of naught and crosses, which was playable on EDSAC, a first stored-program computer that ran a regular computing service [2]. In 1972, the world's first console was invented, Magnavox Odyssey, which sold over 100,000 units in a year. The console came in with a controller and a see-through screen overlay [1].

Video games allow the player to think, speak, and act in a new way. Unquestionably, players come to possess roles that are unapproachable to them [3]. These upper-class virtual worlds are indeed what make video games a powerful way of learning. However, in video games, learning is no longer a way of encountering words and symbols which are separated from the thing's person may learn from these words and symbols or what they are referred. The inverse square law of gravitational excitement is no longer a thing that is possible to be understood from an equation. As a substitute, students can advance their virtual experience by walking in a smaller world than Earth [3]. A style of games like mud-type games, online gaming is not a new concept. Online gaming usually was discarded until now in ways it allows people to play on their personal computers since consoles were not online compatible. However, when Sega Dreamcast was created, all of the popular consoles include such an option, but the percentage of games is not very high. Online gaming is appealing to games, and console developers are far higher than one offline game as online gaming generates monthly income from monthly subscriptions. The reason for this is the future of widespread mass public gaming [1]. In modern days, most of the players are lone teenagers who are seated in front of the computer, playing, which can cause a social phenomenon. An example can be a massively multiplayer online game, in which millions of gamers play at the same time with their reasoning for participation in virtual worlds with their political views and cultures [3]. This paper presents a comprehensive review of games and the impact of video games on them.

This paper is structured as follows. In Sect. 2, the background information required for a better understanding of video games presented in this paper is discussed. In Sect. 3, the related studies on the impact of video games on people are described in detail. Finally, the general conclusion of this paper is explained in Sect. 4.

2 Background

Nowadays, video games are to be said that they started with simple graphics such as Pong, Donkey Kong, Battle Zone, or Centipede. Pong was invented in 1972, which was a relatively basic game that was relative to Ping-Pong, but Pac-Man, which was invented in 1980, showed a significant step forward for its graphical design. It started with it being an average arcade game that leaped through popularity and then was created onto a hugely successful home version. Pac-Man was the most popular video game in America for several years. The console that the gamers used was commonly the ones to generate a sharp video image onto the screen with characters and loud sound effects. Pac-Man, the arcade version, had an 84-circuit chip integrated into the central logical board that backs in the days was one of the reliable devices. The first home console was an all right but less powerful and for most of the gamers not satisfying, but Atari, which created the games, combined a special microprocessor doting to generate an improved video display and sounds [4].

Over the past 30 years, games have become one of the factors of the modern world. Games have become part of the lives of many people and are prevalent not just in the United States but all over the world. Games are very recognized and have a significant impact on people. There are around two billion players in the world [5], which means every 4th person in the world is a player, and the game is one of the most successful things in our world [6]. In the United States alone, computers and consoles in 2001 were very successful because their earnings exceeded $ 6.35 billion, and in the world arena, about $ 19 billion (IDSA 2002). When a foreign company such as Sony released the first Sony PlayStation in the United States in less than 24 h, it earned 150 million dollars, while taking advantage of any competitor at the time in the United States. Since then, this console has become part of one of four homes in the United States, forming a group of 25 million Americans who use the services of Sony [7]. When games began to gain in importance, and the scale at which they began to spread, people began to pay more and more attention to how games, console, and the computer are affecting people, and in particular, the largest sector of people using games: children. So, games become part of the lives of many people, especially children, which suggests that educators still have doubts about whether this is good or bad and what changes it can bring to their student's life. Some educators began to doubt the games and began to fear that the games could increase aggression or violence. Also, it can change the way in how children behave in contact with other children and even isolate themselves from the rest [8]. On the other hand, other educators see games as a huge success. How games motivate them with the help of a vast digital environment; they want to research how motivational components of popular video games might be integrated into the instructional design [9].

3 Related Studies on the Impact of Video Games on People

3.1 Games and People

The results of one study shows that using games, televise or the Internet for several hours a day has a significant impact on children during their adolescence stage [10]. One of the factors of this process is the younger age of the person who begins to use technology. For this reason, even teachers pay attention to how games and the media have an impact on children [11]. Games are so present in the lives of many children, with 97% of these kids in the United States alone spending at least an hour playing games. A large number of psychologists researched the effects of playing games had adverse effects such as depression, violence or addiction. Although games have adverse effects, more research is still needed to understand better how games affect the human mind. Games are changing all the time and how a person perceives these games also change [12, 13].

3.1.1 Impact of Games on Children

Recently, there have also been studies that aim to find the benefits of using games correctly. Because there are games that do not contain much violence but are aimed at developing skills such as concentration, cognitive, building emotions, and learning about social aspects, combining various positive and developmental aspects, including social and medial aspects, can result in improved psychosocial benefits [12]. In research [14] conducted in the field of psychology, the result showed that playing games relate to factors such as coordination and spatial skills as well as visual scanning and hearing improvement. However, studies with children have shown that games that contain violence increase aggression and affect children's behavior [14]. Playing games that contain various physical exercises has effects such as increased heart rate and metabolism, tendonitis, and seizures. Playing games can cause aggressive behavior. So far, there is no direct connection between the game and functioning in school and psychopathology [11]. Although games with harmful aspects are full of adverse effects, they are games that are full of good things and are very important and useful as a learning tool. Most studies, however, are still not fully defined in this matter because there are still not many long-term studies, and many studies give different results [11].

3.1.2 Violence in Games

The potential impact that games which include violence may spread violence and aggression among young people is a topic among scientists, researchers, and the majority of society for many years. Currently, finding the leading cause is difficult because everyone has their opinion on this matter, and it is difficult to know one main reason. So, scholars have debated on this issue all the time. Some scholars have found that the impact of games that contain violence and aggression began to show up and bring to the more significant part of society [15, 16]. Other scientists have found that the adverse effects of these games have little effect on young people and can only affect individuals depending on the circumstances and susceptibility to violence [17–19]. Other scholars argue that the impact of games on behavior and susceptibility to aggression in young people is zero, or the methods they use are not good enough to determine or draw any conclusions due to methodological difficulties or problems [20–22]. Some researchers have stated through their research that playing games cause more and more violent feelings and thoughts, measured by inventory [23–25]. Others studied children how they would play with other children after they had previously played games with violence, as demonstrated by the increase in aggressive play [26]. Other studies on similar situations have shown a more aggressive behavior of only girls [27]. Other researchers have shown increased aggression in children who played with violence than in children who did not play them, and no effects in children who watched television [28]. Recent studies have shown that there are no changes in children who play games with violence [29]. In 1997 there was a shooting in West Paducah, in which a student shot other students, which ended fatally for three students and several victims [30]. Two years later, two other students made the most significant school shooting in the United States at Columbine High School near Denver, Colorado, in the suburbs of Littleton [31]. In addition to the tremendous amount of brutality, violence, and blood, there was another thing that connected these two tragic events. These are video games that have become part of young people from the 70s of the 20th century, which began with the appearance of the first video game [32].

From the psychologists' research on the perpetrators and the circumstances of these two shootings, they were connected by a tremendous desire to play games and in particular, shooters. First of all, it is visible in the other situation where the perpetrators had obsessions for these games in which only shooting and murdering opponents was.

Furthermore, the worst part was the fact that one of the perpetrators adapted this game to a similar scenario of this tragedy that happened [33]. The pattern of results obtained suggests that playing violent games may have an immediate effect on state hostility, but not on state anxiety. Concerning the psychophysiological effects, after many scientific and research studies, it can be concluded that playing games may be hostile to public opinion but does not introduce social anxiety. In contrast, the influence of games on the mind or body is still not entirely clear. Research shows that there are no immediate effects or changes in behavior, but, according to research, games have a more significant impact on women than on men [34]. Studies of people who are already aggressive or playing games like this may have softening effects. However, studies have shown the opposite effect, and playing games with violence may have different effects depending on the aggressiveness of the person, which is consistent with research conducted by the media [35]. That is why what the media say may not be accurate because how the game affects a person is composed of several factors and circumstances. Therefore, people who are more susceptible to games should not play this type of game [36].

3.1.3 Negative Impact of Extended Play In-Game

Technology is the thing that drives our world and the people who use it in everyday life. The development of technical aspects, such as the internet and computers, has promoted the stage of life. In the sector of education and business and, above all, health and entertainment. So, like any great thing or innovation attracts many people, which makes people more and more addicted over time. Well, apart from good self-feelings, electronics devices such as computer or console have several adverse effects [37]:

- Radiation
  Most monitors have a cathode ray tube (CRT), which causes radiation, this lamp emits X- rays. X-rays are very harmful to health. Insomnia, migraine, and cancer, and tumors may be one of the symptoms. Just placing the laptop on a lap or stomach can lead to male infertility, or such radiation can also cause skin irritation [38].
- Stress
  Another sign of prolong using a computer for too long is that the user is more likely to experience stress. Stress may be influenced by many factors, such as poor working conditions, poor health, and pressure at work. This condition can lead to constant headaches, fatigue, and low concentration. In the worst case, a susceptible person can lead to depression or mental disorders [37].
- Obesity
  People who use a computer or console usually use them a few hours a day, sitting all the time comfortably. There are around 2 billion people in the world who are overweight or obese. Such people are less physically active, which, when combined with unhealthy food, gives a terrible mix for health. Children, in particular, are at risk because children and teenagers are the greater society of players. Symptoms occur through obesity, which leads to diabetes and in the worst case, to heart disease [39].
- Headache
  As well as any prolonged use of a different type of electrical device can cause migraines as well as headaches. According to research, many things cause a headache, such as

weak or dim lighting, various patterns, or image on the computer. Besides, bad posture can also contribute to headaches [37].

- Vision Problems
  Using the monitor or television for too long is harmful to the eyes. According to research, the long-term use of visual cognition with the electronic screens of a computer, telephone, or tablet leads to computer vision syndrome. The employee who uses the computer spends around 7 h in front of the computer [40].
- Muscle Problems
  The most common way to use a computer is to sit on a chair in front of a desk. Spend most of the time, look at the monitor that is on the desk. According to research, more extended periods of sitting, whether, on a chair or a couch before the console, the muscles start to be fatigue and sore. There is also numbness in the arms, back, chest, and feet. Furthermore, all this is caused by poor posture when sitting at the computer or the couch for several hours [41].

3.1.4 Phenomena of Popular Games

Throughout the years, the generation of games become more successful, but at the same time, the category they contain is more realistic and gruesome. Brand new video games which are based on CD-ROM type of technology, people often use this technology to create music or for uploading a computer software is changing into a film in which we practically expect of a video game. This type of game is a big step forward that is far beyond the use of simple graphics likes Space Invaders. Space Invaders was so famous for estimated years of 15 to 20 years ago, or small animated cartoon figures created in the Nintendo System that have surpassed the video game market in recent years [42].

A delight phenomenon created by the adventure impacted video games with terms of social, psychological and educational significance, is also regarded by the size of the video game industry. The new evolution of video game character technology and video games influence the storytelling mage huge improvement. More and more people start to recognize games, not just games but something where people can experience something new [37]. Most Americans well know the existence of games. Periodically, articles are published about new games in the newspaper or New York Times, was it consistently carries a feature on new games every Thursday on its "Circuits" section. Time and Newsweek magazines also contain articles about the industry and various games, many magazines are fond of video games, and hundreds if not thousands of Internet sites are devoted to video games. Video Game companies created their internet sites where users can find a variety of different information about the specific game. The main component of the video game is interactivity, which can create image-less fiction records, which might be thought of as an original art form version of video games without the use of animated characters. The progression of games covers from relatively coding "bang-em-up" wrestling games to innovation science fiction and adventure games to a postmodern progressive novel [37].

3.1.5 Content of Games Made for Teenagers

These days, children are mainly exposed to violence in video games, the use of blood and sexual themes with gambling, and media remains the source of public health concern. Even so, the content in games played by the older children and adults has not been evaluated or compared with the rating of information assigned to a consumer by the Entertainment Software Rating Board (ESRB). ESRB stands for Entertainment Software Rating Board. This type of board creates, in turn, a rating system that delivers viable purchases of video games (including parents) with approximate age based on the game category, which includes violence, sexual images, and the use of bad/swear words among the players. The ESRB trusts that these guidelines could be used in a way the parents can downsize the child's time play on video games that contains unfit content [43].

The examination of all content descriptors which were trusted to the 396 T-rated video game titles displayed 373 (94%) in the usage of violence, 102 (26%) for blood, 60 (15%) for sexual images and themes, 57 (14%) for swearing, 26 (7%) for the usage of suggestive humour, 6 (2%) for drugs, and none for gambling. We played a random sample of 81 games in which we were able to find that 79 (98%) of players are involved in violence for a moderate of 36% games played. 73 (90%) required a player to injure a character, 56 (69%)required the player to kill, 34 (42%) demonstrated blood, 22 (27%) demonstrated sexual themes, 22 (27%) contained swearing, 12 (15%) showed usage of substances, and 1 (1%) involved gambling [43]. Games were more likely to illustrate the females by making them incompletely nude or were engaged in sexual behaviors other than males. Fifty-one observations were done in which we identified the content that could authorize a content descriptor of 39 video games (48%) that ESRB was not entrusted into the content descriptor. We were also able to find that the ESRB tasked out seven content descriptors for seven games (9%) that were not observed in what content was indicated within the 1 h of the game being played. The content that was examined suggested that the significant amount of the content used in T-rated games will surprise the teenage player and their parents in the presence of the content being used without ESRB content descriptors. Parents and physicians need to be cautious of popular T-rated games that are mostly like to be a root of exposure to a broad range of fantastic content [43].

3.2 Virtual Reality

Virtual reality, also known as VR, is a type of technology that grants permission for a user to interact with a computer-based environment simulation that can be a real-world or an imaginary world. They range from being able to create a game or having a little walk around the virtual universe to being able to stroll around our own dream house also to be able to experience a walk-in alien planet [44].

Virtual reality is a different way in which we can use computers; it rules out the separation between the user and machine, being able to provide more first-hand and unlearned interaction with information [45]. Virtual reality is used everywhere. Users will not be able to imagine life without using Virtual Reality technology. In this paper, we will point out the qualities of Virtual Reality and its history. We will also point out the importance of development, which gives birth to new technology. Nowadays, we use mail for communication if the person is not sitting next to the user but, by the usage of technology, distance is not a matter. This type of technology contributes to an enormous scope to allow the user to explore the 3D world and users' imagination. It has several applications, from entertainment to product developments. It is still in the development stage with a large scale of users creating their customizable applications and setups to meet their expectations [44].

3.2.1   Use of Virtual Reality in Education

Educating the present and the future generation of children from America to live in an informatics society is included as a critical issue. It is recognized to provide life-long education for people and to support a flexible workplace. Virtual Reality technology is globally proposed as a significant technological advance that can give support for such education. There are many ways in which Virtual Reality is expected to advance learning. One unique capability is the ability to authorize students to visualize mental concepts, to see the events at atomic or planetary scales, and to be able to attend environments. Also, to be able to interact with a variety of events at the time, distance, or safety factors that make it unavailable. These types of activities reinforced by this capability advance the present educational thinking that allows students to better master, retain, and generalize the new knowledge by being actively involved in constructing that knowledge in a learning-by-doing situation [46]. The potential in the usage of Virtual reality to be able to support education is globally recognized. Several programs are designed to be introduced to a significant number of students and teachers. To allow technology has been authenticated. A large number of academic schools have constructed a research program to examine the key issues, and some of the public schools are learning the technology. It is proved to be seen practical use an estimated number of 20 or more public schools and colleges and many more to have been used in evaluations or research efforts. The large scale of educational uses of Virtual Reality technology was able to involve students to use pre-developed Virtual Reality applications in which the students one by one visit the virtual world to be able to learn some of the basic concepts or for example to be able to construct an understanding of different periods in history. Time by time, students may be required to construct their virtual world to lead the research of understanding and display of their grasp of non-scientific or scientific material [46].

Virtual reality was first used to help disabled children, but it has additionally expanded to the field of education. The technology was firstly used for on how to learn to use a wheelchair and driving among the children with sensory-motor disorders, which showed significant results. The success showed supported the search for further usages of Virtual Reality, which eventually led to a new application in science educations. The improvements have since helped the students to learn scientific phenomena and manage experiments in the field of chemistry, physics, and biology [47]. The capabilities of VR technology allow the students to observe the effects of changing physical laws, to see the events of atomic or planetary scale, to be able to picture the abstract concept and to be able to visit environments and interact with them as demonstrated above. Other benefits contain the ability to acknowledge good practices such as demonstrate numeral representations and placing at least more or fewer instructions under the learner's control [46].

3.2.2 Virtual Reality and Games

New technology opens up new possibilities. In this case, it is the same with games. Virtual reality technology can be accessed using the VR set. Thanks to this concept, many new projects have been opened. Game designing uses these technologies but not all games are used for entertainment purposes. Some games are designed to help people, for example, with their phobias. New moots are used, new concepts are created, and new types of games appear on the squads of stores [48]. In the beginning, several game concepts were created. Players have increasingly started playing games using VR. This enabled better and more powerful games to be created. Then experimentation began and more and more various genres of games in VR began to appear. Based on research, scientists have come to the point that playing games generate a variety of ideas in a participative and targeted manner [3].

Virtual reality games are starting to appear more and more. These types of games can slowly begin to displace normal games, just as they did with classic games. Thanks to the fast development of games, better and better ways and solutions appear to facilitate the creation of games. In recent years, VR games have been thought to be seen as larger than normal games [12]. VR games allow personal interaction in the virtual world. With the help of scanners, the real traffic is moved to the virtual world, which means that a person can experience to some extent how it would be there. This is a very interesting concept because it is only the beginning of this technology and is still being improved to more effectively reach the virtual world. In addition, this technology can be used for many good purposes such as mental therapy [49].

3.3 Mental Health

3.3.1 Importance of Good Mental Health

Mental health is a personal matter and Individual for every human being, especially the state in which the mind is. Factors such as society, the environment, or culture can affect how the mind is shaped and may have positive or adverse effects. However, ultimately, only the owner of this mind can influence the state of his or her mind [50]. Normal behavior or standard mental health is challenging because it depends on the place, culture, time, and social group. Namely, a different state or nationality has a different standard than the one in which the person lives. Mental health is of value for many people. Taking all these facts into account makes this harder to ascertain the correct standard of healthy mental state or mental illness. During consideration, if a person is sick or healthy mentally, it is required to a distinction between attributes and actions is required. Considering long-term behavior, whether a person is more or less healthy depends on that person's persistent attributes. However, through actions, it is also possible to state the psychological state in one short, direct situation [50].

The positive state of mental health considers the combination of being fully functional and subjective well-being. Positive mental health gives positive feelings and proper function in society. The positive state can be Considered in two separate philosophical terms: the hedonic perspective, which talks about the importance of honesty and friendliness, and the eudemonic perspective that determines behavior and thinking that the person feels fulfillment and commitment [49]. A state in which a person is entirely mentally healthy is a state in which the person's thinking is positive. Positive thinking is essential for people, families, and society. When a person is satisfied, his or her productivity and involvement in society increases. People who have weak mental health increase spending on mental support and their contribution to society is getting worse. All these negatives impacts may contribute to the economic problem, which results in a low quality of life and severe problems. Mental health is critical in society, and the mental problem is not only burdening of one but all the people closest to this person and society are affected [51].

3.3.2 Work of Game with the Human Mind

Nowadays, games are so popular that millions of adults play them and above all, millions of young people. In the states in 2015, around 40% of people play for at least a few hours a day. Games have gained popularity because they can enormously drag people into their world. They use better and better patents and technologies that sometimes a person feels as if they were already inside the game. Furthermore, each new game adds something new and different from other games. Studies have shown that high-quality games increase concentration, help in learning, and change behavior [52, 53].

The human mind is a very complicated place, and because games are generally available, many people use them, mainly children. Games have begun to gain popularity ever since they also began to teach people many things. Most of the games have a message that is to be given to the user. The games can be used for good or evil purposes. However, players spend a considerable amount of time in a given game. Players begin to identify with the character or with what is happening in a particular game. The more addictive the game, the easier it is to start memorizing and learning those things that happen in a given game. Furthermore, after some time, the player starts learning more and more. Eventually, it begins to affect the behavior or perception of the person [54]. Games are now available all over the world and can be used for a variety of purposes, but some games can be made for better purposes such as education and health care. To create a game that could be more attention to the term as mental health in three steps: the first to increase the reach to all people even to those who have not previously used them. Secondly, increase the number of visitors through the development of educational games and, thirdly, the use of mechanics in the field of therapeutics and educational functions [52].

3.3.3 VR and Mental Health

Over the past decade, plenty of virtual reality (VR) applications has been created to help people who have mental health problems and also understand and evaluate these problems. Sophisticated applications allow users to be physically fully immersed and experience many things in a virtual environment. This experience happens because the user is, in a certain sense, excluded from the real world to the virtual world through image and sound stimuli from the application. Modern devices such as gloves for data transfer allow a user to feel with the user's fingers what is happening in the simulation. So, a person can experience with the help of the three senses touch, hearing, and sight what is happening in the virtual world. These simulations allow the user to experience in a very detailed way what is done in virtual reality, and it has a significant influence on the mind of a person [55]. Many applications Virtual reality is created for mental therapy to treat all kinds of phobias. For example, some phobias can be cured, such as fear of height, arachnophobia, or cockroaches. Other uses of virtual reality are used to treat post-traumatic stress disorder or test anxiety disorder. Some applications are used to help in rehabilitation and help cognitive assessment of people who have schizophrenia, dementia, or brain injuries or stroke. The greatest success is noted in the fight against phobias. Even though treatment in this way is easy and cheaper, under certain conditions, there is also a risk that the phobia may get worse or harm treatment. On the other hand, thanks to the fact that this treatment can cure phobias that can be expensive and dangerous under normal conditions, e.g., in the case of flying phobia. Additionally, the patient feels safe and is not directly exposed to his fear, and confidentiality is maintained because everything usually happens in the therapist's office [55].

Virtual reality, like any entertainment, can addictive interaction in a world where it attracts players with beautiful visual effects, well-composed sounds, and other sensory stimuli. All effects are made in such worlds is to engage players more, and this kind of interaction can have a therapeutic effect on the user. On the other hand, research into the use of VR in medications has also been successful, but the number of participants is not insignificant in such tests. Research is still needed within this period to determine the usefulness of virtual reality clearly. However, promising results of the intervention in virtual reality have been revived in the treatment of Post-Traumatic Stress Disorder (PTSD) in virtual Iraq. VR games are popular, so probably more research in this direction will be conducted [52].

3.4 Alternatives Ways to Video Games

3.4.1 Children and Their Time

Today, children spend more time at home than ever before, because many electronics are now readily available, which means that all kinds of entertainment at home are available. This situation makes children more vulnerable than adults to the harmful effects of this type of environment. According to research, children are spending more time at home all over the world. Most of these children are at the age of 5 to 12 years [56]. In the last decade, all sorts of new technologies have been created that have entertainment goals. Such devices are television, consoles, telephone, and portable consoles. Nowadays, children are overwhelmed by screen entertainment. Research carried out in 2004–2007 results from average child spend about 6 h a day before the screen, which is a more or less equal time that children spend at school [57]. The problem that children spend a significant amount of time in front of computers or consoles is, in most cases, that both parents work, and there is no time to raise a child. Lack of time to meet with children is one of the reasons why children fall in front of computers. Another case is after a hard day, the parent has no strength and is not thinking about what his child is doing. In the last case, the parent is not caring about what the child is doing. The lack of any interest in what the children do with their time is irresponsible from the parents' side. This kind of situation leads to where game raises these children [58].

3.4.2 Reducing the Time that Children Spend with Video Games

The first step to change usually is to change his habits. It is best to start slowly. At first, the parent should reduce the time that a child spends playing games. It is best to start by moving the computer and the console from the child's room, this will make the child spend 40 min less a day playing. Parents should go with their children. The study shows that children who travel with their parents spend 30 min less playing each day. Besides, to prevent a child from playing the wrong game, a parent should check what the game contains, as it may contain inappropriate content for a young person [59]. Creating a schedule by the parent and child how much time a child spent playing games and how much time the child will be able to play next week. To convince the child more, a parent should do some challenges, such as spending less time in front of the screen than last week. To encourage children, more parents can also use the time with games as a reward for doing homework. Parents should not use games as a moment of peace, on the contrary, parents, and children should spend more time, e.g., cooking together a complicated recipe in this way, encourage the child to try other things. The most important thing for a parent is to be patient and not give in [59]. There few alternatives to video games and television:

Outdoor: Playing outside is very important for a young person because it allows him to develop in many ways. The cultivation of sports or games that require the whole mass of movement is an excellent chance for a child to be able to develop the body but also to have a great time. The child also has a chance to meet new people and connect with other children. A child can make new friends and spend time with them. By exploring, the child learns and develops his mind. All this happens in the open air. It is an excellent way for a child to grow in the right way [60].

Indoor: When a child cannot go outside due to bad weather or late hours, there are still things better than sitting in front of a computer. Cooking with parents brings much fun and teaches children how to cook various recipes. Spending time playing board games or card games develops the mind of a young man and teaches a child to make different decisions and, above all, develops imagination. Painting and creative creation of various things by a child develop his talents and also develops imagination. Reading books with parents or telling different stories is also a great way to spend time together and develop a child's mind [59].

3.5 Devices and Software

3.5.1 VR Set

When on the market, there was inexpensive virtual reality equipment that allows research into which the researcher can conduct observations of naturally moving objects. One known such system is HTC Vive, which includes goggles which serve as a display from a computer and besides tracking systems in a designated room. It is all at a reasonable price if the sophisticated tracking precision and sufficient accuracy allow this device to be used for many tests [61]. Figure 1 represents HTC VIVE set. This set contains HTC goggles, two pads and adapters. Adapters track the movement of goggles and pads and send information to the computer. Goggles and pads allow interaction with a virtual environment. The operation of viral graphics consists of the integration of images from graphics sounds from the program and other sensory data such as a plugin with gloves in real-time into one virtual world. The best thing is that the user can feel most things when interacting with a given object. The image from the virtual world is transmitted by the head-mounted display set (HMD).

Fig. 1. Picture of all components from HTC Vive Set [62]

This type of goggles which look like helmet usually contains two small screens built-in. The newer type of this type of goggles has built-in headphones. Everything the user does is tracked and sent to a computer that will adapt everything to the user's actions. Minimum system and hardware requirements are, for example, a Pentium IV computer with a minimum 2 GHz circuit power, 40 GB memory as well as sound and audio functions [55].

3.5.2 Unity

Unity is a game engine, and it was developed in Denmark by Unity Technologies. This engine integrates a custom rendering engine with the NVidia PhysX physics engine and Mono. Mono is open-source, and it is an implementation of Microsoft's.NET libraries. The Unity engine works with complete documentation with examples for its entire API. This complete documentation is the most significant advantage. It allows for increased productivity when compared to other engines such as Source or Unreal, which functionality only provides partial documentation for non-subscribing customers. There is plenty of online developer in the community, which can often help or provide assistance for new developers. The Unity Technologies developers also are very willing to add new concepts and features to Unity at a user's request, which will never happen in case of using a big developer's engine such as Unreal. Several of the features existing as a result of requests from different developers of the SARGE [63]. Figure 2 represents a graphical user interface of Unity during the curation of 3D project. On the left side objects, on the right-side properties of a specific object, on the bottom list of the object that can be added. In the middle is windows which show the 3D project.

In the field of physics properties, objects can be several factors that can be used to determine bounciness, springiness, mass, also features such as detection of a collision. The psychic is simulated by NVidia's PhysX engine, which is used by many games that are made for AAA purposes. Rendering properties include even features such as shader

Fig. 2. Unity example of unity project [64]

and texture that affect the appearance of the visible objects. The built-in rendering software uses a simplified shader language designed with DirectX9 or OpenGL 2.0 software, depending on the target device. Unlike other gaming links such as Unreal or Source to create the game, the cost per license alone would cost $ 300,000, while Unity provides free access only for brushes over $ 100,000, a user must buy the license [63].

3.5.3   C# Programming Language

C # is easy-to-use, object-oriented, one of the new languages, and values security, such a programming language is C#. This programming language combines the excellent performance of application programming with C++ and C output. This language was designed by a team of developers and was the ultimate technical reference to the C # language [65].

4   Conclusion

Since the creation of games, a lot has changed in the appearance and message of the original series of games. New technologies implemented in games attract more and more people. It often happens that violence is the main factor in these games. Especially that many people can learn something useful from games or just the opposite. Games are for people, and everyone likes some games, whether it is classic computer games. The more games there are, the more games there will be players. Everyone can find something for themselves and conclude the games. With more and more players, games have become part of the modern world. Thanks to the successes in the new markets, games are of increasing importance—most on the American market. With the spread of games, people pay more and more attention to what games bring to their lives. Most games are used for entertainment purposes. Some people use them for education. There are also people who only want to make as much money as possible from them. Young people most like games. It allows them to learn new things, increase their perceptiveness and draw conclusions. They are increasing physical fitness if games contain factors such as physical movement. Games allow the player to expand his or her imagination and take dull moments away. Games have many advantages, but they also have disadvantages.

Many popular games contain mainly violence. Violence is already part of the games. Although violence is part of the games, it is still unclear what effects it can have. It is known, however, that depending on the individual factors of this type of game can be harmful. Games of violence can affect human behavior in society, especially in children. Other cases may affect aggressive behavior or aggravation of negative feelings. The debate on the effects of this type of game has been conducted for a long time. Much research has been carried out, and many applications have been released. Most say that this game has psychological and social effects, especially for children. Games are entertainment and a break away from reality. This makes the player spend more and more time playing games. This can lead to adverse psychological and physical effects, for example, radiation, stress, obesity, headache, vision problems and muscle problems. In addition to games, another technology that is rapidly evolving is virtual reality. Let it create something new in virtual reality. One limit in virtual reality is imagination. This new technology is expanding massively, mainly for developmental purposes and for the treatment of various phobias. Cat games are created for virtual reality, and they are often needed to use a set of goggles and a mouse pad that allows the player to interact in the game on a similar basis as in reality. This allows for a completely new gaming experience, but also new threats. Mental health is an essential part of every human being. On mental health has many internal and external associates that can affect his condition. It is vital to keep it in good condition as it may have adverse effects. Games that emanate bad aspects can, over time, significantly affect human behavior. It can also affect human behavior in society. They are more vulnerable to young people and people in stressful situations. Youth is a significant period for many people. Because during this period a young person can get to know the world, shape his views on various topics and meet many people. It is hard to do when young people spend all their time in front of the screen. Gaming absorbs them to spend most of the day playing games. When the world outside offers many new experiences. Especially parents should know about how important this period is for their children and how their games may have an impact on their children. So, people should be able to spend time without electronic devices and with their family at home or outside.

References

1. Rutter, J., Bryce, J.: Understanding Digital Games. Sage, London (2006)
2. Bryce, J., Rutter, J.: Gender dynamics and the social and spatial organization of computer gaming. Leis. Stud. **22**(1), 1–15 (2003)
3. Shaffer, D.W., et al.: Video games and the future of learning. Phi Delta Kappan **87**(2), 105–111 (2005)
4. Berger, A.A.: Video Games: A Popular Culture Phenomenon. Transaction Publishers, New Brunswick (2017)
5. Santos, I.K.d., et al.: Active video games for improving mental health and physical fitness—an alternative for children and adolescents during social isolation: an overview. Int. J. Environ. Res. Public Health **18**(4), 1641 (2021)
6. Mayer, R.E.: Computer games in education. Annu. Rev. Psychol. **70**, 531–549 (2019)
7. Nagasaka, K.: Sony QRIO. In: Goswami, A., Vadakkepat, P. (eds.) Humanoid Robotics: A Reference, pp. 187–200. Springer, Dordrecht (2019). https://doi.org/10.1007/978-94-007-6046-2_16

8. Bègue, L., et al.: Video games exposure and sexism in a representative sample of adolescents. Front. Psychol. **8**, 466 (2017)
9. Rodán, A., et al.: Boys and girls gain in spatial, but not in mathematical ability after mental rotation training in primary education. Learn. Individ. Differ. **70**, 1–11 (2019)
10. Jenkins, R.: Children spend twice as long looking at screens than playing outside, study finds (2018)
11. Emes, C.E.: Is Mr Pac Man eating our children? A review of the effect of video games on children. Can. J. Psychiatry **42**(4), 409–414 (1997)
12. Granic, I., Lobel, A., Engels, R.: The benefits of playing video games. Am. Psychol. Assoc. **69**(1), 66–78 (2013)
13. Mohammed, M., Al-Sharify, T., Kolivand, H.: Real-time cloth simulation on virtual human character using enhanced position based dynamic framework technique. Baghdad Sci. J. **17**(4), 1294 (2020)
14. Chuang, T.-Y., Chen, W.-F.: Effect of computer-based video games on children: an experimental study. In: 2007 First IEEE International Workshop on Digital Game and Intelligent Toy Enhanced Learning (DIGITEL 2007). IEEE (2007)
15. Anderson, C.A., et al.: Longitudinal effects of violent video games on aggression in Japan and the United States. Pediatrics **122**(5), e1067–e1072 (2008)
16. Anderson, C.A.: An update on the effects of playing violent video games. J. Adolesc. **27**(1), 113–122 (2004)
17. Giumetti, G.W., Markey, P.M.: Violent video games and anger as predictors of aggression. J. Res. Pers. **41**(6), 1234–1243 (2007)
18. Kirsh, S.J.: Seeing the world through Mortal Kombat-colored glasses: violent video games and the development of a short-term hostile attribution bias. Childhood **5**(2), 177–184 (1998)
19. Markey, P.M., Scherer, K.: An examination of psychoticism and motion capture controls as moderators of the effects of violent video games. Comput. Hum. Behav. **25**(2), 407–411 (2009)
20. Durkin, K., Barber, B.: Not so doomed: Computer game play and positive adolescent development. J. Appl. Dev. Psychol. **23**(4), 373–392 (2002)
21. Olson, C.K.: Media violence research and youth violence data: Why do they conflict? Acad. Psychiatry **28**(2), 144–150 (2004)
22. Savage, J., Yancey, C.: The effects of media violence exposure on criminal aggression: a meta-analysis. Crim. Justice Behav. **35**(6), 772–791 (2008)
23. Anderson, C.A., Ford, C.M.: Affect of the game player: short-term effects of highly and mildly aggressive video games. Pers. Soc. Psychol. Bull. **12**(4), 390–402 (1986)
24. Calvert, S.L., Tan, S.-L.: Impact of virtual reality on young adults' physiological arousal and aggressive thoughts: Interaction versus observation. J. Appl. Dev. Psychol. **15**(1), 125–139 (1994)
25. Graybill, D., Kirsh, J.R., Esselman, E.D.: Effects of playing violent versus nonviolent video games on the aggressive ideation of aggressive and nonaggressive children. Child Study J. **15**(3), 199–205 (1985)
26. Schutte, N.S., et al.: Effects of playing videogames on children's aggressive and other behaviors1. J. Appl. Soc. Psychol. **18**(5), 454–460 (1988)
27. Cooper, J., Mackie, D.: Video games and aggression in children1. J. Appl. Soc. Psychol. **16**(8), 726–744 (1986)
28. Silvern, S.B., Williamson, P.A.: The effects of video game play on young children's aggression, fantasy, and prosocial behavior. J. Appl. Dev. Psychol. **8**(4), 453–462 (1987)
29. Graybill, D., et al.: Effects of playing versus observing violent versus nonviolent video games on children's aggression. Psychol. J. Hum. Behav. **24**(3), 1–8 (1987)
30. Braun, S., Pasternak, J.: Student Opens Fire on Prayer Group, Kills 3. Los Angeles Time, California (1997)

31. Brooke, J.: Terror in Littleton: The Overview; 2 Students in Colorado School Said to Gun Down as Many as 23 and Kill Themselves in a Siege, vol. 21. New York Times (1999)
32. Calvert, C.: Violence, video games, and a voice of reason: judge Posner to the defense of kids' culture and the first amendment. San Diego L. Rev. **39**, 1 (2002)
33. Moser, R.S., Frantz, C.E.: Shocking Violence: Youth Perpetrators and Victims - A Multidisciplinary Perspective. Charles Thomas Publisher (2000)
34. Anderson, C.A., Bushman, B.J.: Effects of violent video games on aggressive behavior, aggressive cognition, aggressive affect, physiological arousal, and prosocial behavior: a meta-analytic review of the scientific literature. Psychol. Sci. **12**(5), 353–359 (2001)
35. Bushman, B.J.: Moderating role of trait aggressiveness in the effects of violent media on aggression. J. Pers. Soc. Psychol. **69**(5), 950 (1995)
36. Arriaga, P., et al.: Violent computer games and their effects on state hostility and physiological arousal. Aggressive Behav. Official J. Int. Soc. Res. Aggression **32**(2), 146–158 (2006)
37. Berry, B.: 7 worst common health problems caused by computer use (2017)
38. Carbonari, K., et al.: Increased micronucleated cell frequency related to exposure to radiation emitted by computer cathode ray tube video display monitors. Genet. Mol. Biol. **28**(3), 469–474 (2005)
39. Deitel, M.: Overweight and obesity worldwide now estimated to involve 1.7 billion people. Obesity Surg. **13**(3), 329 (2003)
40. Rosenfield, M.: Computer vision syndrome: a review of ocular causes and potential treatments. Ophthalmic Physiol. Opt. **31**(5), 502–515 (2011)
41. Seghers, J., Jochem, A., Spaepen, A.: Posture, muscle activity and muscle fatigue in prolonged VDT work at different screen height settings. Ergonomics **46**(7), 714–730 (2003)
42. Provenzo, E.F., Jr.: Video Kids: Making Sense of Nintendo. Harvard University Press, Cambridge (1991)
43. Shaker, N., Togelius, J., Nelson, M.J.: Procedural Content Generation in Games. Springer, Cham (2016). https://doi.org/10.1007/978-3-319-42716-4
44. Mandal, S.: Brief introduction of virtual reality & its challenges. Int. J. Sci. Eng. Res. **4**(4), 304–309 (2013)
45. Bricken, M., Byrne, C.M.: Summer students in virtual reality: a pilot study on educational applications of virtual reality technology. In: Virtual Reality, pp. 199–217. Elsevier (1993)
46. Youngblut, C.: Educational Uses of Virtual Reality Technology (No. IDA-D-2128). Institute for Defense Analyses. Alexandria, VA (1998)
47. Inman, D.P., Loge, K., Leavens, J.: VR education and rehabilitation. Commun. ACM **40**(8), 53–59 (1997)
48. Rendon, A.A., et al.: The effect of virtual reality gaming on dynamic balance in older adults. Age Ageing **41**(4), 549–552 (2012)
49. Huppert, F.A.: Positive mental health in individuals and populations (2005)
50. Jahoda, M.: Current concepts of positive mental health (1958)
51. Rohrer, J.E., Pierce, J.R., Jr., Blackburn, C.: Lifestyle and mental health. Prev. Med. **40**(4), 438–443 (2005)
52. Fleming, T.M., et al.: Serious games and gamification for mental health: current status and promising directions. Front. Psych. **7**, 215 (2017)
53. Read, J.L., Shortell, S.M.: Interactive games to promote behavior change in prevention and treatment. JAMA **305**(16), 1704–1705 (2011)
54. Fudenberg, D., et al.: The Theory of Learning in Games, vol. 2. MIT Press (1998)
55. Gregg, L., Tarrier, N.: Virtual reality in mental health. Soc. Psychiatry Psychiatr. Epidemiol. **42**(5), 343–354 (2007)
56. Silvers, A., et al.: How children spend their time: a sample survey for use in exposure and risk assessments. Risk Anal. **14**(6), 931–944 (1994)

57. Rideout, V.: Parents, Children & Media: A Kaiser Family Foundation Survey. Henry J. Kaiser Family Foundation, Oakland (2007)
58. Hayes, C.D., Kamerman, S.B.: Children of Working Parents: Experiences and Outcomes. ERIC (1983)
59. Kris, A.: Alternatives to TV and Video Games for Your Elementary School Child. The Parent Institute (2004)
60. Rivkin, M.S.: The Great Outdoors: Restoring Children's Right to Play Outside. ERIC (1995)
61. Niehorster, D.C., Li, L., Lappe, M.: The accuracy and precision of position and orientation tracking in the HTC vive virtual reality system for scientific research. i-Perception **8**(3), 2041669517708205 (2011)
62. HTC Corporation Website (2011). https://www.vive.com/uk/product/vive-pro-full-kit/?gclid=CjwKCAjw7P1BRA2EiwAXoPWA2AsKNJcZPEeSsWcxlKxT9PZEgzKEMoxWxmuQyMrxQAThHS7lQRThoCHDEQAvD_BwE
63. Craighead, J., Burke, J., Murphy, R.: Using the unity game engine to develop Sarge: a case study. In: Proceedings of the 2008 Simulation Workshop at the International Conference on Intelligent Robots and Systems (IROS 2008) (2008)
64. Unity website (2020). https://unity3d.com/unity/beta/2019.3
65. Hejlsberg, A., Wiltamuth, S., Golde, P.: C# Language Specification. Addison-Wesley Longman Publishing Co., Inc. Boston (2003)

Review of Gamified MOOC's Impact Toward Learner's Motivation in Learning Effectiveness Context

Wei Kian Tan[1], Mohd Shahrizal Sunar[2,3]([✉]), and Eg Su Goh[2,3]

[1] Raffles University, 80000 Johor Bahru, Johor, Malaysia
alextanwk@raffles-university.edu.my

[2] Media and Game Innovation Centre of Excellence, Institute of Human Centered Engineering, Universiti Teknologi Malaysia, 81310 Johor Bahru, Malaysia
{shahrizal,eg.su}@utm.my

[3] School of Computing, Faculty of Engineering, Universiti Teknologi Malaysia, 81310 Johor Bahru, Johor, Malaysia

Abstract. Massive Open Online Courses (MOOC) have become a strong support for building a ubiquitous learning environment typically during Covid19 pandemic. Although more and more Internet users are willing to try MOOC, the problems corresponding to users' free and autonomous learning are a poor learning experience, low long-term attractiveness to users, and low completion rate of courses. The fundamental reason is that online learning behaviour cannot be well motivated and maintained. A key design concept related to the MOOC is gamification design - the application of game design elements to non-gamification scenarios. Some MOOC has integrated different gamification method to attract users. However, the academic community's attitude towards gamification still inconsistent, and even some studies believe that the level of user motivation in the gamified design condition will decrease. From the perspective of user information behaviour, this paper follows the logical route of "motivation-behaviour" and analyse the perceptual challenge and perceptual attention, learning results and cognitive user participation. From the MOOC context, this paper discusses the technical application factors that affect user behaviour and enriches the research direction in the field of information behaviour. Lastly, this study puts forward some development suggestions to MOOC operators to comprehensively improve the perception challenge and attention of MOOC users and enhance their learning effect.

Keywords: MOOC · Competitive gamification design · Collaborative gamification design · Motivation factor · Learning effectiveness

© ICST Institute for Computer Sciences, Social Informatics and Telecommunications Engineering 2022
Published by Springer Nature Switzerland AG 2022. All Rights Reserved
Z. Lv and H. Song (Eds.): INTETAIN 2021, LNICST 429, pp. 189–207, 2022.
https://doi.org/10.1007/978-3-030-99188-3_12

1 Introduction

Under the catalysis of Internet 3.0, education is continuously undergoing deep cross-border integration with the new generation of information technology. As a new and vital learning model, MOOC triggered a new wave of online learning and made researchers concerned about the latest development of education continue to think about promoting more effective teaching in MOOC.

1.1 Research Background

With the rise of online learning courses, the scale of Massive Open Online Courses (MOOC) has actively expanded while more learning applications have become more widely used especially during Covid 19 Pandemic [1]. However, the high dropout rate and low completion rate of courses hindered the sustainable development of the learning platform [2]. As a novice way to stimulate and maintain learning motivation, gamification design has won the favour of many learning platforms to attract potential users. So far, the research on the factors affecting the behaviour of MOOC participants has mostly focused on individual characteristic, motivation, cognition, emotion, society landscape only [3]. This research will focus on the influence of user motivation on learning effect under the conditions of MOOC gamification design. According to the concept of "motivation factor-behaviour result", clarify the influence of different gamification on motivation level and the effect of motivation factor on the final learning effect [4]. This paper synthesizes all relevant research results related to motivation and immersion theory, MOOC and gamification design.

2 Theoretical Basis

Different researchers have classified motivation according to various criteria. Thus there is no consistency about existing taxonomies and other categories. The following three are the most widely used in this paper.

2.1 Malone's Intrinsic Motivation Theory

Motivation is derived from the Latin word "Movere", which means to promote and cause activity. Motivation is the inner psychological power of individual activities guided by goals (a key driving factor to stimulate and maintain individual behaviour) [5]. Efficient learning activities cannot lack the support for learning motivation.

Through the research on computer games, Malone identified three types of motivational factors related to learning: challenge, curiosity, and fantasy, and proposed the "intrinsic motivation" theory, which directly reveals the motivational drive of gamification elements and mechanisms in learning activities [6]. First, a system must provide a sense of challenge can essentially motivate learners [7], and secondly, stimulating curiosity will attract learners [8]. Thus, it's emotionally attractive fantasies could engage the users to participate in learning activities [9]. Malone believes that people are immersed in games not because of external rewards, but because of the existence of intrinsic motivation.

1) **Challenge:** Compeau et al. believe that challenges provide individuals with opportunities to develop abilities and enhance self-efficacy, which is related to improving learning outcomes [10]. Applying gamified design elements can create challenges in online learning platforms. Recent research results in the field of education are consistent with Malone's research, players must work hard to overcome the challenges which lead to uncertain ending/result [4].

2) **Curiosity:** Second key motivation factor, including cognitive curiosity and perceptual curiosity. Loewenstein proposed that when users perceive their lack of knowledge, they will have cognitive curiosity, which will encourage users to participate in the learning process to improve their knowledge structure [11]. Clark and Paivio believed that in the learning process, sensory stimuli such as novel colours, sounds, images, etc. will trigger perceptual curiosity and make users focus to the learning task at hand [12]. In short, a proper gamified design could promote curiosity that enhances participation (engagement) and learning outcomes (fill up knowledge gaps).

3) **Fantasy:** Another motivation that workable in a learning environment. Fantasy occurs when people imagine something in their mind. Malone pointed out that fantasy could enable learners to meet their emotional needs and experience power, reputation and wealth that are not available in real life [13]. On the other hand, it allows learners to acquire knowledge and establish a connection with the real world. Research on online training shows that learning materials in a virtual context could improve learner's participation and learning effects [14].

Compared with ARCS Motivation and Flow theories, Malone's intrinsic motivation theory has two unique advantages in guiding the research on the influence of gamification design on motivation. First of all, Malone's theory was developed by observing children playing various computer games, so it is particularly suitable for guiding the selection of game elements. Park and Liu et al. integrated gamification elements based on Malone's intrinsic motivation theory in their learning platform. Research has shown that gamification systems can have a positive impact on learners' learning effects [4, 6, 15]. Therefore, this study includes Malone's intrinsic motivation theory.

2.2 ARCS Motivation Theory

Professor Keller proposed the ARCS motivation theory in 1983 through his research on motivation theories [16]. ARCS was summarised from Attention, Relevance, Confidence and Satisfaction [17].

a. **Attention:** It refers to attracting and maintaining the learners' interest in the learning process. It can arouse the learners' attention by arousing perception, stimulating inquiry, and using variability.

b. **Relevance:** It reflects that the teaching objectives and content should be related to the learner's own needs and knowledge background to make it feel personally relevant, such as establishing a virtual situation associated to the learner's current experience or interest.

c. **Confidence:** It refers to the establishment of self-confidence by various methods such as solving difficulties and achieving success, such as providing students with tasks and challenges within the scope of their ability to help them establish a correct view of attribution.

d. **Satisfaction:** It refers to allowing learners to experience the joy and value of learning by obtaining positive results and feeling fair, and to be satisfied in the learning process, such as learning new knowledge/skills and obtaining rewards.

Research shows that the ARCS motivational design model is one of the most effective instructional design models to reduce the dropout rate of online education [18]. Therefore, this study draws on the ARCS motivation theory as the theoretical basis to study the background of user learning behaviour of online learning platforms.

2.3 Flow Theory

Flow Theory was proposed by Csikszentmihalyi [19]. In his research, he found that immersion is a state of full-heartedness. When people engaged by the activities they are participating in, they will be highly concentrated. Creativity and potential can be effectively stimulated, focusing only on specific goals and ignore irrelevant things and ideas. Jackson and Marsh summarised nine factors that produce immersive experience: challenge-skills balance, action-awareness merging, clear goals, instant feedback, concentration on the task at hand, sense of control, loss of self-consciousness, a transformation of time and autotelic experience [20].

As one of the primary research contents of positive psychology, immersion experience has attracted more and more attention in the fields of education, psychology and information technology. Current research related to immersive experience focuses on exploring the self-affirmation brought by immersion and the subsequent behaviour of users [21]. Immersive experience has a very positive impact on learning activities, helps to explore behaviours, and promotes the mastery of information technology [22]. Users have an immersive experience in gamification design will stay energetic and passionate. Therefore, the gamification design of online learning platforms should fully consider the elements of "immersion" experience [23]. This article summarises the motivation factors involved in the above three theories, as shown in Table 1.

Through the above research conclusions, it shows that challenges and attention as motivational factors could trigger the immersive experience. Csikszentmihalyi believes that the challenge is the key to maintaining the immersive experience between the individual and the task. When the individual's skill level and the challenge are balanced, immersive experience will exist. Rheinberg et al. proposed that users feel the immersion only when attention and challenge-skill level exist at the same time [24].

Table 1. Motivation factor.

Factor	Malone intrinsic motivation theory	ARCS motivation theory	Flow theory
Challenge	X		X
Curiosity	X		
Fantasy	X		
Attention		X	X
Relevance		X	
Confidence		X	
Satisfaction		X	

3 Massive Open Online Class (MOOC)

The continuous opening and sharing of educational resources have led to the emergence of Massive Open Online Courses (MOOCs), which have swept the world at an astonishing speed and become a new research hotspot in the field of open education. It is a new online course model that is free and open to society and a way of learning across time and space in the education field in recent years [25]. MOOC provides rich teaching resources (mostly in the form of multimedia), interactive forums, and learning communities. Based on the student-oriented and teacher-led teaching philosophy, MOOC organises large-scale distributed worlds in a network environment with similar goals, interests, and prior knowledge and complex types. Besides, students with different habits manage to stimulate their interest in learning in the MOOC platform which allows socialising individual learning and life-long learning experience [26].

3.1 Classification of MOOC

Since the development of MOOC in 2008, 2 main branches have evolved: Connectivist MOOCs (cMOOCs) and Expanded/Extension MOOCs (xMOOC) [27]. cMOOCs based on the relevance theory of learning, which is typically represented by the Connectivism and Connective Knowledge (CCK08) online courses offered by Canadian scholars Stephen Downes and George Siemens [28]. xMOOCs is based on behaviourist learning theory, represented by Coursera, Udacity and edX [29, 30, 31]. With the coexistence of cMOOCs and xMOOCs, if universities and social organisations do not distinguish between these two types of MOOC when building MOOC, it will have many unfavourable consequences.

3.2 cMOOCs

Learning theory is a systematic interpretation of the essence of learning and its formation mechanism, conditions and laws [32]. Its fundamental purpose is to provide people with a basic understanding of learning, to lay a more scientific foundation for forming their views on education and teaching. The theoretical basis of cMOOCs is the relevance theory of learning. Connectivism is a new learning theory proposed by George Simmons for the digital age in 2004 [33]. It is an integration of principles explored through chaos, network, complexity and self-organisation theory. Connectivism regards learning as the process of network formation and believes that the essence of learning is the process of creating networks and forming connections. It has two meanings: one is to use the internet to support the learning process, and the other is how to learn on the internet. The existing cMOOCs emphasise creation, creativity, autonomy, social-networking learning. They focus on the generation of knowledge and encourage learners to find resources on the Internet to learn independently, aiming to let learners study by themselves [34]. Therefore, cMOOCs exhibit the primary characteristics of connective-based learning theory.

The cMOOCs is a single independent course, and each cMOOCs has its course content. Individual teachers assemble and implement on the Internet, use diversified platforms, and can use various social software. Learners can choose freely according to their conditions or preferences. The cMOOCs course model encourages learners to participate in multiple blogs, forums and other platforms. Besides, cMOOCs is a distributed learning environment that emphasis student autonomy [35]. Moreover, universities and institutions are not participating in the course planning while only the educators arrange the courses from the beginning until the end alone [36]. The organisers of these popular cMOOCs courses are mostly scholars who study cMOOCs.

For cMOOCs, new learners will be instructed to operate and participate in the platform. At the same time, the beginners have advised on learning skills, and learners are encouraged to tutor and support each other. In terms of resource connection, Stephen Downes developed the gRSShopper application, which is a tool used to aggregate key content in cMOOCs courses. In the cMOOCs course, gRSShopper not only aggregate the resources discovered and suggested by the learners, but also get the posts and Twitter messages in the discussion area, and finally combine these resources into a daily news release to send to the learners [37]. These can effectively help learners build their learning network and support their learning.

In cMOOCs, learners allowed open discussions, and there is no strict right or wrong in evaluating learners [38]. Therefore, in the course of cMOOCs course operation, there is not too much timely feedback on the learning process of learners, and there is no too much learning. The evaluation of the learner's learning effect. Learners can decide how much material they read, how much time they spend studying, and what form of study they use. Learners can also interact with teachers in real-time. As for the effect of learning, teachers use RRS aggregated resources for comprehensive evaluation. Learners could conduct mutual evaluation among themselves. The evaluation standard of cMOOCs is whether learners can successfully carry out autonomous learning without the support and help of educators.

3.3   xMOOCs

Unlike cMOOCs, the theoretical basis of xMOOCs is behaviourist learning theory [39]. Behaviourism's explanation of learning emphasises the acquisition of observable behaviours. What an individual learns are determined by environmental stimuli. When the connection between environmental stimuli and individual behavioural reflections has reinforced, the corresponding behavioural habits form "learning" [40]. The theory has four fundamental viewpoints: a) learning is a process of stimulus-response connection; b) learning is a process of trial and error; c) learning is a process of student observation and imitation; d) learning is a process of operational reinforcement. xMOOCs pays attention to augmentation process, knowledge repetition, and traditional learning methods such as video demonstrations, short quizzes and tests [41]. Therefore, xMOOCs show the characteristics of behaviourist learning theory.

xMOOCs has a strong organisation and operation team. The team is composed of project managers, lecturers, teaching assistants, course volunteers, producers, filming teams, technical support teams together with a large amount of capital investment. To implement xMOOCs, learners only need to complete all the course learning, discussion and testing processes of their elective courses on a single platform. The platform generally cooperates with many world-renowned universities. Universities could publish and share their courses on the MOOC platform with learners around the world for their elective courses [42]. For example, Coursera and edX have gathered courses from famous schools and educators from all over the world.

Compared with cMOOCs, the learning support services of xMOOCs are more technical. The number of xMOOCs courses continues to increase, and the number of learners participating is also enormous. The large-scale and open characteristics of xMOOCs determine the demand for learning support services and attract learning support service providers on the market [43]. Example, Class-Central provides indexing functions, CourseBuffet, Knollop, and CourseTalk that provide evaluation and recommendation functions, CourseMiner provides community functions and Pearson and ProctorU that provide examination functions. The xMOOCs platform cooperates with these learning support service websites to provide a better environment for learners to learn.

Different from cMOOCs, learners can obtain instant learning feedback in the process of learning xMOOCs [27]. A quiz will be embedded in the lecture video to test the learner's mastery of the knowledge base on the section of the content. Else, a final exam will be prepared to obtain the learning effect of the learner's entire unit or the entire course. The evaluations are all carried out on the platform. After completion, the intuitive evaluation results will be displayed. Learners could check their learning condition in time. Teachers can analyse the test results of learners to understand their mastery of knowledge and recommend personalised learning resources. The evaluation standard of xMOOCs is whether learners have the same or similar knowledge as educators [44]. Table 2 will analyse the difference between cMOOCs and xMOOCs.

4   MOOC Gamification Design

Professor Richard Batle, a pioneer of multiplayer online games [45]. The original intention was to "turn things (or work) that are not games into games". In 2003, Nick Pelling adopted the concept of "gamification" when designing the game interface of electronic devices [46]. Until 2010, the term "gamification" began to be widely used [47].

Table 2. Comparison of cMOOCs and xMOOCs.

Subject	CMOOCs	XMOOCs
Learning Theory	Connectivist learning theory, focusing on knowledge creation	Behavioural learning theory, focusing on knowledge repetition
Course Organization	Educator-oriented	A strong teaching team supports the courses
Course Implementation	Distributed on various platforms	Centralized, on a unified platform
Course Content	Unstructured, through various resources created when learners participate in topic discussions	Structured, mainly through videos and lectures for teaching
Course Range	Narrow, mainly in the particular module / subjects	A wide range of subject areas
Learning Support	Conduct tutorials, use tools to aggregate resources and send daily emails / notification	The platform cooperates with learning support service providers to provide learners with learning support services
Feedback	Limited instant feedback	Instant pre-set feedback
Learning Evaluation	Teachers conduct comprehensive evaluations through aggregated resources; learners evaluate each other	Quiz and peer assessment
Evaluation Standard	Could learners successfully carry out autonomous learning without the support and assistance of teachers	Does the learner acquire the same or similar knowledge as the teacher

4.1 Gamification

The concept of "gamification" can be traced back to 1978. It was introduced by The definition of gamification proposed by Deterding in 2011 has been widely recognised [48]. Generally speaking, gamification is the application of game design elements to non-game situations. Early Game-Based Learning (GBL) explored the integration of learning activities into mature and complete games [49]. Glover believes that gamification design requires the addition of a game layer to a well-established online learning system to provide more design flexibility [50]. Besides, he believed gamification is only an auxiliary design - a game element that exists in the learning activity, rather than direct learning in the game. Based on studies, individual performance and satisfaction are expanded by implementing appropriate gamified elements [51]. At present, gamification has become part of the core structure in the online learning platforms.

In the context of the information system, the positive influence of motivation on user information behaviour has been supported by a considerable number of scholars. Gorbunovs et al. researched computer-supported collaborative learning through investigation methods and found that in the learning process, there is a correlation between learners' motivation and knowledge acquisition and learning activities [52]. Kormos and Csizer put forward the factors that affect the learning effect of learners in the network environment and believes that learning motivation is an important personal factor that affects the ability of autonomous learning [53]. Prasetya research shows that learning motivation can effectively improve learning effects and attractiveness [54]. Reinhold et al. found that learners' motivation has a significant and positive impact on learning effects through random sampling methods [55]. Although there have been a lot of proofs for the internal logical relationship of "motivation factor-behaviour result", there are still few studies to analyse in-depth whether online learning platform gamification design can affect the relationship between motivation and learning effect. Secondly, which motivational factors are more conducive to improve learning effects still need to be discussed in depth.

4.2 MOOC Gamification

Low effective participation and high dropout rate are the two major problems that currently exist in MOOC learning. Although MOOC is a comprehensive learning resource, a large number of studies have shown that more MOOC learners are more willing to skip other course links and only spend time watching the course videos. However, the problem of high dropout rate makes the viewing of course videos in MOOC learning also worrying. Relevant studies show that among all users who register for courses, no more than 50% of users persist until the end of the course [56, 57]. In other words, a large number of MOOC learners did not even insist on watching the course videos.

In response to the above problems, researchers in many countries have begun to try to integrate gamification and MOOC. They believe the addition of gamification elements can stimulate the learning motivation of MOOC learners, thereby solving the two major problems in current MOOC learning. For example, ESADE Business School (Spain) integrates two online games MetaVals and Hot-ShotBusiness in MOOC courses to help learners learn financial concepts and investment [58]. Saudi Arabia's mainstream MOOC platform RWAQ, through the integration of gamification, makes the courses more effective. The completion rate has increased to 20%–25%, far exceeding the global average of the completion rate of MOOC courses of no more than 10% [59]. German researchers have integrated gamified competition elements with peer evaluation, which improves the enthusiasm of MOOC learners to participate in peer evaluation [60]. Based on this, it is recommended that the current MOOC platform should integrate with gamification [61, 62]. In addition to related research, many mainstream MOOC platforms, such as Coursera, edX and Udacity have begun to increase support for gamification elements.

Although the enthusiasm for gamification design in the practical world is high, and each MOOC has launched its own gamification design to attract users, the research results of the academic world have shown inconsistencies. Hew's research shows that the introduction of gamification design in curriculum learning has no significant impact on learners' learning effects [63]. Hanus believes that adding gamification design will harm learners' learning effects [64]. De-Marcos et al. confirmed that gamified online learning experience could fully improve teaching effects [65].

Table 3 and 4 summarise the gamification elements and motivation mechanism used by cMOOCs and xMOOCs.

Table 3. cMOOCs gamification.

Gamified MOOC platform		Moodle	Google classroom	Blackboard	Gami press
Gamification elements	Point	✓	✓	✓	✓
	Progress bar	✓		✓	✓
	Badges	✓	✓	✓	✓
	Level	✓	✓		✓
	Leader board	✓	✓	✓	✓
	Achievement	✓		✓	✓
	Mutual assistant	*	*		*
	Challenge (ad-hoc)	✓	✓	✓	✓
Motivation mechanism	Emotion		*		*
	Relevance of content	*	*	*	*
	Narrative	*	*	*	*
	Progress	✓	*	✓	✓
	Relationships	✓	✓	✓	✓

✓ - Yes, * - Depends on user setting/plugins

Table 4. xMOOCs gamification.

Gamified MOOC Platform		Coursera	edX	Udacity	Udemy	Edmodo
Gamification elements	Point	✓	✓	✓	✓	✓
	Progress bar		✓	✓	✓	
	Badges	✓	✓	✓	✓	✓
	Level			✓	✓	✓
	Leader board	✓	✓	✓		
	Achievement					
	Mutual assistant		*			✓
	Challenge (ad-hoc)	✓				✓
Motivation mechanism	Emotion					*
	Relevance of content	*	*	*	*	*
	Narrative	*	*	*	*	*
	Progress	✓	✓	✓	✓	✓
	Relationships	✓	✓	✓	✓	✓

✓ - Yes, * - Depends on user setting/plugins

In general, the gamification components used in these cases are focusing on points, badges, and rankings. On the other hand, gamification motivation mechanisms mainly involved emotions, progress, and relationships. The current integration of gamification and MOOC has two main characteristics. First, the gamification element embeds on existing MOOC platform via plugins. Secondly, learning materials (knowledge-based videos) embedded in a game platform. Currently, the main research gamification elements include leaderboards, badges, competitions, teams, etc. Gamification systems have a high degree of user communication and interaction [66]. According to the way of communication between users, those gamification design could be classified into two categories: competitive and cooperative [67]. This paper will explore the role of cooperative and competitive gamification design in MOOC platform. It mainly explores the influence of differences in motivation factors under different conditions and different gamification design conditions of competition and collaboration on the relationship between user motivation factors and learning effects.

4.3 Overview of Competition and Collaboration

Competition and collaboration are two common social phenomena, which can be seen everywhere in all aspects of life and study, from individuals to groups.

Competition is also the psychological and behavioural needs of individuals or groups trying to overcome the opponent, aiming to pursue attractive goals. Competition is the most epidemic gamification design in MOOC platforms, including leaderboards, championship and other elements. Competition could be adopted to stimulate learning motivation. Maller has done a comparative experiment and divided students into a control group and a competition group. The results show that the learning motivation of the competition group is significantly higher than that of the control group [68]. On the contrary, individuals with improper competitive psychology may have negative emotions such as tension, anxiety and low self-esteem due to irrational motivations and attitudes, which are not conducive to mental health and interpersonal relationship development [69].

Collaboration refers to the behaviour of multiple individuals working together for a common goal, resulting in beneficial results for all parties. Many studies have shown that cooperative behaviour has a positive impact on learners' interpersonal attraction and motivational motivation [70, 71]. The collaboration gamification design includes team formation, mutual help Q&A, check-in reminder, etc. Miquel and Duran propose in research that cooperative learning experience encourages learners to correctly recognise their abilities, reflect on themselves in the process of collaboration with others, and feel the learning content is directly related [73].

Competition and collaboration are of great significance to life, study, and work. They can enrich our interpersonal relationships and give us more opportunities for conversation in an online environment that lacks communication. This paper summarises the definition of collaboration and competition as shown in Table 5. Through the research on the characteristics of competition and collaboration, we could justify the possible impact of competition and collaborative gamification design.

Table 5. Competition v.s. collaboration.

	Competition	Collaboration
Positive meaning	Arouse achievement motivation and stimulate potential	Learn from others and improve efficiency
	Know your own strengths and weaknesses	Establish good interpersonal relationships
	Reflect self-worth and promote innovation	Get encouragement and help
Negative meaning	Too eager for quick success	Dependence, sit back and enjoy
	Produce unhealthy emotions such as tension and anxiety	Reduce the sense of responsibility and shirk each other's accountability
	Harm the interests of others	Laziness, loss of self-motivation

4.4 Perceive Challenge and Attention

Challenge is one of the essential motivation factors suggested in Malone's intrinsic motivation theory. Learners should receive appropriate challenges with a relevant degree of difficulty and complexity. At the same time, the challenge has a positive inherent motivational effect, which provides learners with an opportunity to develop their abilities thus enhance their sense of self-efficacy, which is related to strengthen the learning outcomes [74]. The ARCS motivation theory also proposes that all the tasks/mission must be sufficiently challenging as the difficulty should within the scope of the learner's ability. Those learners shall feel the opportunity to succeed, achieve results, and build self-confidence. Martelli 's research defines the perceptual challenge as the difficulty and complexity experienced by users in the process of acquiring knowledge [75].

ARCS Motivation Theory proposes that attention is another key motivation factor. It is necessary to attract and maintain the learner's attention during the learning process to arouse interest. First, the system inspires learners' interest via new, engaging, uncertain or conflicting content. Second, inspiring inquiry aims to construct problem situations to stimulate learners' desire to participate in exploration, analysis and problem-solving. In short, a system that promotes curiosity and increase attention could enhance learners' sense of participation and learning outcomes.

4.5 Gamification Design Conditions

Gamification systems have a high degree of user interaction. According to the way of interaction between users, the gamification design of MOOC platforms can be divided into two categories: competitive and cooperative [68].

A fundamental design element of a gamified information system is competition. Reeves considers one of the ten main characteristics of successful game design is competition [76]. However, competition creates the risk of losing motivation. The mass still believes that competition failure will lead to negative emotions and reduce the fun. Previous research has shown that losing in the game can negatively affect happiness and intrinsic motivation [77]. Although losing in the game may have a negative impact, a large amount of literature has also confirmed the positive impact of competition. In this paper, we will study the influence of motivational factors on learning effects under the conditions of competitive gamification design.

Regarding collaboration gamification design, some scholars believe that cooperation can put learners in a situation of equal respect, solidarity and mutual assistance. Collaboration gamification design elements (such as teaming, reminders, and likes) may have a certain effect on the formation and development of learning motivation. Cooperative gamification design conditions will not produce the anxiety or depression that may occur under competitive conditions. At the same time, it will not make learners have the idea of giving up after the competition fails.

4.6 The Moderating Role of Gamification Design

At present, there are few studies on the question of what motivational factors are more helpful to improve the learning effect under which gamification design conditions. By increasing the mission difficulty and creating competitive situations are effective ways to increase the challenge. In games, competition is regarded as a source of challenge, which gives the game an inherent motivational effect. Research has confirmed the role of competition as a source of player motivation and participation, although there may be individual differences [77]. Reeves et al. found that competition can increase the desire to do a good job and the sense of challenge, both of which can promote intrinsic motivation [78]. In a competitive external environment, users often face a series of major challenges such as ranking declines and slow progress. The pressure that users can feel increases, which stimulates them to learn more, which can strengthen the perception of challenge and the effect of learning impact. Competition could make individuals pay more attention to their abilities. When they value abilities or perceive challenges, individuals might become more engaged and perform better.

Collaboration can cultivate positive interpersonal relationships and connections between teammates, and guide individuals to value teamwork and personal contributions in it. Huang et al. believes that collaboration will affect intrinsic motivation in many ways so that each individual can experience the benefits of being a team member, work for a common goal, and develop a sense of belonging with their teammates [79]. The research of Wong and Yang showed that when players get instant feedback and can communicate smoothly with other participants, they will have more sense of composure, which may be a reason why people are addicted to the Internet. Under the condition of collaboration gamification design, team reminders, supervision, communication with teammates and peers, personal responsibility and sense of mission could prompt users to focus and strive to perform better and be more engaged.

In summary, this research believes that under the conditions of competitive gamification design, the perceptual challenge is one of the important motivational factors, which will have a significant impact on the learning effect of MOOC platform users. Table 6 summarise the gamification elements required when designing gamified MOOC based on competitive and collaborative context.

Table 6. Gamification elements for competitive and collaborative condition.

Category	Gamification elements
Competitive gamification design	Points
	Levels
	Leaderboard
	Scoring board
Collaborative gamification design	Points
	Levels
	Group scoring board
	Member reminder
	Mutual assistant (from group members)

5 Conclusion

The spectrum of online learning platform perceptual challenge is based on the following rules (Competition condition - Collaboration condition - Non-gamified condition). Participating in leaderboard score competition and group collaboration to complete tasks in the online learning process could improve users' perception of challenge. The pressure and tension in the competition process have a greater impact on users' perceptual challenge performance. Gamified MOOC users' perceptual attention is higher under collaborative condition compared with competition condition. Excessive attention to the leaderboard during the competition may distract users to a certain extent.

Regarding the moderating effect of gamification design conditions on the relationship between motivational factors and learning effects, the tense atmosphere under competitive conditions or the result of competition failure will make users lose confidence and motivation to continue working hard. Perceptual attention has a stronger positive impact on online learning platform users' learning outcomes and cognitive participation under the conditions of collaborative gamification design. Under collaborative conditions, the increased attention from teammates' reminders and self-responsibility supervision can further enhance users' learning results and cognitive participation. Regarding user perception and attention under competitive conditions are higher than non-gamification design conditions. One is that competitive conditions might cause users to pay too much attention to elements such as leaderboards, leading to competition for competition. The situation of competition may distract users' concentration to some extent. Second, some users find it difficult to accept the result of competition failure, and they will have a misleading mentality and give up their attention to follow-up learning.

Regarding the perceptual challenge under the conditions of competitive gamification design, the positive impact on the learning results and cognitive participation of online game platform users is higher. Although the competitive gamification design can fully enhance the perceptual challenge and make users feel pressure and tension, it has not produced the expected adjustment effect. Users only fight for the first place and ignore other things as they disgusted with the elements of competition or use deceptive means to participate in the competition. Under the condition of collaborative gamification design, the user's perceptual attention could be enhanced, whether it is due to the supervision and reminder of the collaborator or the promotion of self-fulfilment and responsibility. In this process, it positively regulates the relationship between perceptual attention and learning effect. The gamified system will prompt users to participate in the learning process and bringing higher progress to themselves and their peers.

In summary, intense competition did not bring about the desired effect. For one of the currently widely used gamification design elements in the leaderboard, nearly half of the research subjects denied its role. For precise mapping and gamification design, user/player type should be considered in future development. The gamified MOOC should be design using game elements based on user types as particular game element might not be suitable and some might negatively affect some user types. The influence of the skill level of peers and competitors on the learning effect of users is worthy of attention in future research.

Acknowledgement. This research was partially supported by Ministry of Higher Education and Media and Game Innovation Centre of Excellence, Institute of Human Centered Engineering, Universiti Teknologi Malaysia, Skudai, Johor, Malaysia through Malaysia Research University Network research grant (R.J130000.7809.4L870).

References

1. Yang, R.: China's higher education during the COVID-19 pandemic: some preliminary observations, pp. 1–5. Higher Education Research & Development (2020)
2. Goopio, J., Cheung, C.: The MOOC dropout phenomenon and retention strategies. J. Teach. Travel Tour. 1–21 (2020)
3. Zhang, M., Yin, S., Luo, M., Yan, W.: Learner control, user characteristics, platform difference, and their role in adoption intention for MOOC learning in China. Australas. J. Educ. Technol. **33**(1) (2017)
4. Van Roy, R., Zaman, B.: Need-supporting gamification in education: an assessment of motivational effects over time. Comput. Educ. **127**, 283–297 (2018)
5. Kulkarni, T.D., Narasimhan, K., Saeedi, A., Tenenbaum, J.: Hierarchical deep reinforcement learning: integrating temporal abstraction and intrinsic motivation. In: Advances in Neural Information Processing Systems, pp. 3675–3683 (2016)
6. Corona Martínez, D., Real García, J.J.: Using Malone's theoretical model on gamification for designing educational rubrics. In: Informatics, vol. 6, no. 1, p. 9. Multidisciplinary Digital Publishing Institute (2019)
7. Alsawaier, R.S.: The effect of gamification on motivation and engagement. Int. J. Inf. Learn. Technol. **35**(1), 56–79 (2018)
8. Svendsen, B., Burner, T., Røkenes, F.M.: Intrinsically motivating instruction—Thomas Malone. In: Akpan, B., Kennedy, T.J. (eds.) Science Education in Theory and Practice. Springer Texts in Education, pp. 45–53. Springer, Cham (2020). https://doi.org/10.1007/978-3-030-43620-9_4
9. Malone, T.W.: What makes things fun to learn? A study of intrinsically motivating computer games (1981)
10. Compeau, D., Gravill, J., Haggerty, N., Kelley, H.: Computer self-efficacy. In: Human-Computer Interaction and Management Information Systems: Foundations, pp. 225–261 (2006)

11. Golman, R., Loewenstein, G.: Curiosity, information gaps, and the utility of knowledge. Inf. Gaps Utility Knowl., 96–135 (2015)
12. Paivio, A., Clark, J.M.: Dual coding theory and education. Pathways to literacy achievement for high poverty children, pp. 1–20 (2006)
13. Gachkova, M., Somova, E.: Plug-in for creation of gamified courses in the e-learning environment moodle. In: IOP Conference Series: Materials Science and Engineering, vol. 618, no. 1, p. 012079. IOP Publishing (2019)
14. Cordova, D.I., Lepper, M.R.: Intrinsic motivation and the process of learning: beneficial effects of contextualization, personalization, and choice. J. Educ. Psychol. **88**(4), 715 (1996)
15. Park, J., Liu, D., Mun, Y.Y., Santhanam, R.: GAMESIT: a gamified system for information technology training. Comput. Educ. **142**, 103643 (2019)
16. Simsek, A.: Interview with John M. Keller on motivational design of instruction. Contemp. Educ. Technol. **5**(1), 90–95 (2014)
17. Li, K., Moore, D.R.: Motivating students in massive open online courses (MOOCs) using the attention, relevance, confidence, satisfaction (ARCS) model. J. Formative Des. Learn. **2**(2), 102–113 (2018)
18. Li, K., Keller, J.M.: Use of the ARCS model in education: a literature review. Comput. Educ. **122**, 54–62 (2018)
19. Nakamura, J., Csikszentmihalyi, M.: The concept of flow. In: Nakamura, J., Csikszentmihalyi, M. (eds.) Flow and the Foundations of Positive Psychology, pp. 239–263. Springer, Dordrecht (2014). https://doi.org/10.1007/978-94-017-9088-8_16
20. Jackson, S.A., Marsh, H.W.: Development and validation of a scale to measure optimal experience: the flow state scale. J. Sport Exerc. Psychol. **18**(1), 17–35 (1996)
21. Tsao, Y.C., Shu, C.C., Lan, T.S.: Development of a reminiscence therapy system for the elderly using the integration of virtual reality and augmented reality. Sustainability **11**(17), 4792 (2019)
22. Van Schaik, P., Martin, S., Vallance, M.: Measuring flow experience in an immersive virtual environment for collaborative learning. J. Comput. Assist. Learn. **28**(4), 350–365 (2012)
23. Zhang, Y., Chen, J., Miao, D.: Zhang, C (2018) Design and analysis of an interactive MOOC teaching system based on virtual reality. Int. J. Emerg. Technol. Learn. (iJET) **13**(07), 111–123 (2012)
24. Rheinberg, F., Vollmeyer, R.: Flow experience in a computer game under experimentally controlled conditions. Zeitschrift fur Psychologie **211**(4), 161–170 (2003)
25. Reich, J., Ruipérez-Valiente, J.A.: The MOOC pivot. Science **363**(6423), 130–131 (2019)
26. Steffens, K.: Competences, learning theories and MOOC s: recent developments in lifelong learning. Eur. J. Educ. **50**(1), 41–59 (2015)
27. Ping, W.: The latest development and application of massive open online course: from cMOOC to xMOOC. Mod. Distance Educ. Res. **3**(005) (2013)
28. Siemens, G., Downes, S.: Connectivism & connective knowledge. Universidad de Manitoba (2008)
29. O'Brien, K., Forte, M., Mackey, T., Jacobson, T.: Metaliteracy as pedagogical framework for learner-centered design in three MOOC platforms: Connectivist. Open Praxis **9**(3), 267–286 (2017)
30. Anyatasia, F.N., Santoso, H.B., Junus, K.: An evaluation of the Udacity MOOC based on instructional and interface design principles. In: Journal of Physics: Conference Series, vol. 1566, no. 1, p. 012053. IOP Publishing (2020)
31. Gimeno-Sanz, A., Navarro-Laboulais, C., Despujol-Zabala, I.: Additional functionalities to convert an xMOOC into an xLMOOC. In: Delgado Kloos, C., Jermann, P., Pérez-Sanagustín, M., Seaton, D., White, S. (eds.) EMOOCs 2017. LNCS, vol. 10254, pp. 48–57. Springer, Cham (2017). https://doi.org/10.1007/978-3-319-59044-8_6

32. Lopatiev, A., Ivashchenko, O., Khudoliy, O., Pjanylo, Y., Chernenko., Yermakova, T.: Systemic approach and mathematical modeling in physical education and sports (2017)
33. Zou, M., Chen, R., Su, M.: How to make traditional advanced mathematics classrooms walks out of MOOC storm. In: 2018 International Conference on Social Science and Education Reform (ICSSER 2018). Atlantis Press (2018)
34. Wang, Z., Anderson, T., Chen, L.: How learners participate in connectivist learning: an analysis of the interaction traces from a cMOOC. Int. Rev. Res. Open Distrib. Learn. 19(1) (2018)
35. Bozkurt, A., Honeychurch, S., Caines, A., Bali, M., Koutropoulos, A., Cormier, D.: Community tracking in a cMOOC and nomadic learner behaviour identification on a connectivist rhizomatic learning network. Turkish Online J. Distance Educ. 17(4), 4–30 (2016)
36. Foroughi, A.: MOOCs: the enduring importance of "teacher presence." J. High. Educ. Theory Pract. 16(6), 76 (2016)
37. Downes, S.: Applications, algorithms and data: open educational resources and the next generation of virtual learning (2017)
38. Joksimović, S., et al.: Exploring development of social capital in a CMOOC through language and discourse. Internet High. Educ. 36, 54–64 (2018)
39. Mahmod, M.A., Ali, A.M., Shah, A.: Massive open online courses as an augmentation of e-learning: a review. Int. J. Perceptive Cognit. Comput. 4(2), 1–4 (2018)
40. Dai, H.M., Teo, T., Rappa, N.: A understanding continuance intention among MOOC participants: the role of habit and MOOC performance. Comput. Hum. Behav. 112, 106455 (2020)
41. Newfield, C.: Aftermath of the MOOC wars: can commercial vendors support creative higher education? Learn. Teach. 9(2), 12–41 (2016)
42. Kaplan, A.M., Haenlein, M.: Higher education and the digital revolution: about MOOCs, SPOCs, social media, and the Cookie Monster. Bus. Horiz. 59(4), 441–450 (2016)
43. Renz, J., Schwerer, F., Meinel, C.: openSAP: Evaluating xMOOC usage and challenges for scalable and open enterprise education. Int. J. Adv. Corpo. Learn. (iJAC) 9(2), 34–39 (2016)
44. Ramírez-Montoya, M.S., Mena, J., Rodríguez-Arroyo, J.A.: In-service teachers' self-perceptions of digital competence and OER use as determined by a xMOOC training course. Comput. Hum. Behav. 77, 356–364 (2017)
45. Chou, Y.K.: Actionable Gamification: Beyond Points, Badges, and Leaderboards. Packt Publishing Ltd., Birmingham (2019)
46. Rigóczki, C., Damsa, A., Györgyi-Ambró, K.: Gamification on the edge of educational sciences and pedagogical methodologies. J. Appl. Techn. Educ. Sci. 7(4), 79–88 (2017)
47. Morschheuser, B., Hassan, L., Werder, K., Hamari, J.: How to design gamification? A method for engineering gamified software. Inf. Softw. Technol. 95, 219–237 (2018)
48. Deterding, S., Dixon, D., Khaled, R., Nacke, L.: From game design elements to gamefulness: defining "gamification". In: Proceedings of the 15th International Academic MindTrek Conference: Envisioning Future Media Environments, pp. 9–15 (2011)
49. Mavromihales, M., Holmes, V., Racasan, R.: Game-based learning in mechanical engineering education: case study of games-based learning application in computer aided design assembly. Int. J. Mech. Eng. Educ. 47(2), 156–179 (2019)
50. Glover, I.: Play as you learn: gamification as a technique for motivating learners. In: Edmedia+ innovate learning, pp. 1999–2008. Association for the Advancement of Computing in Education (AACE) (2013)
51. Nor, N.N., Sunar, M.S., Kapi, A.Y.: User experience of gamified virtual reality (VR) in sport: a review. In: Santos, H., Pereira, G., Budde, M., Lopes, S., Nikolic, P. (eds.) SmartCity 360 2019. LNICST, vol. 323, pp. 440–449. Springer, Cham (2020). https://doi.org/10.1007/978-3-030-51005-3_36

52. Gorbunovs, A., Kapenieks, A., Cakula, S.: Self-discipline as a key indicator to improve learning outcomes in e-learning environment. Procedia Soc. Behav. Sci. **231**, 256–262 (2016)
53. Kormos, J., Csizer, K.: The interaction of motivation, self-regulatory strategies, and autonomous learning behavior in different learner groups. TESOL Q. **48**(2), 275–299 (2014)
54. Prasetya, D.D., Wibawa, A.P., Ahmar, A.S.: Design of web-based lightweight interactive multimedia for distance learning. In: Journal of Physics: Conference Series, vol. 1028, no. 1 (2018)
55. Reinhold, S., Gegenfurtner, A., Lewalter, D.: Social support and motivation to transfer as predictors of training transfer: testing full and partial mediation using meta-analytic structural equation modelling. Int. J. Train. Dev. **22**(1), 1–14 (2018)
56. Rivard, R.: Measuring the MOOC dropout rate. Inside High. Educ. **8** (2013)
57. Ricart, S., Villar-Navascués, R.A., Gil-Guirado, S., Hernández, M., Rico-Amorós, A.M., Olcina-Cantos, J.: Could MOOC-takers' behaviour discuss the meaning of success-dropout rate? Players, auditors, and spectators in a geographical analysis course about natural risks. Sustainability **12**(12), 4878 (2020)
58. Cheek, D.W.: A panoramic view of the future of learning and the role of design(ers) in such experiences. In: Hokanson, B., Clinton, G., Tracey, M. (eds.) The Design of Learning Experience. ECTII, pp. 5–37. Springer, Cham (2015). https://doi.org/10.1007/978-3-319-165 04-2_2
59. Adham, R., Parslow, P., Dimitriadi, Y., Lundqvist, K.Ø.: The use of avatars in gender segregated online learning within MOOCs in Saudi Arabia-A Rwaq case study. Int. Rev. Res. Open Distrib. Learn. **19**(1) (2018)
60. Staubitz, T., Petrick, D., Bauer, M., Renz, J., Meinel, C.: Improving the peer assessment experience on MOOC platforms. In: Proceedings of the Third ACM Conference on Learning @ Scale, pp. 389–398 (2016)
61. Martínez-Núñez, M., Fidalgo-Blanco, Á., Borrás-Gené, O.: New challenges for the motivation and learning in engineering education using gamification in MOOC (2015)
62. Gené, O.B., Núñez, M.M., Blanco, Á.F.: Gamification in MOOC: challenges, opportunities and proposals for advancing MOOC model. In: Proceedings of the Second International Conference on Technological Ecosystems for Enhancing Multiculturality (2014)
63. Klemke, R., Antonaci, A., Limbu, B.: Gamifire - a scalable, platform-independent infrastructure for meaningful gamification of MOOCs. In: Liapis, A., Yannakakis, G., Gentile, M., Ninaus, M. (eds.) GALA 2019. LNCS, vol. 11899, pp. 256–265. Springer, Cham (2019). https://doi.org/10.1007/978-3-030-34350-7_25
64. Hew, K.F., Huang, B., Chu, K.W.S., Chiu, D.K.: Engaging Asian students through game mechanics: findings from two experiment studies. Comput. Educ. **92**, 221–236 (2016)
65. Hanus, M.D., Fox, J.: Assessing the effects of gamification in the classroom: a longitudinal study on intrinsic motivation, social comparison, satisfaction, effort, and academic performance. Comput. Educ. **80**, 152–161 (2015)
66. De-Marcos, L., Garcia-Lopez, E., Garcia-Cabot, A.: On the effectiveness of game-like and social approaches in learning: comparing educational gaming, gamification & social networking. Comput. Educ. **95**, 99–113 (2016)
67. Fan, J., Wang, Z.: The impact of gamified interaction on mobile learning APP users' learning performance: the moderating effect of users' learning style. Behav. Inf. Technol., 1–14 (2020)
68. Liu, D., Santhanam, R., Webster, J.: Toward meaningful engagement: A framework for design and research of gamified information systems. MIS Q. **41**(4) (2017)
69. Maller, J.B.: Cooperation and competition: an experimental study in motivation. Teach. Coll. Contrib. Educ. (1929)
70. Tauer, J.M., Harackiewicz, J.M.: The effects of cooperation and competition on intrinsic motivation and performance. J. Pers. Soc. Psychol. **86**(6), 849 (2004)

71. Tran, V.D.: Does cooperative learning increase students' motivation in learning? Int. J. High. Educ. **8**(5), 12–20 (2019)
72. Liao, C.W., Chen, C.H., Shih, S.J.: The interactivity of video and collaboration for learning achievement, intrinsic motivation, cognitive load, and behaviour patterns in a digital game-based learning environment. Comput. Educ. **133**, 43–55 (2019)
73. Miquel, E., Duran, D.: Peer learning network: implementing and sustaining cooperative learning by teacher collaboration. J. Educ. Teach. **43**(3), 349–360 (2017)
74. Panadero, E., Jonsson, A., Botella, J.: Effects of self-assessment on self-regulated learning and self-efficacy: four meta-analyses. Educ. Res. Rev. **22**, 74–98 (2017)
75. Martelli, E.: International student perceptual challenges and coping within higher education (2020)
76. Bharathi, A.K.B.G., Singh, A., Tucker, C.S., Nembhard, H.B.: Knowledge discovery of game design features by mining user-generated feedback. Comput. Hum. Behav. **60**, 361–371 (2016)
77. Vansteenkiste, M., Deci, E.L.: Competitively contingent rewards and intrinsic motivation: can losers remain motivated? Motiv. Emot. **27**(4), 273–299 (2003)
78. Reeves, N., West, P., Simperl, E.: A game without competition is hardly a game: the impact of competitions on player activity in a human computation game. In: AAAI (2018)
79. Huang, S.C., Etkin, J., Jin, L.: How winning changes motivation in multiphase competitions. J. Pers. Soc. Psychol. **112**(6), 813 (2017)

On-Device Image Labelling Photo Management System Using Flutter and ML Kit

Tan Chi Wee[✉] [ID] and Ken Ng Chen Kee

Tunku Abdul Rahman University College, 53300 Kuala Lumpur, Malaysia
chiwee@tarc.edu.my

Abstract. Automatic image annotation is the process by which the system automatically assigns relevant labels (metadata) to a digital image. This type of computer vision technique is mainly used in image retrieval systems to organize all the data and seek the interest of images from databases. This technique is also considered as a type of multi-class image classification. Regarding the past related work that had been done by the researchers, annotating digital images have also been used for the Academic Health Care Environment to solve the difficulty of business and graphic arts commercial-off-the-shelf (COTS) software in multi-context authoring and interactive teaching environments. As many pre-trained machine models have been created for the past few years, the requirement for existing models still needs a large set of data to be imported, and the usage of CPU hours is tremendously expensive. Google cloud API can outperform existing models in terms of computational complexity in obtaining image labels. The ML Kit firebase associated with Google Cloud Vision API is idealistically suited in this application, which can be useful in returning a set of labels that comes with a score that indicates confidence the ML model has in its relevance. With all of these labels, assembling all images on related labels is no longer a troublesome issue, and it can be quickly searched by querying on the back-end part.

Keywords: Computer vision · Object recognition · Artificial intelligence · Flutter · Machine learning

1 Introduction

The fundamental basis of image annotation technology is multi-class image classification. Many researchers try to make use of this technique into the mobile application because the trends of using mobile applications are proliferating. Mobile applications are portable to be used everywhere else, so, understandably, making use of mobile applications can effectively increase the living standard. There is a related work which uses the multi-classification approach to detect the malware which was intentionally installed into the local device to steal the user's sensitive information. There are numerous advancements in machine learning that contribute to cybercrime, especially malware. Multi-class classification is useful for assigning multiple labels in the application in order to have classes such as (i.e., spyware, rootkit, ransomware, etc.). This is to contain and cluster

Z. Lv and H. Song (Eds.): INTETAIN 2021, LNICST 429, pp. 208–222, 2022.
https://doi.org/10.1007/978-3-030-99188-3_13

all the malware families and their samples [1]. Moreover, there is an investigation on evaluating whether the performance of Google Cloud Vision API for image labelling is outperformed existing Machine Learning (ML) models in describing labelling. There are three methods proposed to annotate the images. The first method is directly processed by Google cloud vision. This method lacks considerations on the synonyms, so the accuracy is not on the ideal baseline. For the second method, validation is done to indicate whether the labels generated by Google Cloud Vision API were consistent with the instance label, and make a comparison using WordNet. The third method is released for a reason to solve the problem caused by the category labels named by a dataset. In this paper, we try to bring two gulfs, which is multi-class image classification into a mobile app with the help of Flutter and Google Cloud Vision without the needs of internet connection. In other words, the image labelling and recognition process are able to work offline independently. The rest of this paper is organized as follows: Section 2: literature review; Sect. 3: the proposed method and architecture; Sect. 4: all the experimental results and discussion are shown here; and finally, the conclusion is described in Sect. 5.

2 Literature Review and Related Work

2.1 Google Cloud Vision

Google Cloud Vision is an image recognition technology that allows a user to remotely process the content of an image and to retrieve its main features. By using a specialized REST API, called Google Cloud Vision API, developers exploit such a technology within their own applications. Currently, this tool is in limited preview and its services are accessible for trusted tester users only. The drawback of this service is that it requires network connection and cannot work standalone.

2.2 Flutter

Flutter is a framework developed by the Google team, which is built to focus on the development of both android and iOS. By using this framework has relatively some advantages in terms of optimization, Flutter uses widgets and dart programming language to create mobile or web applications from a single code base with high performance, and because the code is simplified, so the maintainability of the software is also high.

Every component in flutter is called a widget. A widget is formed by combining several other widgets, for example, Container widget consists of Align widget, Padding widget as well as `DecoratedBox` widget, etc. Creating a user interface in flutter is as similar to a person building a Lego toy by combining every piece of bricks. When each child widget inherits from its parent widget, it forms a hierarchical tree. If there is a need to respond to events, developers can simply use the framework to replace the necessary widget by looking at the constructed tree without deep diving into the codes.

2.3 Widget Lifecycle Events

In Flutter, there consists of two types of widgets to be used in the application, Stateless and Stateful widget. Stateful widget is used when there is the need for interaction from the user to change the current state of the widget, and the state of the stateless widget is unchangeable. Both of these widgets have a `build()` method which serves the purpose of building the widget itself. In this `build()` method, the parameter called `BuildContext` is an instantiation of the widget to indicate the location of this widget in the tree.

Stateless Widget. A stateless widget does not change dynamically, even the configuration has been modified. For example, the screen displays an image with a predefined name (usually the title does not change frequently). This type of widget has only one class; there consists of three ways of calling the stateless widget to be built. One method is that when the widget is first created, the parent of the widget changes and `InheritedWidget` has affected the widget.

Stateful Widget. The state of the `StatefulWidget` will be changed dynamically based on its configuration. For example, if the screen consists of a button which is to calculate a sum of an equation, in this case, the state(value) will be changed when the user clicks on the button. This type of widget is mutable, which means it can vary based on user interaction. Two classes are stated in this type of widget, State and Stateful widget. `StatefulWidget` class is rebuilt whenever the widget's configuration is different from the previous one. However, state class is still the same unless the `Stateful-Widget` is removed from the tree, then it will trigger the State class to be instantiated. New changes value will not repaint on to the screen without calling the `setState()` method. This is to notify the flutter's framework to listen to the changes of the widget and recall back to `build()` method to rebuild a new UI screen.

2.4 Widget Lifecycle Events

In [2], Abdalbasit Mohammed Qadir & Peter Cooper proposed a cargo tracking system that tracks the location of the cargo by integrating the GPS provided by Google and use Flutter framework as its codebase. Their objective is to develop a system which is applicable for cross-platform as well as Web applications. An example of a login screen is provided below (Fig. 1):

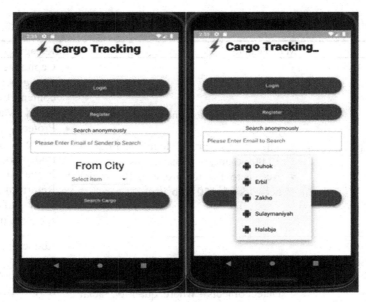

Fig. 1. An example of flutter application

They managed to build the login screen using only a single code base supported by the IOS and Android platforms. They indicate they can write a manageable code and simplify the time-consuming process for working on both platforms.

2.5   Object Detection and Image Labelling

Image annotation is a process of creating a set of data for those computer vision models. This helps the machines to automatically assign metadata into a digital image using relevant keywords and labels. This kind of technique commonly can be found in the image retrieval system, which can easily facilitate the machine to locate particular images from a database.

2.6   Comparison of Image Recognition Tool in the Market

Siham Bacha & Nadjia Benblidia [3] proposed a scheme by combining both content-based and context-based image annotation for automatic image annotation on mobile phones. The combination of these two approaches is to provide a standard feature understanding about the image in different aspects and to improve the description of the image on the high-level concepts. The significant drawbacks of this concept are that the combination brings heavy computation to achieve the final annotation for the AIA system [4].

Zhen Li et al. [5] proposed an image annotation system for media sharing that optimizes the content, context analysis and their integration to label images extracted from the client's mobile (Table 1).

Table 1. Image recognition tools in comparison.

Name	Main Features	Advantages
Talkwalker	• Analyse both text and images, in conjunction • The largest brand logo database - 30,000 logos, objects, scenes • Access to Twitter firehose, 10+ social networks & 150 websites	• Capitalize on user-generated content to boost brand awareness • Protect your brand against trademark abuse • Prove the true Return of investment of your sponsorship
Google Cloud	• Assign labels to images and categorize • Detect objects – where, quantity, facial attributes, landmarks, logos, text OCR • printed and handwritten, explicit content	• Reduce purchase friction with user-friendly mobile UX • Users can upload photo of an item & find similar to purchase
amazon Rekognition	• Easy to use API that doesn't require machine learning expertise • Analyse video and images - objects, people, text, scenes, activities, inappropriate content	• Consistent response times regardless of volume of requests • Facial analysis reveals age range, and sentiment • great for retail
clarifai	• Retrieve images that are similar to query image • Humans used to increase accuracy – for content moderation • Geolocation filter with pre-set parameters – latitude, longitude	• Identify suspicious behaviour happening on your property • Product discoverability based on visual features

(continued)

Table 1. (*continued*)

		– product recommendation
LOGOGRAB	• Find logos in infinite number of social media images, videos, GIFs • Extensive library of global and regional brands and marks	• Protect your brand with counterfeit detection • Deliver better customer service, real-time product demos, customer onboarding
IBM Watson	• Train with your own images to achieve unique, powerful results • Build custom classifiers by uploading training images for an application that can detect and tag images	• Computer vision service can learn any new object or person, & attribute – e.g., identifying car type and damage to estimate repair costs • Analyse visual content to optimize processes & ROI, decrease operational costs
imagga	• Auto tagging, auto categorizing, colour extraction, custom training, face recognition available to data sensitive businesses	• Empower product discoverability • Automated adult image content moderation • Analyse users' social media image content
CloudSight	• Users can expect an average response time of less than 250ms • Recognize objects by scanning phone around room • Filter and categorize images, monitor for inappropriate content	• Make things discoverable on your ecommerce site or through augmented product and image details such as

(*continued*)

Table 1. (*continued*)

		brand, style, type, and more • Let users sell items on your platform by uploading a picture
EyeEm	• AI used to find the best images to license to brands & agencies • Photos automatically tagged and captioned with objects and keywords to make searchable library	• Maximize engagement by determining the discoverability of each photo • Train the tool to maintain a consistent visual language on a global scale • Monitor and measure campaign metrics in real-time to improve content reach

In the content-based analysis, all the previously suggested tags from the media are corporate with the locations using the Gaussian Mixture Model (GMM). The intent of the user community facilitated the tagging process of the annotation system to suggest tag in future tagging. In order to reduce the computational cost for the content analysis process, a bag-of-words (BoW)-based approach with spatial pyramid matching [6] based on dense SIFT is adopted. According to them, by combining the content and context-based information, it brings about 16% and 15% performance improvement to the accuracy and recall rate for the tagging system.

L. Yu, J. Xie and S. Chen [7] proposed a scheme to solve the over-segmentized problem obtained from the segment-based conditional random field (CRF). It makes no sense in terms of statistical information if the extracted segment is too small. In other words, significant segments may not be consistent with the object boundaries, usually would bring error-prone to the process of labelling. The authors of this paper proposed a single-layered segment-based CRF, instead of a multi-layered based CRF, so multi-scale features of pixels, segments and regions can be combined. A modified version of the TextonBoost algorithm is used to determine which object class belongs to which pixel. This brings slightly better results to the recognition accuracy. Although high accuracy is obtained, the authors proposed the segment-based CRF to solve the problem of inaccurate boundaries caused by the pixel-based CRF. Another problem will also arise when pixels and segments are integrated further. In order to alleviate this problem, a region-based CRF is proposed to the model co-occurrence. The authors take this co-occurrence CRF as a post-processing method which results in the process being very fast and able to overcome some co-occurrence constraints violation errors.

3 Proposed Method

In this proposed method, the architecture in Flutter is divided into three different layers and an API provider, it is relatively significant to understand how the data is processed in the entire system and associated with external plugins (Fig. 2).

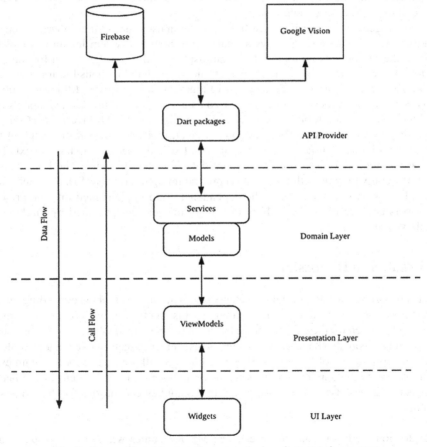

Fig. 2. Proposed architecture for an on-device photo tagging system

The architecture in Flutter is divided into three different layers and an API provider, it is relatively significant to understand how the data is processed in the entire system and associated with external plugins. The widgets in the user interface (UI) layer are a user control that inherits from the `DiagnosticableTree`. It plays a vital role in how the system layout is supposed to look like. It contains no logic other than displaying data on the screen for the user to view the result. In the presentation layer, the view model responsible for preparing and managing the data for an Activity or a Fragment. The purpose of this view model is to retrieve all the processed or unprocessed data from each of the defined models and combine them into an informative view and then pass it to the UI layer to perform the following rendering process. For the domain layer, models represent the shape of the data. A class in dart is used to describe a model. Particular services in the context class will be provided in order to retrieve stored data from the database. The last stage of the architecture diagram is the application programming interface (API), provider. Each plugin has its dart package. Once the dependencies are implemented into the project, developers are free to use these libraries to call the services provided by firebase or google vision.

The widgets in the user interface (UI) layer are a user control that inherits from the `DiagnosticableTree`. It plays a vital role in how the system layout is supposed to look like. It contains no logic other than displaying data on the screen for the user to view the result. In the presentation layer, the view model responsible for preparing and managing the data for an Activity or a Fragment. The purpose of this view model is to retrieve all the processed or unprocessed data from each of the defined models and combine them into an informative view and then pass it to the UI layer to perform the following rendering process. For the domain layer, models represent the shape of the data. A class in dart is used to describe a model. Particular services in the context class will be provided in order to retrieve stored data from the database. The last stage of the architecture diagram is the application programming interface (API), provider. Each plugin has its dart package. Once the dependencies are implemented into the project, developers are free to use these libraries to call the services provided by Firebase or google vision.

4   Result and Discussion

In this proposed, every image can be categorized with different labels depending on the extracted context information from the image. This can be very useful and convenient for a user to search for the wanted image based on the generated labels. Any inconsistent generated tags can also be modified, which is also a robust feature to enhance the flexibility and correctness of these tags. Processed image will not be re-process again even the user restarts the application. This feature can ensure the time taken for the heavy process in the classifying phase. There are two main key capabilities for this proposed system:

– Production-ready for common use cases: ML Kit comes with a set of ready-to-use APIs for common mobile use cases: recognizing text, detecting faces, identifying landmarks, scanning barcodes, labelling images, and identifying the language of text. Simply pass in data to the ML Kit library, and it gives the information that user need.

– On-device or in the cloud: ML Kit's selection of APIs run on-device or in the cloud. Our on-device APIs can process the data quickly and work even when there's no network connection. Our cloud-based APIs, on the other hand, leverage the power of Google Cloud's machine learning technology to give the user an even higher level of accuracy.

4.1 List of Categories

A total of 400+ categories can be recognized, each of the image can consist of either zero or more than one label(s) (Table 2 and Figs. 3 and 4).

Table 2. Categories that can be used to classify image, i.e., image label

Object and scene recognized				
Team	Monochrome	Speedboat	Penguin	Carnival
Bonfire	Chair	Trunk	Shikoku	Snowboarding
Comics	Poster	Coffee	Palace	Waterskiing
Himalayan	Bar	Soccer	Doily	Wall
Iceberg	Shipwreck	Ragdoll	Polo	Rocket
Bento	Pier	Food	Paper	Countertop
Sink	Community	Standing	Pop music	Beach
Toy	Caving	Fiction	Skiff	Rainbow
Statue	Cave	Fruit	Pizza	Branch
Cheeseburger	Tie	Pho	Pet	Moustache
Tractor	Cabinetry	Sparkler	Quilting	Garden
Sled	Underwater	Presentation	Cage	Gown
Aquarium	Clown	Swing	Skateboard	Field
Circus	Nightclub	Cairn terrier	Surfing	Dog
Sitting	Cycling	Forest	Rugby	Superhero
Beard	Comet	Flag	Lipstick	Flower
Bridge	Mortarboard	Frigate	River	Placemat
Tights	Track	Foot	Race	Subwoofer
Bird	Christmas	Jacket	Rowing	Cathedral
Rafting	Church	Pillow	Road	Building
Park	Clock	Bathing	Running	Airplane
Factory	Dude	Glacier	Room	Fur
Graduation	Cattle	Gymnastics	Roof	Bull
Porcelain	Jungle	Ear	Star	Bench

(continued)

Table 2. (*continued*)

Object and scene recognized

Team	Monochrome	Speedboat	Penguin	Carnival
Twig	Desk	Flora	Sports	Temple
Petal	Curling	Shell	Shoe	Butterfly
Cushion	Cuisine	Grandparent	Tubing	Model
Sunglasses	Cat	Ruins	Space	Marathon
Infrastructure	Juice	Eyelash	Sleep	Needlework
Ferris wheel	Couscous	Bunk bed	Skin	Kitchen
Pomacentridae	Screenshot	Balance	Swimming	Castle
Wetsuit	Crew	Backpacking	School	Aurora
Shetland sheepdog	Skyline	Horse	Sushi	Larva
Brig	Stuffed toy	Glitter	Loveseat	Racing
Watercolor paint	Cookie	Saucer	Superman	Airliner
Competition	Tile	Hair	Cool	Dam
Cliff	Hanukkah	Miniature	Skiing	Textile
Badminton	Crochet	Crowd	Submarine	Groom
Safari	Skateboarder	Curtain	Song	Fun
Bicycle	Clipper	Icon	Class	Steaming
Stadium	Nail	Pixie-bob	Skyscraper	Vegetable
Boat	Cola	Herd	Volcano	Unicycle
Smile	Cutlery	Insect	Television	Jeans
Surfboard	Menu	Ice	Rein	Flowerpot
Fast food	Sari	Bangle	Tattoo	Drawer
Sunset	Plush	Flap	Train	Cake
Hot dog	Pocket	Jewellery	Handrail	Armrest
Shorts	Neon	Knitting	Cup	Aviation
Bus	Icicle	Centrepiece	Vehicle	Fog
Bullfighting	Pasteles	Outerwear	Handbag	Fireworks
Sky	Chain	Love	Lampshade	Farm
Gerbil	Dance	Muscle	Event	Seal
Rock	Dune	Motorcycle	Wine	Shelf
Interaction	Santa claus	Money	Wing	Bangs
Dress	Thanksgiving	Mosque	Wheel	Lightning
Toe	Tuxedo	Tableware	Wakeboarding	Van
Bear	Mouth	Ballroom	Web page	Sphynx

(*continued*)

Table 2. (*continued*)

Object and scene recognized

Team	Monochrome	Speedboat	Penguin	Carnival
Eating	Desert	Kayak	Ranch	Tire
Tower	Dinosaur	Leisure	Fishing	Denim
Brick	Mufti	Receipt	Heart	Prairie
Junk	Fire	Lake	Cotton	Snorkeling
Person	Bedroom	Lighthouse	Cappuccino	Umbrella
Windsurfing	Goggles	Bridle	Bread	Asphalt
Swimwear	Dragon	Leather	Sand	Sailboat
Roller	Couch	Horn	Basset hound	Bride
Camping	Sledding	Strap	Pattern	Swamp
Playground	Cap	Lego	Supper	Pie
Bathroom	Whiteboard	Scuba diving	Veil	Bag
Laugh	Hat	Leggings	Waterfall	Joker
Balloon	Gelato	Pool	Lunch	News
Concert	Cavalier	Musical instrument	Odometer	Newspaper
Prom	Beanie	Musical	Baby	Piano
Construction	Jersey	Metal	Glasses	Plant
Product	Scarf	Moon	Car	Passport
Reef	Vacation	Blazer	Aircraft	Waterfowl
Picnic	Pitch	Marriage	Hand	Flesh
Wreath	Blackboard	Mobile phone	Rodeo	Net
Wheelbarrow	Deejay	Militia	Canyon	Icing
Boxer	Monument	Tablecloth	Meal	Dalmatian
Necklace	Bumper	Party	Softball	Casino
Bracelet	Longboard	Nebula	Alcohol	Windshield
Cookware and bakeware	Computer	Stairs		

Sky	96%
Cloud	95%
Building	94%
Infrastructure	89%
Asphalt	88%
Fixture	84%
Tree	80%
Road	79%
Composite Material	77%
Vehicle	73%
Engineering	71%
City	70%
Event	68%
Building Material	67%

Fig. 3. Sample photo 1, TAR UC main gate with its' image label

Food	98%
Tableware	92%
Fruit	92%
Ingredient	91%
Rangpur	91%
Plant	88%
Natural Foods	86%
Recipe	84%
Lime	84%

Fig. 4. Sample photo 2, fruit in a tableware with its' image label

4.2 Strength and Uniqueness

The classifier supports multiple categories' detection to a single image. In this context, the incorrect label(s) can be modified in order to correct the wrongly labelled categories for the particular image. Generated labels are stored in the client's local disk to ensure the next visit to the application will not re-classify again.

The system is able to generate tags to every image during the initialization stage. All the processed images can also be customized if they were wrongly labelled. And for the last objective stated, the application does not need to internet connection in order to perform classification, so this is also considered a success in achieving the objective written at the beginning. However, the application system still has a lot of room to improvement and the image labelling model have a lot of potential to be further enhanced.

As the number of images stored in a user's local device is increasing tremendously, people are interested to know what the image is all about. Therefore, a smart gallery application associated with the image labelling service is proposed in this project. Label all images with tags during the initializing stage is necessary, so that every image can be categorized into different sections with meaningful context. In order to make it more marketable, application programming interface such as Google Map, Social Share and Google search based on the selected tag are integrated with the system as well. In addition, a part of the system is also highly marketable which is the support of custom tags. The user of the application has the flexibility to edit those tags if those images are wrongly labelled. The first operation they can do is to create a tag and transfer to it. If the selected tag has already existed in the following labels, then it will not recreate another same label to the user. Another alternate operation is that they can remove the image from the labels, so by this way, all those inaccurate labelled images can be eliminated from the particular tag.

Dart is the backend tool attached with the flutter framework [8]. As there is a lack of plugins for monitoring changes in media store (It is a media provider that provides all the collection of images, audio, video from the storage devices). In this case, we need an approach to refresh all the new images captured from the external sources. Along with this project, a plugin for Flutter called `flutter_restart` also being proposed and developed with aims of refreshing all the images captured from external sources. This plugin has made for public can be downloaded from https://pub.dev/packages/flutter_r estart [9].

5 Conclusion

The core focus of the project is to create labels for image and photo with and on-device image labelling photo management system using Flutter and machine learning concept which make possible for users to search for related images based on the label on the image. Automatic generation of relevant textual annotations for images can play a crucial role in the performance of image search and image categorization. The effectiveness of browsing an image using annotations can be exclusively faster and even save much time if the system consists of an incredibly large number of images. Traditionally, an image can only exist in one folder, but it could have a decent amount of tags in one image. Although duplication of the same image can be done for both folders, however, this will cause memory wastage problems for the client's phone. By using image annotation technique, saving different key pairs for an image is way more efficient in terms of storage size.

References

1. Alswaina, F., Elleithy, K.: Android malware permission-based multi-class classification using extremely randomized trees. IEEE Access **6**, 76217–76227 (2018). https://doi.org/10.1109/ACCESS.2018.2883975
2. Qadir, A.M., Cooper, P.: GPS-based mobile cross-platform Cargo tracking system with web-based application. In: 2020 8th International Symposium on Digital Forensics and Security (ISDFS), June 2020, pp. 1–7 (2020). https://doi.org/10.1109/ISDFS49300.2020.9116336

3. Bacha, S., Benblidia, N.: Combining context and content for automatic image annotation on mobile phones. In: 2013 International Conference on IT Convergence and Security (ICITCS), December 2013, pp. 1–4 (2013). https://doi.org/10.1109/ICITCS.2013.6717813
4. Zhang, D., Islam, M.M., Lu, G.: A review on automatic image annotation techniques. Pattern Recognit. (2012). https://doi.org/10.1016/j.patcog.2011.05.013
5. Li, Z., Yap, K.-H., Tan, K.-W.: Context-aware mobile image annotation for media search and sharing. Signal Process. Image Commun. **28**(6), 624–641 (2013). https://doi.org/10.1016/j.image.2013.01.003
6. Li, Z.W., Zhang, J., Liu, X., Zhuo, L.: Creating the bag-of-words with spatial context information for image retrieval. Appl. Mech. Mater. **556–562**, 4788–4791 (2014). https://doi.org/10.4028/www.scientific.net/AMM.556-562.4788
7. Yu, L., Xie, J., Chen, S.: Conditional random field-based image labelling combining features of pixels, segments and regions. IET Comput. Vis. **6**(5), 459–467 (2012). https://doi.org/10.1049/iet-cvi.2011.0203
8. Ng, K.: Introducing flutter and getting started. In: Beginning Flutter®, pp. 1–23. Wiley (2019)
9. Tan, C.K., Chi, W., Ng, K.: flutter_restart | Flutter Package (2020). https://pub.dev/packages/flutter_restart

The Dynamic Scattering Coefficient on Image Dehazing Method with Different Haze Conditions

Noor Asma Husain[✉] and Mohd Shafry Mohd Rahim

School of Computing, Faculty of Engineering, Universiti Teknologi Malaysia, Johor Bahru, Malaysia
nasma4@live.utm.my, shafry@utm.my

Abstract. The dust, mist, haze, and smokiness of the atmosphere typically degrade images from the light and absorption. These effects have poor visibility, dimmed luminosity, low contrast, and distortion of colour. As a result, restoring a degraded image is difficult, especially in hazy conditions. The image dehazing method focuses on improving the visibility of image details while preserving image colours without causing data loss. Many image dehazing methods achieve the goal of removing haze while also addressing other issues such as oversaturation, colour distortion, and halo artefacts. However, some of the approaches could solve these problems and be effective at a certain level of haze. A volume of various haze level data is required to demonstrate the efficiency of the image dehazing method in removing haze at all haze levels and obtaining the image's quality. This study proposed a new dataset by simulating synthetic haze in images of outdoor scenes. The synthetic haze simulation is based on the meteorological range and works on specific haze conditions. In addition, this paper introduced a dynamic scattering coefficient to the dehazing algorithm to determine the appropriate visibility range for different haze conditions. These proposed methods improve on the current state-of-the-art dehazing method in terms of image quality measurement results.

Keywords: Haze · Scattering coefficient · Image dehazing · Atmospheric scattering model

1 Introduction

Air pollutants such as dust, sand, water droplets or ice crystals are responsible for the phenomenon of haze, fog, and mist atmospheric. These weather phenomena mainly differ in material, size, shape, and concentration. The haze seems to create a clear grey or blue hue and decreases visibility [1]. The haze of outdoor images is an estimated degradation, especially in computer visions, where the image contrast decreases when the light is scattered in particulate matter suspended. This causes low contrast and poor image visibility. The lack of details caused by haze makes images visually unattractive

Z. Lv and H. Song (Eds.): INTETAIN 2021, LNICST 429, pp. 223–241, 2022.
https://doi.org/10.1007/978-3-030-99188-3_14

and presents human and engine vision challenges, which restrain the identification, tracking or navigation of objects [2, 3].

The contributions control the optical thickness of the medium between the camera sensor and the captured object. Scattering and absorption reduce direct transmission from the image to the camera, creating another layer of ambient scattered light, known as air-light, as seen in Fig. 1. Koschmieder [4] proposed a haze-explained atmospheric scattering model in which poor image quality was caused by horizontal airlight dispersion and reflection, as well as propagation-based attenuation. Due to the attenuated direct transition, the scene's strength is diminished, and the scene's appearance is washed out due to the airlight. Earlier research has shown considerable improvement in approaches that use hazy images. Nayar and Narasimhan [1] estimate their depth, Cozman and Krotkov [5], with the use of atmospheric signals. Since then, many explicit methods have been established for enhancement of visibility and can be broken down into four categories: multi-picture methods [6], filter-based methods [7], proven depth or geometry methods [8] and single-picture methods. [9, 19].

Most of the dehazing single-image algorithms recently introduced different approaches to restoring the hazy look to a natural hazel-free image. Researchers have developed different methodologies on the same principle to retrieve the clean scene from the haze. An accurate medium of the transmission map is the primary purpose. The results of Tan [9] and Fattal [10] improved visibility for one image and automatically eliminated haze in a single image without further information, for example, known geometric information or user feedback. One of the system's drawbacks is the presence of a halo around the depth discontinuity due to local window activity. In his early investigation, Tan [9] received a less reliable estimate. Fattal [10] only functions successfully at low haze and its output decreases at medium and high haze. Fattal [15] proposes another approach based on colour lines but with low brightness. He et al. [11] and his colleagues discovered that most outdoor items have at least one colour channel significantly dark in clear weather. One of the techniques' drawbacks is their computational time, especially in real-time applications where the depth of the input scenes varies from frame to frame. Tarel and Hautiere [12] introduce a fast visibility restoration method with a complexity that is linear to the number of image pixels.

Meng et al. [13] expand the concept of the dark channel by introducing the lower limit before defining the initial transmission values. The transmission of He et al. [11], Meng et al. [13] is also a bit underestimated because the lower transmission boundary is essentially predicted. Estimates from He et al. [11] and Meng et al. [13] become more accurate with the increase in the haze. Ancuti proposes a colour distortion method for image fusion [14]. Tang et al. [16] provide a learning framework. The random forest regressor is used to learn how to associate the features with the transmission. The process yields multi-scale characteristics such as dark channel, maximum local contrast, hue disparity, and maximum regional saturation. Zhu et al. [17] propose Color Attenuation Prior (CAP), which is based on the difference between the saturation and brightness of the hazy image pixels. By using colour attenuation for model parameters to estimate the transmission depth prior to a supervised learning process. Cai et al. [18] propose a learning-based system in which a regressor is trained to predict the value of the transmission from its surrounding patch. The learning techniques, however, rely heavily on the white balancing stage with proper light colour. If minor mistakes in environmental colour measurements arise, their output decreases rapidly. Berman et al. [19] proposes a non-local prior algorithm. Berman makes a minor estimation error at medium hazards, but the error increases at low and heavy haze. Earlier research investigated the problems that were discovered when dealing with haze at various levels. Some of the approaches did not cater to dense haze levels or low haze levels [11, 19]. As a result, it emphasises the significance of image dehazing assessment at various haze levels. A dataset volume is required to meet this requirement to evaluate the efficiency of the image dehazing method in removing haze at all haze levels.

Although many algorithms are proposed for image dehazing, there are insufficient proven criteria or benchmarks for the evaluation of different haze levels. Six datasets for objective analysis algorithm were proposed in the works in advance: FRIDA [20], D-hazy [21], CHIC [22], HAZERD [23], O-HAZY[23] and I-HAZY [25]. FRIDA is highly specialised and presents numerous synthetic hazy road images from the driver's perspective. Indoor scenes not characteristic of the traditional dehazing programme, D-hazy uses depth images from Middlebury [26] and NYU depth V2 [27]. CHIC utilises a fog machine in an indoor setting and offers two indoor scenes with known objects and two scenes with window-viewed outdoor content.

This paper proposes a new dataset that simulates synthetic haze at four different levels based on the meteorological range, as shown in Table 2. The aim is to identify haze level in various atmospheric conditions [28, 29]. The datasets could evaluate the efficiency of future image dehazing to remove haze at any levels. Therefore, this paper also proposes the enhancement dehazing method with a dynamic scattering coefficient to improve the quality of the image in different atmospheric conditions.

Table 1. Haze databases.

Year	Method	Scene	Depth-based
2012	FRIDA [20]	Outdoor	Free-Space Segmentation (FSS)
2016	DHAZY [21]	Indoor	Stereo image
2016	CHIC [22]	Indoor	Actual distance
2017	HAZERD [23]	Outdoor	Fusing structure from motion and lidar
2018	IHAZY [25]	Indoor	Stereo images
2018	OHAZY [24]	Outdoor	Stereo images
2020	VHAZE* [29]	Outdoor	Actual distance

Our dataset

2 Atmospheric Scattering Model

The atmospheric scattering model proposed by Koschmieder [4] has two mechanisms, which are direct attenuation, $J(x) t(x)$, and air-light, $A(1-t(x))$, as shown in Fig. 1.

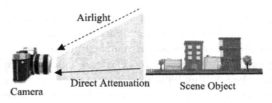

Fig. 1. Atmospheric Scattering phenomena

Haze algorithm combined these mechanisms, given by [3], as follows:

$$I(x) = J(x)t(x) + A(1 - t(x)) \tag{1}$$

where $I(x)$ is the haze image, $J(x)$ is the haze-free image, $t(x)$ is direct transmission, and A is the air-light. In early work, the most haze-opaque pixel was used to estimate air-light. Tan [9] chose the brightest pixel. Fattal [10] used it as an initial guess for an optimization query. The pixels with the highest intensity can be bright object instead of air-light. He et al. [11] states that the brightest pixel should be chosen between the pixels of the darkest channel with the highest brightest values. This is a functional method that generates reliable results. The most difficult part is to estimate the transmission maps $t(x)$ between the lightning of the camera and the scene. Distance, $d(x)$ from the camera observer is the point of the scene. The transmission of haze is physically associated with depth has been observed. Depth assessment is a major yet computer vision challenge [30].

$$t(x) = e^{-\beta d(x)} \tag{2}$$

For calculation of direct transmission, the atmospheric scattering component, β, distance or depth of the scene, $d(x)$, between the observation and the target object are used. It should be noted that the scene's depth is the most important information [4]. Since the scattering coefficient can be regarded as a constant homogenous state of the atmosphere, the medium transmission, $t(x)$, can easily be calculated with Eq. (2) if the depth is known. $t(x)$ in the scalar [0,1] represents a transmission map. Some issues, such as halo artefacts, may result in an incorrect transmission map estimate. Once the air-light and transmission map has been calculated, the hazy image, $J(x)$, can be restored to a haze-free appearance using Koshmieder's [4] Eq. (3):

$$J(x) = \frac{I(x) - A}{t(x)} + A \tag{3}$$

Equation (3) illustrates the formula from Eq. (1) for restoring a hazy image using estimated transmission and air-light. Most dehazing approaches used this formula, and instead of directly using the scattering coefficient, they proposed various techniques to obtain a transmission map. This paper improved the dehazing method by incorporating a dynamic scattering coefficient into our methodology, detailed in the following section.

3   Methodology

This section explains the research framework in Fig. 2 for the proposed dehazing algorithm. The haze simulation is determined using the model of atmospheric scattering in

Eq. (1). To get a haze image, $I(x)$ it requires a haze-free image, $J(x)$, air-light value, A and transmission value, $t(x)$. The default RGB value of an air-light is set to $[1, 1, 1]$. A clear image with a known distance $d(x)$ between the camera and the target is captured. The scattering coefficient is derived based on the captured distance map. Then it will calculate the transmission map value as in Eq. (2). Based on the air pollutant index and environmental conditions, the picture taken must be on a clear day to be classified as a haze-free image. The synthetic haze images were simulated in a clear image, which referred to the meteorological range [30]. The simulation creates four different haze conditions in a haze-free image.

This dehazing algorithm is primarily calculated by using Eq. (1) to apply the atmospheric scattering model. This process of pre-processing employs gamma correction on the hazy input image. Next, quadtree decomposition estimates air-light based on the corrected image brightness [31]. Following that, the scene depth estimated with Dark Channel Prior is used to compute haze thickness [11]. Based on the estimated scene depth, we compute the mean value to obtain the appropriate scattering coefficient value, β, based on the visibility range of the hazy image. Estimation of the visibility range uses a new visibility scale within the intensity range $[0, 1]$. In this framework, a visibility scale is an improvement that results in a dynamic transmission map. As a result, the visibility scale, based on mean value measurement, determines an appropriate scattering coefficient.

The scattering parameter β depends on the weather condition as in Table 2. The value of the visual range is specified as the distance at which the apparent contrast between an observer's dark object and the horizon sky is equivalent to an observation threshold of noticeable contrast, which is typically set at 0.02 in light conditions. Specifically, this scattering parameter is obtained from the visible range, R_m, via the relation $\beta = -ln(\epsilon)/R_m$ [23, 30]. Then, based on visibility range mapping, the new visibility scale refers to Table 1 to determine the scattering coefficient. Following that, based on the scattering coefficient and depth map parameter, the transmission map estimation in Eq. (2) was derived. Finally, the transmission and air-light values were incorporated into Eq. (3) to produce a dehazed image. Image enhancement, which is contrast stretching, is used in post-processing. The dehazed images are compared to the ground truth image using image quality assessments such as MSE, PSNR, and SSIM [32]. To experiment, the dehazing code was written in MATLAB 2017b and executed on a CPU (Intel i5 7200, 2.5 GHz 8 GB).

4   Haze Simulation Algorithm

In order to evaluate image quality, the synthetic haze image is used for the input image. The ideal image quality value must be achieved between the original image and the dehazed image. As a result, it can aid in the creation of a high-quality, haze-free image. As shown in Table 3, four visibility ranges are applied as a synthetic haze to the ground truth image dataset in this section: 1 km, 2 km, 3 km, and 4 km.

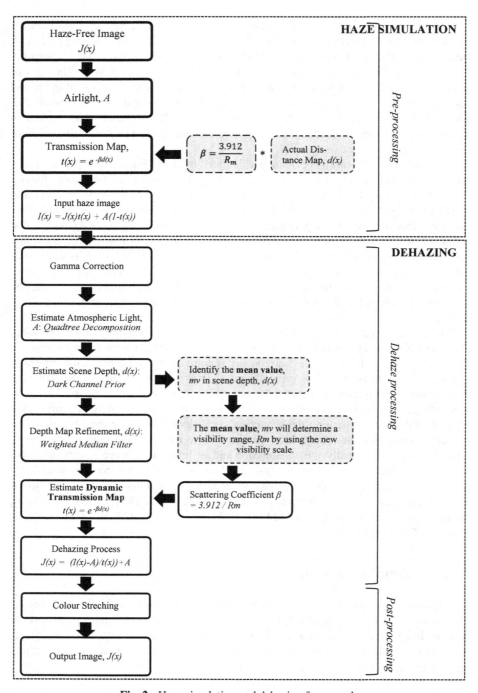

Fig. 2. Haze simulation and dehazing framework

Table 2. The weather conditions visibility range and its scattering coefficient [30]

No.	Weather condition	Visibility range, km	Scattering coefficient, β
1	Dense fog	<50 m	> 78.2
2	Thick fog	50 m–200 m	78.2–19.6
3	Moderate fog	200 m–500 m	19.6–7.82
4	Light fog	500 m–1000 m	7.82–3.91
5	Thin fog/dense haze	1 km–2 km	3.91–1.96
6	Haze	2 km–4 km	1.96–0.954
7	Light haze	4 km–10 km	0.954–0.391
8	Clear	10 km–20 km	0.391–0.196
9	Very clear	20 km–50 km	0.196–0.078
10	Exceptionally clear	>50 km	0.078
11	Pure air	277 km	0.0141

Table 3. The synthetic haze datasets with different four haze levels

Visibility Range, km	1 Dense haze	2 Haze	3 Haze	4 Light haze	Ground Truth
Dataset					

The process of the haze simulation algorithm is summarized as follow:

> *BEGIN: Input haze-free image: J(x)*
> **Step 1:** *Define default airlight value, A = [1,1,1]*
> **Step 2:** *Define a transmission map, t(x)*
> **Step 3:** *Measure scene depth,* $d(x)$ *with Distance Calculator*
> *for each haze visibility range, R_m [1,2,3,4] in kilometre*
> **Step 3.1:** *define the scattering coefficient,*
> $$\beta = \frac{3.912}{R_m}$$
> **Step 3.2:** *calculate the transmission value,* $t(x) = e^{-\beta d(x)}$
> **Step 3.3:** *calculate I(x) = J(x)t(x) + A(1-t(x))*
> *end*
> *END: Output hazy image: I(x)*

The synthetic haze image is used to evaluate the quality of the process by assessing the image quality. The optimal value for the measurement of the image quality between the input and the dehaze image must be achieved. The production of a high-quality, haze-free image can be beneficial. Consequently, with hazy simulation, we proposed a new data set. Air Pollutant Index (API) for government agencies is used in determining or predicting polluted air. An overview of the Malaysian outdoor scene on a clear day that takes into consideration the weather is good and the air pollutants index is good, as shown in Table 4. The API range of 300 to 500 showed a hazardous air quality with a higher environmental and health impact potential. Since each pollutant varies in concentration, API values are grouped into a standardised public health warning [33].

Table 4. Air pollutant index category

Category	Air pollutant index	Visibility range (MI)	Visibility range (km)
Good	0–50	>10	>16.1
Moderate	51–100	5–10	8.05–16.1
Unhealthy for sensitive group	101–150	3–5	4.83–8.05
Unhealthy	151–200	1.5–3	2.41–4.83
Very unhealthy	201–300	1	1.61–4.83
Hazardous	300>	<1	<1.61

In order to enhance the efficiency of the dehazing method, various haze conditions provided by Zhang can be demonstrated [23]. Zhang [23] creates five scenarios from light fog to thick fog. The weather affects the scattering parameter. This scattering parameter is calculated from the visible range, R_m, using the relation $\beta = \frac{-ln(\in)}{Rm}$ [30]. The values of these properties simulate hazy images and capture haze-free images with a distance $d(x)$ calculated in kilometres (km) by the Distance Calculator application, as shown in Fig. 3. The visibility ranges from 1 to 10 km are referred to as simulating a synthetic haze [24]. In this paper, four different haze conditions were used, listed in Table 2: 1 km, 2 km, 3 km, and 4 km.

Based on the features of the haze-free data set in Table 5, the synthetic haze is simulated into four categories based on the haze weather in Table 2. In order to define the transmission map with Eq. (2), We used an actual distance (in kilometres). The transmission was calculated as step 4.2:

$$t(x) = e^{-\beta d(x)}$$

For example,
for 1 km,

$$t(x) = e^{-(3.91)(0.2))} = 0.457$$

Table 5. The properties of haze-free dataset

Venue	UTM KL entrance
Time	Monday, 12 March 2018 1:18 PM
API	22 – Good
Temperature	31 °C - Clouds and Sun
Distance	200 m
Device	Canon EOS 5D Mark III, Lens 17 mm
Dimensions	864 × 576 pixels
Image type	PNG
Properties	ISO 250, Aperture f/4, Shutter Speed 1/1000 s

Fig. 3. The captured clear image and distance measurement with the Distance Calculator application.

for 2 km,

$$t\left(x_{|\beta=1.96|}\right) = e^{-(1.96)(0.2))} = 0.676$$

Step 3.3 is to execute the hazy image using Eq. (1) after the transmission value has been defined as in Eq. (2). As a result, the proposed dehazing algorithm will make use of this haze dataset.

5 Image Dehazing Algorithm

The dehazing algorithm is depicted as a procedure for implementing the dehazing algorithm's enhancement with the dynamic scattering coefficient. To obtain a dehazed image, it was applied to each different synthetic haze dataset, which included light haze, moderate haze, and dense haze.

The proposed Dehazing algorithm

Input haze image: I(x)
Step 1: *Apply Gamma Correction to the input image.*
Step 2: *Estimate airlight, A with Quadtree Decomposition of DCP*
Step 3: *Measure Scene depth with Dark Channel Prior, d(x)*
Step 4: *Refinement depth with Weighted Median Filters*
Step 5: *Define mean value, mv from the known depth information.*
Step 6: *Determine the scattering coefficient value from the R_m visibility scale, β =*
3.912 / R_m
Step 7: *Estimate transmission, $t(x) = e^{(-\beta * d(x))}$*
Step 8: *Recover the scene radiance, $J(x) = \frac{I(x) - A}{t(x)} + A$*
Step 9: *Post-processing with Contrast Stretching to J(x)*
Output scene radiance: J(x)

5.1 Depth Estimation

Gamma correction was applied to an image input from a simulated synthetic haze image
to control its brightness. The quad-tree decomposition algorithm then chooses the sub-
block with the highest average value among the four divided blocks. The air-light estimate
from the quad-tree subdivision is obtained repeatedly from a grey scaled hazy image
up to a predetermined number of times. The air-light can be calculated as the pixel
colour vector between pixels in the final selected area with the lowest Euclidean norm.
Air light can thus be estimated more precisely by lowering the Euclidean norm [31]. A
form of haze-free outdoor image statistics is the dark channel prior [11]. It focuses on a
critical observation: most local patches in haze-free outdoor images contain some very
low-intensity pixels in at least one colour channel. Using this before the haze imaging
model, we can directly estimate the thickness of the haze and retrieve a high-quality
haze-free image. The previous dark channel was founded on the following observations
from haze-free outdoor images: In most non-sky patches, at least one colour channel has
a very low intensity of specific pixels. Because of the additive air-light, a hazy image is
brighter than its haze-free counterpart, where transmission is low. As a result, in areas
with a denser haze, the dark channel in the hazy image will be more intense. A dark
channel is defined as follows:

$$d = \min_{y \in \Omega(x)} (\min_{c \in \{r,g,b\}} J^c(y) \qquad (4)$$

where J^c is the intensity of a colour channel $c \in \{r, g, b\}$ of an RGB image, and x
is a local patch centred on pixel. Then, according to Eq. (4), the dark channel $d(x)$ is
chosen as the lowest value among the three-colour channels and all pixels in $\Omega(x)$. Thus,
the visual intensity of the dark channel is a rough estimate of the haze thickness [11].
The methods for smoothing the depth map are different from many other techniques for
dehazing. The methods of filtration include Gaussian, soft matting, bilateral, and guided

filters. In addition, to improve computational efficiency, a weighted median filter [34] is used to refine the rough approximation and smooth the image. In addition, a weighted median filter [34] is used to refine the rough approximation and smooth the image to improve computational effectiveness.

5.2 Dynamic Scattering Coefficient

At Step 7, the dark channel estimates the scene depth, and the transmission map is computed. In the previous method, the scattering coefficient value was typically set to a constant value. However, almost all existing algorithms for single image dehazing are based on constant assumptions, a more flexible model has highly sought after. This paper suggested a new dynamic scattering coefficient, depending on haze thickness for each image. The scattering coefficient will be computed using the mean value and the mv in-depth map estimation. First, we estimated the visibility range, R_m using the mean value, mv, and a visibility scale ranging from 0.5 m to 10 km, based on the meteorological range in Table 2. Then, we divided that range into intensity values (0, 1) and created a visibility scale as follows:

$$visibility\ scale\ range = \frac{1}{10\,km - 0.05\,km} = \frac{1}{9.95\,km} = 0.1005 \qquad (5)$$

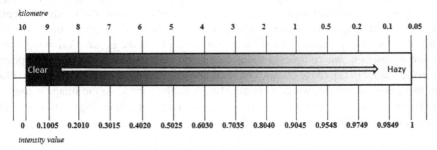

Fig. 4. The proposed new visibility scales to mapping visibility range based on mean values from scene depth intensity.

The example of visibility scale mapping:

if {*mean value*} < 0.1005
  {*visibility range*} = 10;
elseif {*mean value*} < 0.2010

  .

elseif {*mean value*} < 1
  {*visibility range*} = 0.1;
elseif {*mean value*} >=1
  {*visibility range*} = 0.05;

Table 6. The visibility range to its corresponding scattering coefficient

Visibility range, R_m	Scattering coefficient, β
1	3.9120
2	1.9560
3	1.3040
4	0.9780
5	0.7824
6	0.6520
7	0.5589
8	0.4890
9	0.4347
10	0.3912

The mean values, mv, of the depth map intensity must be mapped to this scale to determine the scattering coefficient, as shown in Table 6. The transmission map will be estimated using the scattering coefficient. Because hazy images have varying haze thicknesses, this dynamic scattering coefficient in the dehazing algorithm efficiently produces a better haze-free image. Instead of the constant assumption, this proposed method will set the parameter value based on the depth of the scene. Following transmission estimation, we completed the dehazing process by reversing the atmospheric scattering model in Eq. (3) to obtain a haze-free image. In Fig. 5, we improved the result with image enhancement, which is contrast stretching to increase the image's contrast by extending its range of intensity values through a range of values. Figure 6 depicts the entire dehazing process.

Dehaze image before contrast   Dehaze image after contrast
          stretching   stretching

Fig. 5. A comparison between before and after image enhancement.

6   Image Dehazing Result

This section demonstrates how we used our dehazing method to achieve a haze-free image. The example dataset from a hazy image, scene depth estimation, depth refinement, transmission estimation, dehaze image, and image enhancement are shown in Fig. 6. This process has proven to be effective in removing haze. We proved this method by comparing our results to the ground truth image, as explained in the following section.

| (a) | (b) | (c) | (d) | (e) | (f) |

Fig. 6. The steps of the dehazing process (a) Hazy image (b) Scene depth (c) Depth refinement (d) transmission map (e) Dehaze image (f) Image enhancement

7   Benchmark for Comparative Analysis

The main objective of simulating different conditions of haze is to show that the dehazing algorithm can remove haze at all hazy conditions while maintaining image quality. Therefore, the following dehazing methods were compared: Dark Channel Prior [11], Colour Attenuation Prior [17], DehazeNet [18], Haze-Line [19], and Multi-Layer Perceptron [35], respectively. In order to assess the results of such dehazing procedures the Mean-Squared Error (MSE), Peak-Signal-to-Noise Ratio (PSNR), and the Measurement of the Structural Same Index (SSIM), are used [32]. The results of dehazing methods are shown visually in Tables 7 and quantitatively in Table 8.

The Dark Channel Prior method is capable of removing haze at all levels of haze. The sky, on the other hand, appears oversaturated. Colour Attenuation Prior is an efficient way to reduce haze in a light hazy condition while still appearing natural. However, it was not successful in dense haze conditions. The images that resulted are still hazy. The DehazeNet result appears to be ideal for removing haze in all conditions while maintaining quality, especially in dense haze conditions. However, in the hazy light conditions, it was still at a disadvantage compared to CAP. The Haze-Line method result looks are over contrast and unnatural in all conditions. On the other hand, the Multi-Layer Perceptron method removes haze, but it appears to reduce contrast, making the image darker.

Table 7. The result of dehazing method for VHAZE images (a) Hazy Image (b) Dark Channel (c) Colour Attenuation Prior (d) DehazeNet (e) Haze Line (f) Multilayer Perceptron (g) Proposed

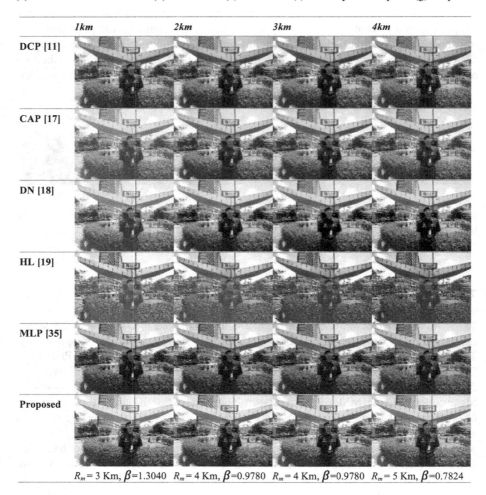

	1km	*2km*	*3km*	*4km*
DCP [11]				
CAP [17]				
DN [18]				
HL [19]				
MLP [35]				
Proposed				

R_m= 3 Km, β=1.3040 R_m= 4 Km, β=0.9780 R_m= 4 Km, β=0.9780 R_m= 5 Km, β=0.7824

However, in all hazy levels, our proposed method outperforms the other method in MSE, PSNR, and SSIM. At the MSE value, the difference error between the original and dehazed images is the least. On the other hand, PSNR value is the most better-quality value and at SSIM is a higher value match to the benchmark than others. Furthermore, each level of haze has been estimated with a suitable coefficient to remove haze. This analysis demonstrated that our dehazing method could overcome haze at various haze levels using synthetic haze images and produce optimal quality in the dehazing method.

Table 8. An image quality assessment for first result of dehazing methods

(km)	IQA	DCP [11]	CAP [17]	DN [18]	HL [19]	MLP [35]	Own
1	MSE	0.0071	0.0092	0.0035	0.0191	0.0056	**0.0002**
	PSNR	21.5075	20.3531	24.5885	17.1888	22.4973	**37.5957**
	SSIM	0.9230	0.9339	0.9663	0.8584	0.9540	**0.9964**
2	MSE	0.0101	0.0018	0.0015	0.0199	0.0075	**0.0005**
	PSNR	19.9742	27.3890	28.3691	17.0133	21.2236	**33.1622**
	SSIM	0.9099	0.9751	0.9740	0.8541	0.9493	**0.9936**
3	MSE	0.0111	0.0030	0.0034	0.0240	0.0076	**0.0008**
	PSNR	19.5365	25.2879	24.6757	16.1977	21.2168	**30.7357**
	SSIM	0.9042	0.9667	0.9342	0.8451	0.9449	**0.9901**
4	MSE	0.0117	0.0038	0.0047	0.0307	0.0075	**0.0008**
	PSNR	19.3360	24.1465	23.2813	15.1217	21.2335	**31.1194**
	SSIM	0.9014	0.9590	0.9096	0.8282	0.9417	**0.9878**

The real hazy images shown in Table 9 have been used as a dataset to apply to our dehazing method. These images were captured in Malaysia's outdoor scene with different API values, which consisted of Moderate, Unhealthy and Very Unhealthy conditions. Even these datasets do not provide a haze-free image as a benchmark, but the result shows the capability to remove haze with a suitable scattering coefficient. Table 10 is a dehazing result from a sample dataset in the latest dehazing study. We also applied our dehazing method by using this dataset to prove the efficiency of our method.

The result gives an estimate of the visibility range for each haze image. Our method was successful in removing haze from all haze levels at various haze levels. Furthermore, by determining the appropriate scattering coefficient for each level, the enhancement method contributed to dynamic transmission. This dynamic transmission was successful in reducing issues like over-enhanced and dense haze. Although it produces better results, this enhancement method has limitations when applied to indoor images and images with unreal haze. Even though the proposed dehazing method successfully removed haze and produced a better result, it still requires improvement in the new proposed visibility scaling, as shown in Fig. 4. The visibility range derived from the visibility scale would seem inaccurate in mapping the actual haze image condition.

Table 9. Real-world haze images in Malaysia based on the air pollutant index

Date and Time	7 August 2019 4.26 pm	18 Sept 2019 9.10 am	19 Sept 2019 7.59 am
API	51-100 Moderate (75*)	101-200 Unhealthy (188*)	201-300 Very Unhealthy (271*)
°C	32°C Broken Clouds 6km	28°C Broken clouds 2km	25°C Dense Fog 1km
Range	8-16 km	2-5 km	1-2km
Haze Image			
DCP			
CAP			
DN			
HL			
MLP			
Own			
	R_m = 5 km, β=0.7824	R_m = 4 km, β=0.9780	R_m = 4 km, β=0.9780

Table 10. The result of dehazing method for random hazy images (a) Hazy Image (b) Dark Channel (c) Colour Attenuation Prior (d) DehazeNet (e) Haze Line (f) Multilayer Perceptron (g) Proposed

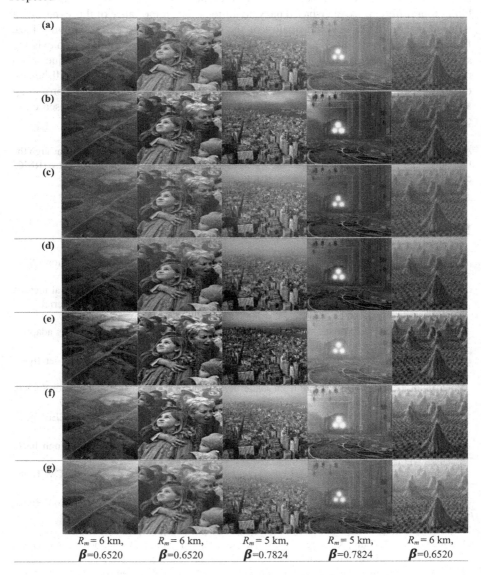

$R_m = 6$ km,	$R_m = 6$ km,	$R_m = 5$ km,	$R_m = 5$ km,	$R_m = 6$ km,
$\beta = 0.6520$	$\beta = 0.6520$	$\beta = 0.7824$	$\beta = 0.7824$	$\beta = 0.6520$

8 Conclusion

Many applications, such as computer vision, surveillance systems, and remote sensing, benefit from the dehazing method. As a result, many dehazing efforts have been made to improve image quality by removing haze. However, the remaining problems are insufficiently recovered from the denser haze or low haze and cause the haze's thickness issues. Therefore, a new synthetic haze was presented in a single image dataset, simulating four different, weather-based hazy conditions. The importance of this experiment is to ensure the efficiency and quality of the dehazing method while removing haze from different haze levels. Furthermore, the results were visually compared to existing state-of-the-art schemes to validate the significance of the proposed technique. As a result, various standard datasets will yield better haze-free images, which will benefit other downstream applications. Furthermore, this approach will be studied by providing a dehazing algorithm that addresses all of the dehazing problems in future research in the visibility scales.

Acknowledgements. This research was funded by the Ministry of Higher Education through the Fundamental Research Grant Scheme and managed by the Research Management Centre (RMC) of Universiti Teknologi Malaysia Vot No. R.K130000.7856.5F036.

References

1. Narasimhan, S.G., Nayar, S.K.: Vision and the atmosphere. Int. J. Comput. Vision **48**(3), 233–254 (2002)
2. Xue, R., Zhong, M., Zhang, E., Zhao, S., Zhang, D.: Real-time image haze removal method for fire scene images. In: 2018 6th International Conference on Machinery, Materials, and Computing Technology (ICMMCT). Atlantis Press (2018)
3. Dong, T., Zhao, G., Wu, J., Ye, Y., Shen, Y.: Efficient traffic video dehazing using adaptive dark channel prior and spatial-temporal correlations. Sensors **19**(7), 1593 (2019)
4. Koschmieder, H.: Theorie der horizontalen sichtweite. In: Beitrage zur Physik der freien Atmosphare (1924)
5. Cozman, F., Krotkov, E.: Depth from scattering. In: Proceedings of IEEE Computer Society Conference on Computer Vision and Pattern Recognition, pp. 801–806, June 1997
6. Narasimhan, S.G., Nayar, S.K.: Contrast restoration of weather degraded images. IEEE Trans. Pattern Anal. Mach. Intell. **25**, 713–724 (2003)
7. Schechner, Y.Y., Narasimhan, S.G., Nayar, S.K.: Polarization-based vision through haze. Appl. Opt. **42**, 511–525 (2003)
8. Kopf, J., et al.: Deep photo: model-based photograph enhancement and viewing. ACM Trans. Graph. **27**, 1–10 (2008). In Siggraph ASIA
9. Tan, R.T.: Visibility in bad weather from a single image. In: IEEE International Conference on Computer Vision and Pattern Recognition, pp. 1–8. IEEE (2008)
10. Fattal, R.: Single image dehazing. ACM Trans. Graph. **27**(3), 72 (2008)
11. He, K., Sun, J., Tang, X.: Single image haze removal using dark channel prior. IEEE Trans. Pattern Anal. Mach. Intell. **33**(12), 1956–1963 (2011)
12. Tarel, J.P., Hautiere, N.: Fast visibility restoration from a single colour or grey level image. In: IEEE International Conference on Computer Vision, pp. 2201–2208. IEEE (2009)
13. Meng, G., Wang, Y., Duan, J., Xiang, S., Pan, C.: Efficient image dehazing with boundary constraint and contextual regularization. In: Proceedings of the IEEE International Conference Computer Vision, Washington, D.C., USA, pp. 617–624 (2013)
14. Ancuti, C.O., Ancuti, C.: Single image dehazing by multi-scale fusion. IEEE Trans. Image Proc. **22**(8), 3271–3282 (2013)

15. Fattal, R.: Dehazing using colour-lines. ACM Trans. Graph. **34**(1), 1–14 (2014)
16. Tang, K., Yang, J., Wang, J.: Investigating haze-relevant features in a learning framework for image dehazing. In: Proceedings of the IEEE Conference Computer Vision Pattern Recognition, Columbus, Ohio, USA, pp. 2995–3002 (2014)
17. Zhu, Q., Mai, J., Shao, L.: A fast single image haze removal algorithm using colour attenuation prior. IEEE Trans. Image Process. **24**(11), 3522–3533 (2015)
18. Cai, B., Xu, X., Jia, K., Qing, C., Tao, D.: DehazeNet: an end-to-end system for single image haze removal. IEEE Trans. Image Process. **25**(11), 5187–5198 (2016)
19. Berman, D., Treibitz, T., Avidan, S.: Non-local image dehazing. In: Proceedings of the IEEE Conference Computer Vision and Pattern Recognition, Las Vegas, Nevada, USA, pp. 1674–1682 (2016)
20. Tarel, J.P., Hautiere, N., Caraffa, L., Cord, A., Halmaoui, H., Gruyer, D.: Vision enhancement in homogeneous and heterogeneous fog. IEEE Intell. Transp. Syst. Mag. **4**(2), 6–20 (2012)
21. Ancuti, C., Ancuti, C.O., Vleeschouwer, C.D.: D-HAZY: a dataset to evaluate quantitatively dehazing algorithms. In: IEEE International Conference on Image Processing, pp. 2226–2230, September 2016
22. El Khoury, J., Thomas, J.-B., Mansouri, A.: A color image database for haze model and dehazing methods evaluation. In: Mansouri, A., Nouboud, F., Chalifour, A., Mammass, D., Meunier, J., ElMoataz, A. (eds.) ICISP 2016. LNCS, vol. 9680, pp. 109–117. Springer, Cham (2016). https://doi.org/10.1007/978-3-319-33618-3_12
23. Zhang, Y., Ding, L., Sharma, G.: HazeRD: an outdoor dataset for dehazing algorithms. In: Proceedings of the IEEE International Conference Image Processing, Beijing, China, pp. 3205–3209 (2017)
24. Ancuti, C.O., Ancuti, C., Timofte, R., De Vleeschouwer. C.: O-HAZE: a dehazing benchmark with real hazy and haze-free outdoor images. In: IEEE/CVF Conference on Computer Vision and Pattern Recognition Workshops (CVPRW) (2018)
25. Ancuti, C.O., Ancuti, C., Timofte, R., De Vleeschouwer, C.: I-HAZE: a dehazing benchmark with real hazy and haze-free indoor images. In: IEEE/CVF Conference on Computer Vision and Pattern Recognition Workshops (CVPRW) (2018)
26. http://vision.middlebury.edu/stereo/data/scenes2014
27. http://cs.nyu.edu/~silberman/datasets/nyudepthv2.html
28. Husain. N.A., Mohd Rahim, M.S., Kari, S., Chaudry, H.: The simulation of synthetic haze based on visibility range for dehazing method in single image. In: 5th International Conference on Engineering and Technology (ICET 2020), Melbourne, Australia, pp. 20–22, March 2020
29. Husain, N.A., Mohd Rahim, M.S., Kari, S., Chaudry, H.: VRHAZE: the simulation of synthetic haze based on visibility range for dehazing method in single image. In: 6th International Conference on Interactive Digital Media (ICIDM 2020), International Virtual Conference, 14–15 December 2020
30. McCartney, E.J.: Optics of the Atmosphere: Scattering by Molecules and Particles. Wiley, New York (1976)
31. Dubok, P., et al.: Single image dehazing with image entropy and information fidelity. In: ICIP, pp. 4037–4041 (2014)
32. Wang, Z.A., Bovik, C., Sheikh, H.R., Simoncelli, E.P.: Image quality assessment: from error visibility to structural similarity. IEEE Trans. Image Process. **13**(4), 600–612 (2004)
33. O'Neil, S.M., Lahm, P.W., Fitch, M.J., Broughton, M.: Summary and analysis of approaches linking visual range, PM2.5 concentrations, and air quality health impact indices for wildfires. J. Air Waste Manag. Assoc. **63**(9), 1083–1090 (2013)
34. Zhang, Q., Xu, L. Jia, J.: 100+ times faster weighted median filter. In: IEEE Conference on Computer Vision and Pattern Recognition (CVPR) (2014)
35. Salazar-Colores, S., Cruz-Aceves, I., Ramos-Arreguin, J.M.: Single image dehazing using a multi-layer perceptron. J. Electron. Imaging **27**(4), 0430 (2018)

Adaptive Gamification: User/Player Type and Game Elements Mapping

Ryan Macdonell Andrias[1,2], Mohd Shahrizal Sunar[1,3(✉)],
and Stephen Laison Sondoh Jr.[4]

[1] Media and Game Innovation Centre of Excellence, Institute of Human Centered Engineering,
Universiti Teknologi Malaysia, Johor, Malaysia
ryan@ums.edu.my, shahrizal@utm.my
[2] Faculty of Computing and Informatics, Universiti Malaysia Sabah, Kota Kinabalu, Malaysia
[3] School of Computing, Faculty of Engineering, Universiti Teknologi Malaysia, Johor, Malaysia
[4] Faculty of Business, Economics and Accountancy, Universiti Malaysia Sabah,
Kota Kinabalu, Malaysia
jude@ums.edu.my

Abstract. Gamification is defined as the use of game design elements in non-game contexts. It is noteworthy that a user preference towards a game mechanic and game element is different as an individual. A common approach to satisfy user expectations is to include multiple game elements to accommodate all the user/player types. However, this approach may cause the user interface to be crowded with irrelevant game elements. This research proposes a method for adaptive gamification design with proper mapping of user/player type and game elements. 915 questionnaires (HEXAD user type) were analysed. Using matrix multiplication/matrix product, we can use correlation analysis to generate two primary relationship output: 1) HEXAD user type with game elements, 2) Six HEXAD user types. The game elements are grouped following Self-Determination Theory (SDT); Competence, Relatedness and Autonomy. Rewards are the fourth category, as extrinsic motivation. The fundamental game components that need to be given extra attention during gamification application development are learning, social comparison/pressure, non-linear gameplay and point features. In the meantime, less attention to leaderboard and creativity tools. The adaptive user types and game elements mapping can be used as a clear guideline for the gamification designer to develop an engaging application.

Keywords: Gamification · Adaptive gamification · User type · Player type · Self-Determination Theory (SDT)

1 Introduction

Gamification is commonly defined as the use of game design elements in non-game contexts [1]. The main reason to add game design elements in a non-gaming context is to motivate and engage the user to act continuously. Bounty Tasker, Beeminder and

Z. Lv and H. Song (Eds.): INTETAIN 2021, LNICST 429, pp. 242–256, 2022.
https://doi.org/10.1007/978-3-030-99188-3_15

Duolingo are some of the gamification applications available in the market. It is noteworthy that an individual personal preference towards game mechanics and game elements is different [2, 3]. Therefore, a gamification application should be designed to fulfil a particular user preference [4]. However, most of the gamified applications available in the market are being developed with fixed game elements such as points, badges, and leaderboards without the adaptivity approach [2]. A recent trend in gamification research is moving towards an adaptive approach [5–7]. The adaptive system can be either towards the game features or the content to suit individual needs.

Many user/player type topologies are available, such as Bartle's taxonomy, BrainHex, HEXAD and Ferro's classification. Most of the player type can be identified using the questionnaire as an instrument, and it can be mapped with specific game features. As an example, by using the HEXAD questionnaire, output, as shown below, can be derived (Table 1).

Table 1. Example of hexad user type classification.

User type	Percentage
Achiever	18%
Disruptor	4%
Free spirit	22%
Philanthropist	26%
Player	14%
Socialiser	16%

From the table above, it is challenging to design and develop a gamification application that suits a specific player type as the user comprises a combination of different types. A common way to satisfy user expectations is to include multiple gamification features to accommodate all the player types. However, this approach has a high risk of over-burdening the application user interface [2, 8].

In this article, we propose an approach to map HEXAD gamification user types with suitable game elements. Our goal is to create an adaptive gamification application with proper mapping of user/player type and game elements.

2 Related Works

2.1 Player/User Type

Bartle's Taxonomy is one of the most common gamers classifying approaches, categorising players according to the playing style. Richard Bartle has identified four types of players; Achiever, killer, socialiser and explorer [9]. Achiever: a player who strives to perform and accomplish an objective involves collecting points and level up. Killer: a hostile player that likes to create chaos either toward the games or other players.

Explorer: a type of player that keen to explore the games freely. Socialiser: a player that prefers to interact with other players while playing the games. However, Yee's [10] has validated Bartle Taxonomy with empirical data using factor analysis. The result has revealed only three major components: achievement (Achiever), social (Socialiser) and immersion (Explorer).

Another type of player classification is the Four Fun Keys Model [11], which comprises easy fun, hard fun, people fun and serious fun. Demographic Game Design model (DGD1) game player model is based on Myers-Briggs taxonomy (MBTI). There are four types of players in DGD1: Conqueror, Manager, Wanderer and Participant. Demographic Game Design 2 (DGD2) model is the extension of DGD1. It is based on Barens's Temperament Theory [12]. Meanwhile, the BrainHex Player Taxonomy [13] was formulated based on the neurobiological result based on earlier demographic game design models (DGD1 and DGD2). Seven types of players are identified: Seeker, Survivor, Daredevil, Mastermind, Conqueror, Socialiser and Achiever. HEXAD user type [14] has identified six gamification users: socialiser, free spirit, Achiever, Philanthropist, player and disrupter. Table 2 is the mapping between game player/user type and Bartle's taxonomy.

Table 2. Game player type and Bartle taxonomy mapping.

Bartle's taxonomy				
	Achiever	Socialiser	Killer	Explorer
Yee's	Achievement, immersion	Social		Immersion
4 fun keys	Hard fun	People Fun		Easy Fun
DGD1	Conqueror, manager	Participant		Wanderer
DGD2	Strategic, logistical	Diplomatic		Tactical
BrainHex	Achiever, conqueror, mastermind	Socialiser		Seeker
HEXAD	Achiever	Socialiser	Disrupter	Free spirit

2.2 HEXAD Gamification User Type

HEXAD gamification user type is based on user intrinsic and extrinsic motivational factors. There are six user types: Socialiser, Free Spirit, Philanthropist, Player, Achiever and Disrupter. Socialiser is a type of user that seeking social connection and relatedness as motivation. The free spirit is interested in autonomy and self-expression. Meanwhile, Achiever is motivated to gain mastery status by completing challenges and obstacles. A philanthropist user is inspired by a sense of meaning, purpose and altruism. The player user type is driven only by external rewards. Finally, the disrupter prefers to create chaos within the gamified environment.

2.3 Adaptive Gamification

A comprehensive table to relate between personality types, traits, player types with game features (game elements and game mechanics) has been proposed [15, 16]. The authors compiled findings from various researchers in the area of psychology, game and Gamification. The table can be used as guidance for the gamification developer. However, to include all the game elements will make the application interface messy and crowded. As an example, for Achiever and Disrupter players, each type has six features. Kocadere and Caglar [17] stressed that a specific game element might positively impact a user but negatively impact another user. For example, teamwork elements will negatively impact the achievers, free spirit and disruptors but positive towards Socialisers.

Monterrat, Lavoué [18] have proposed an adaptive game feature system based on the individual user's interaction. The adaptive system captures two types of interaction: turning on and off the game feature and how often the user interacts with the feature. It is implemented by using a trace analysis system and Ferro's player classification as a design guideline.

Aldemir, Celik [20] have conducted a case study that involved 118 respondents. Students use the gamification application and, at the end of the course, been interviewed to record game mechanics and game elements' effect on their learning process. Nine main themes were identified and suggested to design an educational gamification application. The themes are narrative, reward, constraints, points, win-state, leader board, badge and teams. Although this approach can be used to develop the gamification application; however, it does not offer an adaptive capability to suits individual users and biased to game features that already pre-selected.

Kocadere and Caglar [17] conduct a similar case study as Aldemir, Celik [20]. However, it started with distributing Bartle's Taxonomy Questionnaire to identify the student's player type. Then, for seven weeks, the 41 selected students will use and experience an educational gamified application. At the end of the case study, one prominent participant for each player type is interviewed to capture game mechanics and elements either positively or negatively impact the learning process. However, according to Kotsopoulos, Bardaki [21], it is impossible to categories a user to a specific player type, which the authors point out that a user has a combination characteristic. Furthermore, Kocadere and Caglar [17] case studies are based on pre-selected game features.

Lavoué, Monterrat [2] have conducted a case study to derive an adaptive model from linking learners with game features using the matrix calculation method. The authors are using the BrainHex questionnaire to identify the player type. Two approaches are used to obtain the matrix of game elements and the player type; expert judgment (6 people) and student ranking. A comparison between experts and students' assessment reveals that expert evaluation correlates with the BrainHex player profile. One of the authors' problems is that the students' rating value does not match the player type's game feature. An example of a linear model, $R = B A$. This example comprises four users (u1–u4), three-game features (f1–f3) and a 2-factors player model: Conqueror (C) and Socialiser (S) (See Fig. 1).

Table 3 below shows Expert A-matrix, which comprise of game feature and BrainHex player type.

Kotsopoulos, Bardaki [21] approach is similar to Lavoué, Monterrat [2] to find the relationship between player types and game elements. Two questionnaires are distributed among students to identify HEXAD player type and the importance of game elements based on individual ratings. The authors use SPSS software to analyse the responses using

R

Adaptive Features

	f1	f2	f3
u1	10	00	05
u2	00	06	12
u3	06	03	09
u4	-08	03	02

=

B

BrainHex

	c	s
u1	10	00
u2	00	12
u3	06	06
u4	-08	06

x

A

Game element & player type

	f1	f2	f3
c	1	0	½
s	0	½	1

Fig. 1. Example of matrix multiplication/matrix product calculation.

Table 3. Example of expert A-matrix.

	Stars	Leaderboard	Tips	Walker	Timer
Seeker	0.5	0	0.75	0.88	0
Survivor	0.13	0.5	0	0	0.38
Daredevil	0.63	0.63	0	0.13	0.88
Mastermind	0.63	0.63	0.38	0.25	0.25
Conqueror	0.75	1	0.13	0.38	0.75
Socialiser	0.13	0.13	1	0.25	0
Achiever	1	0.75	0.13	0.88	1

descriptive statistical analysis and correlation analysis. Achiever and Philanthropist were the most extensive characteristics; however, the author's result cannot map Achiever with any game elements. It most likely shares a common problem with Lavoué, Monterrat [2], students giving a mismatch value to represent a game feature rating.

3 Methodology

3.1 Respondents Profile

Nine hundred fifteen undergraduate students participate in this experiment, which comprises 656 females and 259 males; age is between 19–26. The questionnaire is distributed via online using google form to University Malaysia Sabah students.

3.2 Process

The process of creating user/player type and game elements mapping followed these steps:

Step 1: Produce game element and user type-Matrix

The game element and user type-Matrix table is created based on an article written by Tondello, Wehbe [14]. The game element's effect on HEXAD user type is coded with a specific value according to the reported correlation value.

Step 2: Date Collection
Distribute the HEXAD questionnaire, consisting of 24 items among the students via an online URL.

Step 3: Data Analysis
After the responses have been collected, the data were analysed using Statistical Package for the Social Sciences (SPSS) and SmartPLS to identify:

- HEXAD user type distribution.
- User type and Game elements matrix
- User types matrix
- Relationship between types of users and game elements.

The approach to generate the matrix was adopted from Lavoué, Monterrat [2].
Step 4: Data Interpretation
Interpret the analysis result.

4 Result

4.1 HEXAD User Type

The HEXAD user type distribution for the experiment is shown in Table 4. The free spirit and philanthropist type are the highest, and disruptors are the lowest percentage, similar to Andrzej Marczewski's finding from the Gamified.uk website.

Table 4. Example of hexad user type classification.

User type	Percentage
Achiever	17%
Disruptor	12.4%
Free spirit	18%
Philanthropist	18.2%
Player	17.1%
Socialiser	17.3%

4.2 User Type and Game Element - Matrix

Table 5 below is the User type and Game element - matrix table created based on Tondello, Wehbe [14] research finding. The number is based on the correlation value identified in the article.

Table 5. User type and game element – matrix.

User type	Achiever	Disruptor	Free spirit	Philanthropist	Player	Socialiser
Challenges	0.463	0.207	0.412	0.212	0.317	0
Quests	0.266	0	0.236	0	0.245	0
Learning	0.215	0	0.391	0	0	0
Progression	0.239	0	0.204	0	0.302	0.17
Certificates	0.229	0	0.2	0	0.228	0.142
Social comparison	0	0	0	0	0.239	0.152
Social competition	0.161	0.32	0.249	0	0.239	0.216
Social discovery	0	0.179	0	0	0.217	0.205
Social network	0	0.197	0	0	0.143	0.15
Teams	0	0.169	0	0	0.192	0.179
Knowledge sharing	0	0.167	0.138	0.352	0.231	0.184
Creativity tools	0	0.252	0.23	0	0	0
Exploratory task	0	0	0.352	0.139	0.152	0
Nonlinear gameplay	0	0	0.221	0.179	0	0
Badges	0.208	0	0	0	0.271	0.164
Leaderboard	0	0.17	0	0	0.276	0.199
Points	0.172	0	0.201	0	0.259	0.168

4.3 Correlation Between HEXAD User Types

Table 6 shows the correlation between the six types of users in HEXAD. Based on the results, we can state the following:

- All types of users have a statistically significant linear relationship ($p < .01$) except the association between disrupter and socialiser as well as disrupter and Philanthropist (no correlation).
- Philanthropist and Socialiser have a strong correlation ($r > .5$)
- Moderate correlation ($.3 < |r| < .5$) between Achiever, Free Spirit, Philanthropist and Socialiser.
- The is no strong and moderate correlation between disruptors with other user types. It is either weak ($r < .3$), or without relationship.

Table 6. Correlation between HEXAD user types

User type	Achiever	Disruptor	Free spirit	Philanthropist	Player
Disruptor	.182**				
Free spirit	.449**	.200**			
Philanthropist	.474**	0.048	.447**		
Player	.245**	.149**	.307**	.220**	
Socialiser	.374**	0.043	.357**	.572**	.218**

** **Correlation is significant at the 0.01 level (2-tailed).**

4.4   Relationship Between Game Elements and HEXAD User Types

Table 7 shows the relationship between game elements and HEXAD user types. This table is essential as it will describe the game element that correlates with user type. Based on the results, we can state the following:

Positive Relationship

- Achiever is having positive relationship with all competence game elements (Challenges, Quests, Learning, Progression and Certificates).
- Player and Socialiser have positive relationship with all relatedness game elements (Social comparison, Social competition, Social discovery, Social network, Teams and Knowledge Sharing).
- Free Spirit is having a positive relationship with all autonomy game elements (Creativity tools, Exploratory task and Nonlinear gameplay).
- Player and Socialiser have positive relationship with all rewards game elements (Badges, Leaderboard and Points).

No Relationship

- Achiever and Socialiser have no relationship with all autonomy game elements (Creativity tools, Exploratory task and Nonlinear gameplay).
- Philanthropist does not have any relationship with all rewards game elements (Badges, Leaderboard and Points).

Table 7. Correlation between game elements and hexad user types.

	Game elements	Achiever	Disruptor	Free spirit	Philanthropist	Player	Socialiser
Competence	Challenges	0.41	0.27	0.34	0.19	0.32	0
	Quests	0.47	0	0.39	0	0.49	0
	Learning	0.43	0	0.72	0	0	0
	Progression	0.39	0	0.31	0	0.44	0.28
	Certificates	0.35	0	0.28	0	0.5	0.29
Relatedness	Social comparison	0	0	0	0	0.76	0.51
	Social competition	0.19	0.54	0.27	0	0.32	0.29
	Social discovery	0	0.54	0	0	0.5	0.49
	Social network	0	0.7	0	0	0.39	0.42
	Teams	0	0.32	0.17	0.45	0.34	0.28
	Knowledge sharing	0	0.57	0	0	0.49	0.47
Autonomy	Creativity tools	0	0.8	0.46	0	0	0
	Exploratory task	0	0	0.67	0.28	0.35	0
	Nonlinear gameplay	0	0	0.64	0.53	0	0
Rewards	Badges	0.41	0	0	0	0.6	0.38
	Leaderboard	0	0.48	0	0	0.6	0.44
	Points	0.29	0	0.31	0	0.49	0.33

5   Discussion

5.1   Designing a Gamification Application

The player and user type research show that a person is not inclusive to one user category. In other words, a player can have characteristics from a combination of either all types [22]. Therefore it is essential to carefully consider a well-balanced as an overall combination [23]. The player type analysis provides useful information on the prevalent user type for a developer. It is a valuable tool for a specific group of people, such as in an organisation or students with a particular demographic group. For example, in a study conducted at a workplace, for energy saving to become a daily habit, the gamified application should include progression, level and points game design elements [21]. Table 7 above clearly indicates that certain game elements affect users with either strong, weak or no correlation.

One of the most popular motivation theory which often been used in gamified education is Self-Determination Theory (SDT) [24, 25]. The SDT focuses on intrinsic motivation to improves performance, increases sustainability and encourages growth [26, 27]. Intrinsic motivation can be defined as an activity purely performed by an individual for pure internal satisfaction. A person feels excited about doing any task when that person is motivated internally.

SDT consists of three fundamental human needs: competence, autonomy, and relatedness. Competence represents the feeling of being able to handle the task at hand successfully. Autonomy means the more an individual can manage a situation, the greater the probability that he will succeed. Lastly, relatedness is the feeling of social connection with others. Figure 2, 3, 4 and 5 shows users preferential game elements based on the average value. It is structured in four primary categories; competence, relatedness, autonomy and rewards. Rewards such as badges, points, certificates and leaderboard can induce extrinsic motivation.

Learning, social comparison/pressure, non-linear gameplay and point features are the fundamental game elements that need to be given extra consideration. Meanwhile, less attention is paid to leaderboard and resources for creativity tools.

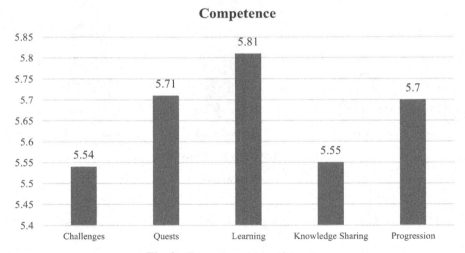

Fig. 2. Competence game elements.

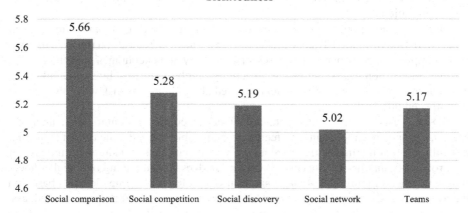

Fig. 3. Related game elements.

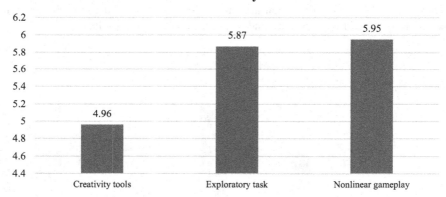

Fig. 4. Autonomy game elements.

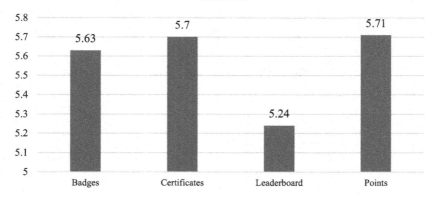

Fig. 5. Rewards game elements.

In the end, we can reduce game elements selection to accommodate all user types and basic human needs, according to SDT. This approach can prevent a high risk of over-burdening the user interface [2, 8]. We can also control the inclusion of a game element that harms a user [17].

5.2 Adaptive Gamification (User Type and Game Elements Mapping)

The entire gamification system should be designed to adapt to the specific needs of each player [4]. It is challenging to develop a gamification application that suits the specific user. However, one of the approaches that can be explored is using the adaptive technique. A highly adaptive gamified application that can match the intended game mechanics and elements is required among learners-players' diversity [30]. The gamified application should be able to provide features that are suitable for a user adaptively. Adaptation of game elements can lead to an increase in participants for active users [30]. The authors

Table 8. Adaptive user type and game elements mapping

	User ID	2	6	56	755
User Type	Achiever	3.7	7	5.3	6.7
	Disruptor	2.5	4	4	3.5
	Free Spirit	5.3	7	5.3	6.7
	Philanthropist	4.8	6.3	5	7
	Player	6	6.8	5.5	2.5
	Socialiser	3.8	6.5	4.8	7
Competence	Challenges	4.6	6.5	5.1	5.5
	Quests	5	6.9	5.4	5.3
	Learning	4.7	7	5.3	6.7
	Knowledge Sharing	4.6	6.2	5	5.4
	Progression	4.8	6.8	5.3	5.4
Relatedness	Social comparison	5.1	6.7	5.2	4.2
	Social competition	4.2	6.1	4.9	5
	Social discovery	4.2	5.9	4.8	4.3
	Social network	3.9	5.6	4.7	4.3
	Teams	4.2	5.8	4.8	4.3
Autonomy	Creativity tools	3.8	5.4	4.6	5
	Exploratory task	5.4	6.8	5.3	5.8
	Nonlinear gameplay	5.1	6.7	5.2	6.8
Rewards	Badges	4.7	6.8	5.3	5
	Certificates	4.8	6.9	5.3	5.6
	Leaderboard	4.4	6	4.9	4.2
	Points	4.9	6.8	5.3	5.4

also suggested that adaptation should not be based on users' choice but rather on indirect measurements through a questionnaire or user interaction.

Table 8 is generated based on matrix multiplication or matrix product between HEXAD user types and user type and game element-matrix. Based on the result, we can see that different user preferences prioritise. Besides, gamification designer can construct a more effective technique by understanding the importance of the game elements for a specific player.

6 Conclusion

The user type profile may be derived from a combination of either all types. The user profile analysis will give some clear insight into the prominent and less prominent characteristics of an individual user or group of people. The gamified application should be design using game elements that suitable for a user because a particular game element may not be appropriate, and some might negatively affect some user types.

This adaptive user type and game element mapping can also help gamification designers choose which Gamification features to incorporate into the gamified application. It is recommended to suit a user type with the suitable game elements by using an adaptive approach. Using matrix multiplication or matrix product and correlation analysis, we can map user types with game elements. The mapping generated can be used by a gamification designer to develop a more engaging application.

Acknowledgement. This research was supported by Ministry of Higher Education and Media and Game Innovation Centre of Excellence, Institute of Human Centered Engineering, Universiti Teknologi Malaysia, Skudai, Johor, Malaysia through the Malaysia Research University Network research grant (R.J130000.7809.4L870) with the title, Gamification Platform and Virtual Environment for University 4.0.

References

1. Deterding, S., Sicart, M., Nacke, L., O'Hara, K., Dixon, D.: Gamification: using game-design elements in non-gaming contexts. In: CHI'11 Extended Abstracts on Human Factors in Computing Systems; Vancouver, BC, Canada, pp. 2425–2428. ACM (2011). 1979575
2. Lavoué, É., Monterrat, B., Desmarais, M., George, S.: Adaptive gamification for learning environments. IEEE Trans. Learn. Technol. **12**(1), 16–28 (2018)
3. Knutas, A., Ikonen, J., Maggiorini, D., Ripamonti, L., Porras, J.: Creating student interaction profiles for adaptive collaboration gamification design. Int. J. Hum. Cap. Inf. Technol. Prof. **7**(3), 47–62 (2016)
4. Nicholson, S.: A RECIPE for meaningful gamification. In: Reiners, T., Wood, L.C. (eds.) Gamification in Education and Business, pp. 1–20. Springer, Cham (2015). https://doi.org/10.1007/978-3-319-10208-5_1
5. Böckle, M., Novak, J., Bick, M.: Towards adaptive gamification: a synthesis of current developments. In: Proceedings of the 25th European Conference on Information Systems, ECIS 2017 (2017)

6. Gallego-Durán, F.J., Molina-Carmona, R., Llorens-Largo, F.: Measuring the difficulty of activities for adaptive learning. Univ. Access Inf. Soc. **17**(2), 335–348 (2017). https://doi.org/10.1007/s10209-017-0552-x

7. Jianu, E.M., Vasilateanu, A.: Designing of an e-learning system using adaptivity and gamification. In: 2017 IEEE International Systems Engineering Symposium (ISSE), pp. 1–4 (2017)

8. Monterrat, B., Lavoué, É., George, S.: A framework to adapt gamification in learning environments. In: Rensing, C., de Freitas, S., Ley, T., Muñoz-Merino, P.J. (eds.) EC-TEL 2014. LNCS, vol. 8719, pp. 578–579. Springer, Cham (2014). https://doi.org/10.1007/978-3-319-11200-8_78

9. Bartle, R.: Hearts, clubs, diamonds, spades: players who suit MUDs. J. MUD Res. **1**, 19 (1996)

10. Yee, N.: The demographics, motivations, and derived experiences of users of massively multi-user online graphical environments. Presence Teleoper. Virtual Environ. **15**(3), 309–329 (2006)

11. Lazzaro, N.: Why We Play Games: Four Keys to More Emotion Without Story. CRC Press, Boca Raton (2004)

12. Berens, L.V.: Understanding Yourself and Others: An Introduction to Temperament. Telos Publications, Candor (2000)

13. Nacke, L.E., Bateman, C., Mandryk, R.L.: BrainHex: preliminary results from a neurobiological gamer typology survey. In: Anacleto, J.C., Fels, S., Graham, N., Kapralos, B., Saif El-Nasr, M., Stanley, K. (eds.) ICEC 2011. LNCS, vol. 6972, pp. 288–293. Springer, Heidelberg (2011). https://doi.org/10.1007/978-3-642-24500-8_31

14. Tondello, G.F., Wehbe, R.R., Diamond, L., Busch, M., Marczewski, A., Nacke, L.E.: The gamification user types hexad scale. In: Proceedings of the 2016 Annual Symposium on Computer-Human Interaction in Play, Austin, Texas, USA, pp. 229–243. ACM (2016). 2968082

15. Ferro, L.S.: An analysis of players' personality type and preferences for game elements and mechanics. Entertain. Comput. **27**, 73–81 (2018)

16. Ferro, L.S., Walz, S.P., Greuter, S.: Towards personalised, gamified systems: an investigation into game design, personality and player typologies. In: Proceedings of the 9th Australasian Conference on Interactive Entertainment: Matters of Life and Death, Melbourne, Australia, pp. 1–6. ACM (2013). 2513024

17. Kocadere, S.A., Caglar, S.: Gamification from player type perspective: a case study. Educ. Technol. Soc. **21**(3), 12–22 (2018)

18. Monterrat, B., Lavoué, É., George, S.: Toward an adaptive gamification system for learning environments. In: Zvacek, S., Restivo, M.T., Uhomoibhi, J., Helfert, M. (eds.) CSEDU 2014. CCIS, vol. 510, pp. 115–129. Springer, Cham (2015). https://doi.org/10.1007/978-3-319-25768-6_8

19. Gonzalez, C.S., Toledo, P., Munoz, V.: Enhancing the engagement of intelligent tutorial systems through personalization of gamification. Int. J. Eng. Educ. **32**(1), 532–541 (2016)

20. Aldemir, T., Celik, B., Kaplan, G.: A qualitative investigation of student perceptions of game elements in a gamified course. Comput. Hum. Behav. **78**, 235–254 (2018)

21. Kotsopoulos, D., Bardaki, C., Lounis, S., Pramatari, K.: Employee profiles and preferences towards IoT-enabled gamification for energy conservation. Int. J. Serious Games **5**(2), 65–85 (2018)

22. Zichermann, G., Cunningham, C.: Gamification by Design: Implementing Game Mechanics in Web and Mobile Apps, p. 208. O'Reilly Media, Inc., Sebastopol (2011)

23. Kim, B.: Designing Gamification in the Right Way, pp. 29–35. American Library Association (2015)

24. Bozkurt, A., Durak, G.: A systematic review of gamification research: in pursuit of Homo Ludens. Int. J. Game Based Learn. **8**(3), 15–33 (2018)
25. Tobon, S., Ruiz-Alba, J.L., García-Madariaga, J.: Gamification and online consumer decisions: is the game over? Decis. Support Syst. **128**, 113167 (2020)
26. Ryan, R.M., Deci, E.L.: Self-determination theory and the facilitation of intrinsic motivation, social development, and well-being. Am. Psychol. **55**(1), 68 (2000)
27. Riley, G.: The role of self-determination theory and cognitive evaluation theory in home education. Cogent Educ. **3**(1), 1163651 (2016)

Federated Parking Flow Prediction Method Based on Blockchain and IPFS

Xuesen Zong[1($\boxtimes$)], Zhiqiang Hu[1], Xiaoyun Xiong[1], Peng Li[2], and Jinlong Wang[1]

[1] Qingdao University of Science and Technology, Qingdao, China
1119698476@qq.com
[2] Qingdao Yilian Information Technology Co. LTD., Qingdao, China

Abstract. Aiming at the problem of privacy security of parking data and low generalization performance of parking flow prediction model, a federated parking flow prediction method based on blockchain and IPFS is proposed. In this method, blockchain and IPFS are applied to the federated learning frame-work. Under the condition of ensuring the privacy and security of parking data, blockchain is used to replace the central server of federated learning to aggregate multi-party local models. Through blockchain and IPFS, the model data in the training stage of the parking flow prediction model are stored and synchronized quickly, which improves the generalization performance of the model and further improves the training efficiency of the model. In addition, in order to improve the participation enthusiasm of all participants, an incentive mechanism based on data volume contribution and model performance improvement contribution is designed. The experimental results show that the method can improve the generalization performance of the model and improve the training efficiency of the parking flow prediction model, and provide a reasonable reward allocation.

Keywords: LSTM · Federated learning · Blockchain · IPFS · Parking flow prediction · Incentive mechanism

1 Introduction

Parking flow prediction plays an important role in intelligent parking management. For office parking lot, it needs accurate and real-time parking flow prediction to analyze parking planning and formulate reasonable parking resource allocation strategy [1, 2]. However, for different office parking lots, due to the difference of parking flow in the same period, the generalization performance of the parking flow prediction model in some office parking lots is low. How to scientifically improve the generalization performance of the parking flow prediction model to provide timely and effective reference is of great significance.

Statistical learning method is a traditional solution [3, 4], which is mainly divided into Auto-regressive Integrated Moving Average (ARIMA) [3] model and Kalman filter model [4]. However, due to the change of parking flow shows some nonlinear characteristics, and changes rapidly with time, the fitting degree of this method for parking

Z. Lv and H. Song (Eds.): INTETAIN 2021, LNICST 429, pp. 257–275, 2022.
https://doi.org/10.1007/978-3-030-99188-3_16

flow data is low. Then, the prediction method of parking flow based on machine learning models such as K-Nearest Neighbors (KNN) [5], Support Vector Regression (SVR) [6] and Long Short-Term Memory (LSTM) [7] appeared. By training the model with parking data, the parking flow data were better fitted. However, with the emphasis on user privacy and data security, it was difficult to achieve the above method to train the parking data set model. In order to solve this problem, Google proposed a new privacy protection technology—Federated Learning in 2016 [8]. It was a collaborative method of distributed machine learning, which made the original data remain in local devices and could maintain the integrity of users' data privacy. Therefore, it was widely used in many fields. For example, federated learning had been applied to the financial sector, with examples of microcredit risk management and anti-money laundering [9]. Nevertheless, federated learning relied on a central server to aggregate the local model. Once the central server fails, it interrupted the training of the model and cause a single point of failure. In response to this problem, some scholars proposed to replace the central server with blockchain [10–13], stored and updated the federated model by using blockchain, and avoided the problem of single point failure by decentralizing. However, the above literature did not consider the low training efficiency of the federated model. When the parameters of the parking flow prediction model were large, there would be excessive demand for blockchain storage space in the direct chain storage of model data, and the storage and query of model data were slow, resulting in a long training time of the model.

In addition, federated learning methods lack incentives to improve the enthusiasm for participants. In the process of model training, not all participants contribute data actively. If there was no feasible incentive mechanism, participants with high-quality data might not participate actively, and ultimately affect the performance of the federated model. Therefore, it was necessary to add incentives to federated learning methods to encourage participants to actively participate in training. Kim et al. [11] proposed a reward based on data volume of participants, the greater data volume of participants, the more reward. Whereas, the greater data volume did not mean the greater the improvement in model performance, and for participants with the same amount of data but different data quality, it was impossible to distinguish the contribution of the two to the federated model. Therefore, this method had certain one-sidedness. Other researchers [14, 15] proposed to evaluate the performance improvement on the federated model before and after the participants' data training by setting a public validation set. However, for the data with strong privacy, it could not provide a public validation set for this method. In addition, there was also an one-sidedness to evaluate the contribution of the participants only from the model performance and ignore the amount of data.

In view of the low efficiency of model training and one-sidedness of incentive methods in current methods, this paper designs a federated parking flow prediction meth-od based on blockchain and IPFS. This method constructs a parking flow prediction model based on LSTM network, trains the parking flow prediction model under the federated learning framework to ensure the privacy of parking data, and uses blockchain to replace the central server to aggregate the local model to realize decentralization under the federated learning framework to prevent single-point faults. At the same time, based on the tamper resistance of blockchain, it further ensures the safety of model data.

The contributions of this paper are itemized as follows.

(1) Improving the efficiency of model training: By combining blockchain and IPFS, it realizes the on-chain and off-chain storage of model data, improves the storage and query efficiency of model data, so as to improve the training efficiency of the federated parking flow prediction model.

(2) Providing a contribution incentive mechanism: A contribution incentive mechanism is designed to comprehensively evaluate the data volume of participants and the performance improvement on the federal model without setting a public validation set, so as to provide reasonable incentive allocation and improve the enthusiasm of participants.

2   Correlative Knowledge

2.1   LSTM Neural Network

Recurrent Neural Network (RNN) abandons the full connection mode of the general fully connected neural network of the hidden layer, introduces the concept of time series and adopts the 'recursive connection' mechanism to retain the time series characteristics of the sequence, and retains the previous input information on the network [14]. Because there are enough hidden layer neurons in RNN, it can accurately fit the predicted time series. However, the traditional RNN has the problems of gradient disappearance and gradient explosion during training. In this regard, Hochreiter and Schmidhuber proposed the LSTM model [17], which is a storage unit composed of several gates. The gate can control the transmission of information about the sequence, obtain the long-term dependence on time series, effectively avoid the problem of gradient disappearance, and achieve good results in the prediction of time series data.

A typical LSTM model is controlled and protected by forgetting gate f, input gate i and output gate o (see Fig. 1). The forgetting gate f is used to discard unimportant information in the previous time step, the input gate i selects useful information from the input, and the output gate o controls the output of the current LSTM model. The state update of each gate is as follows:

$$f_t = \sigma \left(w_f \cdot \left[h_{t-1}, x_t \right] + b_f \right) \tag{1}$$

$$i_t = \sigma \left(w_i \cdot \left[h_{t-1}, x_t \right] + b_i \right) \tag{2}$$

$$o_t = \sigma \left(w_o \cdot \left[h_{t-1}, x_t \right] + b_o \right) \tag{3}$$

where h_t is the hidden state of time step t, x_t is the input of time step t, w_f, w_i and w_o are the weight values for each gate, b_f, b_i and b_o are the offset of each gate, σ is sigmoid activation function. The cell state C_t is constantly updated over time. Firstly, $\tilde{C}_t$ is obtained from Eq. (4), and C_t is updated according to Eq. (5). w_c and b_c represent the weight value and offset respectively, tanh is activation function. The output value h_t is controlled by the output gate unit and the cell state activated with tanh, as shown in Eq. (6). In short, LSTM uses gate units to enhance the memory of the recurrent neural network, reduce the amount of data carried by the intermediate process, and has better prediction results than RNN [18].

$$\tilde{C}_t = \tanh(w_c \cdot [h_{t-1}, x_t] + b_c) \tag{4}$$

$$C_t = f_t * C_{t-1} + i_t * \tilde{C}_t \tag{5}$$

$$h_t = o_t * \tanh(C_t) \tag{6}$$

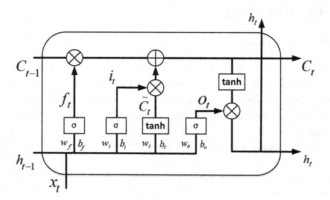

Fig. 1. LSTM network structure.

2.2 Federated Learning

Federated learning is essentially a distributed machine learning technology that can effectively reduce the risk of data privacy caused by source data in traditional ma-chine learning sets [9]. Its working principle mainly includes multiple participants and central servers (see Fig. 2). Participants (mobile phones, tablets, IoT devices, etc.) jointly train the model under the coordination of the central server. Participants use local data to train the local model. The central server uses the model average to aggregate the local model to obtain the global model, and finally obtains a model that is close to the centralized machine learning effect after multiple iterations.

An iterative process of federated learning is as follows:

① Each participant downloads global model parameters from the central server.
② Participants use local data to train local models.
③ Each participant uploads local model parameters to the central server.
④ The central server receives the model data of each participant and obtains the global model parameters by weighted aggregation.

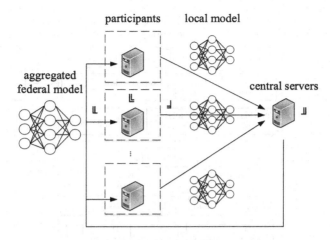

Fig. 2. Federated learning framework.

2.3 Blockchain

As the core technology of the digital cryptocurrency system represented by bitcoin, blockchain has the characteristics of traceability, transparency, tamper-proof and decentralization [19]. It uses the hash algorithm to calculate the head of each data block to obtain a hash value, connects blocks to form a data chain. In the data block, the transaction information in the current time is recorded and saved by Merk-le tree information, each data block is composed of block head and block (see Fig. 3).

The core technology of blockchain is distributed ledger, asymmetric encryption, consensus mechanism and smart contract. Among them, distributed accounts can be completed by multiple nodes in different places, and each node records a complete account. Asymmetric encryption makes data accessible only after authorized, which ensures the security and privacy of data. Consensus mechanism is to solve all ac-counting nodes how to reach a consensus, identify the validity of a record, but also a means to prevent tampering. smart contract is based on trusted and non-tampering data, which can automatically execute some predefined rules and clauses. Blockchain can be divided into three types: public chain, private chain and alliance chain. Among them, public chain is completely decentralized, and anyone can add data to public chain. Private chain is commonly used within the company or organization, and all operating permissions are controlled by the company or organization, with a high degree of centralization. The alliance chain is managed by several organizations or institutions. Each organization or institution controls a limited number of nodes, and the membership of members needs permission from the organization or institution.

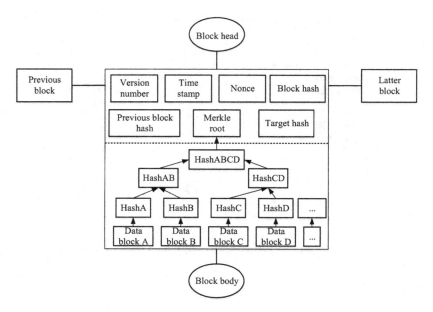

Fig. 3. Data block structure.

2.4 IPFS

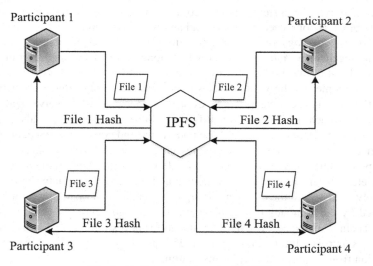

Fig. 4. Participants interact with IPFS.

IPFS provides distributed file storage system and content addressable technology to access stored files, which is convenient to connect with P2P network [20]. All peer points in IPFS computing network can access the unique Hash of files. Hash is modified every time the file is updated. IPFS is also known as version control system, which ensures the security, reliability and scalability of existing file storage and sharing systems [21]. The same transaction has the same hash in IPFS, which ensures the originality of the content. IPFS hash is spread to all peers, which also ensures the consistency between peers. Star file system provides high throughput content addressing block storage model to ensure transaction security. When multiple participants interact with the IPFS network, each participant uploads files to the IPFS network for storage, and then obtains the returned file Hash (see Fig. 4).

3 Federated Parking Flow Prediction Method Based on Blockchain and IPFS

The method in this paper is established under the framework of federated learning combined with blockchain and IPFS network. It is considered that multiple participants are required to train the federated parking flow prediction model at the same time. In order to prevent the leakage of parking data and the abuse of information, strict licensing management is needed. Therefore, the blockchain type in this article uses the alliance chain. In addition, the participants involved in the model training process need to register in the alliance chain, and the information of the registered participants will be sent to the participants nodes assigned to them. Through the participant registration contract, the elliptic curve encryption algorithm is used to generate the unique public-private key pair for the participants, and the participants registration information is bound to the public-private key pair. Finally, the participants node returns the public-private key pair to the corresponding participant.

3.1 Training of Federated Parking Flow Prediction Model

The overall framework of this method is mainly composed of local participants, blockchain networks and IPFS networks (see Fig. 5). Local participants are responsible for training local models. The trained local models are uploaded and stored in the IPFS network, and the returned local model Hash is stored in the blockchain network through the participant node calling smart contracts. In the blockchain network, the local model parameters are aggregated through smart contracts, and the aggregated global model parameters are stored in the IPFS network. The Hash of the returned global model parameters is stored in the blockchain network through smart contracts, and sent to the local participants through smart contracts. Then, the global model is obtained from the IPFS network. Finally, the local model is updated to the global model for the next round of model training. Next, the key components and processes of this method are described in detail.

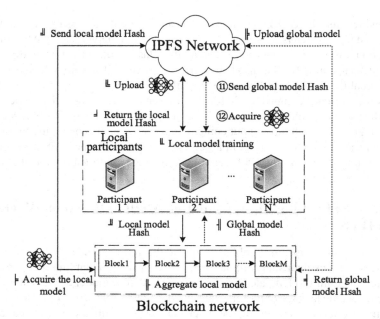

Fig. 5. Federated parking flow prediction method framework based on blockchain and IPFS.

1) Parking flow prediction model

In this paper, the prediction model of parking flow is constructed based on LSTM network, which is divided into two LSTM layers and a full connection layer. The cur-rent parking flow is predicted by combining the previous parking flow data. Due to the working mode of the office building personnel takes a week as a cycle, and its parking behavior also exists in a week as a cycle, with a total of 168 periods. There-fore, the input layer dimension of LSTM is set to 168, the hidden layer unit is

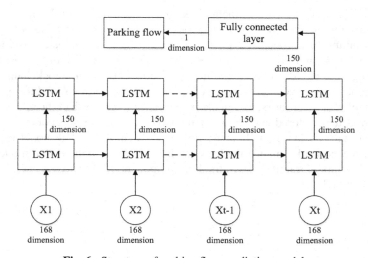

Fig. 6. Structure of parking flow prediction model.

set to 150, and the full connection layer is calculated to generate a one-dimensional parking flow data output with 150-dimensional data as input, where Xt is the model input value at t time (see Fig. 6).

2) Smart contract design

A smart contract is a self-executing contract that defines rules for negotiation, verifies the execution of rules and executes protocols using formal code. The method of this paper sets up the registration contracts of participants, upload contracts, download contracts, send contracts and aggregation contracts. The participant registration contract receives the participant's user name, user password and encrypted identity card number, generates a unique public-private key pair for it using the elliptic curve encryption algorithm, and binds the participant registration information to the public-private key. The encryption of ID card number is to prevent the information leakage of participants caused by hacker intrusion. The upload contract receives the user's name of the participants and the Hash information of the local model, and stores it on the chain in the form of key value pairs after encryption using the elliptic curve encryption algorithm. The download contract to receive the participant user name, using elliptic curve encryption algorithm to decrypt the Hash model information. The send contract is responsible for sending Hash for global model parameters to all participants. The aggregation contract sets the weighted average rule of model parameters, and automatically monitors the upload state of the Hash information of the local model of each participant. When each participant uploads, the local model aggregation is automatically performed, and the aggregated global model is stored in IPFS, and the Hash information of the global model is stored in the blockchain through the upload contract. The weighted average formula for model parameters is shown in formula (7), where w is a global model parameter, k is the number of local participants, n is the total amount of data for all local participants, n_i is the amount of data for local participant i, and w_i is the local model parameter for local participant i.

$$w = \sum_{i=1}^{k} \frac{n_i}{n} w_i \tag{7}$$

3) Model training process

The local model and global model training process of this method are described below (see Fig. 7). Firstly, the upload state of each local model of the local participant is defined as *model_state*, the state of the local participant obtaining the global model is *model_get*, and the update state of the global model is *model_aggregation*, and each state is initialized as 0. Then, each participant uses local data to train the local model, uploads the trained local model to IPFS, and uploads the hash value of the returned local model to the blockchain network with the upload state *model_state* of the local model as 1 through the participant node. The aggregation contract in the blockchain network monitors and queries the upload status of the local model of each participant. When the upload status query of the local model of all participants is 1, the Hash value of the local model of each participant is obtained, and further the local model of each participant is obtained by using the Hash value through the IPFS network, and the upload status *model_state* of the local model of each participant is

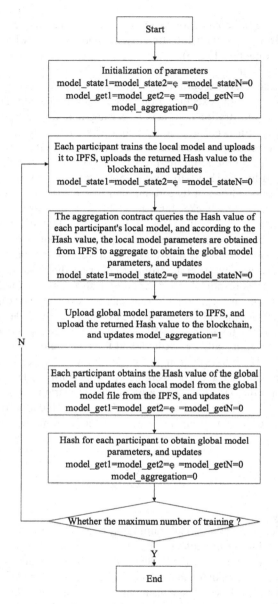

Fig. 7. Model training process.

modified to be 0. Then, the local model of all participants is aggregated according to the weighted aggregation rule set in the aggregation contract, so as to obtain the global model and upload it to the IPFS network. The Hash value of the returned global model is uploaded to the blockchain network, and then the global model is modified to update the state *model_aggregation* as 1. Each participant uploads the

Hash value of the local model, and then queries the update state *model_aggregation* of the global model through each participant node. When the *model_aggregation* is 1, each participant obtains the Hash of the global model from the blockchain network through the participant node, and further obtains the global model from the IPFS network. The state *model_get* of the global model obtained by the local participant is modified to 1. When all local participants obtain the global model, the update state *model_aggregation* of the global model is modified to 0, and the state *model_get* of the global model obtained by the local participant is 0. Then, each local participant updates the global model to the local model for the next round of the local model. When the maximum number of training rounds is reached, the model training is completed.

3.2 Incentive Mechanism

The incentive mechanism designed in this paper is divided into two parts (see Fig. 8). One part is to evaluate the contribution of each participant's data volume, and the other part is to evaluate the contribution of each participant's model performance improvement. Finally, the two parts are integrated to obtain the total contribution of each participant, calculate the allocation proportion of each participant and store it in the blockchain. The following two parts are introduced.

Firstly, the calculation method of data volume contribution is introduced. Let D_i^n denote the number of local training sets of participant i, then the data contribution D_i of each participant can be calculated by formula (8), where N is the number of participants.

$$D_i = \frac{D_i^n}{\sum\limits_{j=1}^{N} D_j^n} \tag{8}$$

Next, the calculation method of model performance improvement contribution is introduced. Firstly, $M_{\{i\}}$ is defined as the sub-federated model trained by the data of other participants except participants, and M is the main-federated model trained by all participants. Each participant uses its local validation set to evaluate the accuracy of the main-federated model and the sub-federated model, respectively. The model accuracy calculation formula is as follows:

$$R = 1 - \sqrt{\frac{1}{m} \sum_{i=1}^{m} \left(y_i - \hat{y}_i \right)} \tag{9}$$

where R is the accuracy of the model, m is the number of validation sets, y is the true value of the validation set, and $\hat{y}$ is the predicted value of the model. The model accuracy of each federated model $M_{\{i\}}$ and the main-federated model M in the local validation set of each participant j is denoted as $R_j^{M_{\{i\}}}$ and R_j^M, respectively. Let S_i denote the average model accuracy of sub-federated model $M_{\{i\}}$ and main-federated model M in

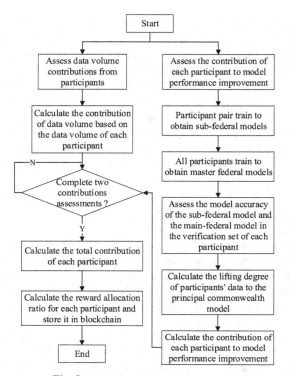

Fig. 8. Incentive Mechanism Process.

the verification set of each participant, as shown in Eq. (10).

$$S_i = \sum_{j=1}^{N} \left(R_j^M - R_j^{M\{i\}} \right) \tag{10}$$

We believe that S_i can reflect the degree of performance improvement of the federated model. The larger S_i is, the higher the improvement of the data of the participant i on the federated model is, and the greater the contribution of the participant to the performance improvement of the model is. On the contrary, if S_i is smaller and close to 0, it is believed that the federated model has a good prediction performance for the data of the participant, then the contribution of the participant to the federated model is small. If S_i is negative, this shows that the data of the participant will reduce the performance of the federated model, then consider not providing incentives or rejecting its participation. In order to intuitively reflect the improvement of the performance of the federated model by the participant data, the contribution of each participant to the model performance improvement can be defined by the following calculation:

$$C_i = \frac{S_i}{\sum_{j=1}^{N} S_j} \tag{11}$$

The total contribution η_i of the participant i is then obtained by formula (12), where λ and $\mu \in [0, 1]$ is the weight of the data volume contribution and the model performance enhancement contribution, respectively, and $\lambda + \mu = 1$.

$$\eta_i = \lambda D_i + \mu C_i \tag{12}$$

According to the contribution value of each participant, the distribution proportion of the reward value G_i of each participant in the federated model training can be calculated as:

$$G_i = \frac{\eta_i}{\sum\limits_{j=1}^{N} \eta_j} \tag{13}$$

4 Experimental Results and Analysis

4.1 Experimental Parameter Settings

In the method of this paper, the local model training is realized based on Python 3.8 and Pytorch deep learning framework. The blockchain adopts the Hyperledge Fabric 2.0 framework, and relies on the mature security mechanism of Fabric to ensure the security mechanism of the method. The consensus mechanism adopts the Raft of Fabric, and the smart contract is realized by Golang programming. The experimental device is a notebook with 16 GB memory, and 6-core Intel Core i7 processor. It runs three virtual machines with 4 cores and 4 GB of memory, each virtual machine with Ubuntu 18.04 system. The experimental data are selected from the parking data collected from three real parking lots in Qingdao, Shandong Province, China from April to September 2020, and the specific information is shown in Table 1. For example, parking lot 2 has 400 parking spaces, with full-day traffic between 650 and 800 on working days and between 100 and 250 on rest days.

4.2 Experimental Data Processing

Check and clear abnormal data for three parking data to ensure the effectiveness of all parking data. Subsequently, the parking flow in each period is further counted for each parking data, and the 0–1 standardization is used to normalize the parking flow data. In addition, according to the time sequence, the parking data from April to August are used as the historical dataset, and the parking data in September are used as the test dataset.

Table 1. Experimental data information.

Parking lot	Number of parking spaces	Parking flow on working days	Parking flow on rest day
1	450	800–900	100–300
2	400	650–800	100–250
3	300	400–550	50–150

4.3 Experimental Result Analysis

This experiment is divided into two parts: model training and model contribution evaluation. The model training part uses the historical dataset of each participant to train the parking flow prediction model, and obtains the global parking flow prediction model. According to the trained global parking flow prediction model and the test dataset of each participant, the root mean square error of the prediction results is calculated respectively, and used as the evaluation standard of the model performance. The model contribution evaluation part evaluates the model contribution of each participant, calculates the reward allocation value of each participant according to the incentive mechanism, and stores it in the blockchain for participants to query.

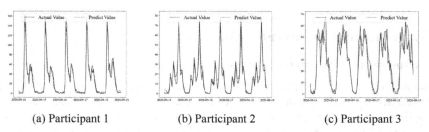

(a) Participant 1   (b) Participant 2   (c) Participant 3

Fig. 9. Model performance after centralized data training based on LSTM model.

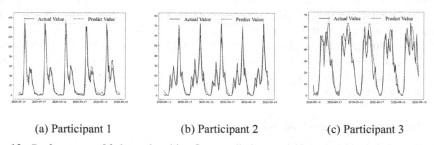

(a) Participant 1   (b) Participant 2   (c) Participant 3

Fig. 10. Performance of federated parking flow prediction model based on blockchain and IPFS.

In order to compare the performance of the federated parking flow prediction model, the method proposed in this paper is compared with the method based on LSTM centralized data training [8]. The performance of the model trained based on LSTM centralized data on the three participants' parking data validation sets (see Fig. 9). The performance of the federated learning model trained by the method proposed in this paper on the three participants' parking data validation sets (see Fig. 10). Table 2 shows the root mean square errors of the above two methods on the three participants' parking test datasets. Through observation and comparison, the performance of the federated model is slightly lower than that of the model based on LSTM centralized data training, but it meets the security of data privacy and meets the actual needs.

In order to measure the model training efficiency of the method in this paper, a total of 15 tests were conducted in the same environment with the federated learning method

Table 2. Model root mean square error statistics.

participants	Centralized data training method based on LSTM model	Federated parking flow prediction method based on blockchain and IPFS
Participant 1	5.442978220296002	6.621649297039326
Participant 2	3.85194816705429	4.176416201840635
Participant 3	2.052104307244879	2.391470359073033

based on blockchain. In each test, a total of 10 rounds of federated learning model training were conducted, and 50 rounds of local model training were conducted by each participant in each round. Statistics single model training time, single model upload time, single model query time, federated model training time as shown in Table 3.

Table 3. Average training time of model.

Test variables	Federated learning method based on blockchain and IPFS	Federated learning method based on blockchain
Single local model training time	10.95 s	10.6 s
Single local model upload time	0.97 s	2.71 s
Single local model query time	2.04 s	2.45 s
Global model aggregation time	12.04 s	14.82 s
Federated model training time	7 m 14 s	8 m 33 s

In addition, in order to reflect the advantages of using IPFS, the model data size is expanded by 2 to 4 times, and the model data upload time based on blockchain federated learning method is compared, as shown in Table 4. Among them, the model upload time of the federated learning method based on blockchain and IPFS is stable at 0.97 s, which does not change with the increase of model data size. The model upload time of the federated learning method based on blockchain increases with the increase of model size, which further reflects the effectiveness of this method to improve the efficiency of model training.

Table 4. Performance comparison based on IPFS.

Model data size	Federated learning method based on blockchain and IPFS	Federated learning method based on blockchain
5.05M	0.97 s	2.71 s
10.10M	0.97 s	4.04 s
15.15M	0.97 s	5.77 s
20.20M	0.97 s	9.08 s

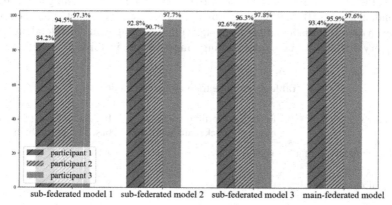

Fig. 11. Accuracy of sub-federated model and main-federated model in validation sets of participants.

Calculating the model accuracy of sub-federated models $M_{\{1\}}$, $M_{\{2\}}$, $M_{\{3\}}$ and main-federated model M on each participant validation set based on incentive mechanism for three participants (see Fig. 11). It can be seen from the graph that for the participant 1, the model accuracy of the sub-federated model $M_{\{1\}}$ and the main-federated mode M on its validation set is quite different, which shows that the participant 1 should make a greater contribution to the model performance of the main federated model M, and for the participant 2, the model accuracy of the sub-federated model $M_{\{2\}}$ and the main federated model M on its validation set is also quite different, which also shows that the participant 2 has a greater contribution to the model performance of the main federated model M, and for the participant 3, the model accuracy of the sub-federated model $M_{\{3\}}$ and the main federated model M on its validation set is basically the same, which shows that the participant 3 has little improvement in the model performance of the main federated model, so the model performance contribution should be small.

In the experiment, when the data volume of each participant is the same, by setting the contribution weight of data volume and the contribution weight of model performance improvement, the reward allocation proportion of each participant is obtained according to the formula (12) and formula (13) (see Fig. 12). Among them, the reward allocation proportion of participant 1 is the largest, accounting for 47.55%, which is because the accuracy of the federated model is the largest, followed by the reward allocation proportion of participant 2, accounting for 36.79%, and the reward allocation proportion of participant 3 is the smallest, which is because the accuracy of the federated model is the smallest.

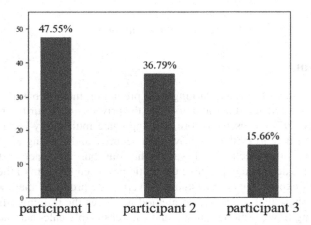

Fig. 12. Proportion of reward value allocation among participants.

Finally, considering the scenario that blockchain will generate concurrent transactions among multi-participant nodes during model training, a generation time of block test is performed to determine whether it can meet participants' daily applications. The test environment is as follows: Each participant node continuously sends 1000 model data to test whether the average generation time of block meets the requirements, that is, less than the set maximum generation block waiting time. In the experiment, the maximum generation block waiting time is set to be 1 s according to the generation block routine of Fabric alliance chain, and three participants are set, so the maximum block transaction number is set to be 3. A total of 15 tests were conducted, and the average generation block time was calculated after each test (see Fig. 13). It can be seen from the figure that the generation block time showed a gentle upward trend at the beginning, reaching the maximum generation block time in the 10th test, and then fluctuated around the average generation block time. The reason for this phenomenon is that with the increase in the number of tests, more memory space, and the rate of data processing is reduced. After 15 tests, the average generation block time of processing model parameters is 0.541 s, and the maximum generation block time is 0.643 s, which is far less than the set maximum generation block waiting time of 1s. Therefore, the Fabric alliance chain selected in this paper can effectively deal with 3000 transaction requests submitted by 3 participating nodes, which can meet the normal application requirements.

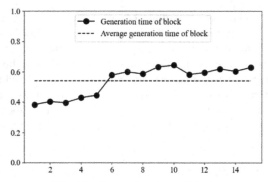

Fig. 13. Generation time of block.

5 Conclusion

This paper proposes a federated parking flow prediction method based on blockchain and IPFS, and uses federated learning to solve the privacy and security of parking data. Blockchain and IPFS are used to store and aggregate multi-party local parking flow prediction model data to further improve data security and training efficiency. At the same time, an incentive mechanism based on the contribution of each participant to the federated model is designed to promote the participation enthusiasm of the participants. Finally, relevant experiments are designed to verify the proposed method. The experimental results show that the proposed method improves the training efficiency of the federated parking flow prediction model and can reasonably calculate the contribution rewards of each participant. Although the performance of the federated parking flow prediction model is slightly lower than that of the traditional method, the data security is improved, which provides some reference for the training of the parking flow prediction model.

References

1. Wang, F.Y.: Parallel control and management for intelligent transportation systems: concepts, architectures, and applications. IEEE Trans. Intell. Transp. Syst. **11**(3), 630–638 (2010)
2. Wang, Y., Guo, L.Y., Cheng, X.: Short-term traffic flow forecasting optimization method based on deep learning. Comput. Eng. Appl. **56**(16), 211–217 (2020)
3. Williams, B.M., Durvasula, P.K., Brown, D.E.: Urban freeway traffic flow prediction: application of seasonal autoregressive integrated moving average and exponential smoothing models. Transp. Res. Rec. **1644**(1), 132–141 (1998)
4. Okutani, I., Stephanedes, Y.J.: Dynamic prediction of traffic volume through kalman filer theory. Transp. Res. Part B Methodol. **18**(1), 1–11 (1984)
5. Zhang, T., Chen, X., Xie, M. P.: Short term traffic prediction method based on K nearest neighbor nonparametric regression. Syst. Eng. Theory Pract. **1**(2), 376–384 (2010)
6. Castroneto, M., Jeong, Y.S., Jeong, M.K.: Online-SVR for short-term traffic flow prediction under typical and atypical traffic conditions. Expert Syst. Appl. **36**(3), 6164–6173 (2009)
7. Li, X.D., Cen, Y.F., Cen, G.: Prediction of short-term available parking space using LSTM model. In: 2019 14th International Conference on Computer Science & Education (ICCSE), Toronto, Ontario, Canada, vol. 20, pp. 631–635 (2019)

8. Mcmahan, H.B., Moore, E., Ramage, D.: Communication-efficient learning of deep networks from decentralized data. Artif. Intell. Stat. **1**(28), 1273–1282 (2017)
9. Yang, Q., Liu, Y., Chen, T.: Federated machine learning: concept and applications. ACM Trans. Intell. Syst. Technol. (TIST) **10**(2), 1–19 (2019)
10. Ma, C., Li, J., Ding, M.: When federated learning meets blockchain: a new distributed learning paradigm. IEEE Internet Things J. **20**(9), 1–7 (2020)
11. Kim, H., Park, J., Bennis, M.: Blockchained on-device federated learning. IEEE Commun. Lett. **24**(6), 1279–1283 (2020)
12. Qu, Y., Pokhrel, S.R., Garg, S.: A blockchained federated learning framework for cognitive computing in industry 4.0 networks. IEEE Trans. Ind. Inform. **17**(4), 2964–2973 (2021)
13. Luo, C.Y., Chen, X.B., Ma, C.D.: Online federal incremental learning algorithm for blockchain. J. Comput. Appl. **41**(2), 363–371 (2021)
14. Kang, J.W., Xiong, Z.H., Niyato, D.: Incentive mechanism for reliable federated learning: a joint optimization approach to combining reputation and contract theory. IEEE Internet Things J. **6**(6), 10700–10714 (2019)
15. Li, Y., Chen, C., Liu, N.: A blockchain-based decentralized federated learning framework with committee consensus. IEEE Netw. **35**(1), 234–241 (2021)
16. Phan, M.C., Hagan, M.T.: Error surface of recurrent neural networks. IEEE Trans. Neural Netw. Learn. Syst. **24**(11), 1709–1721 (2013)
17. Hochreiter, S., Schmidhuber, H.: Long short-term memory. Neural Comput. **9**(8), 1735–1780 (1997)
18. Zhao, R., Wang, D., Yan, R.: Machine health monitoring using local feature-based gated recurrent unit networks. IEEE Trans. Ind. Electron. **65**(2), 1539–1548 (2018)
19. Ma, L., Pei, Q., Qu, Y., Fan, K., Lai, X.: Decentralized privacy-preserving reputation management for mobile crowdsensing. In: Chen, S., Choo, K.K., Fu, X., Lou, W., Mohaisen, A. (eds.) SecureComm 2019. LNICST, vol. 304. Springer, Cham (2019). https://doi.org/10.1007/978-3-030-37228-6_26
20. Alessi, M., Camillo, A., Giangreco, E.: Make users own their data: a decentralized personal data store prototype based on ethereum and IPFS. In: 2018 3rd International Conference on Smart and Sustainable Technologies, Split, vol. 7, pp. 1–7. (2018)
21. Randhir, K., Rakesh, T.: Implementation of distributed file storage and access framework using IPFS and blockchain. In: 2019 Fifth International Conference on Image Information Processing (ICIIP), Shimla, India, vol. 11, pp. 246–251 (2019)

Augmented Reality

Investigating the Motivational Effect of Fantasy and Similarity Through Avatar Identification in AR Game-Based Learning

Tengjia Zuo$^{(\boxtimes)}$, Erik D. van der Spek , Jun Hu , and Max V. Birk

Industrial Design, Eindhoven University of Technology, Eindhoven, The Netherlands
{t.zuo,e.d.v.d.spek,j.hu,m.v.birk}@tue.nl

Abstract. When children engage in virtual learning, they frequently experience a lack of motivation and concentration. Virtual and augmented reality Game-based learning (GBL) is a promising option for increasing learning motivation and can provide a more immersive context. While AR fantasy makes learning more engaging, avatar self-similarity provides players with approachable and straightforward circumstances to begin. However, little is known about how to combine learning with captivating fantasy and engaging self-similarity. Therefore, it is essential to understand how to adjust the similarity and fantasy levels in a game's design to more effectively integrate learning information and increase player motivation. To examine the motivation for fantasy play in gameplay, a key concept titled player identification is introduced. This paper presents an experiment conducted using our designed AR Game, MathMythos, with four conditions. We explore the relationship between fantasy, similarity, motivation, and identification in AR GBL. By exploring the correlation between player identification and enjoyment in fantasy/real-world and similar/dissimilar contexts, this study shows children would enjoy the game more in a fantasy context if they experienced stronger avatar identification in the gameplay. For game designers, this study emphasizes the fantasy and similarity aspects of avatar design and inspires designers to weigh these factors appropriately for their GBL context and design purpose.

Keywords: Fantasy · Player identification · Augmented Reality · Serious games

1 Introduction

Student engagement is a well-established predictor of subsequent academic achievement, and therefore a lack of motivation ('amotivation') [1] can lead to underperformance and dropping out [2, 3]. Research suggests game-based learning (GBL), which incorporates entertaining and playful elements into learning content, can increase motivation [4] in learning mathematics [5, 6], language [7], and life-skills [8], among others. However, GBL does not always increase motivation to engage with the learning content [9]. Therefore, more in-depth, empirical knowledge on how to design GBL to be more motivating could shed light on why some games fail while others succeed in creating compelling games for learning and subsequently help game designers create more efficacious GBL.

© ICST Institute for Computer Sciences, Social Informatics and Telecommunications Engineering 2022
Published by Springer Nature Switzerland AG 2022. All Rights Reserved
Z. Lv and H. Song (Eds.): INTETAIN 2021, LNICST 429, pp. 279–294, 2022.
https://doi.org/10.1007/978-3-030-99188-3_17

An important concept related to player motivation is fantasy play, the act of playing among children with themes and roles that require imagination and make-believe [10, 11]. While performing a cognitive task such as mathematics, fantasy play can allow students to enter and stay in the "magic circle" [12, 13] of the game world without consciously thinking about mathematical challenges [14]. Malone et al. coin Endogenous Fantasy and Exogenous Fantasy that describes approaches to intrinsically integrating fantasy elements with learning content: by making fantasy elements linked to learning content or separating fantasy elements from learning content and setting them as external rewards, respectively [15]. Research suggests Endogenous Fantasy appears to have a greater potential for generating intrinsic motivation [16].

To create a GBL experience that incorporates endogenous fantasy, Designers should place fantasy game features in an authentic learning context [17], where contemporary technology can assist. Augmented Reality, a technology that enables virtual overlay on tangible materials and the physical world [18], could transport users to a world where tangible reality and imaginary virtuality coexist. Such technology brings a more immersive and potentially more motivational experience than Non-AR games for children's education [19]. To fully utilize AR's affordances, judicious design of digital overlays such as avatars and stories is critical [20]. The unanswered concern is whether more realistic or fanciful stories/avatars settings will lead to more engaging authentic learning environments.

Research by Van der Spek et al. indicates people enjoyed fantasy avatars and dialogues in a GBL more, but the alien context of the fantasy could impede learning compared with a more grounded real-life setting [21]. While similarity or alienness is another dimension that can exist both in fantasy and real-life settings, two dimensions were considered in our designed game Mathmythos AR: fantasy and similarity. Therefore the game includes four different avatar designs: similar fantasy (fantasy human), dissimilar fantasy (fantasy animal), dissimilar real-life (real-life animal), and similar real-life (real-life human). With this game, we conducted a study to explore children's motivation in GBL and how they are influenced by levels of fantasy and similarity settings in augmented reality contexts.

To further understand how levels of fantasy and similarity may influence player motivation, we introduce the concept of player identification. Player identification, a vital catalyst to fantasy play, is found increasing users' autonomy and motivation through avatar customization in previous research [22]. An open question, in this case, is whether children want to "escape" the boring learning real-world settings in the textbook [23] and enjoy learning more when playing with fantasy avatars, or whether the more grounded setting makes it easier to insert themselves in the player character. Therefore, the following research questions are proposed: 1. Do players have distinct avatar identifications (similarity and wishful identification) for a fantasy or a real-life avatar setting, for a similar or a dissimilar avatar setting? 2. How do high or low levels of fantasy and similarity settings in games affect their motivation in GBL through player identification?

This research focuses on the "Invitation stage" of gameplay [24]— where potential players are attracted by the GBL design. Players are then invited into the magic circle and become motivated to explore the game. Therefore learning outcomes are not the current primary focus. Through a quasi-experimental using MathmythosAR, we would like to highlight the effect of fantasy and similarity on player identification and motivation in AR GBL design, inspiring the integration research and innovation practice of AR fantasy in GBL.

2 Related Work

2.1 Motivation

Deci & Ryan differentiate two types of motivation in their refined and expanded self-determination theory: intrinsic motivation and extrinsic motivation. While the first describes a type of motivation that derives from one's inner satisfaction of needs, the other refers to a type of motivation caused by external rewards [1]. Based on that, the self-determination-theory continuum [25] was designed to understand different motivations. In that continuum, Amotivation is defined as a human's unmotivated or non-autonomous state [26]. As the level of self-determination increases, there is extrinsic motivation, next to which is intrinsic motivation. An intrinsic motivation inventory (IMI) for game-play was developed to quantify motivation levels [25]. Aspects of interest/enjoyment, perceived competence, effort/importance, tension/pressure are included in that scale. To explore motivation towards playing in virtual worlds, IMI was later converted to a version that suits the context of gameplay [27].

Motivation and children's education is a topic that has raised increasing attention in recent decades [15]. Despite individual differences, it is still a common phenomenon that children prefer playing a video game to learning from a textbook [28]. Because children have the proneness to be attracted by novelty and playfulness, Game-based learning is widely adapted and researched to improve children's learning motivation [27]. However, parts of GBL have proven to be efficient, while others have not, depending on the game setting, the learning content, and how the playfulness was embedded into the learning content [29]. Although GBL can increase children's motivation, the gap between digital games and physical learning material remains the same. One promising approach is to enhance physical interaction in virtual learning through contemporary technologies [30].

2.2 Augmented Reality for Learning

Augmented Reality (AR) is a technology that supports interactive experiences towards the real world while presenting a virtual overlay over the real-world object [31]. By superimposing graphics, 3D models, animation [19] into physical materials like books, blocks, or physical spaces, AR bridges the virtual and physical world with interaction and immersion [32]. As a tool that enhances players' experience, AR has been widely adopted in physical education, nature and science education, language, and mathematics learning [5, 33–35]. Various design research with traditional learning as a pretest and an AR as a posttest was conducted in recent research to show the advantages of employing AR in learning [35]. With the interactive virtual overlay varies, AR allows multiplayer physical interaction in a common space and creates social learning contexts [36]. AR textbooks are preferred by children over regular textbooks [19]. Because of the immersive and unique experience that AR provides, current research has found that it boosts children's learning motivation and engagement [37].

Strategies for designing AR learning have been the key to follow in recent research. Li et al. discover that incorporating a diegetic progress map into the design of an augmented reality mechanic provides players with significantly more motivational pull than a non-diegetic one [34]. Fan et al. indicate 3D multimedia content, location-based design, haptic technology are promising means to maximize AR's affordance. They highlight some keys for designing AR for learning: Smooth transitions from traditional instruction to AR one; Considering the role of teachers; Accessibility for teachers and students; maintenance and updates [20]. While recent research indicates that augmented reality fantasy positively affects children's motivation to learn [5], Miller et al. found users' interaction with AR virtual agents resembling real-life social communication with humans [38]. Because AR facilitates the combination of authentic learning contexts and playful interactions in GBL, it remains to explore how to balance the fantasy and similarity types of the game contexts to achieve a motivating GBL.

2.3 Fantasy and Similarity

Fantasy is initially used to describe an imaginative mental stage [39]. Recent research distinguishes mental activity and game elements parts of fantasy [40]. As a type of activity triggered by imagination, thematic fantasy play describes children's behavior of enacting roles or themes that engender make-believe and imagination [12]. Fantasy play can facilitate the learning process and motivation for children [41, 42]. Research about fantasy as a mental activity mostly focuses on one's proneness towards specific content or state when engaging in play [43]. To identify an individual's tendency to fantasize, Merckelbach, Harald et al. construct a questionnaire to measure fantasy proneness [44]. Beomkyu Choi et al. develop a scale to measure people's state of fantasy when playing games [45]. They propose "identification, analogy, imagination, and satisfaction" as four dimensions of the fantasy state.

Fantasy can also refer to game elements or game types that deviate from the real world [40]. Games with predominantly real-world settings are classified as simulations, whereas games with fictional settings are classified as fantasy [46]. Such situations are regarded as elements of fantasy in game design. Malone and Lepper coined the terms "endogenous" and "exogenous" to refer to two distinct ways of integrating fantasy elements with serious learning: intrinsically related fantasy and extrinsically related fantasy—either to integrate fantasy narrative or mechanics with learning or to simply use fantasy as an external reward for learning [15]. Malone believes that endogenous fantasy increases players' motivation in learning. To enable the motivating effect of endogenous fantasy, representations of learning should use visual features that encourage users' interactive exploration of play and learning [47].

One important visual feature here is avatar self-similarity, which usually describes game avatars' similarity with players in games [48]. Aspects of appearance, personality, abilities, and life experience can all be considered when comparing game avatars to their players. The majority of current research focuses on the similarity of avatar appearances [48, 49]. Since an avatar is a player's virtual self-representation, avatars with similar traits to players can increase players' experience [49]. According to Parmar's research, students learned programming concepts more effectively with self-similar avatars in VR GBL [50].

Players' senses of similarity are not necessarily attributed to real-life-based or fantasy in games. However, the concept of fantasy is often embedded in similar or dissimilar avatars. For example, with both fantastic superpowers, spider-man is designed more similar in appearance to human players, while Broodmother in Dota2 looks more dissimilar to human players (Fig. 1). Spek et al. compare fantasy visual settings and familiar visual settings in serious games. They find fantasy settings can improve the gameplay experience, but a familiar visual setting in serious games can better facilitate learning [21]. It still remains to be explored how the levels of fantasy together with similarity influence players' motivation in GBL.

Fig. 1. The fantasy and similar Spiderman (left), the fantasy and dissimilar Broodmother (right)

2.4 Avatar Identification

One way to understand how avatar design influences players' engagement is through investigating avatar identification. Identifying a fictional character is a pivotal driver to user experience and attraction [51]. Van Looy et al. propose a scale to measure player identification [52]. They validify the player identification questionnaire across three dimensions: avatar identification, group identification, and game identification. Avatar identification, including wishful identification and similarity identification in video gameplay, enables players to transport themselves to different perspectives and temporarily become the game's role. Role-play in games, creating and playing a fictional character with background stories and settings can encourage avatar identification. Research suggests that character customization [53], real-life escaping [52] appear to be positively associated with avatar identification as well. Among these, customizing ones' avatar might boost personal motivation and interest during gameplays [54].

3   The Game Design

To answer our research question, we conducted a study using our own designed game Mathmythos AR. The MathMythos AR is designed to help children aged 9 to 10 practice addition outside the classroom. It is an augmented reality card-based game that encourages children to solve math problems in a fantasy or real-life context. Aiming to explore fantasy and similarity's influence, we provide four avatars and related stories in this game: Rubin the warlock, Buddy the dragon, Luca the student, and Vicky, the cow. Because as humans, players would find an animaloid look relatively dissimilar to general players than humanoid characters, the humanoid character can represent a similar avatar, when the animaloid is the dissimilar type.

Children players will receive four cards when playing as an avatar: a role card that represents themselves, with two virtual buttons, two item cards that contain values to be summed up, one NPC (Non-Player Character) card for triggering the story. Users will first learn the background story and game task via reading the cards' descriptions. After scanning all cards under the camera, virtual 3D models of avatars, items, and NPC will be presented. Player Character avatars will show up with a dialogue indicating the task in this game is to calculate the sum number values on two item cards. With one virtual button covered by the player's hand, random numbers start popping up above the avatar's head, in between where the correct answer lies. The player needs to release the virtual button once the right answer shows up. The second virtual button then needs to be covered to trigger the narrative.

Four different avatars are designed (Fig. 3) with related items, NPC, and narrative in the same gameplay mechanic mentioned above. All the avatars and narratives were designed gender-neutral to avoid possible gender biases. In the Fantasy scenarios, users play Rubin's role, the warlock, to calculate the total power of two magic gems that enable the magic spell to free the friend. Playing as Buddy, the dragon, users need to hatch a dragon egg with an adequate firepower amount. In real-life settings, Luca, the normal student, needs to add up the food's total price on two cards and have them delivered to the brother. When playing Vicky's role, the story is about how the cow Vicky computes the delivery's total weight and sends them to the Horse.

Fig. 2. The experiment settings (the pattern is for anonymization purposes)

4   The Experiment Design

A total of 34 primary school students aged 9 to 10 years old (of whom self-identified as Male $=$ 19, Female $=$ 15) were invited to this research (Fig. 2). All participants from the same classroom at the same primary school were invited to a classroom with settings prepared for the experiment. The procedure lasts approximately 20 min per person. In appreciation of children's time, researchers offered a lecture about Augmented Reality and Design. The content and the experiment's design were approved by the Ethics Review Board at the (anonymous) university in advance. Both children's and their parents' consent for participation was achieved before the experiment. Their teacher provided demographic information and anonymized it according to their student number.

The experiment was designed within-subject to explore the effect of fantasy settings and real-life settings. Two 5-points Likert scale questionnaires were introduced. One is the enjoyment/interest part from the Intrinsic Motivation Inventory (IMI), a dimension that measures children's interest (enjoyment) in different characters during gameplay. The other is the avatar identification part from the Player Identification questionnaire (PI) questionnaire [52] that interprets children's identification regarding different avatars.

Fig. 3. Four avatars with related NPC

Each participant first played a pretest version of the AR card game with only instructional word content at the beginning of the experiment. The form of a five-scale questionnaire and ways of handling reversed questions were introduced beforehand. After that, participants were invited to play four versions of the Mathmythos AR game. These four versions of role-playing contrast 2 × 2 variables, fantasy/real-life versus human/animal player character (Fig. 4). All conditions were presented randomly to the children according to a 4 × 4 Latin Square to minimize potential order effects. Questions in the online questionnaire were presented to children in a random sequence. On average, playing a single condition was approximately 2 min. To avoid boredom among the children, we design the questionnaire with images of all conditions following each question. Additionally, by structuring questionnaires in this approach, children may be encouraged to compare different circumstances and provide more objective evaluations since children are frequently found pleasing adults by providing too positive ratings in studies [14].

Fig. 4. Four conditions

5   Results

5.1   Reliability

The results show good reliability for similarity identification (from 0.8 to 0.9 for all conditions). The wishful identification scale is acceptable in most situations (from 0.6 to 0.8), except for the Human avatar. The reliability is a bit poor, with Cronbach's alpha of 0.5. Besides, Cronbach's alpha for enjoyment is poor, with 0.6 for the Fantasy Animal, 0.5 for the animal, 0.5 for the Fantasy Human, 0.5 for the Human.

5.2 Descriptive Data and Controlled Factors

In general, most children perceive very high enjoyment when playing with all four types of avatars. According to the standard deviation value, a greater spread occurs in Similarity and Wishful Identification data than in Enjoyment data that children reported (Table 1). Previous research indicates that various genders may have a diverse attitude toward gaming [55]. Given the possibility of a gender effect on scores of avatar identification [56] or enjoyment, an independent-sample t-test was undertaken. The finding indicates that there is no discernible gender difference in the enjoyment and avatar identification data gathered.

Table 1. Mean and standard deviation of children's self-reported data

	Similarity identification M (SD)	Wishful Identification M (SD)	Enjoyment M (SD)
Fantasy animal	2.41 (1.12)	2.99 (0.95)	4.44 (0.75)
Fantasy human	2.68 (1.32)	3.31 (1.10)	4.46 (0.78)
Animal	2.15 (0.97)	2.65 (0.98)	4.35 (0.75)
human	2.78 (1.16)	3.08 (0.84)	4.44 (0.72)

5.3 Two-Way Repeated Measures ANOVA

A two-way Repeated Measures ANOVA, setting Fantasy/ Real-life, Humanoid/ Animal-noid as two within-subject factors, is implemented to investigate the RQ1: Do players have distinct avatar identifications (similarity and wishful identification) for a fantasy or a real-life avatar setting, for a similar or a dissimilar avatar setting?

The result from the test of within-subject effects suggests there is a significant difference in users' wishful identification $F(1, 33) = 7.02$, $p = 0.01$ towards fantasy and real-life avatars; A significantly different wishful identification is found $F(1, 33) = 21.31$, $p = 0.00$ towards Humanoid and Animaloid avatars. In general, users perceive significantly stronger wishful identification on Fantasy than Real-life avatars, Humanoid than Animaloid avatars (Fig. 5). In line with our estimation, users' similarity identification is significantly higher $F(1, 33) = 13.28$, $p = 0.00$ with humanoid avatars than animaloid avatars (Fig. 6). No significant effect of the fantasy/real-life and humanoid/animaloid interaction on enjoyment, wishful identification, similarity identification is spotted. There is no significant effect of both factors on user enjoyment.

The ANOVA result shows that Children show a stronger desire to set Fantasy avatars as their wishful identification than Real-life avatars. In parallel, Humanoid characters gain significantly more recognition as their wishful identification than Animaloid characters. Additionally, Humanoid characters are regarded as more similar to them no matter it is with a fantasy setting or not. These findings indicate children are more likely to choose an avatar designed with a similar fantasy, e.g., the magician in our game, as their ideal character in gameplay.

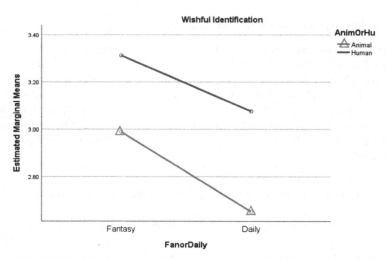

Fig. 5. Plot for effects of two factors on wishful identification

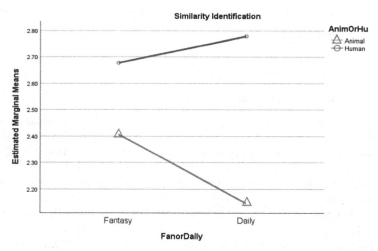

Fig. 6. Plot for effects of two factors on similarity identification

5.4 Partial Correlation

Since both factors of fantasy/real-life and Humanoid/Animaloid affect children's identification, the relationship of identification and enjoyment should be explored by one factor and with the effect of the other factor removed. Therefore two sets of partial correlations are conducted to identify RQ2: How do fantasy and similarity settings in games affect their motivation in GBL through player identification?

To see the effect of fantasy and real-life avatars, the effect of Humanoid and animaloid is controlled. There is a significant correlation between wishful identification and enjoyment $r = 0.26$, $p = 0.03$, similarity identification and enjoyment, $r = 0.25$, $p =$

0.05, with fantasy avatars. Such associations were found insignificant when users were playing with real-life avatars. looking from aspects of Humanoid/ Animaloid, controlling the effect of Fantasy/Real-life., a significant correlation between similarity identification and enjoyment $r = 0.24$, $p = 0.05$ is shown with humanoid avatars. No other significant association is spotted in animaloid avatars.

6 Discussion

The descriptive data, in general, shows children participants enjoy playing all four conditions of the game. These positive scores could be interpreted as a success of implementing AR game design in math education. In alignment with previous work, children have higher motivation and engagement when learning from AR materials than with traditional textbooks [34].

6.1 RQ1: Do Players Have Distinct Avatar Identifications (Similarity and Wishful Identification) for a Fantasy or a Real-Life Avatar Setting, for a Similar or a Dissimilar Avatar Setting?

Our finding regarding similarity identification confirms our expectation: Players perceive more similarity identification toward similar (humanoid) avatars than dissimilar (animaloid avatars); The levels of fantasy in avatar design do not influence players' similarity identification. The findings that players exhibit a higher level of wishful identification with fantasy avatars than with real-life ones are consistent with prior studies: GBL's fantasy settings allow participants to admire super-natural abilities and imaginatively meet their emotional demands [45, 57]. In addition, the result that suggests players also have stronger wishful identification with humanoid avatars similar to players corresponds to Higgins' early formulation of the self-discrepancy theory. Higgins believes the basis of wishful identification is the decrease of self-discrepancy throughout the period of media exposure [58]. A more similar humanoid avatar would have less self-discrepancy between players and avatars, increasing their chances of identifying with the avatars as their desired role.

6.2 RQ2: How Do Fantasy and Similarity Settings in Games Affect Their Motivation in GBL Through Player Identification?

The results suggest our participants enjoy a motivating GBL because fantasy settings encourage wishful and similarity identification. This finding demonstrates that fantasy enables an enjoyable experience via avatar identification, as described by Klimmt et al., where similarity identification facilitates players' mental rapprochement with the avatar [59], and by Bessière et al., where wishful identification enables players to alter their self-perception and feel better about themselves when identifying with a fictional character [60]. The finding that similarity identification facilitates motivation in fantasy conditions may also be explained by the participants' age (9 to 10). Children would like to use fictitious avatars to represent themselves. Pretending play as a superpower avatar is more common at this age [61]. Therefore this could explain why fantasy settings also lead to a rise of similarity identification which increases their GBL motivation.

When looking from aspects of similar humanoid and dissimilar animaloid avatars, the design of the avatars only activates the motivational effect of similarity identification, not wishful identification. To fully activate the motivational effect of wishful identification, fantasy is necessary.

The findings above indicate that children's motivation may be enhanced by wishful identification, i.e., having their imaginative wishes fulfilled via role play and by similarity identification, i.e., feeling a sense of kinship with the avatars. Fantasy settings can trigger the motivational effects of wishful identification. Children who especially enjoy pretending play with novelty, creation, and imagination will also be motivated through similarity identification. On the other hand, the avatar self-similarity is suitable for children in general in terms of motivating their GBL engagement through similarity identification. Further design strategies involving fantasy and similarity should be considered to maximize both affordances.

6.3   Design with Similarity and Fantasy

As Selen Turkay et al. mentioned in their research, games create contexts that allow players to perceive themselves in worlds of imagination [53], fantasy settings create the fictional world, and the similarity allows players to reflect and relate to themselves. With the advantage of enabling players' interest through identification, fantasy settings with authentic learning context can lead to a motivational play without consciously thinking about mathematical challenges.

Even though fantasy fosters a more motivational effect of avatar identification, similar settings can also trigger players' similarity identification which subsequently increases their motivation. Similar humanoid avatar settings can remind players to reflect on themselves through similarity identification [62], which could suit the circumstance while reflecting on what they have learned. Furthermore, a prior study has discovered that similarity identification promotes intuitive control, suitable for players who never played AR GBL before.

In summary, it is mainly recommended that designers use similar fantasy, e.g., the magician avatar in our case, over dissimilar and real-life settings, to achieve more positive effects of avatar identification in AR GBL design. Adjusting priority of applying fantasy and similarity in AR GBL avatar design should consider the learning contexts and target user groups. For children, especially those who are strongly motivated by imagination and novelty, fantasy settings should be considered with priority. If the primary goal is to increase the children's motivation, the design of fantasy components in AR GBL should take precedence. Meanwhile, adding similarity qualities to AR GBL avatar design should be considered because it can assist first-time AR GBL experience players in getting started. For self-driven users, especially those who already have enough motivation for learning, GBL design with similarity could be considered to improve other experiences like learner's reflection and more.

7 Limitation

Although there are two dimensions to design four avatars, the influence of different avatars on enjoyment is still subtle. One reason for the similar positive results on enjoyment could be children tend to give extreme scores and have trouble expressing or understanding neutral attitudes [34]. This could be because the questionnaire selected does not specifically target children. The tension caused by the age difference between experimenters and children also makes them reluctant to give negative reviews of others' work [63]. Future studies should choose or adjust measures for children's participants. Additionally, this study provides just two instances for each dimension. There are more aspects of avatars' design that remain unexplored. In this research, we examine only the motivational effect of fantasy. The influence of AR fantasy on learning outcomes, such as working memory, will be explored in future work.

8 Conclusion

A design study using the game MathMythos AR is conducted to explore the influence of using fantasy/real-world and similar/dissimilar avatars design on children's player identification and motivation in AR GBL. We discover that when players play as fantasy avatars or avatars that resemble them, their wishful identification increases. Players place a higher premium of similarity identification with avatars who resemble them, regardless of whether they are fantasy or real-life based. Additionally, it shows from this study that children's wishful identification and similarity identification are strongly linked with their enjoyment in fantasy settings, while in similar (humanoid) settings, only similarity identification corresponds with enjoyment. Designers are encouraged to create avatars in similar fantasy settings to achieve a motivational effect through avatar identification in GBL. Balancing fantasy and similarity in the design of AR GBL avatars should take into account the learning contexts and target user groups. If the primary objective is to boost the user's motivation, design with fantasy contexts could be a primary choice.

We hope this research can inspire more researchers to explore more aspects of fantasy play, including storytelling, visual effect, immersive technology, and more. This will eventually help designers find solutions to transferring enjoyment and curiosity into learning motivation, making GBL in AR context meaningful and engaging simultaneously.

Acknowledgment. We want to thank Mrs. Wanyu Xu, Miss. Rong Xu and Juqian Street Primary School students for their assistance and participation in our experiment. We wish to express our deep gratitude to Loe Feijs and Xiangsun, who provide technical supports during the game development. We also want to thank CSC for funding the project.

References

1. Ryan, R.M., Deci, E.L.: Self-determination theory and the facilitation of intrinsic motivation, social development, and well-being. Am. Psychol. **55**, 68 (2000)

2. Lee, J., Shute, V.J.: Personal and social-contextual factors in K-12 academic performance: an integrative perspective on student learning. Educ. Psychol. **45**, 185–202 (2010)
3. Lee, J.S.: The relationship between student engagement and academic performance: is it a myth or reality? J. Educ. Res. **107**, 177–185 (2014)
4. Pivec, M., Dziabenko, O., Schinnerl, I.: Aspect of game-based learning. In: 3rd Int. Conf. Knowl. Manag. pp. 2–4 (2003)
5. Zuo, T., Birk, M.V., Van Der Spek, E.D., Hu, J.: Exploring fantasy play in MathMythos AR. In: CHI Play 2020. Ext. Abstr. 2020 Annu. Symp. Comput. Interact. Play. pp. 413–417 (2020)
6. Li, J., Van der Spek, E., Hu, J., Feijs, L.: See me roar: on the over-positive, cross-cultural response on an AR game for math learning. In: Joint International Conference on Serious Games. pp. 54–65. Springer (2018). https://doi.org/10.1007/978-3-030-02762-9_7
7. Ute, R., Michael, C., Peter, V.: Serious Games: Mechanisms and Effects. Google Books (2009)
8. Johnson, W.L.: Serious use of a serious game for language learning. Front. Artif. Intell. Appl. **158**, 67 (2007)
9. Whitton, N.: Motivation and computer game based learning. In: ASCILITE 2007 - Australas. Soc. Comput. Learn. Tert. Educ. pp. 1063–1067 (2007)
10. Asgari, M., Kaufman, D.: Does fantasy enhance learning in digital games? In: Educational Gameplay and Simulation Environments: Case Studies and Lessons Learned. pp. 84–95. IGI Global (2010)
11. Saltz, E., Dixon, D., Johnson, J.: Training disadvantaged preschoolers on various fantasy activities: effects on cognitive functioning and impulse control. Child Dev. 367–380 (1977)
12. Pellegrini, A.D., Galda, L.: The effects of thematic-fantasy play training on the development of children's story comprehension. Am. Educ. Res. J. **19**, 443–452 (1982)
13. Salen, K., Tekinbaş, K.S., Zimmerman, E.: Rules of play: Game Design Fundamentals. MIT Press (2004)
14. Montola, M.: Exploring the edge of the magic circle: defining pervasive games. In: Proc. 6th Digit. Arts Cult. Conf. (DAC 2005). Vol. 1966, pp. 16–19 (2005)
15. Malone, T.W., Lepper, M.R.: Making learning fun, a taxonomy of intrinsic motivations for learning (1987)
16. Kenny, R.F., Gunter, G.A.: Endogenous fantasy-based serious games: intrinsic motivation and learning. Int. J. Soc. Sci. **2**, 8–13 (2007)
17. Grabinger, R.S., Dunlap, J.C.: Rich environments for active learning: a definition. Alt-J. **3**, 5–34 (1995)
18. Azuma, R.T.: A survey of augmented reality. Pres. Teleoper. Virtual Environ. **6**, 355–385 (1997)
19. Radu, I.: Augmented reality in education: a meta-review and cross-media analysis. Pers. Ubiquitous Comput. **18**, 1533–1543 (2014)
20. Fan, M., Antle, A.N., Warren, J.L.: Augmented reality for early language learning: a systematic review of augmented reality application design, instructional strategies, and evaluation outcomes. J. Educ. Comput. Res. **58**, 1059–1100 (2020)
21. Van Der Spek, E.D., Sidorenkova, T., Porskamp, P., Matthias, R.: The effect of familiar and fantasy aesthetics on learning and experience of serious games. Lect. Notes Comput. Sci. (including Subser. Lect. Notes Artif. Intell. Lect. Notes Bioinformatics). Vol. 8770, pp. 133–138 (2014)
22. Birk, M.V., Mandryk, R.L.: Combating attrition in digital self-improvement programs using avatar customization. In: Conf. Hum. Factors Comput. Syst. - Proc. 2018-April, pp. 1–15 (2018)
23. Balfe, M.: Incredible geographies? orientalism and genre fantasy. Soc. Cult. Geogr. **5**, 75–90 (2004)
24. de Valk, L., Bekker, T., Eggen, B.: Designing for social interaction in open-ended play environments. Int. J. Des. **9**, 107–120 (2015)

25. Deci, E.L., Ryan, R.M.: Self-determination theory (2012)
26. Vallerand, R.J., Pelletier, L.G., Blais, M.R., Briere, N.M., Senecal, C., Vallieres, E.F.: The academic motivation scale: a measure of intrinsic, extrinsic, and amotivation in education. Educ. Psychol. Meas. **52**, 1003–1017 (1992)
27. Ryan, R.M., Rigby, C.S., Przybylski, A.: The motivational pull of video games: a self-determination theory approach. Motiv. Emot. **30**, 347–363 (2006)
28. Waal, B. de: Motivations for video game play : a study of social, cultural and physiological factors. http://summit.sfu.ca/item/6647 (1995)
29. Wouters, P., Van der Spek, E.D., Van Oostendorp, H.: Current practices in serious game research : outcomes perspective. Games-based Learn. Adv. Multi-Sens. Hum. Comput. Interf. Tech. Eff. Pract. 232–250 (2009)
30. Wouters, P., Van Oostendorp, H.: Overview of instructional techniques to facilitate learning and motivation of serious games. In: Instructional techniques to facilitate learning and motivation of serious games. pp. 1–16. Springer (2017). https://doi.org/10.1007/978-3-319-392 98-1_1
31. Wu, H.-K., Wen-Yu Lee, S., Chang, H.-Y., Liang, J.-C.: Current Status, Opportunities and Challenges of Augmented Reality in Education 106
32. Li, J., Spek, E.D. van der, Feijs, L., Feng, W., Hu, J.: Augmented Reality Games for Learning: A Literature review (2017)
33. Cai, S., Chiang, F.-K., Sun, Y., Lin, C., Lee, J.J.: Applications of augmented reality-based natural interactive learning in magnetic field instruction. Interact. Learn. Environ. **25**, 778–791 (2017)
34. Li, J., Van Der Spek, E.D., Hu, J., Feijs, L.: Turning your book into a game: Improving motivation through tangible interaction and diegetic feedback in an AR mathematics game for children. In: CHI Play 2019 - Proc. Annu. Symp. Comput. Interact. Play. pp. 73–85 (2019)
35. Fotaris, P., Pellas, N., Kazanidis, I., Smith, P.: A systematic review of augmented reality game-based applications in primary education. In: Proc. 11th Eur. Conf. Games Based Learn. ECGBL 2017. pp. 181–190 (2017)
36. Li, J., Van Der Spek, E.D., Yu, X., Hu, J., Feijs, L.: Exploring an augmented reality social learning game for elementary school students. Proc. Interact. Des. Child. Conf. IDC **2020**, 508–518 (2020)
37. Yuen, S.C.-Y., Yaoyuneyong, G., Johnson, E.: Augmented reality: an overview and five directions for AR in education. J. Educ. Technol. Dev. Exch. **4**, 11 (2011)
38. Miller, M.R., Jun, H., Herrera, F., Villa, J.Y., Welch, G., Bailenson, J.N.: Social interaction in augmented reality. PLoS One. **14** (2019)
39. Malone, T.W.: Toward a theory of intrinsically motivating instruction. Cogn. Sci. **5**, 333–369 (1981)
40. Zuo, T., Feijs, L., Van Der Spek, E.D., Hu, J.: A classification of fantasy in serious games. In: CHI Play 2019 - Ext. Abstr. Annu. Symp. Comput. Interact. Play. pp. 821–828 (2019)
41. Matthews, W.S.: Modes of transformation in the initiation of fantasy play. Dev. Psychol. **13**, 212–216 (1977)
42. Ferguson, C.J., Olson, C.K.: Friends, fun, frustration and fantasy: child motivations for video game play. Motiv. Emot. **37**, 154–164 (2013)
43. Lee, J.: Effects of Fantasy and Fantasy Proneness on Learning and Engagement in a 3D Educational Game (2015)
44. Merckelbach, H., Horselenberg, R., Muris, P.: The creative experiences questionnaire (CEQ): a brief self-report measure of fantasy proneness. Pers. Individ. Dif. **31**, 987–995 (2001)
45. Choi, B., Huang, J., Jeffrey, A., Baek, Y.: Development of a scale for fantasy state in digital games. Comput. Human Behav. **29**, 1980–1986 (2013)
46. Schwartz, L.: Fantasy, realism, and the other in recent video games. Sp. Cult. **9**, 313–325 (2006)

47. Habgood, M.P.J., Ainsworth, S.E., Benford, S.: Endogenous fantasy and learning in digital games. Simul. Gaming. **36**, 483–498 (2005)
48. Jang, Y.B., Kim, W.R., Ryu, S.H.: An exploratory study on avatar-self similarity, mastery experience and self-efficacy in games. Int. Conf. Adv. Commun. Technol. ICACT. **2**, 1681–1684 (2010)
49. Wauck, H., Lucas, G., Shapiro, A., Feng, A., Boberg, J., Gratch, J.: Analyzing the effect of avatar self-similarity on men and women in a search and rescue game. In: Conf. Hum. Factors Comput. Syst. - Proc. 2018-April, 1–12 (2018)
50. Parmar, D.: Evaluating the Effects of Immersive Embodied Interaction on Cognition in Virtual Reality (2017)
51. Regnath, F., Elmezeny, A.: Me, Myself and Others : Connecting Player Identification to Gaming Social Capital (2019)
52. Van Looy, J., Courtois, C., De Vocht, M., De Marez, L.: Player identification in online games: validation of a scale for measuring identification in MMOGs. Media Psychol. **15**, 197–221 (2012)
53. Turkay, S., Kinzer, C.K.: The effects of avatar-based customization on player identification. Int. J. Gaming Comput. Simul. **6**, 1–25 (2014)
54. Birk, M.V., Atkins, C., Bowey, J.T., Mandryk, R.L.: Fostering intrinsic motivation through avatar identification in digital games. In: Conf. Hum. Factors Comput. Syst. - Proc. pp. 2982–2995 (2016)
55. Greenberg, B.S., Sherry, J., Lachlan, K., Lucas, K., Holmstrom, A.: Orientations to video games among gender and age groups. Simul. Gaming. **41**, 238–259 (2010)
56. Rogers, K., Aufheimer, M., Weber, M., Nacke, L.E.: Exploring the role of non-player characters and gender in player identification. In: CHI Play 2018 – Proc. 2018 Annu. Symp. Comput. Interact. Play Companion Ext. Abstr. pp. 271–283 (2018)
57. Asgari, M., Kaufman, D.: Relationships Among Computer Games, Fantasy, and Learning (2014)
58. Higgins, E.T.: Self-discrepancy: a theory relating self and affect. Psychol. Rev. **94**, 319–340 (1987)
59. Klimmt, C., Hefner, D., Vorderer, P., Roth, C., Blake, C.: Identification with video game characters as automatic shift of self-perceptions. Media Psychol. **13**, 323–338 (2010)
60. Bessière, K., Seay, A.F., Kiesler, S.: The ideal elf: Identity exploration in world of warcraft. Cyberpsychol. Behav. **10**, 530–535 (2007)
61. Fein, G.G.: Pretend play in childhood: an integrative review. Child Dev. 1095–1118 (1981)
62. Konijn, E.A., Hoorn, J.F.: Some like it bad: testing a model for perceiving and experiencing fictional characters. Media Psychol. **7**, 107–144 (2005)
63. Miller, K.: Communication Theories. USA Macgraw-Hill (2005)

Research on the Application of Augmented Reality Technology in the Transformation and Development of Cultural and Creative Industries

Feng Liying[1,2], Ng Giap Weng[2], Ma Liyao[3(✉)], Fu Maozheng[1], and Que Xiaoping[1]

[1] Hainan Vocational University of Science and Technology, Hainan, China
[2] Faculty of Computing and Informatics, University Malaysia Sabah, Kota Kinabalu, Malaysia
[3] Faculty of Art and Design, University of Hainan, Hainan, China
fly_liana@126.com

Abstract. In this paper, China Hainan "Li" national woven culture is used as an example, the integration of AR technology and cultural creative industry is the main research object. First, the status quo and problems of cultural creative industry in Hainan are analyzed, and the new trend of the development of Hainan cultural creative industry is further clarified. Second, summarized the four technical characteristics and advantages of Augmented Reality (AR) technology with virtual fusion, real-time interaction, two-way mode and multi-intensity. The application examples of enhanced reality technology are introduced. Finally, this study integrates technology into culture, introduces AR technology to integrate the development of Hainan cultural and creative industrial development, and propose the transformation strategy of cultural industries to integrate scientific and technological innovation. One preliminary result was AR is a promising media to learn, promote and protect Hainan national brocade culture. It concludes generally AR promotes learnning about, and builds back better Hainan's cultural and creative industry.

Keywords: Augmented Reality · Hainan cultural industry · Cultural creativity

1 Introduction

Broadly, cultural and creative industry is a strategic emerging industry cluster in China. Deeply digging regional characteristic culture, tracing historical origin, and perfecting the continuity and promotion of culture are important ways to protect culture. The extraction, application, and innovative development of cultural elements are effective measures for cultural inheritance. For example, The protection, development and inheritance of the brocade culture of the Li nationality in Hainan (Fig. 1 and Fig. 2).

Cultural and creative industry takes cultural content and creative results as an end (core value) for that industry. On the other hand, it takes creation and innovation as the means, it creates and enhances cultural resources with the help of high-tech and others, for example, AR (See Sect. 3) of this work. It provides enjoyable and culturally relevant flow of interactive experience designed for consuming public. In order for that industry to thrive, it should have the characteristics of strong creativity, multi-industry integration, less resource consumption, less environmental pollution, high risk, high added value, sustainable development, cultural value dissemination and others. See also Xiaojun [1].

Hainan province is the largest island in China, inflexed constantly by waves of immigrants of foreign nationalities since the Neolithic age. According to Zhenqing [2], Hainan was mainly the ancestors of Li, Lingao people, the central plains people, immigrants from southeast and southwest of China and other regions. Ling [3] stated that after a long historical evolution and present in Marine culture, li and Miao folk custom, the Red Culture, Nanyang culture, the island culture is given priority to the characteristics of regional culture. In a new era of high-quality development in China, Hainan is an important pivot of China's One Belt and One Road strategy, a free trade port, an island of educational innovation and an island of digital wisdom in China's national strategy [3]. Refer also to Koleski [4]. It not only has a unique geographical advantage, but also has a special political status. At present, although Hainan has abundant cultural resources, the development of cultural and creative industries is relatively low, a complete industrial chain has not been formed, the integration of technology is insufficient, and the added value of products is low. The integration of modern technology represented by AR technology into Hainan's cultural and creative industries will help Hainan to transform into a digital and intelligent island, which has contemporary research significance.

This article puts forward the point of view and attempt to integrate cutting-edge technology into Hainan's cultural industry, which can make up for the lack of attractiveness and single model of Hainan's cultural and creative industry. This point of view and attempt can well promote Hainan's regional culture and enhance consumer experience.

Fig. 1. Traditional Li nationality brocade form and works in Hainan, China

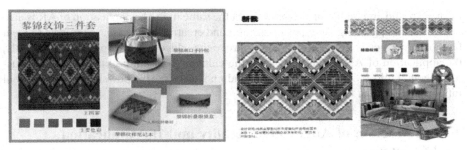

Fig. 2. The creative forms and works of Li Jin culture in China

2 Present Situation and Existing Problems of Hainan Cultural and Creative Industry

For nearly five years, China has issued "Hainan's tourism industry development planning" that includes (a) the construction of Hainan international tourism consumption center of the implementation of the plan, (b) the State Council on overall plan issued by the China (Hainan) free trade area of the notice, (c) the propulsion of Hainan province cultural creativity and design services, (d) related industrial convergence development plan and (e) other series of policies and measures. Although people's understanding of the development of Hainan's cultural and creative industries is deepening, various policies are issued one by one, and the construction process is gradually accelerated, the development of Hainan's cultural and creative industries.

Hainan is still plagued with various problems and contradictions under the new situation of building an international free trade zone, mainly manifested as follows: (a) the contradiction between the high goal of cultural and creative industry construction and the outdated concept of industrial planning under the background of international free trade zone. The contradiction between the lack of high-quality cultural creativity and management personnel and the demand of enterprise development, (b) the contradiction between the demand of regional cultural propaganda and the imperfection of cultural output system, (c) the contradiction between low quality of cultural and creative products and projects and the public's demand for high-quality cultural and creative products and projects, (d) the contradiction between the demand of the times of cultural integration of science and technology and the insufficiency of cultural excavation and scientific and technological means, and finally(e) the positive development of cultural and creative industry and the contradiction between intellectual property protection and development lag. The basic reason lies in the low level of cultural and technological development in Hainan, and many regional cultural resources have not been effectively developed and utilized.

An effective strategy to promote the transformation and upgrading of Hainan's cultural and creative industries is to actively explore, associating the deep integration of Hainan's cultural industry and science and technology. The application of AR (See Sect. 3) is in line with the development of the times and the needs of Hainan to build an international free trade zone. It is helpful for the export of Hainan regional culture, so that citizens and tourists can understand and learn the connotation of Hainan regional culture in an all-round and multi-functional way. At the same time, the application of AR is also conducive to upgrading the types of cultural and creative products and projects to meet the consumer needs of the public and improve the added value of products. Secondly, the application of AR can also promote the cultivation of cultural and creative industry talents, build a digital environment, and enhance the soft power and international influence of Hainan culture.

3 Introduction of Augmented Reality and Its Application Advantages

3.1 Augmented Reality

AR (an interactive and immersive flow of live experience, varying from Reality to Virtual Reality (VR)) is to superimpose ecologically, computer-generated enhanced information (or affordance) into the real environment seen by the observer organically, in real time and dynamically [5]. According to Huishu [6], when the observer moves in the real environment, the enhanced information also changes accordingly [6]. The enhanced information is just as if it exists in the real environment (Fig. 3). In other words, AR as in this work provides one basic structure for learning about Hainan Cultural and Creative Industries through play.

Fig. 3. Application of AR in tourism-scenic AR pray [10]

Traditional VR is dedicated to fully immersing users in the computer-generated virtual world, which requires accurate modelling of the environment and a huge amount of work (Fig. 4). AR to eliminate the modelling for the environment, the core idea is: in the real world fusion computer-generated virtual objects, and make the virtual objects and reality of the world as an organic whole, enhances the user the perception and understanding of the real world, and when the camera motion, virtual objects can be synchronous tracking real environment, real-time registration (Fig. 5).The advantages and characteristics of AR enable it to be applied in many fields such as tourism, entertainment, education, games, museums, clothing, art, exhibition sales, medicine, cultural and creative gifts, and others. See also current works of Asadzadeh [7]. The application of AR in cultural and creative industries can improve the upgrading of manufacturing industry, speed up commercial publicity and marketing (Fig. 6), save time and cost and gain real experience.

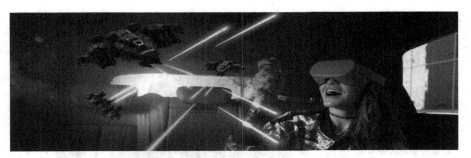

Fig. 4. VR experience form and scene construction [11]

The development of IAT consists of three phases which enable Kinect node and calibration at phase 1, design particle and motion at phase 2, and creating effects on particle visual at phase 3. It is very important to make sure each of the phases should be completed successfully before other phases could proceed. The development stage can be used as a guideline and identified as a strategic plan for developing the project.

At phase 1, the interactive sensor which is Kinect was used and set. The software used in this project called Touch designer. Before this software could be used with the Kinect, it has to be enabled and test. Kinect sensors need to be tested to make sure that their sensor functioning well. During the testing, the calibration needs to be performed. The calibration of the Kinect sensor needs to be tested with the human body part such as the hand, neck, shoulder, and leg. To merge the sensor with the visual, the setup needs to be performed. The setup involves by activating the Kinect calibration with the value of x, y, and z. When the calibration value appears and is verified successfully, the next phases could be started.

AR fast becoming all areas of our lives. Worth mention are ARKit API tool and ARCore.

(a) In June 2017 Apple released the ARKit API tool for developers working on VR and AR applications. The ARKit Tool is designed to accurately map the surrounding using SLAM (Simultaneous Localization and Mapping). Moreover, no external equipment is required to create AR experiences.

- Painting Apps: VR studio (such as Normal) has brought together the HTC VR Kit and iOS beta powered iPad in its new AR app. It has built an AR painting tool that replicates the action of the HTC Vive wearer on the iPad screen.
- Strategy Games: During the Worldwide Developers Conference (WWDC) the audience were given a visual treat. Wingnut AR, a game development studio, showcased a virtual battlefield that could be easily developed into a strategy game.
- Tape Measure: Measurement Cloud, built by Smart Picture 3D, can be used as a measuring tape. Smartphone with this app can do the job.
- Vehicle Purchases: People who are too busy to accompany their children on their first bike or car purchase can use an ARKit built application to preview the vehicle.

Fig. 5. AR application examples

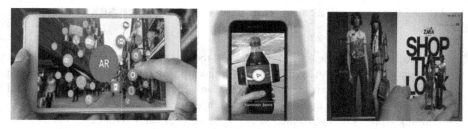

Fig. 6. AR marketing example

Education: Krutosh, an iOS developer, has designed an iPhone application that can bring virtual planets and stars in the living room. This app demonstrates the potential of AR in the field of education.

(b) ARCore also known as Google Play Services for AR, is a software development kit developed by Google that allows for AR applications to be built.
•   ARCore uses three key technologies to integrate virtual content with the real world as seen through smart phone's camera.

- Six degrees of freedom allows smart phone to understand and track its position relative to the world.
- Environmental understanding allows smart phone to detect the size and location of flat horizontal surfaces like the ground or a coffee table.
- Light estimation allows smart phone to estimate the environment's current lighting conditions.
- ARCore has been integrated into a multitude of devices.

Turning to Billinghurst [8], they conducted a systematic study on the usability of AR and reviewed the most influential AR user research from 2005 to 2014, research shows that the application of AR technology has broad prospects. Their work suggests, AR applications have huge development potential and technological dependence in 9 areas such as collaboration, interaction, industry, education, tourism, medical care, games, and navigation. Early research on AR was mainly based on Head-Mounted Displays (HMD), but in the past few years, the use of handheld AR devices has increased rapidly, and more advanced hardware and sensors have emerged. These new wearables and mobile devices have created new research directions, which may affect the categories and methods used in AR user research. Through the development in recent years, especially the arrival of the 5G era in 2019, the superiority of the real-time interaction and perception functions of AR has become more prominent, which has provided great help for our life improvement and technological development.

3.2 Advantages and Characteristics of the Application of AR in Hainan's Cultural Entrepreneurship Industry

Virtual Integration and Real Reproduction. AR used real world virtual environment seamlessly as a whole, letting users feel true integration of harmony. Not only users can feel things in the objective world through VR system, and but also break through the space, time and other constraints [6].

AR integrates Hainan's cultural resources potentially in the following manners. On the one hand, it can quickly identify Hainan's local cultural resources, save users' time and shorten the space distance. On the other hand, it enables through the virtual screen AR glasses, present the dynamic scene, all kinds of cultural and historical past through video, images reappear with rich digital media display of historical context, such as cultural connotation, the greatest degree of let users experience the rich cultural resources in Hainan and the historical background, to deepen the user understanding of Hainan, for the publicity and promotion of history and culture in Hainan play a positive role. Figure 7 demonstrated AR restoration scene of the ancient Chinese Old Summer Palace.

Real-Time Interaction, Immersive Experience. AR is to supplement the real scene, but not completely replace the real scene. Through such a virtual fusion to enhance the user's understanding and feelings of the real environment, so as to achieve the "enhanced" effect. Users can interact directly with virtual objects or virtual environments through interactive devices, which enhances users' perception of the environment. In the development of Hainan cultural resources using AR, real-time interaction between users

Fig. 7. AR historic building restoration [12]

and devices can not only close the psychological distance between users and Hainan, but also allow users to interact according to their own needs. View the details and contents of interest from all angles, especially for some fragile cultural heritage such as Chinese porcelain, or the display of precious brocade from Hainan, as shown in Fig. 8. Immersive interactive experience can not only enrich the content, expand the form, but also get instant feedback through the user's interactive data, and understand the possible problems of the product or project through data analysis, so as to adjust and upgrade in time.

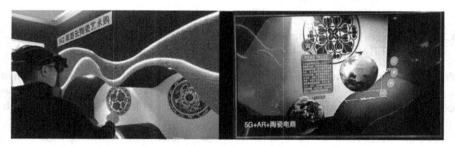

Fig. 8. AR porcelain display

Two-Way Mode to Enhance Effectiveness. Enhanced display technology can be divided into positive and negative two-way enhancement mode. The positive enhancement mode is to supplement and expand the real environment with virtual information to enrich its experience environment and effect. The negative enhancement mode is to adopt the "disappear hidden" mode of material desalination or hiding the real environment in harmony with the real environment. Reduce the perception of the real environment and reduce the impact of disharmony factors on the display effect. Two-way enhancement mode of AR plays a positive role in the development of Hainan cultural resources. For example, the unique Nanyang architectural style of Haikou Arcade old street has become a typical representative of Haikou city style (Fig. 9). The two-way enhancement mode of AR can show the prosperity of and reduce the influence of surrounding modern buildings on its historical and cultural atmosphere.

Fig. 9. The original scene of the old Arcade Street in Haikou and the AR light show effect

Multi-sense Enhancement, The Reality is Not Discernible. AR not only gives people close to real experience in vision, but also can achieve realistic effect in sound, touch and smell. For example, Hainan traditional dance and musical instrument performance is a popular form of cultural entertainment. However, these performances require special auxiliary equipment, manpower cooperation, limited by the venue, personnel, atmosphere and other factors, most of the audience cannot experience the performance brought joy and comfort. By the advantages and characteristics of AR, the development of AR bamboo pole dance, AR octave and other experience projects can not only show consumers the perfect performance of dance and instrumental music, but also meet the comprehensive needs of users in a limited space to obtain visual, auditory, tactile and other senses. As shown in Fig. 10, if the Hainan bamboo pole dance performance is combined with the AR stage scene, virtual bamboo poles and auxiliary personnel are used to reduce venues, tools, and personnel intervention factors, which will bring people a new viewing experience. By using the organic combination of AR and Hainan's characteristic cultural resources, we should explore cultural and creative products and cultural experience projects, select representative cultural heritage content innovation and development, promote the deep integration of Hainan's cultural and creative industry and science and technology. Finally form Hainan's cultural and creative industry development path with outstanding characteristics such as creative product development and sales, cultural project development and experience, non-posthumous cultural heritage, and science and technology promotion.

Fig. 10. Hainan bamboo pole dance show and AR stage scene [13]

By summarizing the research on AR technical characteristics and applications, this article basically divides AR applications into three categories, namely product display, scene display, and interactive experience. Specific examples, technical characteristics and application advantages of the three categories are shown in the table below (Table 1).

Table 1. Features and advantages of AR applications

No.	Application scenario	Technical characteristics	Application advantage
1	**Products Show** Such as cultural relics display, cultural and creative works display, &marketing product display	Element integration, &information interaction,	a. The object is highly protective and has a good protective effect on rare objects and vulnerable objects b. The object has good display ability, which can integrate various elements such as static and dynamic, and express the characteristics and attributes of the object in 360 degrees in all directions c. Break through regional and temporal constraints
2	**Scenario Shows** Such as stage performance, teaching and teaching	Element integration, human-computer interaction, Three-dimensional registration, real-time tracking	a. Expansion of the form of expression b. The richness of content c. Representation of breakthroughs in geography and time and space d.Breakthrough in display range e. Reduce cost control
3	**Interactive experience** Such as game experience, special training, collaboration, &navigation	Fusion of VR elements, Human-computer interaction, three-dimensional registration, Real-time tracking, natural interaction	a. Enrich the experience of the experiencer b. Extend the experience space, increase the difficulty and breadth of the experience c. In high-risk environments, experiencers have high safety d. Break through geographical and temporal constraints e. Reusable, resource sharing

4 Research on Cultural and Creative Development of Hainan Based on AR

Although Hainan's rich cultural resources provide fertile soil for the development of cultural and creative industries, some cultural resources with local characteristics have not been well developed and utilized. For example, Li nationality traditional textile dyeing embroidery technique (Li Jin technology) is a kind of textile skill used by Li nationality women in Hainan Province, China. It integrates spinning, dyeing and embroidery, and makes clothes and daily necessities with cotton, hemp and other fibres. Li Jin technology, which has existed for more than 3000 years, is the oldest cotton textile dyeing and embroidery technology in China and even in the world and is known as the "living fossil" in the textile history of China. However, with the development of science and technology, because of the single way of inheriting Li Jin's skills (and traditions) and the limited object of inheritance, Li Jin's skills are facing a crisis of loss of transmission. UNESCO put it on the list of intangible cultural heritage in urgent need of preservation in 2009.

4.1 Li Brocade Display and Protection Using AR Techniques

Through fusion of AR, and Li brocade development, user in scenic spots, museums, shopping malls, airports, and lounge can quickly through the display device and even open hole, all-round, multi-dimensional, integrated understanding of the history of the Li brocade and weaving process, pattern characteristic, at the same time, appreciate the show can get related audio, can in-depth understanding of the cultural connotation of li brocade.AR will greatly save the display cost of brocade, expand the scope and content of display, and strengthen the effect and influence of display. In recent years, the relevant departments at all levels in China have made great progress in the protection of li brocade culture, but Li brocade's "spinning, dyeing, weaving, embroidery" skills protection results are not balanced, the crisis of technology loss has not been eliminated. At present, the number of people who master the techniques of "dyeing" and "embroidery" is relatively small. The techniques of "dyeing" and "embroidery" are reproduced by virtual technology, and the corresponding resource database is constructed by using digital technology, which can better protect the inheritance of the techniques and attract more people to learn and study the brocade of Li nationality.

4.2 Using AR to Create Brocade Interactive Experience

Users can not only watch and understand Li brocade culture through AR, but also participate in product design and process production through virtual simulation, experience the production process of products, and make their own unique products. Users can feel the charm of traditional skills. Finally, everyone can experience the production of products, everyone is a product designer, everyone studies non-legacy culture, everyone buys non-legacy products characteristic tourism model. Through the interactive experience of AR, we can enhance consumers' cognition and experience of Hainan's traditional brocade skills, and promote the propaganda and promotion of Hainan's national and folk culture.

4.3 AR Was Used to Repair and Restore Li Brocade

Li brocade includes traditional Li costumes, dragon quilts and modern innovative products of Li brocade, among which traditional Li costumes and dragon quilts are generally made with a long history. Most of the existing dragons' quilts were made in the Ming and Qing dynasties. Because the dragons' quilts were cotton textiles and the humid climate in Hainan, after hundreds of years of baptism, some dragons' quilts were damaged in varying degrees. The use of AR to repair and copy the damaged dragon quilts and the traditional costumes of Li nationality is the rescue protection of Li nationality brocade. By respecting the original form and cultural connotation of quilt and traditional dress, use AR technology to virtual display the broken pattern, organization structure, style shape and color attribute of dragon quilt, combine dynamic and interactive technology, reproduce Li nationality textile treasures to users in many directions. Besides, AR can also be used to repair with Hainan ancient buildings, unearthed cultural relics, underwater porcelain and so on, which is helpful to the protection of Li nationality's national characteristics and the spread of Hainan regional culture.

4.4 Using AR to Develop Li Brocade's Innovative Products

Integrating Li brocade culture into our life is the best protection and inheritance. Using AR to explore the development of clothing products and cultural innovation products based on Li brocade culture is the development trend of the times and industries. Taking clothing innovation as an example, this paper uses AR to design Li brocade clothing innovation, and deeply excavates the connotation of Li brocade culture. Assemble the current fashion trend, design elements through real-time digital models, animation and video images for information transmission and processing, forming interactive two-dimensional or three-dimensional dynamic image images superimposed in clothing, make static images dynamic, transfer more information, and bring users a new experience. Besides, it has great prospect and significance to use the AR to develop the virtual fitting, custom-made clothing and online and offline sales of Li traditional clothing and innovative clothing.

In this study, AR is applied in the traditional textile skills of Li nationality, which is conducive to the cultural extension and connotation output of Li nationality brocade, so that more people can understand Hainan's excellent intangible cultural heritage. It is conducive to promoting the development and display of brocade related products, expanding its cultural and creative product structure and display channels, and realizing the transformation of related industries and economic growth. The reproduction of traditional technological weaving process through virtual technology plays a positive role in promoting the protection and inheritance of brocade weaving.

5 Conclusion

In the development of cultural and creative elements, AR is a very important technical tool. At present, the development foundation of Hainan cultural industry is weak, and there are still some outstanding contradictions under the background of international free trade port construction. Relying on modern science and technology to help Hainan's cultural and creative industries to achieve leapfrog development is the realistic need for Hainan to develop the digital economy, and it is also the specific requirement for Hainan to build a major national strategy of "intelligent Hainan" in Hainan. This paper elaborates the path of the integration of Hainan's cultural and creative industries and AR and making full use of the characteristics and advantages of AR to deeply integrate with Hainan's rich cultural resources, promote the promotion of Hainan's characteristic culture, and enhance the soft power and international influence of Hainan's culture. Expand the digital research and development of cultural creative products to promote digital cultural consumption. It will help transform and upgrade Hainan's cultural and creative industries and provide theoretical and practical basis for realizing the goal of regional intelligent development in Hainan.

Fund. This study was supported by the social science planning project of Hainan Province in 2020 (Project Name: Research on the development path of creative tourism in the deep integration of intangible cultural heritage and AR technology in Hainan, project number: HNSK(YB)20-63. And the 2020 Industry-University Cooperation Collaborative Education Project of the Ministry of Education of China (Project Name1: Research on the Design of "Regional" Intangible Cultural Heritage Teaching Platform Based on AR Technology, project number1: 202002015005. Project Name2: Research on the experimental teaching project of tourism, cultural and creative design based on AR/VR technology, project number2: 202002015063).

References

1. Xiaojun, X., Donghai, Z., et al.: On international experience and development strategy of cultural and creative industry in Hainan International Tourism Island. China Nat. Expo **01**, 37–41 (2018)
2. Zhenqing, H.Z.: Sustainable development strategy of Hainan Li nationality cultural eco-tourism. Econ. Persp. **1**(10), 49–50 (2013)
3. Ling, Q.: Accelerating the development of cultural and creative industries and promoting the construction of Hainan International Tourism Island. China Econ. Rev. **28**, 40–42 (2012)
4. Koleski, K.: The 13th Five-Year Plan. U.S. – China Economic and Security Review Commission. Staff Research Report. https://www.uscc.gov/sites/default/files/Research/The%201 3th%20Five-Year%20Plan_Final_2.14.17_Updated%20(002). Accessed 14 Feb 2017
5. Gibson, J.J.: The Theory of Affordances. In Shaw, R., Bransford, J. (eds.). Perceiving, Acting, and Knowing: Toward an Ecological Psychology, pp. 67–82. Lawrence Erlbaum, Hillsdale, NJ (1977)
6. Huishu, Z., Hongchao, P., Wanming, L.: Research on the prediction and application of augmented reality technology in cultural and creative industry. Design **32**(09), 41–43 (2019)
7. Asadzadeh, A. TahaSamad, S., PeymanRezaei, H.: Applications of virtual and augmented reality in infectious disease epidemics with a focus on the COVID-19 outbreak. Inf. Med. Unlock 24, 100579 (2021)
8. Billinghurst, A.D., Linderman, R.W. Swan II, J.E.: A systematic review of 10 years of augmented reality usability studies: 2005 to 2014. Front. Robot. AI, 5(37) (2018)
9. Guowei, Sh., Yongtian, W., Liuyue et al.: Application of augmented reality technology in cultural heritage digital protection. J. Syst. Simul. **04**, 2090–2094 (2009)
10. Tencent video: "Meet the Cheng Huangge" AR pray for travel. https://v.qq.com/x/page/v32 194mzyev.html. Accessed 07 Jan 2021

11. Snowball: Holoride creates a new car entertainment virtual reality experience. https://xueqiu. com/u/7748174714. Accessed 16 Oct 2019
12. Tencent video: AR reproduces the Great Water Method of Old Summer Palace. https://v.qq. com/x/page/m08973sz0zd.html. Accessed 10 Jul 2019
13. Unreal Engine: 2021 CCTV Spring Festival Gala AR Packaging. https://www.sohu.com/pic ture/450877170. Accessed 15 Feb 2021

The Heptagon of AUX Model: Development of a Synergising Model on Aesthetic Experience and User Experience through the Fuzzy Delphi Method Towards Augmented Reality Comics

Mohd Ekram Alhafis Hashim, Muhammad Zaffwan Idris[✉], and Che Soh Said

Sultan Idris Educational University, Tanjong Malim, Perak, Malaysia
zaffwan@fskik.upsi.edu.my

Abstract. This research paper aims to report the development of a synergy model from two different fields of knowledge, namely Aesthetic Experience (AX) and User Experience (UX) using Fuzzy Delphi Method (FDM). This model was put forward in order to fill the theoretical gaps in the context of technology-based arts application, such as augmented reality comics (AR comics). Most technology products only measure UX elements even though there are strong artistic elements on the product and vice versa, when most art products only measured at AX despite using the dominant technology on the product. Constructs and elements were built using a methodological review of six models, three from each AX and UX models. In the methodological review, the elements of AX and UX are synergise and are used as research items as constructs and elements for expert consensus process. A total of ten experts, constitute of half from each comics and AR related expertise were used to gain consensus on 16 constructs and 39 elements of AX and UX. The analysis was conducted based on FDM conditions, namely expert consensus $> 70\%$, threshold value (d) < 0.2, and fuzzy score, amax > 0.5.

Keywords: Aesthetic experience · User experience · Fuzzy delphi method · Augmented reality · comics

1 Introduction

The advent of new media technology since 1995 has allowed for massive changes to the creative world as a holistically. Information is at our fingertips, connect via email and watch videos via the YouTube application. There is no doubt that the comic industry is also moving in line with the technology that is present and with that, comics were produce in the form of web, interactive comics and motion comics. Now with the prevailing of industry revolution 4.0, the comics industry is changing rapidly with the birth of mix-reality technology. Now comics are produced with mix-reality technology with a combination of comics as artform and Human-Computer Interaction (HCI) technology. In reflection, comics are objects of art use aesthetic elements in the production process

Z. Lv and H. Song (Eds.): INTETAIN 2021, LNICST 429, pp. 309–321, 2022.
https://doi.org/10.1007/978-3-030-99188-3_19

and AX during the measurement process. While on the other hand, mixed-reality technology especially AR, is HCI based and uses UX as its measurement method. Of course, there is a big gap when the combination of these two disciplines occurs and need for a new model as a guide line in the production and measurement process.

2   Literature Review

In the literature review, the researcher uses methodological review techniques to obtain the elements of AX and UX and in order to stimulate the research questions namely; what is the similarity and dissimilarity of AX and UX construct and what are the construct and elements suitable to be synergise for AUX model. In the case of AR comic, the two major components are AX for comics and UX for AR then researchers need to cover up these two major theories as a synergy for the new model.

2.1   Aesthetic Experience (AX)

In Hagman [1], Plato states that AX is the reflection of idealistic aesthetic objects such as flowers, mountains, beautiful faces, music, theatre, dance, and painting. The uniqueness of relationship on the aesthetic objects and the preoccupation of experience that is as a source of AX [2]. Aesthetic experience is often associate between perceptions and feelings [3]. In contrast, the sensitivity towards both is integrated with the idealistic feelings such as refine pleasure, delight, awe, admiration, and joy. Furthermore, affects and passions considered to be of unique positive value [4, 5]. However, emotion and sensation are a proponent of mental experience, thus the AX source not only to the object or pleasure but also to the subjective knowledge of the universal idea [6]. Docherty [7] emphasises this subjective knowledge as compiling the universal conceptualisation that shapes the basis of our judgment. Under the circumstances, the AX involves several stages of the mental process, which must be passed. Among them is the stage of creating (artist) appreciation (artist, beholder, expert) and appraisal (artist, beholder, expert). These stages are based on cognitive, emotional and perceptual domains to ensure the synergising of AX. Intensely, other scholars have studied over 50 emotions applied to aesthetic objects and events such as concerts, musicals, dances, art exhibitions and films [8]. Consequently, seven emotional constructs were proposed, namely: negative emotions, prototypical aesthetics emotions, epistemic emotions, nostalgia, animation, sadness and amusement.

In the discipline of comic art, AX element has long been practiced as an affirmation of the imagination and surprise inveighing beyond the soul's pleasure are called playful or humorous. It is necessary to strengthen the integration between humour and AX designed to evoke amusement regardless of what aesthetic paradigm is in the various comic genres such as satire, parody, lampoon, burlesque, caricature, farce, slapstick and limerick.

2.2   User Experience (UX)

The early HCI discover the involvement interaction of computer with humans. However, the massive development of the research has widened the role of HCI to multidisciplinary and encompasses almost all information technology designs and all communication devices. When it comes to human experience in HCI, the concept of the experience itself is more closely related to how the human experience interacts with a technology product. Concerning this, Azzawi [9] outlines the concept of experience in technology, namely, time and experience, as an essential concept in the context of experience because experience has a duration, and judgments of such duration changes as the experience unfold. Discussing the UX, we need to understand the fundamental concepts of UX such as what experience to measure, how to define the experience in order to react to a technology product, and what to do after reviewing each of the potential variables.

Formally, ISO 20101 defines UX as involving human perceptions and responses or expectations of responses using a product, system, or service. It is relevant to the UX, including emotions, beliefs, preferences, perceptions, and physical and psychological responses. Hence, the use of such products also potent reflexes to the behaviour and achievements that occur before usage, during usage, and after usage of the product. Thielsch and Thielsch [10] emphasize that there is a difference between usability and UX. In contrast, UX has a global objective goal to achieve effectiveness, efficiency, and satisfaction and enhance holistic UX from anticipation, interaction, and reflection of the experience. Hassenzahl [11] point out that the focus of UX is on the positive outcome of the interaction and the usability theory, which diffuse on pragmatic aspects that can be objectively defined. If it involves the UX to measure such aspects of the stimulus, product introduction, appeal, aesthetics, trust, and privacy are all subjective and very dynamic affected by various factors.

UX can be a larger entity, encompassing usability and the pragmatic and hedonic aspect of a system [12]. UX can be an AR system element such as the visual, sound, haptic, and 3D environment from an AR point of view. In a practical sense, UX can enhance the user reality and specific content of a system. Nowadays, UX constructs more attention from many studies in HCI, especially in AR products. The user needs to go beyond functionality and shift to experiential perspectives to touch the usability and cognitive, affective, aesthetics, and positive feelings towards the product. Under the circumstances, the knowledge of end-users potentially requisites the analysing what kind of experience is expected to evoke. Concerning this, the research knowledge preparedness to be used in UX design, especially in augmented reality service. The UX itself involves several stages of the mental process, which must be passed. Among them is the stage of developing (developer) to the end-user (target users). In a practical sense, these stages involve several elements likewise, valuable, UX characteristic, emotion, usability, assessable and desirable [13, 14].

Scholars have collected the UX constructs and elements from previous studies using technology, including the usage of AR technology namely; efficiency, increased awareness, inspiration, motivation, creativity, liveliness, meaningfulness, playfulness & entertainment, captivation, intuitiveness, and tangibility [15]. These constructs and elements will be in synergy with AX and UX to obtain expert consensus at the next level, namely the FDM.

2.3 Augmented Reality Comics (AR Comics)

AR is one of the platforms included in MR representing the interoperability platform currently used in various fields. Popular in military, medical and aerospace, AR is now widely used in education, games and arts [16]. The term AR first appeared in 1992 in the HUDSET research project during designing and prototyping processes. In a practical sense, the technology enabling this access interface call heads-up (see-thru) combined with a head position sensor to workplace registration systems [17]. The augment of the visual field of the user information concurrent with reality manufacturing task, overwhelm the human-involve operations, and they call the system is AR technology [18, 19].

AR is a technology that allows an interactive three-dimensional environment and virtual imagery to be overlaid the real objects [20]. This statement is fully supported by other scholar [21], that emphasis an AR system must have the following properties such as, combines real and virtual objects in the real environment, runs interactively in real-time and register real and virtual objects with each other. AR comic was first introduced commercially in 2016 when Stuart Campbell, a comic artist who produced a comic with an AR application and sold it online. Comics have evolved in line with technology but still retain the aesthetic elements. The use of technology enhances the user experience and sensation, while reading comics with the integration of technology and art [22, 23]. In this study the researchers have selected an existing AR comic published by Marvel, entitled Master of the Sun as a stimulus to gain expert consensus by employing the FDM. The comic uses AR technology entirely in conveying the narrative.

3 Fuzzy Delphi Method (FDM)

In this study, the researchers excerpt FDM as a method in order to obtain expert consensus in the context of formulating new constructs and elements to develop an AR comic prototype. The selected experts are heterogeneous and this is in line with the FDM technique itself [24]. The selection of respondents for this phase comprises an appointed panel of experts to validate constructs and elements in the previous MR process. Concerning this, ten panelists are appointed, each representing comics and five others representing AR. Experts' selection is determined by more than ten years in comics industry and has produced conventional and contemporary comics. The criteria considered are qualifications for AR experts, involvement in the new media industry and recognised expertise. Because these two experts are heterogeneous, therefore, a total of ten experts are sufficient to obtain empirical data [25].

A methodological review aims to identify the integration of relevant models and theories. Indeed, for the purpose of critical readings, it was made on three models and the idea of UX [11, 12, 26]. Furthermore, through the process of screening, selection, integration, and formulation are critically coupled with identifying UX elements for AR to get the constructs and elements in the UX. The same concept is applied to the theories and models of the AX. Three models are integrated, filtered, and formulated to identify the elements of AX for comics and further identify the constructs and AX elements. The three models are Redies [27], Leder, et al., [28], and Markovic [29]. On the other hand, the constructs and elements that have been identified and adapted from several studies [15, 30–33]. As shown in Table 1 below:

Table 1. Methodological review proses of construct and element of UX and AX

The construct and element of UX		
No	Construct	Element
1	Efficiency	Time, effort
2	Increase awareness	Feeling of discovery, feeling of insights
3	Inspiration	Cognitive stimulated, encourages, eager to try new things
4	Motivation	Being motivated, Interaction proactivity
5	Creativity	Self-expressive, creative
6	Liveliness	Vivid, dynamic
7	Meaningfulness	Personal meaningful, relevant
8	Playfulness and entertainment	Joy, amusement, playfulness
9	Captivation	Captivate, immerse
10	Intuitiveness	Human likeness, naturalness
11	Tangibility	Concreteness, coherence
The construct and element of AX		
No	Construct	Element
1	Amusement	Love, funny, cheerfulness
2	Paradox of tragedy	Tragic, Grotesque, Macabre, Horrible
3	Mental jolt	Bizarre, fantastic
4	Harmony	Verisimilitude, accuracy
5	Storytelling clarity	Surprise, drama, amazement, authenticity

3.1 FDM Initial Model Formulation

The ensuing process formulation of the AUX model from the result of the findings of the expert consensus in the FDM process earlier. In this process, the acceptable constructs and elements will be arranged to determine through the process of accumulation, merging, and altering constructs and elements appropriate to the AR comic. The ranking of each element will also be studied as a guideline to merge, accumulate or alter the constructs and elements affording to the AX and UX models as well as the SLR process carried out.

16 constructs and 39 elements that have been collected through the methodological review process were used as random items for expert consensus. Seven levels of fuzzy scale were used and FDM analysis was performed based on triangular fuzzy number, defuzzification and ranking. The triangular fuzzy number represents the values m1, m2 and m3, which is the m1 = minimum value, m2 = reasonable value and m3 = maximum value (refer Fig. 1). Purposely, to produce a fuzzy scale in order to translate the linguistic variables into fuzzy numbers (refer Table 2). On account of this, the higher of the fuzzy scale of the exact data will obtain [34]. Conversely, the defuzzification process involves media values between fuzzy numbers (0–1), and the significant value is below 0.2. This means that measure items or constructs are accepted based on expert consensus. Meanwhile, the proses of ranking are to manage the construct and item according to the chronology of the main and ultimate construct that been occur by expert consensus.

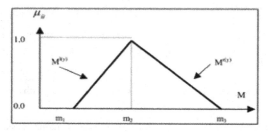

Fig. 1. Triagular fuzzy number

Table 2. Seven-level fuzzy scale of consensus

Linguistic variables	Fuzzy scale
Extremely disagree	(0.0,0.0, 0.1)
Strongly disagree	(0.0, 0.1, 0.3)
Disagree	(0.1, 0.3, 0.7)
Moderate	(0.3, 0.5, 0.7)
Agree	(0.5, 0.7, 0.9)
Strongly agree	(0.7, 0.9, 1.0)
Extremely agree	(0.9, 1.0, 1.0)

Table 3 postulates the value of three main conditions in FDM: Percentage of expert consensus, Threshold (d) value, and defuzzification (Fuzzy score). In this case, the percentage of expert consensus is the main entity, and it is identical significant to be the foundation for the acceptance of constructs and elements, then the threshold value and so on is the fuzzy score [35]. Based on FDM conditions, it must be stress that threshold, $d \leq 0.2$, expert consensus percentage >70% and fuzzy score, Amax > 0.5.

Table 3. Overall acceptance and rejection construct and element of AX and UX

Construct	Element	Percentage	Threshold value	Fuzzy score	Consensus	Ranking
Amusement	Love	40%	0.187	0.653	Reject	
	Funny	70%	0.179	0.767	Accept	2
	Cheerfulness	80%	0.155	0.803	Accept	1
Paradox of Tragedy	Tragic	50%	0.147	0.710	Reject	
	Grotasque	50%	0.165	0.520	Reject	
	Macabre	90%	0.178	0.617	Accept	1
	Horrible	70%	0.233	0.613	Reject	2
Mental Jolt	Bizzare	60%	0.196	0.777	Reject	
	Fantastic	70%	0.135	0.847	Accept	1
Harmony	Verisimilitude	80%	0.145	0.820	Accept	1
	Accuracy	70%	0.172	0.797	Accept	2
Storytelling Clarity	Surprise	90%	0.103	0.910	Accept	1
	Drama	100%	0.126	0.783	Accept	4
	Amazement	80%	0.107	0.863	Accept	2
	Authencity	70%	0.145	0.857	Accept	3
Tangibility	Concreteness	30%	0.221	0.680	Reject	
	Coherence	60%	0.215	0.763	Reject	
Intuitiveness	Human likeness	20%	0.228	0.687	Reject	
	Natural	50%	0.304	0.590	Reject	
Captivation	Captive	50%	0.217	0.807	Reject	
	Immersive	50%	0.264	0.770	Reject	
Playfulness & Entertainment	Joy	20%	0.232	0.733	Reject	
	Amusement	70%	0.205	0.770	Reject	1
	Playfulness	60%	0.192	0.810	Reject	
Meaningfulness	Personal meaningful	80%	0.162	0.757	Accept	1
	Relevant	60%	0.208	0.797	Reject	
Liveliness	Vivid	50%	0.172	0.727	Reject	
	Dynamic	70%	0.157	0.830	Accept	1
Creativity	Self-Expressive	70%	0.191	0.813	Accept	2
	Creative	100%	0.049	0.947	Accept	1
Motivation	Being motivated	70%	0.185	0.837	Accept	1
	Interaction proactivity	70%	0.188	0.737	Accept	2

(continued)

Table 3. (*continued*)

Construct	Element	Percentage	Threshold value	Fuzzy score	Consensus	Ranking
Inspiration	Cognitive stimulated	80%	0.107	0.863	Accept	1
	Encourages	80%	0.155	0.803	Accept	3
	Eager to try new things	70%	0.193	0.847	Accept	2
Increase awareness	Feeling of discovery	70%	0.135	0.847	Accept	1
	Feeling of insights	80%	0.157	0.807	Accept	2
Efficiency	Time	70%	0.135	0.767	Accept	2
	Effort	70%	0.125	0.837	Accept	1

The formulation process begins by analysing constructs with only one element combined with the appropriate construct and has more than one element. With reference to this, for AX, two constructs have only one element, which is the paradox of tragedy (macabre) and mental jolt (fantastic), while for UX two constructs have one element namely liveliness (dynamic) and meaningfulness (personal meaningful) (see Fig. 2). By the same token, some constructs have been retained, and some constructs have undergone a rebranding process in terms of construct names due to the addition of elements that make the construct stronger and more appropriate. The storytelling clarity construct has received additional macabre and fantastic elements from the paradox of tragedy. Mental jolt constructs create the new construct name from storytelling clarity to storytelling only and both elements from the AX component.

The amusement construct from the AX component has received an additional two elements from the creativity construct under the UX component, namely self-expressive and creative. In other respect, the creation of the amusement construct has four elements: self-expressive, creative, funny, and cheerful. For the harmony construct, the elements have been integrated with the liveliness construct from the UX component, which is dynamic. This construct contains three elements: accuracy, verisimilitude, and dynamic. The original construction of the UX component that increases awareness has been changed to mindfulness after being added with the personal element meaningful is a construct from the UX component that is meaningfulness. It must be stressed that the UX component's efficiency construct is maintained and the original construct from the UX component that is motivation has been renamed to the incentive to make it more suitable for the AUX model to be developed.

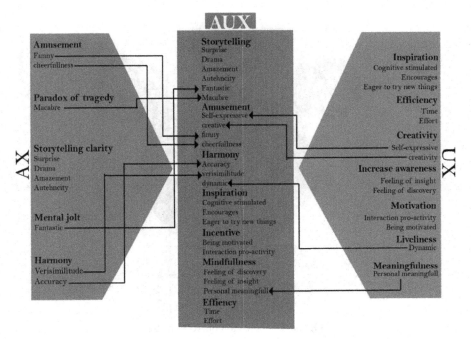

Fig. 2. The formulation of the AUX model

4   The Heptagon of Aesthetic User Experience (AUX) Model

The heptagon of the AUX model (Fig. 3) was taken in conjunction with celebrating the shape of a heptagon that has seven corners representing the seven AUX constructs and 24 elements embedded in it. In such a case, it becomes the basis and guideline for the production of aesthetic products that use HCI devices. The description of each construct and element is as follows:

4.1   Storytelling

Storytelling constructs are among the main agendas in the AUX model as a narrative aesthetic product. In this case, it is supported by an element of authenticity that is able to provide novelty value. In addition, surprise, drama, fantastic and macabre elements can stir emotions and publish a sense of amazement.

4.2   Amusement

Amusement is self-expressive born from a creative point of view, and in the context of AUX, it is a manifestation of self-expression, creativity, funny and cheerfulness. The value of amusement is applied in AUX as a reflection of the basis of the beholder aesthetic object's emotion and aesthetic experience.

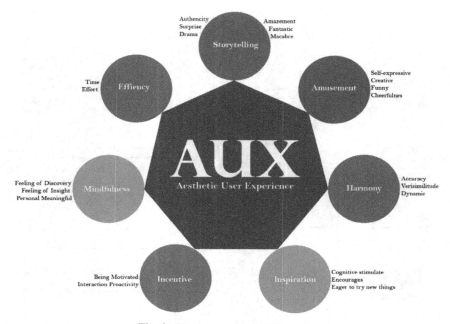

Fig. 3. The heptagon of AUX model

4.3 Harmony

Harmony in the AUX model encompasses the aesthetic and user experience of the aesthetic objects and HCI products. It requires precision from a technical point of view and emotional experience so that the beholder feels something is true and verisimilitude. In addition, it can also implement products that are not static but more dynamic.

4.4 Inspiration

Among the important constructs in AX and UX are cognitive. It plays a big role in stimulating knowledge with existing knowledge and previous experience. It can also be a medium to encourage and shove for the beholder eager to try new things.

4.5 Incentive

The incentive is a construct that aims to inspire always to be motivated. The combination of AUX with the device and the aesthetics of the product provides an experience of interaction with the activities offered, giving positive encouragement to the aesthetic object.

4.6 Mindfulness

Mindfulness is an awareness of the need to explore and experience with aesthetic devices and objects. That being so, the beholder will be able to feel of insight and at the same time, grow an experience termed personal meaningful.

4.7 Efficiency

Undeniably attainment of something efficiently time and effort is an important thing as its main goal. In the context of the AUX model, the beholder's experience with AUX products is related to time and effort.

5 Conclusion

In conclusion, the heptagon of AUX model (Hepta AUX) is a combined model between AX and UX theories for technology-based arts application. It can be used as a guideline for the development and evaluation not only for AR comics but other technology-based arts applications such as digital art installation and VR poster. According to previous studies, most products from mix-reality applications that apply art elements use a lot of UX model while most art objects that apply mix-reality technology only use AX to translate the results of the product. Furthermore, the significant contribution of the Hepta AUX model is that it bridging the two major theories that are different in terms of discipline and body of knowledge, namely AX and UX to be sinergised, thus enable to establish an accurate empirical measurement of commonly neglected area that is technology-based arts application.

References

1. Hagman, H.: Aesthetic Experience Beauty, Creativity, and the Search for the Ideal. Contemporary Psychoanalytic Studies (2005)
2. Perlovsky, L.: Mystery in experimental psychology, how to measure aesthetic emotions? Front. Psychol. **5**, 1006 (2014)
3. Moens, B.G.: Aesthetic experience in virtual museums: a post phenomenological perspective. Stud. Digital Herit. **2**, 1 (2018)
4. Schoeller, F., Perlovsky, L.: Aesthetic chills: knowledge-acquisition, meaning-making, and aesthetic emotions. Front. Psychol. **7**, 1093 (2016). https://doi.org/10.3389/fpsyg.201601093
5. Savaş, E.B., Verwijmeren, T., van Lier, R.: Aesthetic experience and creativity in interactive art. Art Percept. **9**(2), 167–198 (2021)
6. Pelowski, M.: Tears and transformation: feeling like crying as an indicator of Insightful or "aesthetic" experience with art. Front. Psychol. **6**, 1006 (2015). https://doi.org/10.3389/fpsyg.2015.01006
7. Docherty, T.: Aesthetic Education and the Demise of Experience. Manchester University Press, In The new aestheticism (2018)
8. Schindler, I., et al.: Measuring aesthetic emotions: a review of the literature and a new assessment tool. PLoS ONE **12**(6), e0178899 (2017)
9. Al-Azzawi, A.: Experience with Technology: Dynamics of User Experience with Mobile Media Devices. Springer Science & Business Media (2013). https://doi.org/10.1007/978-1-4471-5397-9
10. Thielsch, M.T., Thielsch, C.: Depressive symptoms and web user experience. Peer J **6**, e4439 (2018)
11. Hassenzahl, M.: The hedonic/pragmatic model of user experience. Towards a UX manifesto 10 (2007)

12. Ritsos, P.D., Ritsos, D.P., Gougoulis, A.S.: Standards for augmented reality: a user experience perspective. In: International AR Standards Meeting, pp. 1–9 (2011)
13. Qing-Xing, Q., Zhang, L., Chao, W.-Y., Duffy, V.: User experience design based on eye-tracking technology: a case study on smartphone APPs. In: Duffy, V.G. (ed.) Advances in applied digital human modeling and simulation, pp. 303–315. Springer International Publishing, Cham (2017). https://doi.org/10.1007/978-3-319-41627-4_27
14. Klingbeil, M., Pasewaldt, S., Semmo, A., Döllner, J.: Challenges in user experience design of image filtering apps. In: SIGGRAPH Asia 2017 Mobile Graphics & Interactive Applications, 22. ACM. (2017)
15. Olsson, T., Lagerstam, E., Kärkkäinen, T., Väänänen-Vainio-Mattila, K.: Expected user experience of mobile augmented reality services: a user study in the context of shopping centres. Pers. Ubiquit. Comput. 17(2), 287–304 (2011). https://doi.org/10.1007/s00779-011-0494-x
16. Speicher, M., Hall, B.D., Nebeling, M.: What is mixed reality? In: Proceedings of the 2019 CHI Conference on Human Factors in Computing Systems, ACM (2019)
17. Hamacher, A., Hafeez, J., Csizmazia, R., Whangbo, T.K.: Augmented reality user interface evaluation – performance measurement of hololens, moverio and mouse input. Int. J. Inter. Mob. Technol. (iJIM) 13(03), 95 (2019). https://doi.org/10.3991/ijim.v13i03.10226
18. Cabero Almenara, J., Barroso, J.: The educational possibilities of augmented reality. New Appr. Educ. Res. 5(1) (2016)
19. Larsen, R.R., Sackris, D.: Feeling the Aesthetic: A Pluralist Sentimentalist Theory of Aesthetic Experience (2020)
20. Marques, D.: Augmented reality: the new kid on the block. J. Nat. Sci. Illust. 49(3), 12–14 (2017)
21. Azuma, R., Baillot, Y., Behringer, R., Feiner, S., Julier, S., MacIntyre, B.: Recent advances in augmented reality. IEEE Comput. Graphics Appl. 21(6), 34–47 (2001)
22. Smith, C.: Motion comics: the emergence of a hybrid medium. Writ. Vis. Cult. 7, 1–23 (2015)
23. Vassiliadi, M., Sylaiou, S., Papagiannakis, G.: Literary myths in mixed reality. Front. Digit. Humanit. 5, 21 (2018). https://doi.org/10.3389/fdigh.2018.00021
24. Clayton, M.J.: Delphi: a technique to harness expert opinion for critical decision-making tasks in education. Educ. Psychol. 17(4), 373–384 (1997)
25. Ayub, E., Mohamad, S.N.A., Wei, G.W., Luaran, J.: A learning design strategy framework for content transformation using fuzzy delphi method. Int. J. Inf. Educat. Technol. 10(12), 882–888 (2020)
26. Irshad, S., Awang Rambli, D.R.: Multi-layered mobile augmented reality framework for positive user experience. In: Proceedings of the 2nd International Conference in HCI and UX Indonesia 2016, pp. 21–26. ACM (2016)
27. Redies, C.: Combining universal beauty and cultural context in a unifying model of visual aesthetic experience. Front. Hum. Neurosci. 9, 218 (2015). https://doi.org/10.3389/fnhum.2015.00218
28. Leder, H., Belke, B., Oeberst, O., Augustin, D.: A model of aestjetic appreciation and aesthetic judgements. Br. J. Psychol. 95, 489–508 (2004)
29. Markovic, S.: Components of aesthetic experience: aesthetic fascination, aesthetic appraisal, and aesthetic emotion. i-Perception 3(1), 1–17 (2012). https://doi.org/10.1068/i0450aap
30. Morreall, J.: Comic Relief. Wiley-Blackwell, Oxford, UK (2009). https://doi.org/10.1002/9781444307795
31. Klaehn, J.: The craft of comics: an interview with comic book artists Norm Breyfogle. J. Grap. Novels Com. 6(1), 108–115 (2015). https://doi.org/10.1080/21504857.2014.943414
32. Plutchik, R.: A general psychoevolutionary theory of emotion. In: Theories of Emotion, pp. 3–33. Academic press (1980)
33. Parrot, W.: Emotions in Social Psychology. Psychology Press, Philadelphia (2001)

34. Jamil, M.R.M., Said, S., Azeez, M.I.K.: Kopetemsi guru terhadap pengurusan pengajaran dan pembelajaran: suatu pendekatan kaedah fuzzy Delphi. Jurnal kepimpinan pendidikan **1**(3), 77–88 (2014)
35. Manakandan, S.K., Rosnah, I., Mohd, J.R., Priya, R.: Pesticide applicators questionnaire content validation: a fuzzy Delphi method. Med. J. Malaysia **72**(4), 228–235 (2017)

AREDAPPS: Mobile Augmented Reality Development and Learning Framework Based on Augmented Reality Technology for Engineering Drawing Course

Dayana Farzeeha Ali[1]([✉]) [iD], Marlissa Omar[2]([✉]) [iD], Mohd Shahrizal Sunar[1] [iD], Norasykin Mohd Zaid[1] [iD], Nor Hasniza Ibrahim[1] [iD], and Johari Surif[1] [iD]

[1] Universiti Teknologi Malaysia, 81310 Johor Bahru, Johor, Malaysia
dayanafarzeeha@utm.my
[2] Universiti Kebangsaan Malaysia, 43600 Bangi, Selangor, Malaysia
marlissa@ukm.edu.my

Abstract. Technology in teaching and learning is crucial as we are now focusing on 21st Century Learning. Moreover, the Covid-19 pandemic has affected many sectors, including education sectors, where most educators are continuously looking for approach and tools to enhance their teaching deliveries to ensure students can still learn effectively even though most of the classes are currently conducted online. Other than that, students also have problems with their visualization skills when learning engineering drawing, which caused a lack of understanding of the content, thus making it even harder for them to learn in this situation. Technology such as augmented reality is a well-received technology application due to its benefit in enhancing users' learning experiences, enhancing visualization skills, and supplementing materials more effectively. Thus, this paper aims to describe Augmented Reality Engineering Drawing Apps (AREDApps) development process, a mobile augmented reality apps for orthographic projection topic in engineering drawing subject, highlight the students' perception when using AREDApps during learning and introduce the engineering drawing learning framework based on AREDApps implementation in the classroom. The result indicates that students were mostly satisfied with augmented reality technology to learn orthographic projection. This is because AREDApps helps them supplement the information that cannot be delivered by using modules or PowerPoint presentation such as the three-dimensional representations of the task given to them. The findings of this paper strengthen the facts that augmented reality is a suitable technology to teach complex technical subjects, which requires supplementary materials that can help students to be able to visualize the task effectively.

Keywords: AREDApps · Visualization · Orthographic projection · Engineering drawing · Perception · Framework

1 Introduction

Engineering drawing is known as a universal language for people working in the technical field. It contains complete detail and specification for any design or product, which can

Z. Lv and H. Song (Eds.): INTETAIN 2021, LNICST 429, pp. 322–335, 2022.
https://doi.org/10.1007/978-3-030-99188-3_20

help the production department understand the exact details of a product they need to produce. Even though there are various draughting software available nowadays which provide convenience for people who work in technical fields to produce technical drawings in a shorter time compared to manual drawings, they still need to master the basic of producing technical drawings and able to visualize the design given to them [1]. Insufficient visualization skills are why students face difficulties in producing the representations of an orthographic projection in engineering drawing subject [2]. According to Marunic and Glazar [3], authorities have made various efforts to redesign engineering drawing curricula for undergraduate engineering students where contents addressing visualization skills were included in the curricula. The efforts include introducing a freehand sketching activity involving isometric, orthographic, rotation of objects, and cross-sections of solids. Emphasis on visualization skills is essential because this course requires students to deal with the construction of 2-dimensional and 3-dimensional geometry and the creation of multi-view and pictorial representations.

Mastering technical drawing, primarily through an engineering drawing course, is essential among engineering students. Mastering technical drawing is essential because technical drawings play an essential role in engineering careers. The accuracy of technical drawing in the designing and production process is crucial for any engineering practitioners and the ability to read and interpret the drawings precisely. Failure in reading or interpreting technical drawing might cause a more significant impact on the whole designing and production process [4]. Sorby *et al.* [5] also mentioned in their research that it is essential to represent the problems pictorially before beginning any processes to avoid more complicated problems arises later. Thus, learning how to produce a high-quality technical drawing with a detailed specification can help reduce the errors when interpreting the technical drawings [6]. Proper training on producing, reading, and interpreting technical drawing among students in engineering and technical fields should be further emphasized to avoid misinterpretation and failure to read the drawings throughout their engineering career.

According to Sorby *et al.* [7], students have some issues when learning engineering drawing. Some students have difficulties with understanding and mastering the concept of orthographic applications such as projections, orthographic to isometric transformation and dimensioning [2]. Students also claimed to have problems with their ability to view or visualize objects mentally. These problems are closely related to the issues with lack of visualization skills [2]. Another problem identified in this study is the difficulties in understanding projection views due to the lack of ability to imagine images in three-dimensional scenarios [6]. They tend to have difficulties switching between two-dimensional and three-dimensional scenarios [8], which disrupt the process of producing, reading, and interpreting the drawing. Students lacking in visualization skills tend to use trial and error methods due to the lack of proficiency in solving the problems [9].

The significance of teaching and learning strategies during the teaching and learning process is undeniably essential to securing effective learning. However, the strategies used may vary depending on the course requirements. Failure to adopt appropriate teaching and learning strategies could make it difficult for learners to understand the learning subjects' ideas. Recent educational approaches require educators to integrate real-world situations into the learning process to nurture students' interests through technology-enhanced learning [11]. Among all the technologies used in teaching and learning, augmented reality has been receiving tremendous interests among researchers worldwide.

It is proven to effectively reduce cognitive load and help increases students' learning interests [10, 11]. The advantages that this technology offered are why people in various fields have recently seen this technology as one of the emergent technologies. Other than the education field, augmented reality also has been used in clothing, automobile, and biomedical industry [12]. The idea of this technology had exceeded the needs of different areas, providing a more engaging and efficient environment to compare how it used to be before implementing this technology. The results from all of these studies showed that the application of this technology could elevate students understanding when learning complicated concepts. Other than that, it can also improve students' visualization skills in various course and areas. Other than that, augmented reality also fosters self-directed learning skills.

Researchers in the visualization field claimed that students with excellent visualization skills would do well to visualize three-dimensional objects and better understand the concept of visual representation than those lacking visualization skills [13]. Thus, with the utilization of augmented reality technology that can help to enhance visualization skills as proven by various researchers in various field, this study aims to describe the development of Augmented Reality Engineering Drawing Apps (AREDApps), a mobile augmented reality developed with a purpose to enhance students' visualization skills when learning engineering drawing course, identify students' perception on using AREDApps during the learning process and introduce the engineering drawing learning framework based on the implementation of AREDApps in the classroom.

2 Development of AREDApps

2.1 3D Model Development

During the first stage, which is designing 3D virtual models, the program involved is Autodesk 3D Studio Max. Autodesk 3D Studio Max is a professional program designed to allow users to create 3-dimensional animations, models and images. This program was developed by Autodesk Media and Entertainment, where it is mainly used for games development purposes. This program has modelling and animation capabilities which has been used by various commercial studios as well as visualization studios. The 3D modelling process for all the 3D virtual models was done based on the included exercises in the augmented learning module. In this application, only exercises related to the orthographic projection topics are included. Figure 1 shows the Autodesk 3D Studio Max interface, and Fig. 2 shows the example of 3D modelling produced using the software.

The models are designed using Autodesk 3D Studio Max will then be rendered based on the materials that will allow the models to look more apparent and more attractive. In this study, the researcher chooses to use an ocean blue colour as the material for all the 3D models. Many experts approved that the blue colour can help students learn an intensely challenging topic and improve concentration during the teaching and learning process. Furthermore, the models were then export into.fbx file format to allow the importing process in Unity3D later on during the development of the augmented reality environment.

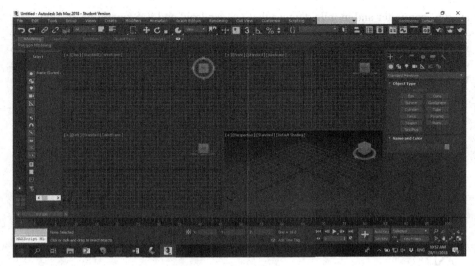

Fig. 1. The interface of Autodesk 3D Studio Max

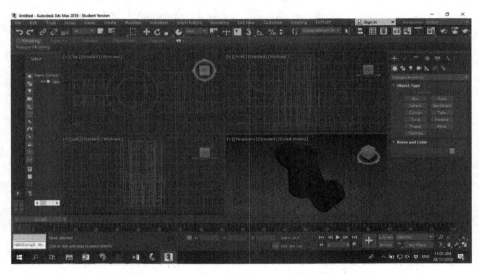

Fig. 2. The example of 3D modeling produced using the software

2.2 Mobile Augmented Reality Development

Once the first stage is completed, the next stage will be developing AREDApps using Unity3D software. Unity3D software is chosen due to the researcher's familiarity with the programming language used in the software, which is the C# programming language. Apart from its use to develop an augmented reality content, it is also widely used to develop games content. Unity3D can develop contents that can be used in various devices such as computer and mobile devices that use Android and iOS operating systems. For AREDApps, the researcher has chosen the Android operating system option as the medium to run mobile apps since most students use Android devices instead of iOS devices. Figure 3 shows the options that the developer can consider when developing using Unity3D.

Fig. 3. Options when developing using Unity3D

On the main menu of AREDApps, several buttons are available to navigate the main menu to the content of AREDApps. The simplicity of the interface is the primary key of the development for users to be able to use it comfortably. Other than that, bright colours provide an attractive learning environment to the users, significantly to help maintain their interests in the teaching and learning process. Figure 4 shows the interface of AREDApps.

In the tutorial video menu interface, several buttons are available where each of the buttons will navigate users to the tutorial video of each type of surface. Apart from that, an animation video is placed at the top of the interface to explain the basic information on orthographic projection. The video explains the meaning of orthographic projection, types of orthographic drawings and their labelling. Users will choose the tutorial video that they want to learn according to their interests and move to the other tutorial video based on their own learning pace. The tutorial video in the app allows users to fast forward, stop and pause according to their interest.

The second button in the main menu will navigate users to the AR camera when they are ready to answer the task for orthographic projection. The questions that users need to solve is designed with the AR Marker. The marker consists of two sides, where the front side is where the AR marker is. Users can scan the marker using the AR camera to view

Fig. 4. Interface of AREDApps

the virtual objects. Meanwhile, the backside of the AR marker is the two-dimensional images of the virtual objects complete with the dimensions. The format of the two-dimensional images is designed according to the content of the orthographic projection syllabus. Users can view and manipulate the three-dimensional virtual objects to help them see the hidden views and draw their respective orthographic projection drawing accurately. Figure 5 shows the example of a marker for AREDApps, and Fig. 6 shows the example of the augmented reality interface of AREDApps.

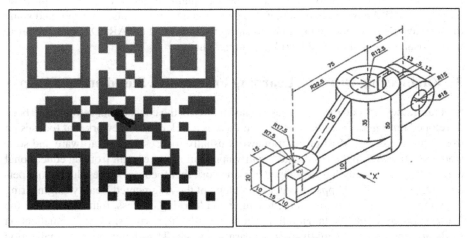

Fig. 5. Marker for Augmented Reality

Fig. 6. Example of Augmented Reality interface of AREDApps

Augmented reality will show the three-dimensional virtual objects for each two-dimensional image that they need to solve, and users will be able to freely manipulate the object as if they are holding the actual object and view the cross-section views of the objects. According to Chen [14], students tend to treat virtual objects in an augmented reality environment as holding an actual object. This approach will encourage them to learn independently while educators will act as their facilitators. This feature is also known as one of the appropriate strategies for effective learning. The development process followed the ADDIE Model to ensure the quality of the developed end-product, which is AREDApps. Other than that, the development process also incorporated some theories and models that are useful in ensuring the quality of the AREDApps to enhance user's visualization skills and learning comprehension.

3   Engineering Drawing Learning Framework Based on AREDApps

Several frameworks on the use of augmented reality in the educational setting have been developed throughout the years. However, there is a lack of a framework that focuses on the learning process. Most of the framework usually focuses on the hardware and software used to develop the augmented reality application rather than from an educational perspective. This study has developed a framework that focuses on the educational perspectives of the AREDApps. In order to implement the Augmented Reality Engineering Drawing Apps (AREDApps) in the teaching and learning process, four elements in the learning process must be taken into account towards improving students' visualization skills and increase their motivation to learn the topic. The elements are visualization strategies, student's centeredness, teaching presence and meaningful learning theory. Figure 7 shows the Engineering Drawing Learning Framework based on AREDApps.

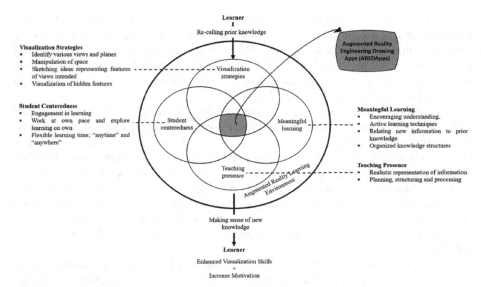

Fig. 7. Engineering Drawing Learning Framework based on the implementation of AREDApps

Educators are responsible for ensuring that all indicators are achieved to further improve teaching quality and enhance student learning. The framework in this study aims to support the learning practices of educators in engineering drawing classrooms using the augmented reality environment produced in this study, the Augmented Reality Engineering Drawing Apps (AREDApps). Using this framework alongside AREDApps as teaching and learning tools, students will be able to make sense of the new knowledge they have constructed in the classroom. Also, it helps to improve student visualization skills and motivate learners to study engineering drawing.

The first element, which is teaching presence, is crucial in the teaching and learning process. Teaching involves educators formulating an opportunity for students to learn [15]. Examples of teaching presence are giving direct instruction such as recommendations or information, facilitating students by posing questions to encourage students' further thoughts on a topic and give feedback to the students by agreeing or criticize their ideas [16]. The study also identified an indirect positive impact between teaching presence and student satisfaction as well as learning performance. There is proven to be equally great importance between teaching presence and levels of learning based on previous studies [17]. Therefore, by incorporating the elements of teaching presence in the teaching and learning process by AREDApps, students will be able to learn actively with their classmates and construct the meaning of the topic they will learn.

The second element in the framework is student-centeredness. Among college students, various issues are being highlighted regarding their learning behaviour. Some of them are low-class attendance, lack of class participation and not conducting reading assignments [18]. This issue is sometimes due to the types of approaches in the teaching and learning process that do not encourage and motivate students to be involved in the classroom. Unattractive teaching practices and lack of sense of community with class-mates are among the reasons that hinder students interests to learn [19]. However, by implementing student-centred learning, educators will be able to create a meaningful learning experience and help them actively learn, apply their skill, care for their learning and the most important thing is learn how to learn. Student-centred learning is often associated with technology-enhanced learning.

Visualization strategies are also one of the elements in the framework developed in this study. Various research has illustrated a potential for visualization skill to be developed and their effect on academic achievement. Visualization skill also becomes increasingly linked to the Science, Technology, Engineering and Mathematics (STEM) field [20]. Using AREDApps, the researcher aims to help educators collectively improve students' learning experience and visualization skills during the teaching and learning of orthographic projection topic in an engineering drawing course. By emphasizing the visualization strategies element in the framework developed from this study, students are expected to see significant improvement in their visualization skills after learning AREDApps.

According to Ausubel in Vallori [21], learning is influenced by the students' prior knowledge. Thus, making meaningful learning is a process that implies knowledge being retained much longer than memorizing. Meaningful learning occurred when learning implemented an active, constructive, and goal-oriented process involving problem-solving while strongly influencing one's prior knowledge [22]. Furthermore, this situation occurs when students can relate new knowledge with their prior knowledge. By giving students materials that they can relate to, students will contextualize what they learned [23]. Meaningful learning is much more preferred than rote learning due to the nature of this learning process that encouraged students to construct meanings from what they learned actively. When meaningful learning occurs, knowledge gained by students will be most likely be stored in the long-term memory storage.

4 Students' Perception on Using AREDApps

This section analyses the students' perception of learning engineering drawing using AREDApps. When developing an application as a tool specifically made for teaching and learning purpose, it is crucial to know the users' perception when using the tool. In this case, it is essential to know the students' feedback on using AREDApps towards improving their learning experiences and visualization skills. A total of 30 students were involved in teaching and learning of engineering drawing course using AREDApps. The students' involved are first-year engineering students in a public university in Malaysia. A questionnaire is developed to identify students' perception of using AREDApps by the researcher, where the students were asked to answer the questionnaire based on the scales provided (SA: Strongly Agree, A: Agree, D: Disagree, SD: Strongly Disagree). After the use of AREDApps, Table 1 shows the students' perceptions when learning using AREDApps.

Table 1. Mean and standard deviation score for students' perception using AREDApps

No.	Items	Mean	Standard deviation	Level
1	AREDApps helps me to memorize the content of this topic	4.20	.484	High
2	AREDApps content delivery is simple, concise and orderly which is easy to follow	3.97	.490	High
3	AREDApps help me in getting better picture (realistic) towards the content of this topic	4.10	.403	High
4	AREDApps helps me to relate the content of this topic with the real world	3.90	.712	High
5	Usage of AREDApps increase my interest towards this topic	4.47	.507	High
6	Usage of animation/graphic/3D model in AREDApps is more helpful to me compared to explanation lecture method alone in understanding the content of this topic	4.23	.626	High
7	I prefer learning through AREDApps compared to printed note	4.53	.629	High
8	By learning using AREDApps, i can reduce my study period compared to learning through printed notes	4.23	.568	High
9	AREDApps helps me to visualize the view of given object more easily	4.63	.490	High
10	AREDApps helps me to visualize side views of each object more easily	4.50	.509	High

5   Discussion

In orthographic projection, students need to master problem-solving skills. According to Frerejan et al. [24], several steps need to be followed for a practical problem-solving approach. Students must be able to explore, construct and understand the concept of this topic for them to solve the problems in this topic. Thus, educators must provide an environment that allows students to implement these steps in their learning. Providing quality teaching presence will positively impact students' learning behaviour, improve their learning motivation, and indirectly improve their learning performance [25].

Using AREDApps allows students to learn at their own pace by exploring all the tutorial videos and solving the exercises with the help of the augmented three-dimensional virtual objects. Other than that, the student-centred learning approach also helps increases retention and understanding of the knowledge. This is because the students apply all learning activities during the teaching and learning process, while educators facilitate the learning process by providing support when there is a complex concept that needs to be clarified.

In this study, visualization strategies consist of few activities such as identify various views and planes, space manipulation, identifying axes, sketching ideas of views, and visualizing the hidden features of the given object. The use of three-dimensional virtual objects in AREDApps provides a realistic experience that promotes visualization activity [26]. By providing means for visualization strategies in AREDApps, it enables the student to improve their visualization skills throughout their learning process. The visualization strategies incorporated in AREDApps enable students to understand the fundamentals of multi-views and allow them to see hidden views, which are difficult to explain only by using two-dimensional representations of three-dimensional objects. When using AREDApps, students can view the objects in three-dimensional views and sketch the respective image simultaneously to ensure the images that they mentally construct are precisely interpreted. Emphasizing all these visualization strategies in the framework can increase the efficiency and effectiveness of implementing AREDApps in engineering drawing classrooms.

Integrating this framework while implementing AREDApps as a teaching and learning aid for orthographic projection topic will help students make sense of new knowledge, enhance their visualization skills, and increase their motivation to learn. With the evidence from this study that proves to learn that using AREDApps positively impacts students' visualization skills, it is recommended for educators to practice using AREDApps in their classroom. Educators need to be able to provide various approaches in their teaching and learning process to help increase their teaching quality and improve students learning experience.

Based on the study results, the respondents in the experimental group are all satisfied and acknowledged that the use of AREDApps in teaching and learning orthographic projection would help them improve their learning experience and help them understand the content of the study lesson. The majority of the students are satisfied and interested in learning using AREDApps. According to the majority of the respondents, AREDApps helps students to visualize the views of the objects easily. This is based on the highest and second highest mean scores among all the items in the questionnaires. The items with the highest mean score are "AREDApps helps me visualize the views of given objects more easily" and the items with the second highest mean score are "AREDApps helps me visualize side views of each object more easily".

AREDApps provides an environment where students can manipulate, hold, and observe virtual 3D objects that then give the object's existence and location. This activity is called perceptual activities that can help improve visualization skills [27]. This statement also supports Piaget's allegations that allowing students to experience an environment involving space and object in space will help improve visualization skills [28]. With the integration of augmented reality environment in AREDApps, students can improve their visualization skills during the teaching and learning process and enable them to perceive correct views of the 3D objects accurately. With the proper design and development of AREDApps, students can experience exciting and efficient teaching and learning process. In this study, the factors that contribute to the effectiveness of AREDApps in increasing student's motivation is the types of technology integrated into

AREDApps, learning materials, and their satisfaction towards AREDApps. The findings in this study are consistent with Sungkur, Panchoo and Bhoyroo [29] that the use of mobile augmented reality helps students visualize and understand complex concepts.

6 Conclusion

In conclusion, visualization skills are essential in Science, Technology, Engineering and Mathematics (STEM) field, and it is essential to emphasize the skill during their early years of study. Furthermore, educators must improve students' visualization skills during an engineering drawing course due to their high spatial content. It is also because visualization skills are one of the predictors of success in engineering and technical career. Producing quality graduates with excellent visualization skills enables them to have good graphical communication skills and problem-solving skills. These skills will contribute to their competence as an engineer in the future. Hence, this study could be an exposure among other engineering drawing educators and other fields to encourage them to implement augmented reality technology in their classroom. With the positive findings on the use of AREDApps in this study as well as the implementation of the learning framework, it is proved that AREDApps and the implementation of the engineering drawing learning framework developed in this study can be used as visualization tool as well as able to increase students' learning motivation and interest. The researcher hopes that this study will serve as a guideline for future researchers and educators to explore further the augmented reality's potential in the educational field, especially in an engineering and technical field, to improve the quality of education in Malaysia.

Acknowledgement. The authors would like to thank the Ministry of Higher Education and Universiti Teknologi Malaysia through Industry-International Incentive Grant (Q.J130000.3017.02M06) and Ministry of Higher Education and Universiti Teknologi Malaysia through UTM Prototype Grant (Q.J130000.2817.00L25) for funding this research.

References

1. Branoff, T.J., Dobelis, M.: The relationship between spatial visualization ability and students' ability to model 3D objects from engineering assembly drawings. Eng. Design Graph. J. **76**(3) (2012)
2. Baronio, G., Motyl, B., Paderno, D.: Technical drawing learning tool-level 2: an interactive self-learning tool for teaching manufacturing dimensioning. Comput. Appl. Eng. Educ. **24**(4), 519–528 (2016)
3. Marunic, G., Glazar, V.: Spatial ability through engineering graphics education. Int. J. Technol. Des. Educ. **23**(3), 703–715 (2013)
4. Shreeshail, M.L., Koti, C.M.: Augmenting the out of classroom learning of machine drawing laboratory course. J. Eng. Educ. Transform. **29**(4), 37–41 (2016)
5. Sorby, S., Veurink, N., Streiner, S.: Does spatial skills instruction improve STEM outcomes? The answer is 'yes.' Learn. Individ. Differ. **67**, 209–222 (2018)
6. Azodo, A.P.: Attitude of engineering students towards engineering drawing: a case study. Int. J. Res. Stud. Educ. **6**(1), 71–84 (2017)

7. Sorby, S., Casey, B., Veurink, N., Dulaney, A.: The role of spatial training in improving spatial and calculus performance in engineering students. Learn. Individ. Differ. **26**, 20–29 (2013)

8. Carrera, C.C., Perez, J.L.S., Cantero, J.D.L.T.: Teaching with AR as a tool for relief visualization: usability and motivation study. Int. Res. Geograph. Environ. Educ. **27**(1), 69–84 (2018)

9. Garmendia, M., Guisasola, J., Sierra, E.: First-year engineering students' difficulties in visualization and drawing tasks. Eur. J. Eng. Educ. **32**(3), 315–323 (2007)

10. Lee, I.J., Chen, C.H., Chang, K.P.: Augmented reality technology combined with three-dimensional holography to train the mental rotation ability of older adults. Comput. Hum. Behav. **65**, 488–500 (2016)

11. Hsu, Y.-S., Lin, Y.-H., Yang, B.: Impact of augmented reality lessons on students' STEM interest. Res. Pract. Technol. Enhanc. Learn. **12**(1), 1–14 (2016). https://doi.org/10.1186/s41039-016-0039-z

12. Parekh, P., Patel, S., Patel, N., Shah, M.: Systematic review and meta-analysis of augmented reality in medicine, retail, and games. Visual Comput. Indust. Biomed. Art **3**(1), 1–20 (2020). https://doi.org/10.1186/s42492-020-00057-7

13. González, N.A.A.: Development of spatial skills with virtual reality and augmented reality. Int. J. Interact. Design Manufact. **12**(1), 133–144 (2017). https://doi.org/10.1007/s12008-017-0388-x

14. Chen, Y.C.: Peer learning in an AR-based learning environment. In: 16th International Conference on Computers in Education, pp. 291–295 (2008)

15. Kennedy, D.M., McNaught, C.: Design elements for interactive multimedia. Austral. J. Educ. Technol. **13**(1) (1997)

16. Nami, F., Marandi, S.S., Sotoudehnama, E.: Interaction in a discussion list: an exploration of cognitive, social, and teaching presence in teachers' online collaborations. ReCALL J. EUROCALL **30**(3), 375–398 (2018)

17. Turula, A.: Teaching presence in telecollaboration. Keeping an open mind. System **64**, 21–33 (2017)

18. Gao, C., Goda, B.: Student-centered learning: create a significant learning experience by using flipped classroom approach. In: Proceedings of the 20th Annual SIG Conference on Information Technology Education, p. 173. ACM (2019)

19. National Academies of Sciences, Engineering, and Medicine. Barriers and opportunities for 2-year and 4-year STEM degrees: systemic change to support students' diverse pathways. National Academies Press (2016)

20. Buckley, J., Seery, N., Canty, D.: A heuristic framework of spatial ability: a review and synthesis of spatial factor literature to support its translation into STEM education. Educ. Psychol. Rev. **30**(3), 947–972 (2018)

21. Ausubel, D.P.: A subsumption theory of meaningful verbal learning and retention. J. Gen. Psychol. **66**(2), 213–224 (1962)

22. Shuell, T.J.: Phases of meaningful learning. Rev. Educ. Res. **60**(4), 531–547 (1990)

23. Ally, M.: Using learning theories to design instruction for mobile learning devices. In: Mobile Learning Anytime Everywhere, pp. 5–8 (2005)

24. Frerejean, J., van Strien, J.L., Kirschner, P.A., Brand-Gruwel, S.: Effects of a modelling example for teaching information problem solving skills. J. Comput. Assist. Learn. **34**(6), 688–700 (2018)

25. Law, K.M., Geng, S., Li, T.: Student enrollment, motivation and learning performance in a blended learning environment: the mediating effects of social, teaching, and cognitive presence. Comput. Educ. **136**, 1–12 (2019)

26. Heo, M., Toomey, N.: Learning with multimedia: The effects of gender, type of multimedia learning resources, and spatial ability. Comput. Educ. **2019**, 103747 (2019)

27. Bryant, C., Frazier, A.D.: Developing visual-spatial thinking in youth using sensorimotor experiences: Approaches from a Piagetian cognitive framework. J. Pedag. Res. **3**(3), 99–112 (2019)
28. Potter, C., van der Merwe, E.: Spatial ability, visual imagery and academic performance in engineering graphics. In: Proceedings of the International Conference on Engineering Education (2001)
29. Sungkur, R.K., Panchoo, A., Bhoyroo, N.K.: Augmented reality, the future of contextual mobile learning. Interact. Technol. Smart Educ. **13**(2), 123–146 (2016)

Assessing the Effectiveness of Augmented Reality Handheld Interfaces for Robot Path Programming

Francesco De Pace[1]([✉])(iD), Andrea Sanna[1], Federico Manuri[1], Damiano Oriti[1], Simone Panicucci[2], and Valerio Belcamino[1]

[1] Politecnico di Torino, Corso Duca degli Abruzzi, 24, 10129 Turin, Italy
{francesco.depace,andrea.sanna,federico.manuri,
damiano.oriti,valerio.belcamino}@polito.it
[2] COMAU S.p.A, Via Rivalta, 30, 10095 Grugliasco, Italy
simone.panicucci@comau.com

Abstract. The Industry 4.0 is changing the very nature of the factories. If, in the past, the industrial facilities were composed by a plethora of devices disconnected from each other, nowadays, the digitalization of the industrial processes allows the devices to continuously exchange data with each other, thus improving the levels of production. Autonomous robots represent one of the main Industry 4.0 pillars. Among them, the collaborative robots are expected to be extensively used on the production lines allowing the companies to face an increasingly competitive market. In order to not be cut off from the production process, the human operators should combine their intrinsic capabilities of adapting to unforeseen scenarios with the high level of accuracy, speed and strength of the robots. Augmented Reality (AR) is another main pillar and it results to be effective for programming the robotic arms. Several AR interfaces have been evaluated in such scenarios in the last decade. However, there is a lack of studies that have deeply analyzed the effectiveness of AR handheld interfaces to control arm robot for tasks that require the creation of robot path in the 3D space. The study presented in this work fits in this context, proposing an evaluation of an AR handheld interface to control a robotic manipulator. The main results suggest that these types of interfaces are slightly adequate for controlling the manipulators, indicating that there is still room for improvements and research.

Keywords: Augmented Reality · Robot path programming · Collaborative robotics · Cobots

1 Introduction

So far, our society went through three different industrial revolutions. At the end of the 18th century, the society moved from an agriculture-based society

Z. Lv and H. Song (Eds.): INTETAIN 2021, LNICST 429, pp. 336–352, 2022.
https://doi.org/10.1007/978-3-030-99188-3_21

to a mechanical one kicking off to the first industrial revolution. The discovery of electricity about a century later ushered in the second industrial revolution, bringing with it revolutionary technologies such as the telegraph and the telephone. The third industrial revolution began in the second half of the twentieth century, marked by the advent of ICT technologies. If the three previous industrial revolutions were marked by mechanization, electrical energy and widespread digitalization [1], we are now on the verge of a fourth industrial revolution, named *Industry 4.0*, in which factories are supposed to be fully autonomous and intelligent. The German government coined the word *Industry 4.0* to describe a high-tech plan for potential manufacturing industries [2]. The idea of Smart Manufacturing is at the heart of this modern movement [3], implying that factories will become smart factories as new technologies such as the Internet of Things and Cyber Physical Systems become more widely adopted [4]. The nine main pillars of Industry 4.0 [4] reflect the nine main innovations that factories are encouraging and employing to enhance all aspects of the manufacturing process. One of the key innovations that can successfully help the fourth revolution is represented by Augmented Reality (AR). It is one of the major Industry 4.0 foundations and it has been used in a great variety of industrial tasks [5]. Another essential pillar is represented by the autonomous robots, which are supposed to boost and increase the efficiency of future factories. It is expected that the autonomous robots will start working side-by-side with the human operators [6], "becoming" the so called *collaborative robots* or *cobots* [7]. In order to reduce the risk of hazards, the industrial robots have traditionally worked in well-defined areas, completely separated by the human operators. The new AR interfaces, on the other hand, offer novel forms of interaction that can ensure the safety of human operators while also allowing to effectively control the robots through innovative interaction paradigms. So far, four different types of interfaces have been used to interact with the manipulators: (i) desktop, (ii) projected, (iii) handheld and, (iv) wearable. However, despite the related state of the art provides a fair amount of works and projects, there is a lack of studies that deeply investigate the effectiveness of the AR interfaces in the Human-Robot Collaborative (HRC) area from a user-centred perspective [7]. Since there will be a considerable increase in the number of robots employed on the production line [8], it is expected that the human operators will share the workspace with the robots and machines, thus collaborating with them and generating new forms of interaction and production [9]. Hence, it becomes of primary importance investigating and developing innovative interfaces aiming at improving the human-robot collaboration guaranteeing the safety oh the human workers. Moving from these considerations, this work presents an AR handheld interface to program robotic manipulators. The interface allows the users to create and manipulate robot end-effector paths in the real space. The interface has been deeply evaluated, collecting both objective and subjective data. The related results have been analyzed providing useful insights about the strengths and weaknesses of the handheld interfaces when used in the HRC area.

2 Background

AR technologies have been researched into three main HRC areas: (i) to visualize the robot workspace (*Workspace* area), (ii) to get a virtual feedback over the robot control (*Control Feedback* area) and (iii) to provide information regarding the task or the robot itself (*Informative* area) [7]. Since this work mainly focuses on the Control Feedback category, this section will presents only a detailed review of the state of the art strictly related to the aforementioned category. However, interested readers are encouraged to refer to [7] for a complete review of the main uses of the AR interfaces in the HRC domain.

Following the definition of the Control Feedback category [7], the AR interfaces are commonly used to (i) provide a feedback over the user's input itself and (ii) to visualize and manipulate the virtual robot paths. Regarding the former, a comparison between an AR gaze-based interface and a gesture based one is proposed in [10]. Both interfaces allow the users to select the real objects that will be manipulated by a robotic manipulator. The motion of a virtual representation of the robotic arm provides the users a feedback on the user's input. Similarly, in [11,12] the users can control a virtual robot using the Wiimote controller and a wearable AR device, respectively. Besides pointing out the motion of the robot through its virtual counterpart, also the real objects of interest can be highlighting using virtual metaphors. Frank et al. [13] proposed a hand-held AR interface to control a robotic arm for a pick-and-place scenario. The device camera is used to capture a live video-stream and the users can select the object of interest by exploiting the touch capabilities of the considered device. Once selected, a virtual asset is superimposed on the real object, highlighting the user's input (the proposed work has been extended in [14] considering also egocentric and exocentric interfaces). The authors of [15–17] proposed a gesture-based AR interface to control a robotic arm for a pick-and-place task. Referring to their most recent work [17], the camera of a handheld device is used to recognize hand gestures that are translated into robot instructions. The AR system has been compared with a kinesthetic approach and with an offline programming method (refer to [18] for a comprehensive definition of the word *kinesthetic*). The main results show that the AR interface greatly lowered the task time and it was more appreciated by the users. The camera of a handheld device is also used in [19] to automatically recognize the real objects that should be manipulated by a robotic arm. The main results indicate that the proposed object detection algorithm is reliable enough to be effectively employed to program a real manipulator. Recently, Chacko and Kapila [20] introduced a smartphone AR interface to control a small-size manipulator. The system is similar to the one proposed in [13] and it has been deeply evaluated involving a considerable amount of users. The main outcomes indicate that the proposed interface allows the users to accurately control the robot arm. Furthermore, the interface obtained high usability scores and low workload scores, suggesting that the proposed solution could be effectively employed for pick-and-place scenarios. Additional works can be found in [21], which details a handheld AR interface to ease the creation of robot programs, and in [22] whose authors proposed an AR interface that allows users to create virtual assembly sequences that will be executed by a robot arm.

Considering the robot path, several works have employed desktop AR interfaces to manipulate virtual paths of robotic manipulators. It is worth noticing that in this work a *virtual path* is defined as a set of connected 3D points created by the user. Chong et al. [23] proposed an heuristic search solution to ease the creation and manipulation of virtual manipulator paths. The users can add, remove and modify the virtual path points using a flat image-based stylus tracked by an external camera. Once the path is defined, if a virtual point is not reachable by the real manipulator, the point color is changed to red to warn the user. Similarly, the accuracy of a desktop AR interface for path programming has been evaluated in [24,25]. The main results show that the interface can achieve an accuracy of 11 mm using a camera placed at 1.5 m from the workspace. Further projects that employ AR desktop interfaces to manipulate robot paths can be found in [26,27]. Projected and wearable interfaces have been also used to manipulate virtual robot paths. Zaeh and Vogle [28] proposed an interactive AR projected interface to program industrial robots. The users can define in the real space a set of virtual points and the related path is then executed by the real manipulator by using a tracked stylus. The outcomes indicate that the proposed system greatly reduced the task time with respect to a kinesthetic approach. Moreover, the adopted tracking methodology can achieve an accuracy of ~0.5 mm. A similar approach is proposed in [29]. The projected AR interface allows the users to control a manipulator during grinding processes of ceramic parts. The main outcomes are in line with the work proposed in [28], showing a considerable reduction of the time required to program the robotic arm. Additional interesting works can be found in [30,31]. Regarding the wearable devices, the interface proposed in [32] provides the users the ability to manipulate the virtual path by exploiting the gestures recognition capabilities of the adopted device. Furthermore, the torques of each joint is also displayed in the real environment. Quintero et al. [33] compared an AR interface based on speech and gestures recognition with a traditional kinesthetic approach. Despite the proposed AR interface required less time to program the robot than the kinesthetic programming method, high levels of mental loads have been detected due to requirements of the speech interface to memorize a set of pre-defined vocal commands. A tracked stylus is used in combination with a wearable device to manipulate virtual paths in [34]. Similarly to the previous works, the proposed interface greatly reduced the execution time for welding and pick-and-place tasks (from 347 s to 63 s and from 117 s to 34 s, respectively). Further research projects regarding the use of wearable AR interfaces in the HRC domain can be found in [35,36].

3   Methodology

To the best of the authors' knowledge, the only work that analyzes the effectiveness of an AR handheld interface to manipulate virtual robot paths can be found

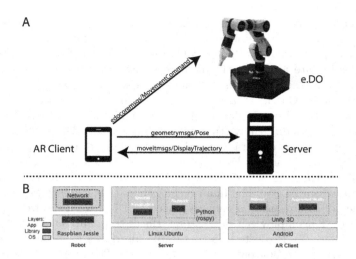

Fig. 1. A: the hardware architecture. B: the software architecture.

in [37]. The proposed solution allows the users to define virtual paths using a smartphone device. Although the interface has been assessed considering both objective and subjective parameters, it presents some limitations that should be overcome: (i) the creation of the virtual path is limited to 2D plane surfaces and (ii) the overall interface accuracy has been determined involving only one single user. The study presented in this work extends the analysis done in [37] by evaluating more challenging tasks, considering both 2D and 3D paths (e.g., virtual robot paths that are not constrained on 2D planar surfaces but they can be specified in the 3D space). Furthermore, the overall interface accuracy has been determined by considering several users, providing useful insights from a user-centred perspective analysis.

To achieve the mentioned goals, the following methodology has been adopted:

- development of an AR handheld interface that allows users to create virtual robot paths in the 3D space surrounding the robot;
- definition of a sequence of tasks to evaluate the proposed AR interface;
- definition of a proper metric to measure the accuracy of the AR interface;
- the choice of the appropriate questionnaires to measure the levels of usability and workload of the AR interface.

In the following section, the proposed system is detailed along with its hardware and software architectures. Furthermore, the handheld AR interface is presented discussing its main functionalities.

4   The Proposed System

The hardware and software architectures are introduced and detailed in this section. Moreover, the proposed AR interface is deeply discussed, describing its main functionalities.

4.1   The System Architecture

Figure 1 shows the system architecture. It is essentially composed by three distinct elements: (i) an Android tablet, (ii) a remote Personal Computer (PC) and (iii) a real manipulator. The tablet runs the AR interface developed using the Unity3D [38] game engine. The Vuforia SDK [39] has been integrated to provide a common reference system between the tablet and the manipulator. The alignment is carried out by tracking an image target positioned at a known location with respect to the real robot. The Unity3D application exchanges data with the remote PC that is responsible of computing the virtual robot path (see Sect. 4.2). The PC runs the Ubuntu 20.04.2.0 [40] distribution and the Robot Operating System (ROS) Melodic [41]. The real manipulator is represented by the COMAU e.DO [42] robotic arm. It consists of a 6 degrees-of-freedom (DOF) ROS-based manipulator equipped with a two-fingers robotic hand. The tablet, the PC and the manipulator are connected on the same Local Area Network (LAN) to effectively exchange data. The advantage of having the inverse kinematic (IK) solver decentralized (i.e., running at the server side) with respect to the real manipulator is straightforward: the propose architecture is *robot independent* and it can be easily extended considering different real manipulators.

The main functioning of the system is the following: when the user adds a new virtual point using the tablet device, the point position and orientation are sent through a TCP socket connection to the PC that in turns computes a possible path using an inverse kinematic algorithm provided by the MoveIt [43] ROS package. Once the path is computed, it is sent back to the Unity3D application and it is displayed in the real environment. Then, in case the user is pleased with the computed path, the application sends the acquired path to the real manipulator through an additional TCP socket connection, starting the motion of the real robot.

In the following section, a detailed description of the proposed AR interface is presented, illustrating the mechanism of virtual path creation and modification.

4.2   The AR Interface

The main functionalities of the proposed interface provide the ability of adding one ore multiple virtual points to the real scene and of visualizing two different versions of the virtual robot path. Specifically, when the user frames the image target, a virtual representation of the e.DO manipulator is superimposed on its real counterpart. However, it has been decided to keep visible only the robot end-effector to reduce the negative effects of possible occlusions. Both the robot

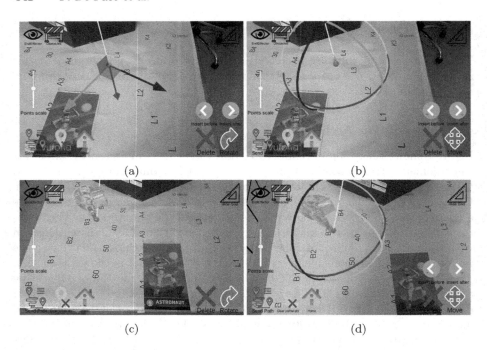

Fig. 2. (a) The VP translational tool. (b) The VP rotational tool. (c) The virtual robot end-effector. (d) The virtual end-effector during a rotational manipulation.

and the image target have been placed on a table with the base of the robot positioned at the same height of the target. The user can add a new virtual point (VP) to the real scene by touching the tablet surface at the desired location. In this work, a VP is represented by a virtual sphere carrying both the positional and rotational information required by the IK solver to compute the end-effector pose. In order to ease the VP addition, a virtual invisible plane is instantiated at the same height of the image target, preventing the user from adding a point below the table, that is, in a position not reachable by the real robot. The new point is added sequentially to the point list (a new point is inserted by default as last element of the list).

When a new VP is rendered into the scene, it is instantiated with a default orientation. Specifically, with the forward vector parallel to the surface normal direction (i.e., the end-effector perpendicular with respect to the surface). If the user selects one of the VPs, its three local axes are displayed and they can be used to drag the point into a new location (Fig. 2a). By changing to the orientation modality, a virtual gimbal is rendered and it can be used to change the VP orientation around its local axes (Fig. 2b).

In order to improve the visualization of the final pose of the robot end-effector, the interface can render a 3D model of the end-effector at the VP location (Fig. 2c). The transformations applied to the VP are mapped directly to the virtual end-effector (Fig. 2d).

To provide the user the ability of adding a VP between two other VPs, the user should select a point and use the arrow buttons positioned at the bottom right-side of the user interface. These two buttons allow the user to add a new VP at the *right-side* and *left-side* of the selected VP, respectively. Referring to Fig. 3, when the user wants to add a new VP at the left-side of P_1, it is verified that $D \geq s$, with D being the distance between two VP and s being the VP diameter, respectively. In case the condition is verified, a new VP of diameter s is rendered at $D/2$ (and the new VP is added to the point list at the specified position), otherwise the dimension of the VPs is iteratively reduced until a suitable position is found. The reduction it is constrained by $s \geq s_{min}$ to ensure a clear visualization of the VPs (the s_{min} value has been experimentally computed). In case the constrain is violated, a message appears informing the user that is not possible to add further VPs.

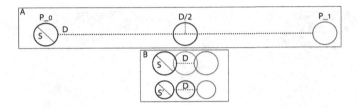

Fig. 3. The blue and red circles represent two VPs (P_0 and P_1, respectively) already added by the user. When the user wants to add a new VP (the green circle) at the left-side of P_1, there can be two different conditions: (a) when $D \geq S$, the VP is successfully added, (b) when $D < S$, the dimension of all the VPs is firstly scaled down and then the green VP is added between P_0 and P_1. (Color figure online)

The next step would be displaying the virtual robot path passing through the user's VPs. However, due to time complexity of the IK solver, the robot path cannot be computed in real-time (i.e., when a new point is added or modified). Hence, a Catmull-Rom virtual spline is firstly displayed starting from the current position of the robot end-effector and passing through the VP added by the user (this process is repeated every time a new VP is added to the scene). Although this spline only approximates the real robot path, it improves the user's understanding of the VP sequence.

Once all the VPs have been added to the real environment, the user can send them to the remote PC through the socket connection. Each VP describes the position and orientation that the end-effector should have in that specific point and the IK solver (running at the remote PC) tries to calculate a suitable path passing through all the VPs added by the user. As the path is computed, it is sent back to the AR application through the same socket connection and the approximated Catmull-Rom spline is modified according to the new path. Furthermore, the virtual robot end-effector starts moving along the virtual path, allowing the user to pre-visualize the movement of the real robot. Finally, the user can send to the real robot the new computed path, starting the real manipulator motion. Figure 4a and Figure 4b show the approximated and real robot virtual paths, respectively.

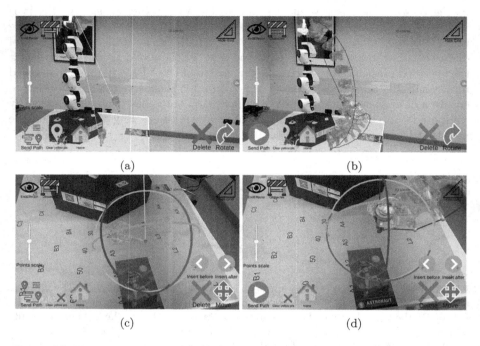

(a)   (b)

(c)   (d)

Fig. 4. (a) The approximated robot path is displayed by means of a yellow virtual line. (b) The same line is modified according to the real path and its color is changed to green. (c) The VP has been added with a wrong orientation. (d) The VP orientation has been successfully updated. (Color figure online)

If the user has added a VP in a position not reachable by the real manipulator, the IK solver would fail in computing a suitable path. In this case, the PC sends a message of error back to AR application that colors in red the VP that has been placed in a wrong position. A VP is considered in a wrong configuration when the end-effector cannot reach the VP position (in terms of X, Y and Z coordinates) or it cannot reach the VP position with the orientation (in terms of quaternion) specified by the user. Hence, to complete the path creation, the user has to modify the position and/or orientation of the VP sending it back again to the remote PC (Fig. 4c and Fig. 4d illustrate a wrong VP and the same VP after having being corrected by the user, respectively).

Although, at the current stage, the system does not provide a real-time objects tracking mechanism, the AR interface provides a collision detection capability: if the spline or one of the VP intersect an obstacle, their color is changed

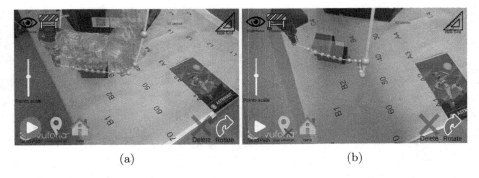

(a)   (b)

Fig. 5. (a) The end-effector path collides with an obstacle. Its color is changed to red to highlight the collision. (b) The collision with the visualization of the end-effector disabled. (Color figure online)

to red, highlighting a possible collision between the object and the real end-effector. To simulate the object detection process, the real objects have been placed at a known location with respect to the image target. Then, their virtual counterparts have been positioned at the same location, allowing to perform the collision detection mechanism (Fig. 5).

Finally, the user can delete one VP at a time by selecting it and by pressing the "Delete" button positioned at the bottom right-side of the user interface. Furthermore, the users can also delete all the VPs at the same time by pressing the "Clear yellow pts" button placed at the bottom left-side of the user interface. A video showing the main functionalities of the proposed AR interface can be found at[1].

5   The User Study

In order to assess the effectiveness of the proposed solution, twelve users have been involved in a user study at Politecnico di Torino university. The study has been divided into two different tasks: (i) 2D translational and rotational (TR_2D) and (ii) 3D translational and rotational (TR_3D) tasks. Generally, the tasks required the users to create a virtual path in the real environment, under some specific conditions. The labels *2D* and *3D* refer to whether the task was constrained on the plane on which the e.DO manipulator has been placed or to the 3D space surrounding the robot, respectively. The label *TR* indicates that the path should be generated using translational and rotational (TR) actions (see Sect. 4.2).

Each task required the creation of one single path, composed by two distinct VPs. In order to assess the accuracy of the proposed AR interface, the VPs

---

[1] https://www.youtube.com/watch?v=xvJhPJ50-xg.

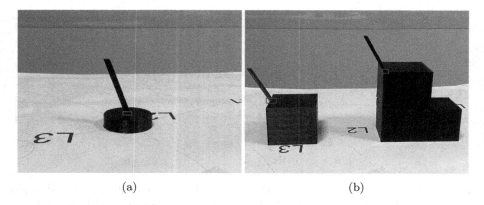

Fig. 6. (a)–(b) The printed models used for the TR_2D and TR_3D tasks, respectively. The red rectangles highlight the position that the end-effector should reach. The stick inclination represents the orientation that the end-effector should have at the specific position. (Color figure online)

had to be placed in a set of known positions with pre-defined orientations (the ground truth points, GTPs). The GTPs thus represented both the position and orientation that the real end-effector should had at the specific positions. The GTPs were represented by some 3D printed models with different shapes and sizes. The models represented in Fig. 6a have been used for the TR_2D task, whereas the models shown in Fig. 6b have been employed for the TR_3D task. The purpose of the vertical stick was twofold: (i) the tip of the stick (highlighted in red in Fig. 6) indicated to the users the position that the end-effector should reach whereas (ii) the stick inclination represented the orientation that the end-effector should have at the specific position. The GTPs have been positioned in pre-defined locations with respect to the image target, thus allowing to compute the GTPs positions and orientations.

Both objective and subjective parameters have been collected and analyzed. Specifically, the objective consisted of: (i) the time required to complete the task, (ii) the number of user's errors, (iii) the number of touch interactions and, (iv) the positional and rotational differences between the VPs and GTPs. The task time represents the time between the starting of a specific task and the positioning of the two VPs (an external operator was monitoring and recording the users' actions). Every time the users were pleased with their positioning of the VPs, the external operator stopped the time. It is worth noticing that although users could be accurate in placing the VPs, the accuracy could not be enough for the IK solver running at the PC side. In this case, the IK solver would send back an error message, highlighting the wrong VP (see Sect. 4.2). Hence, each user could try the creation of a path for at maximum three times and a global time value was computed as the sum of the time values required at each trial (same procedure applied for the touch values). Referring to the VP-GTP differences, two different types of accuracy have been computed, represented by the positional and rotational errors (PE and RE, respectively). PE has been computed following the ISO 9283 standard [44], that is, the square root of the distance between the VP and GTP X, Y and Z coordinates. Similarly, RE has been determined by calculating the distance angle between the VP and GTP rotations. Considering the subjective parameters, four different types of data have been collected: (i) user general data (UGD), (ii) interface usability (I_USA), (iii) interface workload (I_WOR) and, (iv) a global score indicating whether the interface was adequate or not to effectively complete the tasks (GLOS). UGD consisted of sex, age and the level of previous experience with AR and robotics. The I_USA and I_WOR have been assessed using the System Usability Scale [45] and the NASA-TLX [46] questionnaires, respectively. GLOS has been determined using the Single Ease Questionnaire [47].

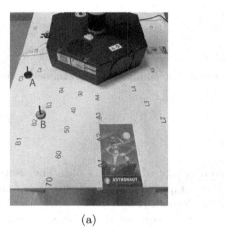 

(a)   (b)

Fig. 7. (a)–(b) The TR_2D and TR_3D tasks, respectively. The users had to generate a virtual path passing through the A and B points.

The overall user study procedure can be summarized as follows: firstly, the user has been introduced to the experiment by letting them try the interface in several trial scenarios. The scenarios have been designed to encourage the users to apply the translational and rotational actions, thus improving the user knowledge of the interface. Moreover, they have been explained the purpose of the 3D printed models, with particular attention for the model sticks. Then, the user filled the UGD section and started the sequence of tasks (TR_2D-TR_3D, refer to Fig. 7). The VPs were already instantiated in the virtual scene at the image target coordinates, thus guaranteeing the same starting conditions across all the users. Then, the user started a task trying to generate a path as quickly as possible. The starting joint robot configuration has been kept the same across all the tasks with the joint values equal to 0°. In case the user generated a virtual path feasible for the real manipulator, he/she had the possibility to send it to the real robot to visualize the real robot motion. After having completed all the tasks, the user had to fill the LUSA, LWOR and GLOS sections of the questionnaire. He/she could also verbally report to the external operator additional comments regarding the overall experience.

In the next section, the related results are presented and discussed.

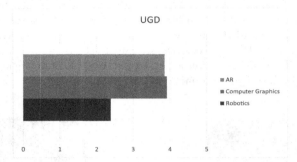

Fig. 8. The UGD outcomes ranging from 0 (not familiar) to 5 (extremely familiar).

6   Results and Discussion

The users were all male with an average age of 27 years old. The users were found to be familiar with AR and the computer graphic context whereas they had moderate knowledge of the robotic domain (Fig. 8).

The LUSA score has been determined by computing the average value that has been used to compute the usability score using the approach presented in [45], whereas the GLOS average value has been normalized in the 1–100 interval. The USA score indicates that the AR interface has been deemed sufficiently appropriate to generate the virtual robot path, although there seems to be space for future improvements. The high standard deviation value of the GLOS outcome suggests a non uniform users' opinion regarding the effectiveness of the AR interface for the evaluated tasks. Regarding the LWOR scores, the relatively high mental and effort values indicate that the users had difficulty in reasoning about the correct VP configuration. Some users reported that the manipulation of the VP rotation was quite hard, whereas the VP translation methodology was appropriate for the considered tasks. Figure 9a and Fig. 9b illustrate the LUSA, GLOS and LWOR results, respectively.

Figures 9c–9d–9e–9f show the objective results. Independently of the data, the collected values have been summed up across all the users computing the corresponding average values. Unsurprisingly, both the task time (Fig. 9c) and number of touch interaction (Fig. 9d) values show higher scores for the TR_3D task with respect to the TR_2D one. Having to manage an extra dimension, the users seem to have encountered more difficulties in the 3D task then the 2D one.

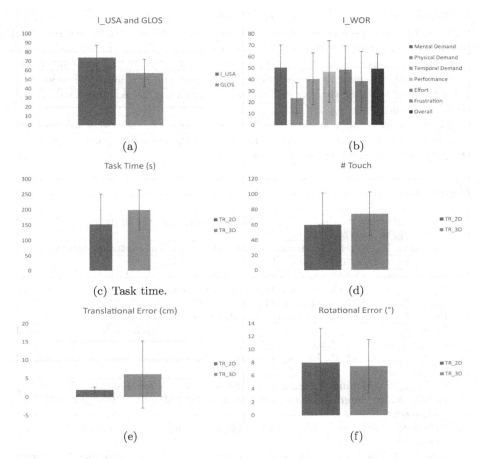

Fig. 9. (a–b) The usability and workload results, respectively. (c–d) The task time and number of touch interactions, respectively. (e–f) The translational and rotational errors, respectively.

The results are partially confirmed by the translational errors (Fig. 9e), whereas the rotational ones (Fig. 9f) appear to be consistent across the task modalities. It is reasonable to assume that there are no significant differences between rotating a VP positioned on a 2D plane and one placed on a 3D model, at a different height with respect to the base plane.

7 Conclusion

This paper proposed the evaluation of an AR handheld interface to program a real robot manipulator. The interface allows the users to generate and visualize virtual robot paths directly in the real environment. By pre-visualizing the robot path, the users can understand if it is adequate for the considered task.

The interface has been evaluated through a series of user tests. The novelty of the work consists into assessing both 2D and 3D tasks, that have not been previously considered in the related state of the art. The main results suggest that the 3D tasks are far more compelling than the 2D ones. Furthermore, the users deemed the interface as fairly appropriate for the evaluated scenario. This outcome suggests that there is still room for improving the AR interfaces in this peculiar domain.

Future works will compare the handheld interface with wearable ones to verify whether a changing in the interaction and visualization paradigms affects the generation of the virtual robot paths.

References

1. Lasi, H., Fettke, P., Kemper, H., Feld, T., Hoffmann, M.: Industry 4.0. Bus. Inf. Syst. Eng. **6**, 239–242 (2014)
2. Hofmann, E., Rüsch, M.: Industry 4.0 and the current status as well as future prospects on logistics. Comput. Ind. **89**, 23–34 (2017)
3. Kagermann, H., Wahlster, W., Helbig, J.: Others recommendations for implementing the strategic initiative Industrie 4.0: final report of the Industrie 4.0 working group. Forschungsunion, Berlin, Germany (2013)
4. Erboz, G.: How to define Industry 4.0: the main pillars of Industry 4.0 (2017)
5. De Pace, F., Manuri, F., Sanna, A.: Augmented reality in Industry 4.0. Am. J. Comput. Sci. Inf. Technol. **6**, 17 (2018)
6. Vaidya, S., Ambad, P., Bhosle, S.: Industry 4.0 - a glimpse. Procedia Manuf. **20**, 233–238 (2018)
7. De Pace, F., Manuri, F., Sanna, A., Fornaro, C.: A systematic review of augmented reality interfaces for collaborative industrial robots. Comput. Ind. Eng. **149**, 106806 (2020)
8. Robotics, I.: Top trends robotics 2020. https://ifr.org/ifr-press-releases/news/top-trends-robotics-2020
9. Gaz, C., Magrini, E., De Luca, A.: A model-based residual approach for human-robot collaboration during manual polishing operations. Mechatronics **55**, 234–247 (2018)
10. Krupke, D., Steinicke, F., Lubos, P., Jonetzko, Y., Görner, M., Zhang, J.: Comparison of multimodal heading and pointing gestures for co-located mixed reality human-robot interaction. In: 2018 IEEE/RSJ International Conference On Intelligent Robots And Systems (IROS), pp. 1–9 (2018)
11. Araque, D., Díaz, R., Pérez-Gutiérrez, B., Uribe, A.: Augmented reality motion-based robotics off-line programming. In: 2011 IEEE Virtual Reality Conference, pp. 191–192 (2011)
12. Sita, E., Studley, M., Dailami, F., Pipe, A., Thomessen, T.: Towards multimodal interactions: robot jogging in mixed reality. In: Proceedings of the 23rd ACM Symposium on Virtual Reality Software and Technology, pp. 1–2 (2017)
13. Frank, J., Moorhead, M., Kapila, V.: Realizing mixed-reality environments with tablets for intuitive human-robot collaboration for object manipulation tasks. In: 2016 25th IEEE International Symposium on Robot and Human Interactive Communication (RO-MAN), pp. 302–307 (2016)
14. Frank, J., Moorhead, M., Kapila, V.: Mobile mixed-reality interfaces that enhance human-robot interaction in shared spaces. Front. Robot. AI **4**, 20 (2017)

15. Lambrecht, J., Krüger, J.: Spatial programming for industrial robots based on gestures and augmented reality. In: 2012 IEEE/RSJ International Conference on Intelligent Robots and Systems, pp. 466–472 (2012)

16. Lambrecht, J., Kleinsorge, M., Rosenstrauch, M., Krüger, J.: Spatial programming for industrial robots through task demonstration. Int. J. Adv. Rob. Syst. **10**, 254 (2013)

17. Hügle, J., Lambrecht, J., Krüger, J.: An integrated approach for industrial robot control and programming combining haptic and non-haptic gestures. In: 2017 26th IEEE International Symposium on Robot and Human Interactive Communication (RO-MAN), pp. 851–857 (2017)

18. Akgun, B., Cakmak, M., Yoo, J., Thomaz, A.: Trajectories and keyframes for kinesthetic teaching: a human-robot interaction perspective. In: Proceedings of the 7th Annual ACM/IEEE International Conference on Human-Robot Interaction, pp. 391–398 (2012)

19. Gradmann, M., Orendt, E., Schmidt, E., Schweizer, S., Henrich, D.: Augmented reality robot operation interface with Google Tango. In: 50th International Symposium on Robotics, ISR 2018, pp. 1–8 (2018)

20. Chacko, S., Kapila, V.: An augmented reality interface for human-robot interaction in unconstrained environments. In: 2019 IEEE/RSJ International Conference on Intelligent Robots and Systems (IROS), pp. 3222–3228 (2019)

21. Kapinus, M., Beran, V., Materna, Z., Bambušek, D.: Spatially situated end-user robot programming in augmented reality. In: 2019 28th IEEE International Conference on Robot and Human Interactive Communication (RO-MAN), pp. 1–8 (2019)

22. Blankemeyer, S., Wiemann, R., Posniak, L., Pregizer, C., Raatz, A.: Intuitive robot programming using augmented reality. Procedia CIRP **76**, 155–160 (2018)

23. Chong, J., Ong, S., Nee, A., Youcef-Youmi, K.: Robot programming using augmented reality: an interactive method for planning collision-free paths. Robot. Comput. Integr. Manuf. **25**, 689–701 (2009)

24. Fang, H., Ong, S., Nee, A.: Interactive robot trajectory planning and simulation using augmented reality. Robot. Comput. Integr. Manuf. **28**, 227–237 (2012)

25. Fang, H., Ong, S., Nee, A.: Robot path and end-effector orientation planning using augmented reality. Procedia CIRP **3**, 191–196 (2012)

26. Fang, H.C., Ong, S.K., Nee, A.Y.C.: Novel AR-based interface for human-robot interaction and visualization. Adv. Manuf. **2**(4), 275–288 (2014). https://doi.org/10.1007/s40436-014-0087-9

27. Pai, Y., Yap, H., Singh, R.: Augmented reality-based programming, planning and simulation of a robotic work cell. Proc. Inst. Mech. Eng. Part B J. Eng. Manuf. **229**, 1029–1045 (2015)

28. Zaeh, M., Vogl, W.: Interactive laser-projection for programming industrial robots. In: 2006 IEEE/ACM International Symposium on Mixed and Augmented Reality, pp. 125–128 (2006)

29. Veiga, G., Malaca, P., Cancela, R.: Interactive industrial robot programming for the ceramic industry. Int. J. Adv. Robot. Syst. **10**, 1 (2013)

30. Reinhart, G., Vogl, W., Kresse, I.: A projection-based user interface for industrial robots. In: 2007 IEEE Symposium on Virtual Environments, Human-Computer Interfaces and Measurement Systems, pp. 67–71 (2007)

31. Tanzini, M., Tripicchio, P., Ruffaldi, E., Galgani, G., Lutzemberger, G., Avizzano, C.: A novel human-machine interface for working machines operation. In: 2013 IEEE RO-MAN, pp. 744–750 (2013)

32. Kyjanek, O., Al Bahar, B., Vasey, L., Wannemacher, B., Menges, A.: Implementation of an augmented reality AR workflow for human robot collaboration in timber prefabrication. In: Proceedings of the 36th International Symposium on Automation and Robotics in Construction (2019)

33. Quintero, C., Li, S., Pan, M., Chan, W., Loos, H., Croft, E.: Robot programming through augmented trajectories in augmented reality. In: 2018 IEEE/RSJ International Conference on Intelligent Robots and Systems (IROS), pp. 1838–1844 (2018)

34. Ong, S., Yew, A., Thanigaivel, N., Nee, A.: Augmented reality-assisted robot programming system for industrial applications. Robot. Comput. Integr. Manuf. **61**, 101820 (2020)

35. Guan, Z., Liu, Y., Li, Y., Hong, X., Hu, B., Xu, C.: A novel robot teaching system based on augmented reality. In: 2019 International Conference on Image and Video Processing, and Artificial Intelligence, vol. 11321, id. 113211D (2019)

36. Manring, L., et al.: Augmented reality for interactive robot control. Spec. Top. Struct. Dyn. Exp. Tech. **5**, 11–18 (2020)

37. Chacko, S., Granado, A., Kapila, V.: An augmented reality framework for robotic tool-path teaching. Procedia CIRP **93**, 1218–1223 (2020)

38. unity.com: Unity. https://unity.com

39. developer.vuforia.com: Vuforia SDK. https://developer.vuforia.com/downloads/sdk

40. releases.ubuntu.com: Ubuntu 20.04.2.0. http://www.releases.ubuntu.com/20.04/

41. wiki.ros.org: ROS Melodic. https://wiki.ros.org/melodic

42. comau.com: COMAU e.DO. https://www.comau.com/en/our-competences/robotics/edo

43. moveit.ros.org: MoveIt. https://moveit.ros.org/

44. Iso.com SO 9283:1998: Manipulating industrial robots - performance criteria and related test methods. https://www.iso.org/standard/22244.html

45. Brooke, J., et al.: SUS: a 'quick and dirty' usability scale. In: Usability Evaluation In Industry, vol. 189, pp. 4–7 (1996)

46. Hart, S., Staveland, L.: Development of NASA-TLX (task load index): results of empirical and theoretical research. Adv. Psychol. **52**, 139–183 (1988)

47. tinyurl.com: Measuring task usability: the single ease question (SEQ). https://tinyurl.com/24p2x2dd

A Prototype Application of StickAR to Enhance Note-Taking Activity by Using Augmented Reality Technology

Adlin Shaflina binti Azizo[1]([envelope]), Farhan bin Mohamed[2] [ID], Chan Vei Siang[3] [ID],
Muhammad Ismail Mat bin Isham[3], Mohd Khalid bin Mokhtar[3] [ID], and Ira Wirasari[4]

[1] Department of Quantity Surveying, Faculty of Built Environment and Surveying,
Universiti Teknologi Malaysia, 81310 Johor Bahru, Johor, Malaysia
adlinshaflina96@gmail.com

[2] UTM-IRDA MaGICX, Institute of Human Centred Engineering, Universiti Teknologi
Malaysia, 81310 Johor Bahru, Johor, Malaysia
farhan@utm.my

[3] Faculty of Engineering, School of Computing, Universiti Teknologi Malaysia,
81310 Johor Bahru, Johor, Malaysia
vschan2@live.utm.my, khalmokh@me.com

[4] Faculty of Creative Industries, Telkom University, 40257 Bandung, Indonesia
irawirasari@telkomuniversity.ac.id

Abstract. This paper presents the work-in-progress StickAR mobile application prototype which enables the users to record real life events such as images or video recordings alongside with their physical notes. It also provides the users with the utility of information retrieval by using the AR scanning interaction to get the relevant information immediately. The StickAR application uses the Unity3D API for frontend, assets management, and server communication logic, meanwhile the Vuforia SDK is utilized for the AR scanning interaction. All the information and assets are stored in the HTTP server. This paper also focused on the reproducible methodology that consists of the use case descriptions and system architecture to build the application. The functionalities of StickAR are demonstrated in the result section which includes the key AR information retrieval feature for immediate access to the requested information based on the physical notes. Its potential and risks are also discussed in the SWOT analysis.

Keywords: Augmented reality · Graphical user interfaces · Mobile application · System development

1 Introduction

Recent research has demonstrated the effectiveness of note-taking to humans as a tool for remembering notes and comprehending details from a reading or lecture [1]. Kobayashi [2] concluded that the importance of note-taking and reviewing can bring a positive

Z. Lv and H. Song (Eds.): INTETAIN 2021, LNICST 429, pp. 353–371, 2022.
https://doi.org/10.1007/978-3-030-99188-3_22

impact to the memory and affect the learning of a student compared to attending the class only. This method can boost the student's performance and their confidence during their studies. Stacy and Cain [3] also argued that training learners in systematic note-taking approaches can help learners encode and study large quantities of learning material. Furthermore, the research on learning performance with digital note-taking tools today is required since a potential physio-cognitive connection between writing and learning is recognised [3]. The note-taking is important as it can be a reference material to memorise or understand before the test.

In the digital age, people prefer to use the smartphone or computer to write the notes and do the revision for their studies [4]. Furthermore, the use of slide, audio, and recording can assist them in understanding the lecture after the class and are easy to bring anywhere. In line with the most recent technological developments, the fourth industrial revolution (4IR), the use of augmented reality (AR) in smartphone applications is becoming more common in order to attract users with the uniqueness and convenience of an application [5]. According to [6], AR technologies are a unique subset of mobile media that has successfully piqued the public's interest by allowing various types of visual media to be presented while simultaneously overlaid onto physical space. Besides, the use of AR interfaces in books can help users in comprehension, memory, concentration, affordance, interactivity, imagination, problem-solving, and level-differentiated learning by providing immersion, presence, and context [7]. Thus, it can provide various enhanced experiences to the user such as links to extra web contents, viewing 3D models for spatial understanding, animation, and multimedia. Furthermore, AR also can be used to integrate the physical medium, for example books, with digital contents.

Recently, digital note-taking applications have become an important application in storing important information instantly [8]. Cloud storage applications also offer users to save a variety of file types, such as images, documents, videos, and audios, in the cloud which can be accessed anywhere, anytime. These applications focus on the digital platform, from data collection to data storage processes and data retrieving. However, traditional hand-written methods are still an effective choice for note-taking and memorisation [1]. Therefore, AR technology is a potential solution for the traditional hand-written format because it can retrieve the supplementary data based on a physical medium. But the current AR-based note-taking applications have limitations include bulky installation [9] and the lack of customization function for students [10] which affect the usability and practicality of the AR-based note-taking applications.

This work-in-progress project aims to incorporate AR and mobile phone technologies into the note-taking activity to enhance the learning experience. StickAR mobile application is an AR note-taking application which provides the users with customizable contents, where they can upload their own multimedia contents, such as images and video recordings. The proposed application also offers navigation functionality to help the users to locate the relevant information instantly.

In the following sections, this paper discusses the literature review, research methodology, as well as result and discussion in Sects. 2, 3 and 4, respectively. The literature review presents the analysis and synthesis of related digital note-taking applications and AR applications for information retrieval. The methodology section includes the use case requirements of StickAR application, its framework design and system development process. In the results section, the user interfaces of the StickAR application are presented. Lastly, the paper is concluded in Sect. 5 with future works and suggestions.

2   Literature Review

2.1   Digital Note-Taking Application

The digital note-taking applications have taken a centre stage in this digitalization era, as they have become one of the staple applications provided by many big technological companies, for instance Google, Microsoft, and Apple. Popular digital note-taking applications, such as Evernote and Microsoft OneNote, have been utilized in various tasks, which ranged from management to education. A market research forecasted the increase of 5.32% in the compound annual growth rate (CAGR) of the global note-taking application market from 2019 to 2026, and the cumulative profit is estimated to reach USD 1.35 billion in 2026 from USD 897.7 million in 2018 [8].

However, traditional hand-written methods are still an effective and popular choice among the users to record important information [1]. The study shows that the note takers using hand-written methods tend to work more efficiently to adapt to their speed disadvantage and they also have less digital distraction [11]. Besides, lectures with image heavy contents are difficult for the digital note-taking application since they can only record text-based content but not illustration [11, 12]. In addition, past research also discovered that the users also wanted the advantages of digitalization in combination with the traditional hand-written method to make the learning process become more active and engaging [11, 13].

On the other hand, the tablet can provide a more attractive solution for the note-taking interaction, for example the stylus or pen-based input can simulate the real writing activity. Despite the usefulness of tablet and its stylus, a research done by Pew Research Center [14] found out that the percentage of tablet ownership among the United State of America (USA) adults is lower than that of smartphone ownership, which is 53% compared to 85% in 2021, as shown in Fig. 1. Therefore, there is a need for an immediate solution that is suitable for the masses. Hence, the AR tracking method for smartphones is the most reasonable and affordable solution.

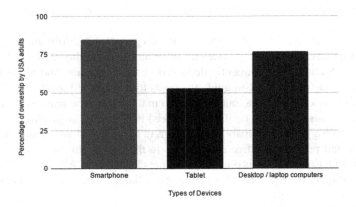

Fig. 1. The ownership percentage of digital devices by the USA adults on February 7, 2021. Adopted from [14].

Besides, users can opt for the commercialized Software as a Services (SaaS) cloud storage application, such as Google Drive, Dropbox, and Microsoft OneDrive. The benefits of these services are they can store a variety of file types and provide free storage with upgradable options to increase the storage size. Their cross-platform feature also helps users synchronize their data across their desktop computers and smartphones which allow them to access the data at anywhere, anytime.

However, studies found that it is difficult for the users to navigate to the relevant files due to the increase of the folder number and complexity of the folder structure [15]. The users also become confused and forget the contents in their cloud storage [16]. The solution to these problems is to leverage the click logs or activity logs of the users to determine the most frequently used or opened files and display them in the application's home page. But there is also a need for storing the additional multimedia information for physical note-taking activity, which can seamlessly link the real-world bookmarks to the relevant digital contents.

2.2   AR Application and Information Retrieval

AR is a display and interaction technology that superimposes virtual objects in the real-world environment. In another word, AR is also a technique which retrieves additional information based on a specific trigger point or event for display purposes. These trigger points or events can be marker-based or geoinformatics-based.

The marker-based AR uses an image that acts as a unique code, and it is recognised by the AR application to trigger the information retrieval event. The Wonderful Augmented Reality and Art (WARna) application provides an intuitive experience for the children to interact with the 3D characters they have coloured [17]. The works by [10, 18] and [19] also showed the popularity of using the AR marker in book publication to display supplementary information to enhance the reading and learning process. In addition, the marker-based AR tracking method can provide more intuitive user interaction and immersive learning environment to the applications, such as the holographic AR display of planets in the real world by using a reflective pyramid [20] and the solution of user interaction issue found in the mobile virtual reality (VR) for welding training application [21].

Meanwhile, the geoinformatics-based AR uses geographic information system (GIS) data as a trigger event where the relevant information is displayed when the users are in a certain location. It is frequently deployed in the navigation and tourism systems, such as the Google Maps AR to guide the users to the selected location [22]. Besides, Lin et al. [23] also proposed a tourism system that retrieves the name of nearby tourist attractions and displays them on the camera feed in the users' smartphone.

AR technology has the capability to integrate the physical world and virtual world to enhance and provide intuitive experiences to the users. This work also anticipated that the information retrieval is one of the features available in AR applications as it can obtain and display the relevant information immediately to the user by interacting with a physical point or event.

2.3   Related Work

Table 1 shows the comparison of features between the traditional note-taking method, existing digital note-taking applications, and online cloud storage. In this work, the digital note-taking application is the combination of Evernote and OneNote, while the online cloud storage includes Google Drive, OneDrive, and Dropbox.

Table 1. Comparison between the traditional note-taking method, related digital note-taking applications, and the online cloud storage applications.

	Traditional note-taking	Digital note-taking application	Online cloud storage
Description	Hand-written note	Writing notes digitally	Cloud storage
Platform	–	Web browser and mobile application	Web browser and mobile application
Medium	Physical	Digital	Digital
Display on	Paper	Screen	Screen
Accepted file format	Text-based, images	Text-based, images, video recordings, audio, documents, and PDFs	Accept all file types, such as images, video recordings, audio, documents, PDFs, zip files, and more
Interaction methods for data input	Writing and drawing by using pen or pencil	Keyboard (key in the data), pen (write or draw), browse and upload files	Browse and upload files
Navigation task	Searching manually through the notebook	Searching, navigate manually	Searching, most frequent files section, navigate manually
Storage size (free version)	–	**Evernote:** 25 MB maximum note size **OneNote:** depends on the size of OneDrive	**Google Drive:** 15 GB **OneDrive:** 5 GB **Dropbox:** 2 GB

As for the related AR-based note-taking application, Mitsuhara et al. [9] was the first project to use marker-based AR and projection-based display technologies to display additional notes alongside the textbook. They set up a specialized frame to hold a video camera to detect the marker in the textbook and a projector to display the additional contents on the page. In 2004, Yang et al. [24] used a head-mounted device (HMD) for AR-based note-taking applications to display 3D curricular contents. The users can use hand gestures to write the note and annotate the 3D models in a virtual 3D space. Suzuki et al. [10] introduced an active textbook (A-txt) for iOS mobile applications. Teachers can upload the customized information and assets, such as diagrams, videos,

3D models, and audios, into the server, and the student can use the application to scan the marker to obtain this information. Yang et al. [24] focused on the interaction with the 3D contents and storytelling, but less concentrated on notes storage and information retrieval. Meanwhile, the customization capabilities in [9] and [10] are only limited to the teachers, and the students can only retrieve the information but cannot edit them. Thus, this project proposed to enhance the AR-based note-taking application in mobile phone and to improve the interaction for information retrieval. In addition, supporting the traditional hand-written method and customizable contents were also the main focus in this research. Table 2 shows the comparison of features between the related AR-based note-taking applications and the proposed StickAR application. Figure 2 shows the chronological order of AR-based note-taking applications.

Table 2. Comparison of related AR-based note-taking applications and the proposed StickAR application.

	Mitsuhara et al. [9]	Yang et al. [24]	Suzuki et al. [10]	StickAR
Description	Note-taking with AR	Note-taking with AR and HMD	Textbook notes with AR	Note-taking with AR
Platform	Mobile application	Mobile, HMD application	Mobile application	Mobile application
Medium	Digital and physical			
Display on	Virtual materials are projected on paper	HMD	Screen	Screen
Accepted file format	Images and text	3D models	Images, video recordings, audio, documents, and PDFs	Images and video recordings
Interaction methods for data input	Browse and upload files (by teachers only)	Select the 3D models from library, hand gesture for writing	Browse and upload files (by teachers only)	Browse and upload files
Navigation task	AR marker navigation	Not stated for information retrieving	AR marker navigation	Navigate manually, AR marker navigation
Storage size (free version)	Not stated	Not stated	Not stated	1 GB maximum note size for free account

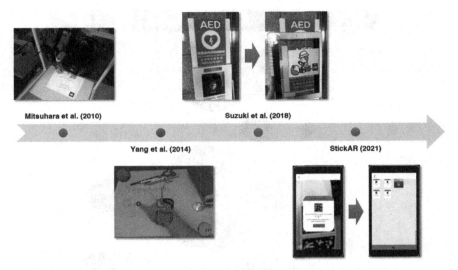

Fig. 2. The chronological order of AR-based note-taking applications.

3 Methodology

In this section, the methodology to develop the StickAR mobile application is described succinctly. This work implemented the prototyping software development model to guide the design and system development stages, as shown in Fig. 3. This method is useful to build the prototype incrementally and evaluate the prototype at each iteration for improvement [25].

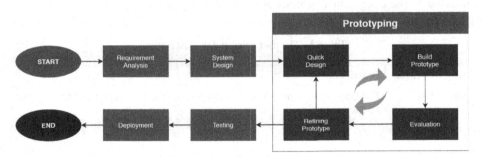

Fig. 3. The software prototype model of StickAR application.

3.1 Requirement Analysis for the StickAR Mobile Application

This section describes the functional requirements in the StickAR System. Figure 4 shows the use case diagram of the StickAR System.

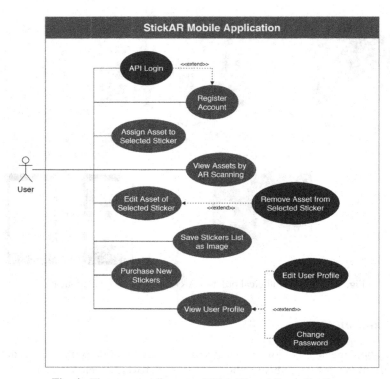

Fig. 4. The use case diagram of StickAR mobile application.

Use Case Actors. Currently, there is only one type of user role, which is User, as shown in Table 3. The User is the consumer and user of the system.

Table 3. The user roles and its descriptions.

ID	User role	Description
UR1	User	The User uses the mobile application to scan the AR marker and manage the assets

Use Case Descriptions. Table 4 shows the requirements and its detailed descriptions.

Table 4. The requirements and its description.

ID	Requirement	Description
RQ1	Register account	User registers a new account
RQ2	API login	User login using Facebook account
RQ3	Assign asset to selected sticker	User assigns assets, such as image and video, to the selected sticker
RQ4	View assets by AR scanning	User views the assets by AR scanning
RQ5	Edit asset of selected sticker	User edits and views the assets of the selected sticker
RQ6	Remove asset from selected sticker	User removes the asset from the selected sticker
RQ7	View user profile	User views the information of the user account
RQ8	Edit user profile	User updates the profile image, username, and email
RQ9	Change password	User updates the password
RQ10	Save stickers list as image	User saves a list of stickers as an image, such as pdf, jpeg, png, for printing
RQ11	Purchase new stickers	User purchases a new sticker pack

3.2 System Design

The system architecture of StickAR mobile application is illustrated as in Fig. 5. The client layer consists of a graphical user interface (GUI) for the users to interact with the application.

The middleware layer contains all the application programming interface (API) and software development kit (SDK) implemented in the StickAR mobile application. The Unity Scripting API forms a major part of the application, which handles the frontend and interaction, browse manager for assets management and server manager to allow the communication between the client and the StickAR HTTP server. The Vuforia SDK provides the VuMark API, which provides the tracking and metadata extraction of the registered StickAR marker. Besides, Facebook Login API is utilized to offer the user with an alternative method to login to the StickAR application.

All the HTTP requests, such as get, update and delete, are sent to the HTTP server to create a new record or update the available record in the database. The HTTP server stack includes the PHP scripts to handle the standard request operation and also the PHP-FFMpeg software to generate the thumbnail of the uploaded video assets. In addition, the information of the users and assets are uploaded and stored in the MySQL database in the resource layer. Both the server and database are hosted in an Ubuntu Linux server. In addition, Table 5 shows the identified software requirements for the system development phase.

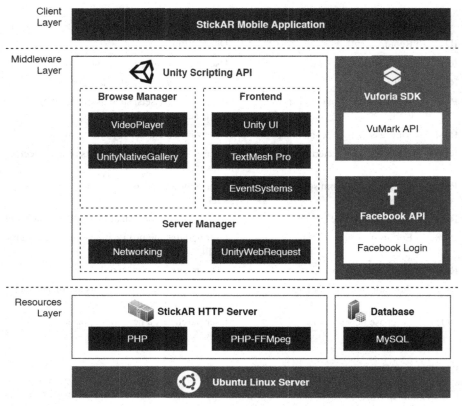

Fig. 5. The high-level architecture design of StickAR mobile application.

3.3 Prototyping

In the system development phase, the prototype was created by using Unity3D for the Android-based mobile application.

The AR function was implemented in the prototype which allows the users to scan the VuMark AR marker for user interaction. The VuMark is one of the AR tracking methods provided by the Vuforia AR SDK that can allow the developer to create a stylish sticker, each with its distinctive code. It is similar to a QR code but for AR application. Figure 6 shows the example of the StickAR markers' design based on the VuMark guidelines in Adobe Illustrator provided by Vuforia [26]. The unique code in the markers is generated by submitting the VuMark design into Vuforia Developer Portal. Each marker represents a unique string of twelve characters specified by the developer.

Besides, the web server function was also created to facilitate the users to upload their information and assets. In addition, the images and videos gallery were created to allow the users to view the assets uploaded to the server in their StickAR mobile application.

Table 5. The software requirements and its description.

Software name	Type	Description
Unity3D version 2019.4.18f1	Game engine	To implement the frontend, interaction, and backend logic of the StickAR mobile application To build the APK files for installation
Vuforia for Unity version 9.8.8	SDK	To implement the AR functionality
PHP	Scripting language	To handle the HTTP requests on the server
PHP-FFMpeg	Software	To generate the video thumbnail of the uploaded video assets
MySQL	Database	To store the users and assets information in the server
Android SDK Platform 10.0 (Q)	SDK	To build the Unity project into an Android APK file for Android deployment

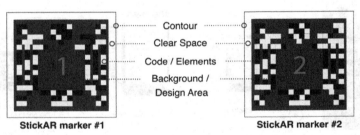

StickAR marker #1   **StickAR marker #2**

Fig. 6. The important parts of StickAR markers, which are based on the VuMark design guidelines [26].

3.4 Deployment

In the deployment phase, the Android application package (APK) file was created and integrated with the web server for users and assets management. The deployment settings and configurations for generating the APK are as follows:

1. Set the display configuration to portrait mode only.
2. Set the minimum API level to Android 4.4 "KitKat" (API level 19).
3. This project is built as a 32-bit application for faster building time and ease of testing.

4   Result and Discussion

4.1   AR Scanning Interaction

The AR scanning interaction is the major contribution of this work. Figure 7 shows the AR scan interaction flow. Users can access the desired StickAR marker folder immediately by using the AR scan functionality. This interaction provides a faster way to locate the folder for various purposes, such as uploading a new asset or viewing the uploaded assets.

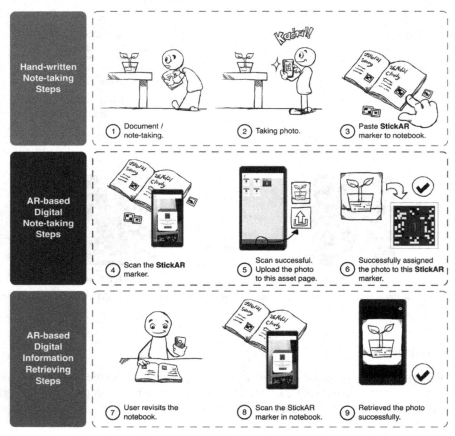

Fig. 7. The AR scan interaction flow for note-taking activity.

This function, which is represented by requirement RQ4, can be performed by the users by clicking on the AR scan button in the home page. Then, the application activates the AR camera for the users to scan the physical StickAR marker. Once the StickAR marker is recognised by the Vuforia, the success panel is displayed on top of the camera view. Next, the users can click on the scan button to open the view assets page relative to the scanned StickAR marker.

Besides, the AR scan interaction also promotes the integration of physical activity with virtual functionalities, such as note-taking. Users can paste the StickAR marker beside their notes, and then, add the multimedia contents, such as images or video recordings, inside the folder through StickAR mobile application which act as a supplementary information.

Figure 7 shows the example of the note-taking process in the real-world scenario. The student documented the growth of the plant in the notebook and used a smartphone to capture the photo of the plant. Then, the student pasted the StickAR marker beside the notes and scanned the marker by using the StickAR application. Lastly, the student uploaded the image of the plant to assign to this marker. Hence, the student can use the StickAR application to scan the AR marker to retrieve the selected image of the plant when he or she revisits the note again.

4.2 Start Pages

Figure 8 shows the graphical user interface (GUI) of the start pages. When the users open the StickAR application, they are first greeted by the start page, as shown in Fig. 8(a). Once the users click on the "Get Started" button, the StickAR application will navigate the users to the sign-in page, as shown in Fig. 8(b).

Users can choose to sign-in by using the StickAR account or Facebook Login. For first-time users, they can create a StickAR account by clicking the "Sign Up" button in the sign-in page to open the create account page, as shown in Fig. 8(c). Both functionalities represent the requirements RQ1 and RQ2.

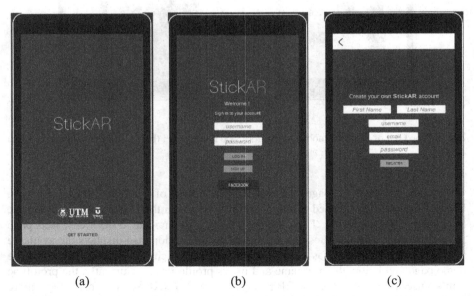

| (a) | (b) | (c) |

Fig. 8. The GUI of StickAR mobile application: (a) start page; (b) sign-in page; (c) create a new user account page.

4.3 Home Page

Once login to the StickAR application, users are directed to the home page, as shown in Fig. 9(a). In the home page, there are three buttons located in the bottom toolbar. Starting from the left, the first button is the hamburger button which opens the side menu panel, as shown in Fig. 9(b). The centre button is the AR scan button to open the AR scanning interaction that is explained in Sect. 4.1, while the right button is the tutorial button which provides fast access to the tutorial page.

In the side menu panel, there are another three buttons, which are the home button, setting button and log out button. Both the home button and logout button are self-explanatory. The setting button can direct the users to user management pages, as presented in Sect. 4.5.

(a)   (b)

Fig. 9. The GUI of StickAR mobile application: (a) home page; (b) activate the hamburger menu panel.

In addition, the home page also shows all the folders of available StickAR markers. Users can view the uploaded assets or add new assets in the folder by clicking on the StickAR marker they want. Then, the application will navigate to the view assets page as presented in Sect. 4.4. Besides, the StickAR application also displays the available storage space of the users as a horizontal scrollbar, which is located at the top of the home page and below the username and user's profile image. Currently, the prototype limits a user to store a total of 1 GB note size to the StickAR server. This is the feature for future application production, where the users can sign up for a free account with a total of 1 GB note size. The StickAR application should also provide an upgradable option to increase the storage capacity if the users require more memory space.

4.4 View Assets Page

There are two ways to access the view assets page. Firstly, it can be accessed through the AR scanning interaction flow, as presented in Sect. 4.1. Secondly, the users can also click on one of the StickAR marker buttons in the home page, as shown in Fig. 9(a). Figure 10(a) shows the GUI of view assets page.

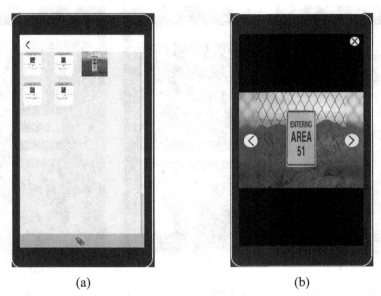

(a)   (b)

Fig. 10. The GUI of StickAR mobile application: (a) assets gallery page; (b) view the image gallery.

Inside the view asset page, users can perform several functionalities for assets management purposes, which are assigning new assets, view and edit the assigned assets, and remove the assets from the StickAR marker. They represented the requirements RQ3, RQ5 and RQ6, respectively.

Users can click on the clip button below to assign a file to this StickAR marker's storage. It will redirect the users to the file browser for them to search for the images or video recordings that they wanted to upload. Once assigned, all the multimedia contents are displayed in the middle of the view assets page in the form of a thumbnail. Then, users can click on one of the thumbnails to open the multimedia gallery, as shown in Fig. 10(b). Therefore, the users can browse through the images or video recordings that are assigned to this StickAR marker.

4.5 User Management Pages

Lastly, the StickAR application provides users with the functionalities to edit their profile information, which are represented as requirements RQ7 to RQ9. Figure 10 shows the GUI of the user setting pages.

Figure 11(a) shows the main user setting page which users can access from the hamburger menu by clicking the "Setting" option as shown in Fig. 9(b). In this page, users can choose to change their username or password. Figure 11(b) and (c) show the interface design of edit profile page and change password page, respectively. In the edit profile page, users can change their full name and profile image.

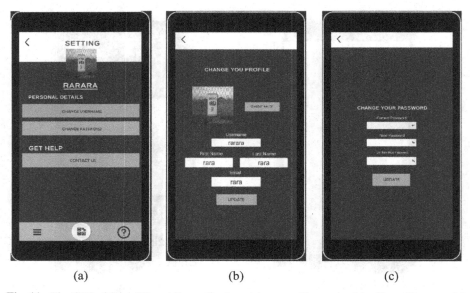

| (a) | (b) | (c) |

Fig. 11. The GUI of StickAR mobile application: (a) user setting page; (b) edit profile page; (c) change password page.

4.6 Discussion

Figure 12 shows the overview of the SWOT (strengths, weakness, opportunities, and threats) analysis which is used to discuss and assess the capabilities and future potential of the StickAR mobile application. The detailed descriptions are presented as follows:

1. **Strengths:** The StickAR mobile application provides the users with many stylish AR stickers, which allows the users to stick them in their notebook to bookmark their experiences in terms of video recordings and images at that physical point by using the AR technology. Compared to other traditional cloud storage applications, StickAR allows the users to obtain the desired data immediately by scanning the AR marker. The other storage application requires the users to search for them manually folder by folder. This feature can become the hypothesis for the user evaluation stage.
2. **Weaknesses:** The current product is still in the work-in-progress and prototyping stages. The function is also limited to the user. Besides, there are some requirements that are not implemented, which is from RQ10 and RQ11. The system also lacks the administrative functions to manage the StickAR markers and users.

3. **Opportunities:** The application provides a new opportunity for the artists and content creators to design the sticker that can be featured in this StickAR application. The AR functionality can also be used in exhibitions, for example museum and art gallery, or book publication which allows the owner and publisher alike to add the relevant information to the StickAR application. Then, the users can view this additional information by using the StickAR mobile application. In addition, the growing market demands of digital note-taking applications also provides a new opportunity to innovate and improve the user experience of these applications.

4. **Threats:** The competition from the existing note-taking applications and cloud storage applications, which offer competitive features and affordable options to the users. This study requires further user evaluation to determine and compare the efficiency of these applications with the proposed method.

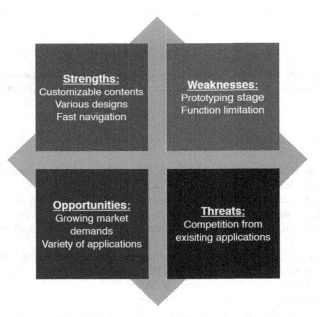

Fig. 12. The overview of SWOT analysis.

5   Conclusion

This paper presents the work-in-progress StickAR mobile application that can help the users to capture important physical events in the form of images or video recordings, along with the hand-written notes. These digital multimedia contents are stored in the StickAR web server by assigning them to a StickAR marker, and the marker can be sticked beside the notes. Then, the users can use the AR scanning interaction method of StickAR mobile application to navigate to the correct supplementary information immediately by using the smartphone's camera to scan the StickAR marker. For the next steps of the StickAR mobile application:

1. Complete all the use case requirements.
2. Create a web application for administration functions.
3. Conduct a formal user evaluation and case studies.

Lastly, there are more suggested future works to improve the features and user experience of the StickAR mobile application:

1. Support text-based entries like Evernote and OneNote.
2. Utilize the 3D capability of AR technology to display 3D contents.
3. Create a new platform for the content creators to provide their custom AR marker design.
4. Collaborate with potential partners, such as museums, art galleries, schools, and publishers.

Acknowledgements. This work is supported by the International Collaboration Grant of Universiti Teknologi Malaysia (UTM) and Telkom University (Tel-U) with vote R.J130000.7301.4B569.

References

1. Rusdiansyah, R.: Note-taking as a technique an teaching reading comprehension. IDEAS: J. English Lang. Teach. Learn. Linguist. Literat. **7**(2), 173–184 (2019)
2. Kobayashi, K.: Combined effects of note-taking/-reviewing on learning and the enhancement through interventions: a meta-analytic review. Educ. Psychol. **26**(3), 459–477 (2006)
3. Stacy, E.M., Cain, J.: Note-taking and handouts in the digital age. Am. J. Pharm. Educ. **79**(7), 1–6 (2015)
4. Darko-adjei, N.: The use and effect of smartphones in students' learning activities: evidence from the University of Ghana, Legon. Lib. Philos. Pract. (e-journal), 1–37 (2019)
5. Walker, Z., Mcmahon, D.D., Rosenblatt, K., Arner, T.: Beyond Pokémon: augmented reality is a universal design for learning tool. SAGE Open **7**(4), 1–8 (2017)
6. Liao, T.: Future directions for mobile augmented reality research: understanding relationships between augmented reality users, nonusers, content, devices, and industry. Mob. Media Commun. **7**(1), 131–149 (2019)
7. Lim, C., Park, T.: Exploring the educational use of an augmented reality books. In: Proceedings of the Annual Convention of the Association for Educational Communications and Technology, pp. 172–182. Association for Educational Communications & Technology, Jacksonville, Florida (2011)
8. Verified Market Research. Global Note-Taking Management Software Market by Type, by Geographic Scope, Competitive Landscape and Forecast. https://www.verifiedmarketresearch.com/product/note-making-management-software-market/. Accessed 16 May 2021
9. Mitsuhara, H., Yano, Y., Moriyama, T.: Paper-top interface for supporting note-taking and its preliminary experiment. In: 2010 IEEE International Conference on Systems, Man and Cybernetics, pp. 3456–3462. IEEE, Istanbul (2010)

10. Suzuki, S.N., Akimoto, Y., Kobayashi, Y., Ishihara, M., Kameyama, R., Yamaguchi, M.: A proposal of method to make active learning from class to self-study using active note taking and active textbook system. Proc. Comput. Sci. **126**, 957–966 (2018)
11. Flanigan, A.E., Titsworth, S.: The impact of digital distraction on lecture note taking and student learning. Instr. Sci. **48**(5), 495–524 (2020). https://doi.org/10.1007/s11251-020-095 17-2
12. Fiorella, L., Mayer, R.E.: Spontaneous spatial strategy use in learning from scientific text. Contemp. Educ. Psychol. **49**, 66–79 (2017)
13. Hayes, G.R., Pierce, J.S., Abowd, G.D.: Practices for capturing short important thoughts. In: CHI 2003 Extended Abstracts on Human Factors in Computing Systems (CHI EA 2003), pp. 904–905. Association for Computing Machinery, New York (2003)
14. Pew Research Center. Mobile fact sheet. https://www.pewresearch.org/internet/fact-sheet/ mobile/. Accessed 15 May 2021
15. Jagerman, R., Kong, W., Pasumarthi, R.K., Qin, Z., Bendersky, M., Najork, M.: Improving cloud storage search with user activity. In: Proceedings of the 14th ACM International Conference on Web Search and Data Mining, pp. 508–516. Association for Computing Machinery, Israel (2021)
16. Khan, M.T., Hyun, M., Kanich, C., Ur, B.: Forgotten but not gone: identifying the need for longitudinal data management in cloud storage. In: Proceedings of the 2018 CHI Conference on Human Factors in Computing Systems, pp. 1–12. Association for Computing Machinery, Montreal (2018)
17. Mokhtar, M.K., Mohamed, F., Sunar, M.S., Arshad, M.A.M., Sidik, M.K.M.: Development of mobile-based augmented reality colouring for preschool learning. In: 2018 IEEE Conference on e-Learning, e-Management and e-Services (IC3e), pp. 11–16. IEEE, Langkawi (2018)
18. Billinghurst, M., Kato, H., Poupyrev, I.: The MagicBook: a transitional AR interface. Comput. Graph. **25**(5), 745–753 (2001)
19. Gudinavičius, A., Markelevičiūtė, G.: Using augmented reality in book publishing from a small language market perspective. Publ. Res. Q. **36**(1), 43–54 (2020). https://doi.org/10. 1007/s12109-019-09704-1
20. Siang, C.V., Isham, M.I.M., Mohamed, F., Yusoff, Y.A., Mokhtar, M.K., Tomi, B., Selamat, A.: Interactive holographic application using augmented reality EduCard and 3D holographic pyramid for interactive and immersive learning. In: 2017 IEEE Conference on e-Learning, e-Management and e-Services (IC3e), pp. 73–78. IEEE, Kuching (2017)
21. Isham, M.I.M., Haron, H.N.H., Mohamed, F., Siang, C.V., Mokhtar, M.K., Azizo, A.S.: Mobile VR and marker tracking method applied in virtual welding simulation kit for welding training. In: 2020 6th International Conference on Interactive Digital Media (ICIDM), pp. 1–5. IEEE, Bandung
22. CNBC. Google Maps has a wild new feature that will guide you through indoor spaces like airports. https://www.cnbc.com/2021/03/30/google-maps-launches-augmented-reality-directions-for-indoor-spaces.html. Accessed 16 May 2021
23. Lin, P.-J., Kao, C.-C., Lam, K.-H., Tsai, I.C.: Design and implementation of a tourism system using mobile augmented reality and GIS technologies. In: Juang, J., Chen, C.-Y., Yang, C.-F. (eds.) Proceedings of the 2nd International Conference on Intelligent Technologies and Engineering Systems (ICITES2013). LNEE, vol. 293, pp. 1093–1099. Springer, Cham (2014). https://doi.org/10.1007/978-3-319-04573-3_133
24. Yang, M., Chiu, Y.: Note-taking for 3D curricular contents using markerless augmented reality. Interact. Comput. **26**(4), 321–333 (2014)
25. Kendall, K.E., Kendall, J.E.: Systems Analysis and Design, 8th edn. Prentice-Hall, New Jersey (2011)
26. Vuforia. VuMark Design Guide. Vuforia Developer Library. https://library.vuforia.com/art icles/Training/VuMark-Design-Guide.html. Accessed 16 May 2021

CMAR: A Conceptual Framework for Designing Mobile Augmented Reality Learning Module for Construction Measurement

Ahmad Faiz Azizi Ahmad Fauzi[1]([✉]) [iD], Kherun Nita Ali[1] [iD],
Norhazren Izatie Mohd[1] [iD], Nurshikin Shukery[1], Mohd Azwarie Mat Dzahir[1] [iD],
Shamsulhadi Bandi[1] [iD], and Mohd Shahrizal Sunar[2] [iD]

[1] Faculty of Built Environment and Surveying, Universiti Teknologi Malaysia, 81300 Skudai, Johor, Malaysia
{ahmadfaizazizi,b-kherun,norhazren,b-nurshikin,mohdazwarie, shamsulhadi}@utm.my
[2] Institute of Human Centered Engineering (iHumEn), Universiti Teknologi Malaysia, 81300 Skudai, Johor, Malaysia
shahrizal@utm.my

Abstract. Augmented Reality (AR) is a technology that allows two- or three-dimensional computer-generated graphics, objects, and information to be displayed as an overlay onto the real environment. With the advancement of mobile devices in term of their sensors (gyroscope, barometer, accelerometer, proximity sensor, camera module), displays and processing power, the potential of using mobile AR in teaching and learning (T&L) is becoming clearer. Construction measurement subject is considered the core subject for a quantity surveying student to master. However, some of the measured elements are difficult for students with low spatial skills to visualize the construction sequence and understand. Therefore, the use of AR would help in enhancing the T&L experience of construction measurement for the students. This paper aims to propose a conceptual framework for designing a mobile AR learning module for construction measurement subject. The Construction Measurement Augmented Reality (CMAR) framework consist of the learning theory, learning content, features and learning outcome.

Keywords: Augmented reality · Construction measurement · Quantity surveying education · Mobile application · CTML

1 Introduction

Mobile devices such as smartphones and tablet are omnipresent in this era. Smartphones have been moulded into a part of people daily life especially students. Students nowadays are not only equipped with smartphones, but they are also technologically literate [1]. Scholars believe that utilizing technology in the teaching and learning process could help in understanding and the learning process [2]. Scholars have suggested that educators

Z. Lv and H. Song (Eds.): INTETAIN 2021, LNICST 429, pp. 372–382, 2022.
https://doi.org/10.1007/978-3-030-99188-3_23

take advantage of the technology that the students are interested in, this is to capture their interest in the learning process.

Therefore, with the implementation of mobile AR, the educators could capture the student's interest in the subject. With the mobile device's advancements in term of sensors (gyroscope, barometer, accelerometer, proximity sensor, camera module), the use of AR could be beneficial. Other than that, the combination of 3D models in the teaching and learning process has been proven beneficial in teaching construction-related subjects due to the ability of computer-generated graphics to realistically represents the building element. With mobile AR, students can use AR as a learning tool because AR application can be made to be used with a smartphone. Therefore, the AR application is easily accessible.

However, despite the various advancement of technology, the teaching and learning process of construction measurement has been limited to the traditional approach which has minimal use of technology [3]. Construction measurement is defined as a skill to interpret drawings, the knowledge of construction technology and the understanding of the standard method of measurement (SMM) and construction measurement is deemed to be one of the most important skills for a quantity surveyor to acquire [4, 5]. Students have to acquire adequate knowledge and understanding of the construction technology to identify the elements and help visualize the construction process [6].

Furthermore, the lack of content specifically for AR is lacking not only in the context of construction measurement but in any other body of knowledge. Therefore, to incorporate AR with construction measurement teaching and learning, this study focused on the conceptual framework needed to design a learning module for construction measurement. To develop the proposed conceptual framework, these objectives are outlined:

1. To discover relevant learning theories associated with AR
2. To identify what features needed to be included in the AR application
3. To identify what is the syllabus for the construction measurement course
4. To determine the expected learning outcome of learning construction measurement using AR

2 Conceptual Framework

The conceptual framework is proposed to be used in designing a mobile AR learning module for construction measurement. The use of AR, CTML, relevant features and construction measurement syllabus would complement the learning process of construction measurement and make learning more effective and accessible. These are the components that would be included in the conceptual framework.

2.1 Cognitive Theory of Multimedia Learning (CTML)

This study incorporates the cognitive theory of multimedia learning (CTML) as the foundation/learning theory of the framework. Shirazi and Behzadan [7] describe the cognitive theories of multimedia learning as three fundamental concepts in the science of learning. Before developing learning tools, it's important to understand how the human information processing system works [8].

As shown in Fig. 1, humans process information across channels and store it in three forms of memories. First is the dual-channel which states that humans have separate channels for processing verbal and visual content or learning materials. Second is the limit of capacity which a person can process a limited amount of material in each channel at one time. The third is active processing where indicates that meaningful learning had occurred when learners are engaged in appropriate cognitive processes during the learning session.

CTML is a simple interpretation of how the human information processing system functions. There are three different sections where different types of memory are stored, as shown in Fig. 1. The sensory memory is the first part, and it focuses on information collected in the same sensory format provided to the user. The sensory memory has a broad memory capacity but only lasts for a short period. Working memory is the second component, which stores and organizes information in a small capacity. Working memory often stores information for a brief period. According to Ebbinghaus [9], long-term memory retains information in an ordered format, has a wide capacity, and lasts for a long time.

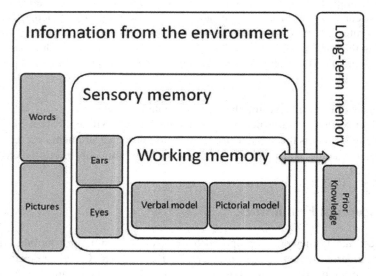

Fig. 1. Cognitive structure and information processing model [5]

Based on these theoretical assumptions, Mayer [11] has developed the principles to design an effective multimedia instruction which includes 12 principles to design an effective multimedia learning module. According to Mayer [11], CTML supports the arguments that students learn better with audio and visual representation together rather than audio or visual alone. CTML provides a framework for improving how students learn with the involvement of technology. CTML provides these design principles for the creation of multimedia instructional technology that focuses on efficiently responding to student's cognitive load. The design principle by Mayer [11] is shown and explained in the table below. These design principles were used as the theory for this study to design a better experience of using AR in construction measurement teaching and learning (Table 1).

Table 1. Mayer's [10] 12 design principle for multimedia instructions

Design principle	Explanation
The coherence principle	When there isn't any extraneous, distracting content, humans learn better
The signalling principle	When humans are shown exactly what to pay attention to on a display, they learn more efficiently
The redundancy principle	People learn more effectively when narration and images are used instead of narration, graphics, and text
The spatial contiguity principle	When related text and visuals are physically close together, humans learn better
The temporal contiguity principle	When related words and images are viewed together rather than sequentially, humans learn better
The segmenting principle	When knowledge is viewed in fragments rather than as a continuous stream, humans learn better
The pre-training principle	Humans learn more easily if they are already acquainted with some of the fundamentals
The modality principle	Humans learn more easily from images and spoken words than from written words
The multimedia principle	Humans learn more easily from both words and pictures than from only words
The personalization principle	Humans learn more from a conversational, casual tone than from a formal tone
The voice principle	A human voice is more effective than a machine voice in teaching humans
The image principle	Humans do not always understand better from a video of another person

There are several scholars [12–21] who discuss the use of the CTML design principle for AR and agrees that not all of Mayer's CTML design principle is included in their use of AR. These scholars only use signalling principle, spatial contiguity principle, temporal contiguity principle, modality principle and multimedia principle in their study and this shows that the principle used is suitable to be used in AR environment.

2.2   Features to be Included in CMAR

The conceptual framework is designed to be used as a mobile application that involves in integrating the mobile device and the multimedia contents. The use of 3D models, computer-generated graphics, 3D text, audio, and video are implemented into the application to generate an AR environment. The inclusion of 3D objects could help in aiding the students in the visualization of the construction elements.

However, to use AR for teaching and learning construction measurements, other features needed to be included to deliver the content. These features were identified by interviewing quantity surveying educators from universities all over Malaysia. The educators interviewed have over 5–10 years of experience in teaching construction measurements. The identified features are that were deemed important to use in teaching and learning construction measurement using AR are:

1. Annotation – extra information on the 3D models (building elements, units)
2. Specifications – Building specifications, materials specifications, and dimensions of the building elements
3. Interactive video – on the construction sequence, construction process of the building elements
4. 3D Models of the building elements
5. Measurement rules – clauses based on Malaysian Standard Method of Measurement 2
6. Guideline to measure the building elements

2.3   Syllabus

Construction measurement is often taught concurrent construction technology. The dominant timing of teaching construction measurement is concurrent, in which construction technology is taught before construction measurement. Therefore, the syllabus from construction technology and construction measurement was included in the conceptual framework.

The syllabus of construction technology and construction is obtained from the Board of Quantity Surveying Malaysia (BQSM) academic accreditation requirements. The academic accreditation requirements show the topics that were taught·in the course and the requirements are used in all universities that offer quantity surveying program. Therefore, the conceptual framework could be used by other universities in Malaysia to develop their CMAR teaching module. Table 2 shows the syllabus that is extracted from the BQSM academic accreditation requirements. The syllabus is the content of the learning module for teaching construction measurement using AR.

Table 2. Construction measurement and construction technology syllabus [22]

Syllabus	
Construction measurement	Construction technology
Intro to measurement (History & Development, QS roles, Intro to SMM, Principle of measurement	Intro to construction technology (Review on construction process, roles of building and design team, classification of work, building trades and elements)
Site preparation	Site preparation and soil investigation
Simple Substructure works - Excavation and foundation	Foundations (Shallow foundations, Piling, Basement)
Internal & External Wall (Brick, block, masonry, precast panels)	Wall and partition (Brickwork, blockwork, masonry, precast panel)
Finishes (Ceiling, wall, floor)	Timber structure (Frame, floor, wall, staircase, roof structure and coverings)
Timber roof (Structure, coverings, drainage)	Reinforced concrete (frame, floor, flat roof, wall, staircase, ramp, precast concrete)
Door and Window	Door and window
Reinforced concrete (Substructure, Frame, Upper floor, Staircase, Roof)	Finishes
Precast concrete (IBS component)	Steel structure
Services Installation (Plumbing & Sanitary, Mech. Engineering, Electrical Engineering)	Demolition and alteration, temporary works
Structural steelwork	External works
Piling works	Civil engineering works
Basement works	Marine and offshore structure
Demolition & alteration works External works Prime cost sum Provisional Sum Preliminaries	Building materials (Concrete, brick, block, masonry, waterproofing and asphalt, roofing, woodwork, structural steelwork, metalwork, finishes, glazing, painting, and decorating, sanitary fitting, and plastic products
Civil measurement	Draughtsmanship
Computer-aided measurement	
Specifications and preambles	

2.4 Student's Actual Use

The input from students was collected by using a questionnaire and is based on the technology acceptance model (TAM) [21]. The construct that was used to evaluate the student's actual use is perceived usefulness (PU), perceived ease of use (PEOU), behavioural intention and attitude (BIA), self-efficacy (SE), subjective norm (SN) and teacher factor (TF).

A total of 332 students from universities that offers quantity surveying participated in answering the questionnaire. Based on the questionnaire results, students intended to use the AR application as a mean to visualise the construction sequence, acquire knowledge, knowledge processing and group sharing.

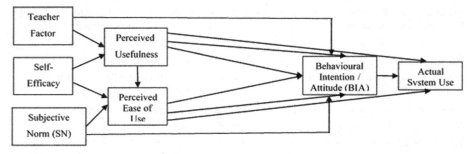

Fig. 2. Proposed technology acceptance model

However, because of the similar attributes of the actual use, acquire knowledge, processing information and group sharing were combined to form knowledge acquisition. With the proper implementation of AR content and designing the syllabus, the intended actual use of the students could be achieved. Therefore, the integration of AR content would enhance the students understanding and learning experience of construction measurement.

2.5 Expected Learning Outcome

Two outcomes are expected from the CMAR framework, which are knowledge transfer and spatial skills. Based on other studies conducted with AR [12–21], most of the expected learning outcome is the transfer of knowledge and spatial skills enhancements. Students are expected to gain knowledge from the AR application and achieve the expected learning outcome from the two syllabus which is construction measurement and construction technology.

For the spatial skills, students are expected to improve their spatial/visuospatial perception, spatial visualisation, mental folding, and mental rotation, with these skills enhanced, students can improve their interpretation of 2D drawing plan and visualise the plan into 3D form. These spatial skills are beneficial for students in construction measurement because it is expected for students to be able to visualise the elements and interpret the construction drawings.

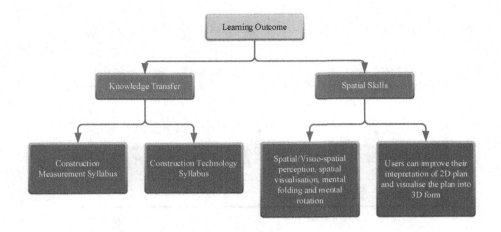

2.6 Proposed Conceptual Framework

The CMAR application is designed to enhance the learning experience of construction measurement. With the accessibility and usability of the application, students could learn and store notes on construction measurement ubiquitously. Figure 2 shows the conceptual framework for designing a learning module for construction measurement using AR. The components of the CMAR conceptual framework involves:

1. Mayer's CTML Design Principles – 5 Design principles for learning using AR. These design principles help educators in designing the learning module based on the design principles requirements.
2. Syllabus – construction measurement and construction technology course outline, the inclusion of construction technology is because the subject is taught concurrently.
3. Features –the application should include these required features. These features were stated by the educators and deemed important in learning construction measurements.
4. Student's Actual Use – This section refers to the student's true intention to use the technology.
5. Learning outcome – Refers to the expected learning outcome when using CMAR which is knowledge transfer and improvement of spatial skills (Fig. 3).

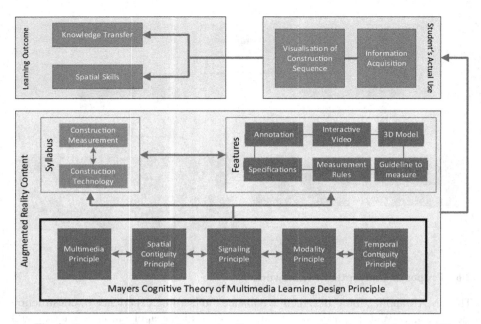

Fig. 3. Framework for designing construction measurement learning module using AR

3 Conclusion

The framework and prototype for applying AR into the teaching and learning of construction measurement are achieved from all findings from the previously stated research objectives. The framework comprises learning theory, features, syllabus, student's actual use and learning outcome as the components. The learning theory implemented into the framework is the Mayers cognitive theory of multimedia learning as the foundation for the framework. The design principles from the theory are selected to fit the use case for the study which is specifically used for AR. The expected learning outcome from the use of AR would be reflecting the whole framework. The combination of learning theory, features, syllabus, student's actual use and learning outcome is essential in developing the framework.

The research findings contribute toward the understanding of cognitive and technology-aided learning which results in a more updated and effective learning experience. AR could be used as an educational tool to enhance learning effectiveness, improve the learning environment, and have ubiquitous access to the learning material.

Acknowledgement. The authors would like to acknowledge Universiti Teknologi Malaysia (UTM), Faculty of Built Environment and Surveying, Institute of human-centred Engineering (iHumEn) and Malaysia Research Universiti Network and Ministry of Education (Grant Number R.J130000.7852.4L871 and Q.J130000.3652.02M84) for providing the funding for this study. The authors would like to thank the parties involved for contributing to this paper.

References

1. Nes, A.A.G., Steindal, S.A., Larsen, M.H., Heer, H.C., Lærum-Onsager, E., Gjevjon, E.R.: Technological literacy in nursing education: a scoping review. J. Prof. Nurs. **37**(2), 320–334 (2021)
2. Potkonjak, V., et al.: Virtual laboratories for education in science, technology, and engineering: a review. Comput. Educ. **95**, 309–327 (2016)
3. Wong, J.K.W., Oladinrin, O.T., Ho, C.M.F., Guilbert, E., Kam, R.: Assessment of video-based e-learning in a construction measurement course. Int. J. Construct. Manag. **22**(1), 1–7 (2018)
4. Hodgson, G.: An e-learning approach to quantity surveying measurement, December 2015, pp. 1639–1649 (2008)
5. Tian, L.C.C., Hogg, K.: Early career training of quantity surveying professionals. Northumbria Res. Link. 10–11 (2009)
6. McDonnell, F.P.: The relevance of teaching traditional measurement techniques to undergraduate quantity surveying students. J. Educ. Built Environ. 1–15 (2010)
7. Shirazi, A., Behzadan, A.H.: Content delivery using augmented reality to enhance students' performance in a building design and assembly project. Am. Soc. Eng. Educ. 1–24 (2015)
8. Shirazi, A., Behzadan, A.H.: Design and assessment of a mobile augmented reality-based information delivery tool for construction and civil engineering curriculum. J. Prof. Issues Eng. Educ. Pract. **141**(3), 4014012 (2014)
9. Ebbinghaus, H.: Memory: a contribution to experimental psychology, no. 3. University Microfilms (1913)
10. Mayer, R.E.: Applying the science of learning: evidence-based principles for the design of multimedia instruction. Am. Psychol. **63**(8), 760–769 (2008)
11. Sommerauer, P., Müller, O.: Augmented reality in informal learning environments: a field experiment in a mathematics exhibition. Comput. Educ. **79**, 59–68 (2014)
12. Liu, D., Valdiviezo-Díaz, P., Riofrio, G., Sun, Y.-M., Barba, R.: Integration of virtual labs into science E-learning. Proc. Comput. Sci. **75**, 95–102 (2015)
13. Gopalan, V., Zulkifli, A.N., Abubakar, J.A.: A study of students motivation based on ease of use, engaging, enjoyment and fun using the augmented reality science textbook. In: A Study of Students' Motivation Based on Ease of Use, Engaging, Enjoyment and Fun Using the Augmented Reality Science, August 2017 (2016)
14. Montoya, M.H., Díaz, C.A., Moreno, G.A.: Evaluating the effect on user perception and performance of static and dynamic contents deployed in augmented reality based learning application. Eurasia J. Math. Sci. Technol. Educ. **13**(2), 301–317 (2016)
15. Joo-Nagata, J., Martinez, A.F., García-Bermejo, G.J., García-Peñalvo, F.J.: Augmented reality and pedestrian navigation through its implementation in m-learning and e-learning: evaluation of an educational program in Chile. Comput. Educ. **111**, 1–17 (2017)
16. Ibrahim, A., Huynh, B., Downey, J., Höllerer, T., Chun, D., O'donovan, J.: Arbis pictus: a study of vocabulary learning with augmented reality. IEEE Trans. Vis. Comput. Graph. **24**(11), 2867–2874 (2018)
17. Wang, T.-K., Huang, J., Liao, P.-C., Piao, Y.: Does augmented reality effectively foster visual learning process in construction? An eye-tracking study in steel installation. Adv. Civil Eng. **2018**, 1–12 (2018)
18. Altmeyer, K., Kapp, S., Thees, M., Malone, S., Kuhn, J., Brünken, R.: The use of augmented reality to foster conceptual knowledge acquisition in STEM laboratory courses—theoretical background and empirical results. Br. J. Educ. Technol. **51**(3), 611–628 (2020)
19. Habig, S.: Who can benefit from augmented reality in chemistry? Sex differences in solving stereochemistry problems using augmented reality. Br. J. Educ. Technol. **51**(3), 629–644 (2020)

20. Thees, M., Kapp, S., Strzys, M.P., Beil, F., Lukowicz, P., Kuhn, J.: Effects of augmented reality on learning and cognitive load in university physics laboratory courses. Comput. Human Behav. **108**, 106316 (2020)
21. Davis, F.D.: Perceived usefulness, perceived ease of use, and user acceptance of information technology. MIS Q. **13**(3), 319 (1989)
22. Board of Quantity Surveyors Malaysia. Quantity Surveying Academic Accreditation Requirements (2019)

Enjoyment as Gamified Experience for Informal Learning in Virtual Reality

Abdul Syafiq Bahrin[1,2,3] (ID), Mohd Shahrizal Sunar[1,2(✉)] (ID), and Azizul Azman[1,2]

[1] School of Computing, Faculty of Engineering, Universiti Teknologi Malaysia,
81310 Johor Bahru, Johor, Malaysia
shahrizal@utm.my
[2] Media and Game Innovation Centre of Excellence, Institute of Human Centred Engineering,
Universiti Teknologi Malaysia, 81310 Johor Bahru, Johor, Malaysia
[3] School of Creative Industry Management & Performing Arts, Universiti Utara Malaysia,
06010 Bukit Kayu Hitam, Kedah, Malaysia

Abstract. Learning in the virtual world informally is still challenging due to some distracting factors. Previous studies show that there is a need for the learning process to informally learn using virtual reality in an enjoyable way through the gamified learning experience, as gamification enhances enjoyment whilst motivate the user to keep exploring the virtual world and learn things informally. This paper aims to discuss the concept of enjoyment as gamified experience for informal learning in virtual reality and propose the model development idea of enjoyable informal learning in virtual reality through the systematic literature review process. Through content analysis, this paper provides researchers with background information on gamification, enjoyment as gamified experience, enjoyable informal learning, virtual reality, virtual reality for informal learning, gamified learning versus game-based learning, related theories, and the initially proposed a broad methodology to be further explored for future study. Future studies may refer to this paper to conduct any related virtual reality system for learning informally in an enjoyable way to the user.

Keywords: Gamification · Enjoyment · Informal learning · Virtual reality · Gamified learning

1 Introduction

Gamification is a rapidly growing phenomenon that uses game mechanics as tools to motivate, engage and enhance gamified experiences [1] in non-game context instead in game context [2]. It is also essential to ensure that most gamified experiences are generally enjoyable [3]. In another word, it is a work of using game mechanics and elements that make the game fun and put them into an enjoyable productive activity, like enjoying learning new things informally [4, 5] or in other term it is called gamified learning [6]. From a theoretical standpoint, gamification can increases the visibility,

Z. Lv and H. Song (Eds.): INTETAIN 2021, LNICST 429, pp. 383–399, 2022.
https://doi.org/10.1007/978-3-030-99188-3_24

performance information, comparability, and immediacy [7]. Visibility can be delivered through, for example, scores gained or badges obtained. Performance information enables comparability for users to access their current limit information from visibility, thus set a new target to mantain or improvise their performance. Immediacy means that users get real-time access or timely information.

Virtual Reality (VR) is one of the most effective platforms for informal learning. This is because over recent years, new development of software and hardware for VR such as Head Mounted Display (HMD) HTC VIVE, and Unity Game Engine, has leveled up the effectiveness of user immersion for entertainment, gaming, and even education. However, there is still an open issue for learning through VR [8]. Even though from previous studies, VR may increase user's receptivity and learning rates [9, 10], some findings opposed it like the increment of user's presence but reduce the capability of learning [11]. The findings from [11] tell that the viewed high-immersive VR was too hedonic to the user, which causes the user to get distracted from focusing on enjoy learning the content, but on the digital environment instead. Being excited and fun to get immersed in the virtual world for the first time also could be one of the possibilities that lead to the result. Hence, there is more room to be explored especially on enjoying learning things informally in a virtual world.

Therefore, this study implements VR by providing enjoyment as gamified experience for informal learning.

2 Literature Review

A previous literature study in related subjects is essential to observe the idea of the selected study. Hence, this section discusses the overview of enjoyment as gamified experience, enjoyable informal learning, virtual reality for informal learning, and the related theories.

2.1 Enjoyment as Gamified Experience

Enjoyment or enjoyable is related to intrinsic motivation [12] which is considered to be a motivation durable form that does not decrease much over time [13]. Therefore, numerous activities including learning aim to enhance the enjoyment by embedding game elements, which is what we called gamification.

Related previous studies have been done by [14] in two experiments. Experiment 1 measures whether game elements enhance enjoyment level and durability specifically for balance exercise. The results for experiment 1 proved that there was a significant result of enjoyment durability through gamification effects. Meanwhile, the game group enjoyment raised while enjoyment falls over time in the control group. Experiment 2 measures whether adding game elements to a walking exercise enhances the level and durability of exercise enjoyment. The results for experiment 2 proved that gamification enhanced enjoyment. However, there was no significant result of enjoyment durability through gamification effects. The conclusion from both experiments verified that enjoyment in an activity can be increased through gamification.

In addition, enjoyment experience also may occur from a variety of factors. It could come through mechanics, dynamics, and emotions [15]. A previous study by [16] showed that a good influence of game mechanics may provide a strong relationship between enjoyment and the duration of a game, but only when the player gain accomplishment. Meanwhile, not just mechanics but also dynamics past research has demonstrated to be a significant role in improving users' enjoyment and concentration [17]. Moreover, emotion is also claimed by [3] to be beyond enjoyment, which caters to positive emotions (e.g. excitement, surprise, triumph over adversity) and negative emotions (e.g. pity, anxiety). Figure 1 summarize the variable used in previous studies to measure enjoyment.

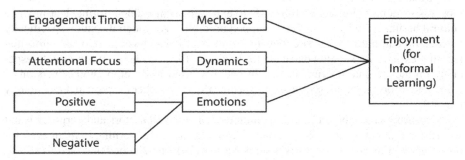

Fig. 1. Summary of key variables of enjoyment for informal learning from previous studies

2.2 Enjoyable Informal Learning

The term of enjoyable informal learning in some previous studies was defined as an experience (in general) where the viewer feels entertained and satisfied while gaining some knowledge at the same time [18, 19]. This study however has specifically defined the term as a gamified learning experience where the viewer feels entertained and satisfied while also gaining some knowledge at the same time. In another word, this term is used to paraphrase the flow of enjoyment as gamified experience for informal learning.

Generally, enjoyment does promote informal learning in many sectors with different purposes. For example, there was a previous study to measure the role of enjoyment in informal learning within the workplace [20]. In their study, the data for enjoyment activities and manager support from 206 respondents (i.e., managers) has been collected with a negative result on manager support for enjoyment. However, the study finds that there is a positive significant result for enjoyment activities with overall informal learning.

Other previous studies also have been done specifically in proposing a model for gamifying informal learning activities using interactive displays [21], to see which selected factors have the most contribution towards informal learning. Those factors are satisfaction, intention to participate, easiness, enjoyment, usefulness, and control. Through empirical evaluation, pre-post attitudinal surveys and cognitive tests, and observation data were recorded in the study. The result shows that user's knowledge acquisition, intention to participate, satisfaction, and enjoyment are significantly improved, with enjoyment as the highest significant P value equal to 0.00. Although the focus and the medium used for the evaluation is not comparable to the immersive VR, the result from the study should be considered as one of the supporting pieces of works of literature for this research.

An instrument for enjoyable informal learning measurement also has been developed by [5], specifically for learning cultural heritage sites. The instrument had gone through content and face validity, followed by reliability analysis to make sure that the initially proposed instrument at an early stage is reliable to be used for the user testing stage. The instrument was later tested on their developed prototype application name AR@Melaka. Data from 200 respondents have been collected and the results show that most respondents were successfully able to experience enjoyable informal learning at a cultural heritage site by using the developed prototype. Although the study specifically focused on cultural heritage site, the core of the study which is the enjoyable informal learning experience should contribute to the body of knowledge in this research; especially on the validate instrument, which could be used to develop another version of enjoyable informal learning instrument specifically for another purpose and technology like VR.

Measuring enjoyable informal learning that caters to all sectors and purposes is not something that can be done in just one research because the learning domain even for informal learning is too vast. This is supported by [20] who claimed that there is still an incomplete understanding of the role of enjoyment in the learning domain, especially informal learning. Thus, there is a need to study each enjoyable informal learning for a specific purpose separately, like using different technology could also lead to different kinds of enjoyment experience for informal learning.

2.3 Virtual Reality

VR is defined as *"a real or simulated environment in which a perceiver experiences telepresence"* [22]. It refers to a computer-generated, information-rich, and three-dimensional environment that provides spatial navigation, enables user control to interact between user and virtual objects [23, 24]. There are four key elements in experiencing VR namely immersion, virtual environment, interactivity, and sensory feedback.

Immersion. There are two types of immersion levels in VR technologies, such as immersive and non-immersive [25]. Immersive VR enables users to experience fully immersive into the virtual environment [26, 27]. It could be in a form of mobile VR (e.g., Samsung Gear, Google Cardboard), high-end Head Mounted Display (HMD) (e.g., HTC Vive series, Oculus series, Samsung Gear, Samsung Odyssey, and Google Cardboard), and enhanced VR (e.g., a combined HMD with other devices such as data gloves, Kinect or bodysuit). On the other hand, non-immersive VR provide less immersive where the user can still aware and recognize the screen or a conventional graphics workstation such as Cave Automatic Virtual Environment (CAVE) system, desktop VR [28, 29], 360-degree videos, and panoramic videos [25]. There was also discussion among scholars about semi-immersive VR from using the CAVE system. However, literature in this study only identified immersive and non-immersive VR exergame studies studied by previous researchers. Thus, this research defined VR immersion as in these two categories as suggested by Radianti et al. (2020).

Immersion is an essential feature in VR as it influences not just the user's sense of presence but also the whole context of user experience as well [30]. Speaking of presence, there is a concern by Basu (2019), mentioned that there is confusion between the term of immersion and presence among the VR community [31]. He further explained that immersion refers to a user's state of mind while presence refers to a user's subjective psychological response towards the system. The state of mind in immersion is a short moment of disbelief that enables the user to move at will in both the real and virtual world [31]. This short moment of disbelief could also relate to a lack of awareness of time and the real environment [32]. Meanwhile, the subjective psychological response in presence is a human response to a VR system with a certain level of immersion, or in a simpler sentence, it is a human reaction to immersion [33]. Immersion and presence might be different based on the above definition, but they are strongly related to each other. This is because a sense of "being there" in a virtual world indicates that the user can feel their body is "being physically there" in a virtual environment instead of the real environment.

Virtual Environment. A Virtual Environment (VE) is the content and the subject matter, represented in visual and/or aural to the user to be immersed in any virtual experiences including VR. It is a medium of communication with broad applications ranging from training and education to exploratory data visualization or analysis to entertainment [31]. The way the VE is presented to the user or the way the story flows at any given time is controlled by the VR system based on the interaction with the user itself [34]. For example, players will go through many different places with a different set of terrain in the VR tour. They will also listen to the three-dimensional audio such as waterfall and birds which is getting louder as they get near to it and vice versa as they passed it farther, which further enhances the user experience in VE. Of course, this is not only limited to the "outdoor" VE, but "indoor" VE as well.

Interactivity. Aside from immersion and VE, interactivity is also an important key to exploring a virtual world. Good interactivity in a VR system should be able to let the user engage with the virtual world and gain feedback appropriately based on their action or condition [31]. There is various form of interaction depending on the system subject matter (e.g., VE, virtual avatar, user interface) in VR system. For example, users can interact with the virtual avatar to get information such as a hint to the next level or learn some knowledge (e.g. historical) from the conversation.

Sensory Feedback. Playing computer games require a user to interact with the system using devices such as mouse and keyboard button most of the time. A good system will provide the programmed feedback based on the button pressed by the user. Sensory feedback does the same but using sensor devices and program instead of a button such as a 3-dimensional camera (e.g., Kinect) to detect movement, gesture, face recognition, facial expression, head, and eye gaze. Aside from visual, sensory feedback also could be in another form such as aural (i.e. spatial audio, voice recognition), and haptic (i.e. touch)

[31]. In another word, it is a method to communicate between humans and computers, which is through human senses.

2.4 Virtual Reality for Informal Learning

VR for informal learning has been studied over two decades ago [35], and nowadays there are numerous studies of VR for education, specifically for informal learning. As can be concluded in Sect. 2.2, learning informally has more significant value when the user learns enjoyably. However, most recent VR studies for informal learning does not support enjoyable informal learning experience, which discussed in the next paragraph.

To improve the learning experience and learning efficiency, a study by [36] has proposed a model of an experiential learning space with VR technology. The study also came out with the conception of experiential learning space with the combination of virtuality and reality. However, the presented paper does not mention any methodology on validation and evaluation of the proposed model, while also lacking literature resources that support the development of the model. Thus, it is suggested that the proposed model could be further studied with the consideration of adding other factors like enjoyment as a part of the learning experience in using VR.

As mentioned in the Introduction section earlier, there were opposite results by [11] where lesser knowledge gained but more presence occur in return. The results have been argued by [37] who claimed to use almost similar experiment that the respondents in [11] had to separate their attention between text and virtual environment, which led to various cognitive load, thus lower the gained knowledge. This is because the results by [37] show significant learning results in VR as the text in their experiment was given in form of cueing tips. The experiments also compared the use of VR with another two learning materials of paper and desktop display. It was found that learning processes are more efficient when using VR than reading texts on paper or interacting with 3D models on a desktop screen. However the measurement in the study is only based on the correct answers, as it is more into formal learning, while the study by [11] was informal learning with learning beliefs, satisfaction, knowledge, and transfer as its main variable to measure. Moreover, the study also does not include enjoyment as one of the factors for learning success.

Although VR has a great effect on the learning process, the learning material structure and organization in a virtual environment could still affect the advantage it. This is because the design of the virtual environment is perceived differently (abstract) to each user. It also has great potential to divert the user's attention from learning the content [37].

2.5 Gamified Learning vs Game-Based Learning

Gamification in the learning context can be referred to as gamified learning. There are similarities between gamified learning and game-based learning among scholars. However, both are not the same thing because each of them has a different approach to learning [6]. Gamified learning approaches focus on modifying or augmenting an existing learning process to develop a revised version that users perceived as game-like

[38], while game-based learning approaches are more into (serious) games implication [39].

Thus, gamification is not a (serious) game. In the context of learning, gamification is a procedure of changing existing learning processes by embedding game elements into them [6, 38, 39]. This study is applying gamified learning as one of the grounded theories discussed in the next subsections.

2.6 Related Theories

The subsection below discussed the related theories that explain the enjoyable informal learning process through game elements for gamified experiences.

Semiotics Theory. Semiotics is called "semeion" from a Greek word, mean signs. These signs are the perceived aspect of communication [40], such as visual (text, image, visual perspective, color, graphic, layout, shape, form, and texture) and aural (music, sound effect, and voice) [41]. This theory explains how the sign is perceived by the user to create a meaningful idea.

There were a few versions of semiotics theories, as discussed by [42]. However, this study found that the extended version of semiotics theory by Barthes [43] to be fit the bill more with the objective of this study. Barthes's theory explains that there is a first and second level of meaning. The first level is called denotation, followed by connotation for the second level. The idea from Barthes' theory is where the signification process from Peirce's theory [44] occurs once to operate iconic sign relationship at denotation level. An iconic sign is resembled and mimetic the object. It means that the user recognizes what kind of each subject they are perceived or exposed to. After that, the same signification process from Peirce's theory occurs once again to operate symbolic sign relationship at connotation level. The symbolic sign is where the "stand for" is understood through the convention. In another word, the sign is "stand for" something else.

This means that the user will recognize each of the objects in the virtual environment at the denotation level. After that on the connotation level, the user will identify the overall meaning behind all the denotation processes through the experienced event within the virtual environment. The identified overall meaning will trigger the learning process. It is important to explain how the learning process works continuously from semiotics theory because learning theory can provide a structure that guides strategies and activities of learning [45]. Thus, the next sub-section discussed on chosen learning theory for this study.

Constructivism Theory. This theory requires the learner to construct knowledge on their own [46], rather than receiving it [47]. It focuses on inventing, creating, developing, and constructing the knowledge [48], rather than transmitting the knowledge [49]. The learning process starts through experience [47] and pre-existing knowledge [50].

There are three major hypotheses concluded from to what extend learners participate in seeking meaningful knowledge, which agreed by many constructivist [48, 51]:

- Learning is the knowledge active formation obtained from experience and environment contact.
- Knowledge is constructed by the learner itself from their own experience and existing knowledge to find out a meaningful context.
- Meaningful knowledge is closely related to the experience. So learners will practice the knowledge in their lives.

Concerning this study, constructivism theory may impact informal learning in virtual reality through meaningful learning content and unique experience. However, to make the learning more enjoyable, this study also suggested the use of gamified learning theory which is discussed in the next sub-section.

Gamified Learning Theory. Gamified learning theory recommended one type of gamification, the inclusion of game fiction or narrative game, which can be used to enhance learning outcomes [52]. In another word, it is defined as the use of narration in a fictional game world [53] to improve instructional outcomes; as narration are much easier to accurately remembered than expository texts [52].

This study finds that gamified learning theory by [54] to be more in line with the objective of this study; as it is focused on gamification that can affect learning:

- Instructional content influences learning outcomes and behaviors.
- Behaviors/attitudes (enjoyment) influence learning.
- Game characteristics influence changes in behaviors/attitudes (enjoyment).
- Game elements affect behaviors/attitudes that moderate instructional effectiveness.
- The relationship between game elements and learning outcomes is mediated by behaviors/attitudes (enjoyment).

From this theory, enjoyment is placed in the behaviors/attitudes as a mediator between the relationship of game elements and learning outcomes. It is somehow explained how enjoyable informal learning could be achieved using VR technology in this study.

Flow Theory. Csikszentmihalyi (1990) is the founder of flow theory, where it has been defined as "the process of optimal experience" where the enjoyment experiences feels by the user through *"a sense of exhilaration, a deep sense of enjoyment that is long cherished, does not come through passive, receptive, relaxing times"* while fully concentrating on conducting a particular task [55]. The sense of flow is best to experienced at the moment when the user's body or mind is widely open to accept any challenging and worthwhile task [55]. There is little similarities with the definition of immersive as defined in Sect. 2.3. However, immersive has more focused on the telepresence experience where user feels like "being somewhere else", while the flow definition are much into a broader context.

In learning, the learner will experience flow at their optimal experience while performing full concentration in learning activity where the challenges are fully connected with their skills [56]. This means that the provided challenge must not exceed the user's capabilities. Else, users might not be able to experience flow due to the difficulties to reach the goal and complete the task. Therefore, in the context of gamified learning environment, there is need for consideration to maintain the user's optimal level on each provided challenge, to make sure the users can always be in the flow state in most of the time. Additionally, there are eight components that represent enjoyment phenomena in this theory [55] such as:

1. We confront tasks we have a chance of completing;
2. We must be able to concentrate on what we are doing;
3. The task has clear goals;
4. The task provides immediate feedback;
5. One acts with deep, but effortless involvement, that removes from awareness the worries and frustrations of everyday life;
6. One exercises a sense of control over their actions;
7. Concern for the self disappears, yet, paradoxically the sense of self emerges stronger after the flow experience is over; and
8. The sense of duration of time is altered.

3   Methodology

Research methodology is a systematic approach to solve the research problem. There is various type of research methodology in a vast research context. However, design science research is one of the best methodologies for this study because it focuses on an artifact-based creation that can provide a solution for the related problem [57, 58], where the form of artifact could be in constructs, model, method or instantiation [59].

This study adapt a design research methodology by Vaishnavi and Kuechler (2015) [60]. It consists of five main phases i) problem identification, ii) proposed solution, iii) design and development, iv) evaluation and v) conclusion as illustrated in "Fig. 1" (Fig. 2).

3.1   Phase 1: Problems Identification

Before the study begin, it is compulsory to determine who are the learners that will learn informally using the VR system. After that, a several questions with potential issues and problems in a form of questionnaires or semi-structured interview will be conducted in a *Preliminary Study*. After that, based on the results from the preliminary study, a research question will be formed to conduct a *Systematic Literature Review (SLR)*. The SLR will further address the issues and problems in the state-of-the-art among scholars, and to highlight the research gap. Issues or problems within preliminary studies and literature studies can be the gist of the research objectives and scopes through thematic analysis and content analysis (Fig. 3).

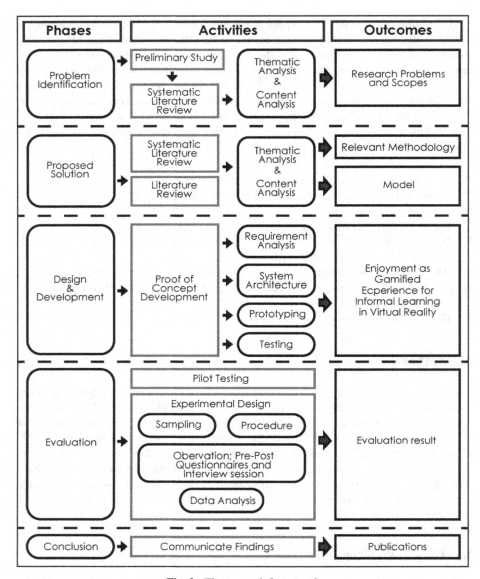

Fig. 2. The research framework

3.2 Phase 2: Proposed Solution

This stage proposed a solution for the identified problem in phase one. Once again, the findings of phase one should be reconfirmed that they are lacking in a particular scoped area in enjoyable informal learning using VR system. Once it is confirmed, another *SLR* will be conducted as a comprehensive method to determine the factors and characteristics of enjoyable informal learning in VR based on the scopes and objectives. A model will

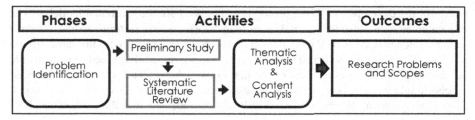

Fig. 3. Problem identification phase

either be produced as main contribution in this phase, or adapted, based on the required research objectives. Nonetheless, it will be a guide for the whole research process, especially to analyze the outcome variables in the evaluation phase. Along the way, a regular *Literature Review* will also be conducted to support the research objectives such as aformentioned grounded theories and the VR system in previous sections. This also includes other related content that needed to be expanded from identified SLR results. Thematic analysis and content analysis will be conducted to themed and organized the findings results to be discussed extensively (Fig. 4).

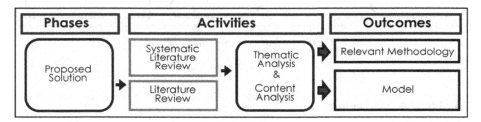

Fig. 4. Proposed solution phase

All the identified factors and features will be extracted, combined, and arranged to construct the hypothetical model, which will be reviewed later by experts to come out with the proposed model of enjoyable informal learning in VR. The selected experts have an experienced in either teaching, researching, or practicing for at least five year in related fields.

3.3 Phase 3: Design and Development

Previous processes resulted in the factors and features of the model. As proof of concept, the model will be tested by implementing it in a prototype development. *Requirement Analysis* will be conducted to determine the relevant evaluation content that reflect the objectives. The structure for the prototype also will be planned accordingly based on the the selected VR system and grounded theories. For instance, as suggested in flow theory, the developed prototype will be matches with the target user's competency (Refer to flow theory section). *System Architecture* is the main representation of the system, as the main purpose is to support the reasoning of the proposed system. *Prototyping* is the actual phase for the development of the prototype. This is where the evaluated model will be implemented for enjoyable informal learning in the VR system. *Testing* is to find any error such as glitches or bugs on the developed prototype. Two experts with the same criteria as in model validation will test the prototype to ensure the developed system would be able to provide the evaluation resuls that answer the research objectives. Previous process might need to be repeated if necessary according to the experts comments. If there is no problem, the next phase will be conducted, which is the evaluation phase (Fig. 5).

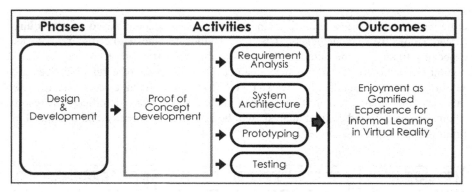

Fig. 5. Design and development phase

3.4   Phase 4: Evaluation

Evaluation will be conducted to determine the user's enjoyable informal learning on the usability of the developed prototype. A questionnaire to measure enjoyable informal learning in VR will be developed, reviewed by ten experts with the same criteria as in model validation and prototype testing. The developed ptotype and questionnaire will be tested by the user in *Pilot Testing* to ensure both are reliable to be used during the actual evaluation process. Sixty participants will conduct the final test on the developed proto-type in an *Experimental Design*. All the participants will be briefed before the evaluation started. After that, they will be asked to complete a demographic pre-questionnaire. After the evaluation ended, each participants will be given the post-questionnaire, which is the developed questionnaire. Semi-structured interview also will be conducted to obtain subjective responds by the participants in a qualitative data. All the evaluation data will be collected and analyzed in descriptive, correlation, t-test, and ANOVA for the next phase (Fig. 6).

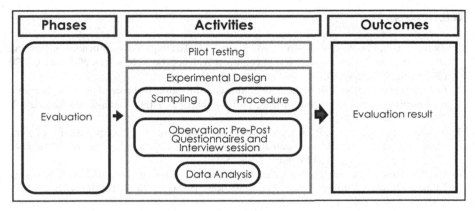

Fig. 6. Evaluation phase

3.5 Phase 5: Conclusion

The conclusion is the final phase in this study, where the overall findings of the study will be described and explained and formulated. The outcome and recommendation for future study will also be discussed and documented for future publications (Fig. 7).

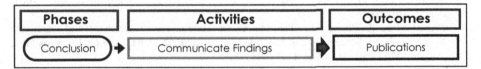

Fig. 7. Conclusion phase

4 Conclusion

This article discussed the important concept of enjoyable as gamified experience for informal learning in virtual technology. It also explains the broad methodology for model development of enjoyable informal learning in VR technology through adapted research design, which can be applied for future studies. Different research content also could benefit from this study as long it is related to the learning-through-VR study.

Acknowledgment. This study is funded by the Ministry of Higher Education (MOHE) scholarship and Media and Game Innovation Centre of Excellence, Institute of Human Centered Engineering, Universiti Teknologi Malaysia, Skudai, Johor, Malaysia under Malaysia Research University Network Grant (R.J130000.7809.4L861) and (R.J130000.7309.4B591).

References

1. Zainuddin, Z., Chu, S.K.W., Shujahat, M., Perera, C.J.: The impact of gamification on learning and instruction: A systematic review of empirical evidence. Educ. Res. Rev. **30**(March), 2020 (2019). https://doi.org/10.1016/j.edurev.2020.100326

2. Groh, F.: Gamification: state of the art definition and utilization. In: Proceedings of 4th Seminar on Research Trends Media Informatics, pp. 39–46 (2012). http://vts.uni-ulm.de/docs/2012/7866/vts_7866_11380.pdf

3. Mullins, J.K., Sabherwal, R.: Beyond enjoyment: a cognitive-emotional perspective of gamification. In: Proc. 51st Hawaii International Conference on System Science, pp. 1237–1246 (2018). https://doi.org/10.24251/hicss.2018.152

4. He, T., Zhu, C., Questier, F.: Predicting digital informal learning: an empirical study among Chinese University students. Asia Pac. Educ. Rev. **19**(1), 79–90 (2018). https://doi.org/10.1007/s12564-018-9517-x

5. Pendit, U.C., Zaibon, S.B., Bakar, J.A.A.: Enjoyable informal learning at cultural heritage site using mobile augmented reality: measurement and evaluation. J. Telecommun. Electron. Comput. Eng. **8**(10), 13–21 (2016)

6. Sailer, M., Homner, L.: The gamification of learning: a meta-analysis. Educ. Psychol. Rev. **32**(1), 77–112 (2019). https://doi.org/10.1007/s10648-019-09498-w

7. Gerdenitsch, C., et al.: Work gamification: effects on enjoyment, productivity and the role of leadership. Electron. Commer. Res. Appl. **43**, 100994 (2020). https://doi.org/10.1016/j.elerap.2020.100994

8. Checa, D., Bustillo, A.: Advantages and limits of virtual reality in learning processes: Briviesca in the fifteenth century. Virtual Reality **24**(1), 151–161 (2019). https://doi.org/10.1007/s10055-019-00389-7

9. Chen, S., Pan, Z., Zhang, M., Shen, H.: A case study of user immersion-based systematic design for serious heritage games. Multimed. Tools Appl. **62**(3), 633–658 (2013). https://doi.org/10.1007/s11042-011-0864-4

10. Roussou, M., Slater, M.: Comparison of the effect of interactive versus passive virtual reality learning activities in evoking and sustaining conceptual change. IEEE Trans. Emerg. Top. Comput. **8**(1), 233–244 (2017). https://doi.org/10.1109/TETC.2017.2737983

11. Makransky, G., Terkildsen, T.S., Mayer, R.E.: Adding immersive virtual reality to a science lab simulation causes more presence but less learning. Learn. Instr. **60**(November), 225–236 (2019). https://doi.org/10.1016/j.learninstruc.2017.12.007

12. Ryan, R.M., Deci, E.L.: Self-Determination Theory: Basic Psychological Needs in Motivation, Development, and Wellness. Guilford Publications (2017)

13. Vansteenkiste, M., Lens, W., Deci, E.L.: Intrinsic versus extrinsic goal contents in self-determination theory: another look at the quality of academic motivation. Educ. Psychol. **41**(1), 19–31 (2006). https://doi.org/10.1207/s15326985ep4101_4

14. van der Kooij, K., van Dijsseldonk, R., van Veen, M., Steenbrink, F., de Weerd, C., Overvliet, K.E.: Gamification as a sustainable source of enjoyment during balance and gait exercises. Front. Psychol. **10**(MAR), 1–12 (2019). https://doi.org/10.3389/fpsyg.2019.00294

15. Robson, K., Plangger, K., Kietzmann, J.H., McCarthy, I., Pitt, L.: Is it all a game? Understanding the principles of gamification. Bus. Horiz. **58**(4), 411–420 (2015). https://doi.org/10.1016/j.bushor.2015.03.006

16. Moll, P., Frick, V., Rauscher, N., Lux, M.: How players play games: observing the influences of game mechanics. In: MMVE 2020 - Proceedings 2020 International Work. Immersive Mixed and Virtual Environment Systems - Part MMSys 2020, pp. 7–12 (2020). https://doi.org/10.1145/3386293.3397113

17. Wang, Y., Rajan, P., Sankar, C.S., Raju, P.K.: Let them play: the impact of mechanics and dynamics of a serious game on student perceptions of learning engagement. IEEE Trans. Learn. Technol. **10**(4), 514–525 (2016). https://doi.org/10.1109/tlt.2016.2639019
18. Ariffin, A.M.: Conceptual Design of Reality Learning Media (RLM) Model Based on Entertaining and Fun Constructs. Universiti Utara Malaysia (2009)
19. Zaibon, S.B., Pendit, U.C., Abu Bakar, J.A.: User requirements on mobile AR for cultural heritage site towards enjoyable informal learning. In: Proceedings of APMediaCast 2015 Asia Pacific Conference Multimedia Broadcasting, no. April, pp. 61–67 (2015). https://doi.org/10.1109/APMediaCast.2015.7210289
20. Tews, M.J., Michel, J.W., Noe, R.A.: Does fun promote learning? The relationship between fun in the workplace and informal learning. J. Vocat. Behav. **98**, 46–55 (2017). https://doi.org/10.1016/j.jvb.2016.09.006
21. Leftheriotis, I., Giannakos, M., Jaccheri, L.: Gamifying informal learning activities using interactive displays: an empirical investigation of students' learning and engagement. Smart Learn. Environ. **4**(1), 1–19 (2017). https://doi.org/10.1186/s40561-017-0041-y
22. Steure, J.: Defining virtual reality: dimensions determining telepresence. J. Commun. **42**(4), 73–93 (1993)
23. Brooks, F.P.: What's real about virtual reality? IEEE Comput. Graph. Appl. **19**(6), 16–27 (1999). https://doi.org/10.1109/38.799723
24. Abu Bakar, J.A.: Architectural Heritage Learning Through Virtual Reality in Museums. International Islamic University Malaysia (2012)
25. Radianti, J., Majchrzak, T.A., Fromm, J., Wohlgenannt, I.: A systematic review of immersive virtual reality applications for higher education: design elements, lessons learned, and research agenda. Comput. Educ. **147**, 103778 (2020). https://doi.org/10.1016/j.compedu.2019.103778
26. Khalifa, M., Shen, N.: System design effects on social presence and telepresence in virtual communities. Icis, 547–558 (2004). http://aisel.aisnet.org/icis2004
27. Martín-Gutiérrez, J., Mora, C.E., Añorbe-Díaz, B., González-Marrero, A.: Virtual technologies trends in education. Eurasia J. Math. Sci. Technol. Educ. **13**(2), 469–486 (2017). https://doi.org/10.12973/eurasia.2017.00626a
28. Robertson, G., Czerwinski, M., van Dantzich, M.: Immersion in desktop virtual reality. In: UIST (User Interface Software Technology Proceedings ACM Symposium, pp. 11–19 (1997). https://doi.org/10.1145/263407.263409
29. Frank, B.D.B.: Immersive virtual reality technology. Commun. Age Virtual Real. **15**(32), 10–5555 (1995)
30. Rose, T., Nam, C.S., Chen, K.B.: Immersion of virtual reality for rehabilitation – review. Appl. Ergon. **69**, 153–161 (2018). https://doi.org/10.1016/j.apergo.2018.01.009
31. Basu, A.: A brief chronology of Virtual Reality. arXiv, pp. 1–18 (2019)
32. Jennett, C., et al.: Measuring and defining the experience of immersion in games. Int. J. Hum. Comput. Stud. **66**(9), 641–661 (2008). https://doi.org/10.1016/j.ijhcs.2008.04.004
33. Slater, M.: A note on presence terminology. Presence Connect **3**, 1–5 (2003)
34. Ghaffari, R., Raj, M., Mcgrane, B.: Method and system for interacting with a virtual environment, 10,300,371 (2019)
35. Roussou, M.: Immersive interactive virtual reality and informal education. i3 spring days, Work. User Interfaces All Interact. Learn. Environ. Child., CD-ROM (2000)
36. Gan, B., Zhang, C., Meng, H.: Construction of experiential learning space model based on virtual reality technology. J. Phys. Conf. Ser. **1486**(4) (2020). https://doi.org/10.1088/1742-6596/1486/4/042001
37. Zinchenko, Y.P., et al.: Virtual reality is more efficient in learning human heart anatomy especially for subjects with low baseline knowledge. New Ideas Psychol. **59**(May), 2020 (2019). https://doi.org/10.1016/j.newideapsych.2020.100786

38. Landers, R.N., Auer, E.M., Collmus, A.B., Armstrong, M.B.: Gamification science, its history and future: definitions and a research agenda. Simul. Gaming **49**(3), 315–337 (2018). https://doi.org/10.1177/1046878118774385
39. Deterding, S., Dixon, D., Khaled, R., Nacke, L.: From game design elements to gamefulness. In: Proceedings of the 15th International Academic MindTrek Conference on Envisioning Future Media Environments - MindTrek 2011, p. 9 (2011). https://doi.org/10.1145/2181037.2181040
40. Huhtamo, E.: Visual communication and semiotics: some basic concepts. Signs (Chic) (2003)
41. Abdul Syafiq, B.: Attributes of Narrative Game Aesthetics for Perceived Cultural Learning, Universiti Utara Malaysia (2017)
42. Moriarty, S.: Visual semiotics theory. In: Smith, K.L., Moriarty, S., Barbatsis, G., Kenney, K. (eds.) Handbook of Visual Communication: Theory, Methods, and Media, pp. 227–241. Routledge (2004)
43. Barthes, R.: Elements of Semiology. Hill and Wang, New York (1968)
44. Peirce, C.S., Weiss, P., Hartshorne, C., Burks, A.W.: The collected papers of Charles Sanders Peirce [electronic resource]. Past masters (1994)
45. Bakar, N.A.A., Zulkifli, A.N., Mohamed, N.F.F.: The use of multimedia, augmented reality (AR) and virtual environment (VE) in enhancing children's understanding of road safety. In: 2011 IEEE Conference on Open Systems, ICOS 2011, 2011, no. September 2014, pp. 149–154. https://doi.org/10.1109/ICOS.2011.6079288
46. Boghossian, P.: Behaviorism, constructivism, and socratic pedagogy. Educ. Philos. Theory **38**(6), 713–722 (2006)
47. Guney, A., Al, S.: Effective learning environments in relation to different learning theories. Procedia Soc. Behav. Sci. **46**, 2334–2338 (2012). https://doi.org/10.1016/j.sbspro.2012.05.480
48. Büyükduman, I., Şirin, S.: Learning portfolio (LP) to enhance constructivism and student autonomy. Procedia Soc. Behav. Sci. **3**, 55–61 (2010). https://doi.org/10.1016/j.sbspro.2010.07.012
49. Obikwelu, C., Read, J.C.: The serious game constructivist framework for children's learning. Procedia Comput. Sci. **15**, 32–37 (2012). https://doi.org/10.1016/j.procs.2012.10.055
50. Thurlings, M., Vermeulen, M., Bastiaens, T., Stijnen, S.: Understanding feedback: a learning theory perspective. Educ. Res. Rev. **9**, 1–15 (2013). https://doi.org/10.1016/j.edurev.2012.11.004
51. Nurul Nadwan, A.: Conceptual design and development model of assistive courseware for young low vision learners (AC4LV), Doctoral dissertation, Universiti Utara Malaysia (2015)
52. Armstrong, M.B., Landers, R.N.: An evaluation of gamified training: using narrative to improve reactions and learning. Simul. Gaming **48**(4), 513–538 (2017). https://doi.org/10.1177/1046878117703749
53. Landers, R.N., Callan, R.C.: Validation of the beneficial and harmful work-related social media behavioral taxonomies: development of the work-related social media questionnaire. Soc. Sci. Comput. Rev. **32**(5), 628–646 (2014). https://doi.org/10.1177/0894439314524891
54. Landers, R.N.: Developing a theory of gamified learning: linking serious games and gamification of learning. Simul. Gaming **45**(6), 752–768 (2014). https://doi.org/10.1177/1046878114563660
55. Csikszentmihalyi, M.: Flow: The Psychology of Optimal Experience. Harper & Row, New York (1990)
56. Sharek, D., Wiebe, E.: Measuring video game engagement through the cognitive and affective dimensions. Simul. Gaming **45**, 569–592 (2014). https://doi.org/10.1177/1046878114554176
57. Höckmayr, B.S.: Engineering Service Systems in the Digital Age (2019)

58. Deng, Q., Ji, S.: A review of design science research in information systems: concept, process, outcome, and evaluation. Pacific Asia J. Assoc. Inf. Syst. **10**(1), 1–36 (2018). https://doi.org/10.17705/1pais.10101
59. March, S.T., Smith, G.F.: Design and natural science research on information technology. Decis. Support Syst. **15**(4), 251–266 (1995). https://doi.org/10.1016/0167-9236(94)00041-2
60. Vaishnavi, V.K., Kuechler, W.: Design Science Research Methods and Patterns. CRC Press (2015)

Virtual Reality

A Systematic Review of Purpose and Latency Effect in the Virtual Reality Environment

Muhammad Danish Affan Anua[1]($\boxtimes$), Ismahafezi Ismail[1], Nur Saadah Mohd Shapri[1], Maizan Mat Amin[1], and Mohd Azhar M. Arsad[2]

[1] Faculty of Informatics and Computing, Universiti Sultan Zainal Abidin, Kuala Terengganu, Malaysia
danish.affan.16@gmail.com

[2] V3X Malaysia SDN. BHD, Johor, Malaysia

Abstract. VR means immersing oneself in a virtual environment where all we see is three dimensional (3D) computer-generated. VR has been around for several decades now, but in recent years, the consistency of experience has dramatically improved. This technology has been recognised worldwide, making the adoption of VR a more progressive widespread occurrence across various fields. VR technology evolves very fast and significant as it merges with artificial intelligence (AI), thus transforming the way people use machines and smartphones in daily life to communicate with the world around them. However, there is a problem commonly faced by the virtual reality user, which is cybersickness or motion sickness in the virtual reality environment. As the result, a systematic review has been made to gain a better understanding and present this information in the form of a written summary of current researches. The study of the previous research publication of review papers was limited around 2017 to 2021 from the Scopus library. Among 187 results, five of them were selected since they met the criteria through the inclusion and exclusion criteria procedure. Eight purposes were found and listed together with the outcomes. This paper also briefly discusses the latency effect and its relationship with motion sickness in the virtual reality environment and system. Understanding the purpose and latency effect in the virtual reality environment can encourage researchers and developers to find a better solution to counter the motion sickness problem.

Keywords: Virtual reality · Motion sickness · System latency

1 Introduction

Within the last few years, researchers have been focusing on the area known as virtual reality. This technology, which comes out with an interactive computer-generated environment, has moved from being focused on gaming to professional development [1]. Although the augmented reality (AR) technology is also one of the most famous and popular multimedia technology [2], it also has a high reputation and well-known across the globe. Recent developments in the field of virtual reality have led to a renewed

© ICST Institute for Computer Sciences, Social Informatics and Telecommunications Engineering 2022
Published by Springer Nature Switzerland AG 2022. All Rights Reserved
Z. Lv and H. Song (Eds.): INTETAIN 2021, LNICST 429, pp. 403–413, 2022.
https://doi.org/10.1007/978-3-030-99188-3_25

interest in many industries from many sectors including education, military, business, medical, agriculture, tourism, and transport. In 1987, the first definition of virtual reality formulated by Jaron Lanier and Steve Bryson described that the use of computer technology to create the illusion of an immersive three-dimensional world in which objects have a sense of spatial presence is known as virtual reality [3].

Experiencing virtual reality technology requires a system with specifically designed computer software that can implement the technology and a head-mounted display (HMD) that allow users to see the virtual environment. The first HMD was invented and developed in Sutherland in 1965, which was introduced as the ultimate display [4] and became available to the public commercially as the revival of virtual reality with HMD at a low price [5]. Many HMDs have been produced by multiple gigantic companies like Google, HTC, Facebook, Sony, and Samsung, allowing users to experience immersive virtual reality with the presence of advanced virtual assisted tools and devices like the Oculus head-mounted display [6].

Nowadays, virtual reality technology is used for various purposes and applications. More importantly, this technology is still able to be developed further from time to time. The latency effect plays a bigger part in virtual reality. By understanding the latency effect in virtual reality, the most common diseases experienced by virtual reality users can be reduced. Thus, virtual reality will have the opportunity to grow and expand beyond the initial creation.

Much research has been conducted to extend the body of knowledge in this domain. However, there are some grey areas with the existing knowledge of virtual reality. One major theoretical issue that has dominated the field for many years concerns the motion sickness effect in virtual reality. It is also known as cybersickness in terms of symptoms as they are similar. The only difference between the terms is that motion sickness is caused in the real world while cybersickness is caused by the virtual one [7].

This paper summarises recent review papers on the virtual reality subject in terms of usage purposes and outcomes of the research in their specific fields. Nonetheless, there is a newer trend regarding this domain that exists and has yet to be reviewed.

2 Past Review

The goal of this chapter is to study, evaluate, and classify the existing works of the past review on the same field. By performing the systematic literature review method (SLR) commonly used by today's reviewers, five publications related to the study were found. This research used a particular string to search for a published review paper in the popular database journal named Scopus, which was set as the title. The string included "systematic review" AND "virtual reality" results in 187 documents. To filter the article for further investigation, this research utilised several inclusion and exclusion criteria. Table 1 and Table 2 below show the criteria in the inclusion and exclusion process.

From the inclusion and exclusion filtration procedure, five publication were selected to be reviewed as they met the criteria above besides being related to the field of study. Table 3 illustrates the summary of five selected papers classified into three subjects; the title, author, as well as purpose and outcome.

Table 1. Inclusion criteria

	Inclusion
1	Publication from 2017 to 2021
2	Keywords: virtual reality, systematic review, review, meta-analysis
3	Articles written in English

Table 2. Exclusion criteria

	Exclusion
1	Articles not related to motion sickness approaches
2	Articles with a similar region of review

Table 3. The previous research summary

	Title	Author	Purpose	Outcome
1	A systematic literature review on virtual reality for learning [8]	Kurniawan, C, et al. (2019)	a) To understand how virtual reality can be used to enhance learning	a) There are four purposes for using VR in learning, which are to improve participants' achievement, enhance the learning, engaging, and motivate the participants b) Two types of devices are used for VR learning, namely, projection divided into a personal and large screen, and an interaction type divided into tracking, haptics, and audio c) Two types of user experience in VR learning, which are single and multi-users. The single-user is the most used for user experience

(*continued*)

Table 3. (*continued*)

	Title	Author	Purpose	Outcome
2	A systematic review of immersive virtual reality applications for higher education: design elements, lessons learnt, and research agenda [9]	J.Radianti, et al. (2019)	a) To identify the design elements of existing research focusing on the application of VR in higher education	a) Learning theory is often not considered in VR application development to accomplish the learning outcome b) VR is still experimental in most domains with the usage that is considered unsystematic c) Acknowledgement about VR application that has been used on the regular basis in some domains, especially for practical knowledge
3	The new era of virtual reality locomotion: a systematic literature review of techniques and a proposed typology [10]	Boletsis, C (2017)	a) An analysis of the literature on the modern age of virtual reality locomotion strategies, which has been studied since 2014 b) Proposed a typology for VR locomotion technique	a) The study of virtual reality locomotion focusing on the physical movement needs to navigate open virtual worlds in continuous motion b) An empirical study is needed with approaches under comparative arrangements
4	A systematic review of a virtual reality system from the perspective of user experience [11]	Y.M. Kim, et al. (2019)	a) To provide a structured methodology to categorise current virtual reality studies b) To categorise and summarise research on user experience in virtual reality c) To state the current limitations for future advancement and development	a) The study of user experiences in virtual reality requires more research, especially into virtual reality device-related issues and technology, as well as the research methodology b) There are bad effects that may not be confirmed in the VR context and yet to be introduced c) Study on utilising the sensor data on virtual reality system might lack performance

(*continued*)

Table 3. (*continued*)

	Title	Author	Purpose	Outcome
5	The use of virtual reality simulation among nursing students and registered nurses: A systematic review [12]	Shorey, S, et al. (2021)	a) To investigate and evaluate the latest evidence on the use of virtual reality as a teaching tool	a) Virtual reality is mostly studied by nursing students and in developed countries b) Virtual reality is budget-saving and saves time compared to mannequin simulation and lectures c) Virtual reality is lack of realistic presence and often has technological issues

Virtual reality is one of the most anticipating domains in research because the technology evolves dramatically throughout the years and still ongoing. The search was carried out using Scopus for systematic literature. Figure 1 displays the publication trends included since 2007 in this review. A significant increase in the number of articles can be seen every year until 2020. Following that, a downtrend to less than 10 publications was observed by the year 2021.

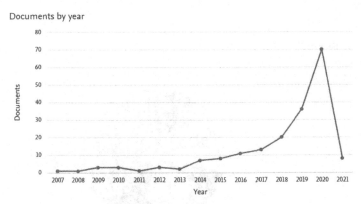

Fig. 1. Document publication trends (Source: Scopus)

From the same source, the documents related to the virtual reality domain came from various types. According to the comparison in Fig. 2, documents published were dominated by reviews, which accounted for 60.4% in the Scopus database, followed by articles, which accounted for 29.4%, and conference papers representing 4.8%.

Documents by type

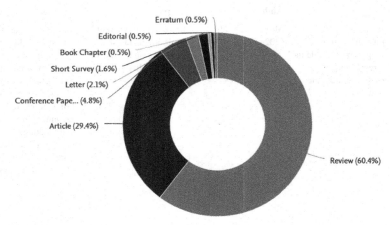

Fig. 2. Document publication trends (Source: Scopus)

In addition, Scopus shows document publications according to the subject area. It was reported that the highest subject area involves medicine with 37.6%. The health professions took second place with 10.9% while computer science came third with 9% in their database. Figure 3 illustrates the comparison among documents published by subject area.

Documents by subject area

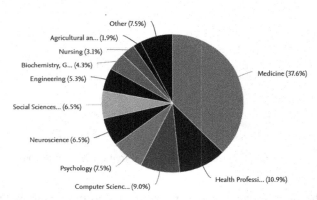

Fig. 3. Document publication comparison by subject area (Source: Scopus)

3 System Latency in VR

Latency is the time taken for a system to react to the actions of the user. The primary factor of the lessened sense of presence is latency in HMD systems [13]. Virtual reality technology can potentially grow further in interacting with computers. However, there are still some disadvantages such as motion sickness and discomfort to the user [14]. Jason (2009) defined the virtual environment as 'Immersive Virtual Environment' (IVE) with the additional requirement that only computer-generated visual cues are visible and divide the IVE system into their primary components: tracking, application, rendering, and display [15]. Figure 4 shows the loop process between the user and the IVE system. The tracking will calculate the user's perspective. Non-rendering aspects of the virtual world are included in the application, such as updating dynamic geometry, user interaction other than perspective manipulation, and physics simulation. The geometric description will transform into a pixel in rendering. The process of the display shows the computed pixel physically to the user from a video signal.

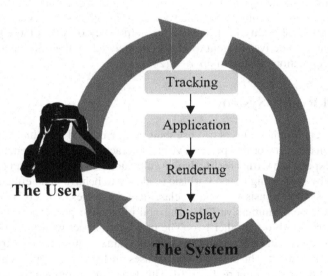

Fig. 4. An immersive virtual environment system consisting of the input from the user that will go through four primary components and produce output to the user.

4 Motion Sickness in Virtual Reality Environment

Motion sickness is produced by motion. Other motions like visual or vehicle motion come from motion sickness in the virtual reality environment. These motions are the contributors to cybersickness [16]. According to Nesbitt K. et al. (2018) "Cybersickness is an uncomfortable side effect experienced by users of immersive interfaces commonly used for Virtual Reality. It is associated with symptoms such as nausea, postural instability, disorientation, headaches, eye-strain, and tiredness." [17]. Some people experience motion sickness in VR, which means that when they put on a headset and enter a virtual world, they feel dizzy or nauseous. Eye fatigue disorientation and nausea are the major signs of VR sickness (Joseph et al., 2000) [18]. These uncomfortable feelings will inhibit future experiences of VR; thus, these problems require an urgent solution.

One of the previous researchers discovered that motion sickness is caused by visual motion in virtual reality [19]. Similar symptoms of motion sickness also came from the lower frame per second of the virtual reality display (FPS). According to Cheng Zang (2020), if the frame per second is limited to below 50 Hz, the user may experience uncomfortable side effects of the virtual reality motion sickness [20]. In addition, the most essential and yet one of the factors that caused the motion sickness effect is the content. Chang E. et al. (2020) stated that the degree of VR constancy and virtual reality sickness is determined by the material used in virtual reality. With developers striving for higher constancy in VR, the content's specifics are becoming more complicated [21].

Despite many factors that contribute to motion sickness in the virtual reality environment, various solutions can reduce the motion sickness effect on users. One of the solutions is using the teleportation technique instead of navigating technique that uses more head movement to complete a task. By teleporting, the user can get a more pleasant experience in virtual reality [22]. Besides, the efficiency of VR is largely determined by its hardware. To deliver content to a user as intended by the developer, a particular hardware specification must be supported [21].

5 Virtual Reality System

In the virtual environment, users can use their eyes, ears, and their hands just like they normally do in the real world to perform virtual interaction [23]. A system needs to allow the users to experience virtual reality. It also cultivates self-determination theory (SDT), a motivation by supporting users' intrinsic tendency to behave in an effective way [2].

The VR system consists of three classified categories, namely non-immersive, immersive, and semi-immersive [24]. The non-immersive provides a less immersive experience compared to the other two. The user can interact with the environment by using only a mouse and joystick [25]. A video game is the best example of a non-immersive environment. The semi-immersive uses the hybrid system and plays a substitute role but not for replacing reality [26]. This type of environment is frequently used for training purpose [27]. For example, the flight simulation. Meanwhile, the immersive category provides the highest experience of immersive virtual reality [24]. For example, the head-mounted display (HMD) device or fully equipped virtual reality room. The Table 4 below shows the virtual reality system category with details and tools.

Table 4. Virtual reality system category

	Category	Detail	Tools
1	Non-Immersive	-Least immersive -Least sophisticated component	-3D environment stereo display monitor or glass
2	Immersive	-Most expensive -Highest level immersion -Feeling of being in a virtual environment (VE)	-Head-mounted display (HMD) -Tracking device -Data glove
3	Semi-Immersive	-A hybrid system or augmented reality -High-level immersion	-Desktop virtual reality -Some physical models

6 Conclusion

This systematic review identified eight purposes for conducting the research related to virtual reality. Among the eight, six of them contributed clear findings to the research while the other two have provided the idea and insight that will help to maintain the relevance of virtual reality technology. This study has also explained the latency effect of the virtual reality environment and its relation with motion sickness and virtual reality system. Each relationship focuses on the definition to provide a better understanding of virtual reality. Understanding the purpose and the latency effect in a virtual reality environment can motivate researcher and developer to achieve a better solution and technique to overcome or at least minimise the motion sickness in virtual reality environment.

Virtual reality technology takes the next advanced step in human-machine interaction. This study proved that virtual reality could provide a massive contribution to many regions and society besides possibly breach a new discovery. Moreover, this study also found some boundaries and limitations to fully utilise the technology to meet their purposes. This study also found that the current findings need to be further studied from every aspect. Modern technology tends to evolve dramatically, but virtual reality technology is believed to possibly maintain its relevance in the future for many years.

Acknowledgement. This research paper is supported by Universiti Sultan Zainal Abidin (UniSZA) using FRGS Racer Fund, project number: RACER/1/2019/ICT01/UNISZA//1. Special Thanks to the Ministry of Higher Education Malaysia (MOHE) and Centre for Research Excellence & Incubation management (CREIM) UniSZA for providing financial support for the research.

References

1. Kamińska, D., et al.: Virtual reality and its applications in education: survey. Information (Switzerland) **10**(10), 318 (2019)
2. Shamsuddin, S., Selman, M., Ismail, I., Amin, M., Rawi, N.: A conceptual framework for gamified learning management system for LINUS students. Indonesian J. Electr. Eng. Comput. Sci. **12**(3), 1380–1385 (2018)

3. Bryson, S.: Virtual Reality: A Definition History - A Personal Essay, December 2013. https://arxiv.org/abs/1312.4322. Author, F.: Contribution title. In: 9th International Proceedings on Proceedings, pp. 1–2. Publisher, Location (2010)
4. LNCS Homepage. http://www.springer.com/lncs. Accessed 21 Nov 2016. Sutherland, I.E.: The ultimate display. In: Multimedia: From Wagner to Virtual Reality, pp. 506–508. Macmillan and Co, London (1965)
5. Wang, J., Lindeman, R.: Coordinated hybrid virtual environments: seam-less interaction contexts for effective virtual reality. Comput. Graph. **48**, 71–83 (2015)
6. Zolkefly, N.N., Ismail, I., Safei, S., Shamsuddin, S.N.W., Arsad, M.A.M.:. Head gesture recognition and interaction techniques in virtual reality: a review. Int. J. Eng. Technol. (UAE) **7**(4.31 Special Issue 31), 437–440 (2018)
7. Martirosov, S., Kopecek, P.: Cyber sickness in virtual reality- literature review. In: Katalinic, B. (ed.) Proceedings of the 28th DAAAM International Symposium, Vienna, Austria, pp. 0718–0726, Published by DAAAM International, ISBN 978-3-902734-11-2, ISSN 1726-9679 (2017)
8. Kurniawan, C., Rosmansyah, Y., Dabarsyah, B.: A systematic literature review on virtual reality for learning. In: Proceeding of 2019 5th International Conference on Wireless and Telematics, ICWT 2019. Institute of Electrical and Electronics Engineers Inc. (2019)
9. Radianti, J., Majchrzak, T.A., Fromm, J. et al.: A systematic review of immersive virtual reality applications for higher education: design elements, lessons learned, and research agenda. Comput. Educ. (2019)
10. Kim, Y.M., Rhiu, I., Yun, M.H.: A systematic review of a virtual reality system from the perspective of user experience. Int. J. Hum. Comput. Interact. **36**(10), 893–910 (2019)
11. Boletsis, C.: The new era of virtual reality locomotion: a systematic literature review of techniques and a proposed typology. Multimodal Technol. Interact. **1**(4), 24 (2017)
12. Shorey, S., Ng, E.D.: The Use of virtual reality simulation among nursing students and registered nurses: A systematic review. Nurse Education Today. Churchill Livingstone (2020)
13. Meehan, M., Brooks, F., Razzaque, S., Whitton, M.: Effects of latency on presence in stressful virtual environments. In: Proceedings of IEEE Virtual Reality, pp. 141–148 (2003)
14. Davis, S., Nesbitt, K., Nalivaiko, E.: A systematic review of cybersickness. In: IE 2014. ACM, New York (2014)
15. Jerald, J.: Scene-motion- and latency-perception thresholds for head-mounted displays (2009)
16. Weech, S., Kenny, S., Barnett-Cowan, M.: Presence and cybersickness in virtual reality are negatively related: a review. Front. Psychol. 10, 158 (2019). https://www.frontiersin.org/article/10.3389/fpsyg.2019.00158
17. Nesbitt, K., Nalivaiko, E.: Cybersickness. In: Lee, N. (ed.) Encyclopedia of Computer Graphics and Games, pp. 1–6. Springer International Publishing, Cham (2018). https://doi.org/10.1007/978-3-319-08234-9_252-1
18. LaViola, J.J.: A discussion of cybersickness in virtual environments. ACM SIGCHI Bull. **32**(1), 47–56 (2000)
19. Weech, S., Kenny, S., Barnett-Cowan, M.: Presence and cybersickness in virtual reality are negatively related: A review. Front. Psychol. **10**, 158 (2019)
20. Zhang, C.: Investigation on motion sickness in virtual reality environment from the perspective of user experience. In: Proceedings of 2020 IEEE 3rd International Conference on Information Systems and Computer Aided Education, ICISCAE 2020, pp. 393–396 (2020)
21. Chang, E., Kim, H.T., Yoo, B.: Virtual reality sickness: a review of causes and measurements. Int. J. Hum. Comput. Interact. **36**(17), 1–25 (2020)
22. Fulvio, J.M., Ji, M., Rokers, B.: Variations in visual sensitivity predict motion sickness in virtual reality. Entertainment Comput. **38**, 100423 (2021)

23. Jung, J., et al.: A review on interaction techniques in virtual environments. In: Proceedings of the 2014 International Conference on Industrial Engineering and Operations Management, pp. 1582–1590 (2014)

24. Bamodu, O., Ye, X.: Virtual Reality and Virtual Reality System Components. Atlantis Press (2013)

25. Henderson, A., Korner-Bitensky, N., Levin, M.: Virtual reality in stroke rehabilitation: a systematic review of its effectiveness for upper limb motor recovery. Top. Stroke Rehabil. **14**(2), 52–61 (2007)

26. Mahmud, N. I. M. M., et al. (2019). Learning performance assessment using mobile-based augmented reality application for preschool environment. Int. J. Recent Technol. Eng. **8**(2Special Issue 3), 436–439 (2019)

27. Tsyktor, V.: What Is Semi-Immersive Virtual Reality? – The Technology Simplified, February 2019. https://cyberpulse.info/what-is-semi-immersive-virtual-reality/

Author Index

Printed in the United States
by Baker & Taylor Publisher Services